THOMAS CARLYLE

VOL. II.

THOMAS CARLYLE

A HISTORY OF THE FIRST FORTY
YEARS OF HIS LIFE

1795–1835

BY

JAMES ANTHONY FROUDE, M.A.

FORMERLY FELLOW OF EXETER COLLEGE, OXFORD

IN TWO VOLUMES

VOL. II.

NEW YORK
CHARLES SCRIBNER'S SONS
1882

Republished, 1970
Scholarly Press, 22929 Industrial Drive East, St. Clair Shores, Michigan 48080

Standard Book Number 403-00210-9
Library of Congress Catalog Card Number: 72-108483

This edition is printed on a high-quality,
acid-free paper that meets specification
requirements for fine book paper referred
to as "300-year" paper

CONTENTS

OF

THE SECOND VOLUME.

vi   *Contents.*

LIFE OF

THOMAS CARLYLE.

CHAPTER I.

A.D. 1828. ÆT. 33.

GOETHE had said of Carlyle that he was fortunate in having in himself an originating principle of conviction, out of which he could develop the force that lay in him unassisted by other men. Goethe had discerned what had not yet become articulately clear to Carlyle himself. But it is no less true that this principle of conviction was already active in his mind, underlying his thoughts on every subject which he touched. It is implied everywhere, though nowhere definitely stated in his published writings. We have arrived at a period when he had become master of his powers, when he began distinctly to utter the 'poor message,' as he sometimes called it, which he had to deliver to his contemporaries. From this time his opinions on details might vary, but the main structure of his philosophy remained unchanged. It is desirable, therefore, before pursuing further the story of his life, to describe briefly what the originating principle was. The secret of a man's nature lies in his religion, in what he really believes about this world, and his own place in it. What was Carlyle's religion ? I am able to explain it, partly from his conversations with myself, but happily not from this source only, into which alien opinions might too probably intrude. There remain among his unpublished papers the fragments of two unfinished essays which he was never able to complete satisfactorily to himself, but which he told me were, and had been, an imperfect expression of his actual thoughts.

We have seen him confessing to Irving that he did not believe, as his friend did, in the Christian religion, and that it was vain to hope that he ever would so believe. He tells his mother, and he so continued to tell her as long as she lived, that their belief was essentially the same, although their language was different. Both these statements were true. He was a Calvinist without the theology. The materialistic theory of things—that intellect is a phenomenon of matter, that conscience is the growth of social convenience, and other kindred speculations, he utterly repudiated. Scepticism on the nature of right and wrong, as on man's responsibility to his Maker, never touched or tempted him. On the broad facts of the Divine government of the universe he was as well assured as Calvin himself; but he based his faith, not on a supposed revelation, or on fallible human authority. He had sought the evidence for it, where the foundations lie of all other forms of knowledge, in the experienced facts of things interpreted by the intelligence of man. Experienced fact was to him revelation, and the only true revelation. Historical religions, Christianity included, he believed to have been successive efforts of humanity, loyally and nobly made in the light of existing knowledge, to explain human duty, and to insist on the fulfilment of it; and the reading of the moral constitution and position of man, in the creed, for instance, of his own family, he believed to be truer far, incommensurably truer, than was to be found in the elaborate metaphysics of utilitarian ethics. In revelation, technically so called, revelation confirmed by historical miracles, he was unable to believe—he felt himself forbidden to believe—by the light that was in him. In other ages men had seen miracles where there were none, and had related them in perfect good faith in their eagerness to realise the divine presence in the world. They did not know enough of nature to be on their guard against alleged suspensions of its unvarying order. To Carlyle the universe was itself a miracle, and all its phenomena were equally in themselves incomprehensible. But the special miraculous occurrences of sacred history were not credible to him. 'It is as certain as mathematics,' he said to me late in his own life, 'that no such thing ever has been or can be.' He had learnt that effects succeeded causes uniformly and inexorably without intermission or interruption, and that tales of wonder were as little the true accounts of real occurrences as the theory of epicycles was a correct explanation of the movements of the planets.

So far his thoughts on this subject did not differ widely from those of his sceptical contemporaries, but his further conclusions not only were not their conclusions, but were opposed to them by whole diameters; for while he rejected the literal narrative of the sacred writers, he believed as strongly as any Jewish prophet or Catholic saint in the spiritual truths of religion. The effort of his life was to rescue and reassert those truths which were being dragged down by the weight with which they were encumbered. He explained his meaning by a remarkable illustration. He had not come (so far as he knew his own purpose) to destroy the law and the prophets, but to fulfil them, to expand the conception of religion with something wider, grander, and more glorious than the wildest enthusiasm had imagined.

The old world had believed that the earth was stationary, and that the sun and stars moved round it as its guar-

dian attendants. Science had discovered that sun and
stars, if they had proper motion of their own, yet in respect of the earth were motionless, and that the varying
aspect of the sky was due to the movements of the earth
itself. The change was humbling to superficial vanity.
'The stars in their courses' could no longer be supposed
to fight against earthly warriors, or comets to foretell the
havoc on fields of slaughter, or the fate and character of a
prince to be affected by the constellation under which he
was born. But if the conceit of the relative importance
of man was diminished, his conception of the system of
which he was a part had become immeasurably more magnificent; while every phenomenon which had been actually
and faithfully observed remained unaffected. Sun and
moon were still the earthly time-keepers ; and the mariner
still could guide his course across the ocean by the rising
and setting of the same stars which Ulysses had watched
upon his raft.

Carlyle conceived that a revolution precisely analogous
to that which Galileo had wrought in our apprehension of
the material heaven was silently in progress in our attitude towards spiritual phenomena.

The spiritual universe, like the visible, was the same
yesterday, to-day, and for ever, and legends and theologies
were, like the astronomical theories of the Babylonians,
Egyptians, or Greeks, true so far as they were based on
facts, which entered largely into the composition of the
worst of them—true so far as they were the honest efforts
of man's intellect and conscience and imagination to interpret the laws under which he was living, and regulate
his life by them. But underneath or beyond all these
speculations lay the facts of spiritual life, the moral and
intellectual constitution of things as it actually was in
eternal consistence. The theories which dispensed with
God and the soul Carlyle utterly abhorred. It was not

credible to him, he said, that intellect and conscience could have been placed in him by a Being which had none of its own. He rarely spoke of this. The word God was too awful for common use, and he veiled his meaning in metaphors to avoid it. But God to him was the fact of facts. He looked on this whole system of visible or spiritual phenomena as a manifestation of the will of God in constant forces, forces not mechanical but dynamic, interpenetrating and controlling all existing things, from the utmost bounds of space to the smallest granule on the earth's surface, from the making of the world to the lightest action of a man. God's law was everywhere: man's welfare depended on the faithful reading of it. Society was but a higher organism, no accidental agreement of individual persons or families to live together on conditions which they could arrange for themselves, but a natural growth, the conditions of which were already inflexibly laid down. Human life was like a garden, 'to which the will was gardener,' and the moral fruits and flowers, or the immoral poisonous weeds, grew inevitably according as the rules already appointed were discovered and obeyed, or slighted, overlooked, or defied. Nothing was indifferent. Every step which a man could take was in the right direction or the wrong. If in the right, the result was as it should be; if in the wrong, the excuse of ignorance would not avail to prevent the inevitable consequence.

These in themselves are but commonplace propositions which no one denies in words; but Carlyle saw in the entire tone of modern thought, that practically men no longer really believed them. They believed in expediency, in the rights of man, in government by majorities; as if they could make their laws for themselves. The law, did they but know it, was already made; and their wisdom, if they wished to prosper, was not to look for what was convenient to themselves, but for what had been decided already in Nature's chancery.

Many corollaries followed from such a creed when sincerely and passionately held. In arts and sciences the authority is the expert who understands his business. No one dreamt of discovering a longitude by the vote of a majority; and those who trusted to any such methods would learn that they had been fools by running upon the rocks. The science of life was no easier—was harder far than the science of navigation : the phenomena were infinitely more complex; and the consequences of error were infinitely more terrible. The rights of man, properly understood, meant the right of the wise to rule, and the right of the ignorant to be ruled. 'The gospel of force,' of the divine right of the strong, with which Carlyle has been so often taunted with teaching, merely meant that when a man has visibly exercised any great power in this world, it has been because he has truly and faithfully seen into the facts around him ; seen them more accurately and interpreted them more correctly than his contemporaries. He has become in himself, as it were, one of nature's forces, imperatively insisting that certain things must be done. Success may blind him, and then he mis-sees the facts and comes to ruin. But while his strength remains he is strong through the working of a power greater than himself. The old Bible language that God raised up such and such a man for a special purpose represents a genuine truth.

But let us hear Carlyle himself. The following passages were written in 1852, more than twenty years after the time at which we have now arrived. Figure and argument were borrowed from new appliances which had sprung into being in the interval. But the thought expressed in them was as old as Hoddam Hill when they furnished the armour in which he encountered Apollyon.

They are but broken thoughts, flung out as they presented themselves, and wanting the careful touch with which Carlyle finished work which he himself passed through the press; but I give them as they remain in his own handwriting.

SPIRITUAL OPTICS.

Why do men shriek so over one another's creeds? A certain greatness of heart for all manner of conceptions and misconceptions of the Inconceivable is now if ever in season. Reassure thyself, my poor assaulted brother. Starting from the east, a man's road seems horribly discordant with thine, which is so resolutely forcing itself forward by tunnel and incline, victorious over impediments from the western quarter. Yet see, you are both struggling, more or less honestly, towards the centre—all mortals are unless they be diabolic and not human. Recollect with pity, with smiles and tears, however high thou be, the efforts of the meanest man. Intolerance coiled like a dragon round treasures which were the palladium of mankind was not so bad; nay, rather was indispensable and good. But intolerance, coiled and hissing in that horrid manner, now when the treasures are all fled, and there are nothing but empty pots new and old—pots proposing that they shall be filled, and pots asserting that they were once full—what am I to make of that? Intolerance with nothing to protest but empty pots and eggs that are fairly addle, is doubly and trebly intolerable. I do not praise the tolerance talked of in these times; but I do see the wisdom of a Truce of God being appointed, which you may christen tolerance, and everywhere proclaim by drum and trumpet, by public cannon from the high places, and by private fiddle, till once there be achieved for us something to be intolerant about again. There are a few men who have even at present a certain right, call it rather a certain terrible duty, to be intolerant, and I hope that these will be even more, and that their intolerance will grow ever nobler, diviner, more victorious. But how few are there in all the earth! Be not so much alarmed at the opulences, spiritual or material, of this world. Whether they be of the hand or the mind, whether consisting of St. Katherine's docks, blooming cornfields, and filled treasuries, or of sacred philosophies, theologies, bodies of science, recorded heroisms, and accumulated conquests of wisdom and harmonious human utterances—they have all been amassed by little and little. Poor insignificant transitory bipeds little better than thyself have ant-wise accumulated them all. How inconsiderable was the contribution of each; yet working with hand or with head in the strenuous ardour of their heart, they did what was in them; and here, so magnificent, overwhelming, almost divine and immeasurable, is the summed-up result. Be modest towards it; loyally reverent towards it: that is well thy part. But begin at last to understand withal what thy own real relation to it is; and that if it, in its greatness, is divine, so then in thy littleness art thou [not so?] *Lass Dich nicht verblüffen*, 'Don't let thyself be put upon' [no]. 'Stand up for thyself withal.' That, say the Germans, is the eleventh commandment; and truly in these times for an ingenuous soul there is not perhaps in the whole Decalogue a more important one.

And in all kinds of times, if the ingenuous soul could but understand that only in proportion to its own divineness can any part or lot in those divine possessions be vouchsafed it, how inexpressibly important would it be! Such is for ever the fact; though not one in the hundred now knows it or surmises it. Of all these divine possessions it is only what thou art become equal to that thou canst take away with thee. Except thy own eye have got to see it, except thy own soul have victoriously struggled to clear vision and belief of it, what is the thing seen and the thing believed by another or by never so many others? Alas, it is not thine, though thou look on it, brag about it, and bully and fight about it till thou die, striving to persuade thyself and all men how much it is thine. Not *it* is thine, but only a windy echo and tradition of it bedded in hypocrisy, ending sure enough in tragical futility, is thine. What a result for a human soul! In all ages, but in this age, named of the printing press, with its multiform pulpits and platforms, beyond all others, the accumulated sum of such results over the general posterity of Adam in countries called civilised is tragic to contemplate; is in fact the raw material of every insincerity, of every scandal, platitude, and ignavia to be seen under the sun. If men were only ignorant and knew that they were so, only void of belief *and sorry for it*, instead of filled with sham belief and proud of it—ah me!!

The primary conception by rude nations in regard to all great attainments and achievements by men is that each was a miracle and the gift of the gods. Language was taught man by a heavenly power. Minerva gave him the olive, Neptune the horse, Triptolemus taught him agriculture, &c. The effects of *optics* in this strange camera obscura of our existence, are most of all singular! The grand centre of the modern revolution of ideas is even this— we begin to have a notion that all this *is* the effect of optics, and that the intrinsic fact is very different from our old conception of it. Not less 'miraculous,' not less divine, but with an altogether totally new (or hitherto unconceived) *species* of divineness; a divineness lying much nearer home than formerly; a divineness that does not come from Judæa, from Olympus, Asgard, Mount Meru, but is in man himself; in the heart of everyone born of man—a grand revolution, indeed, which is altering our ideas of heaven and earth to an amazing extent in every particular whatsoever. From top to bottom our spiritual world, and all that depends on the same, which means nearly everything in the furniture of our life, outward as well as inward, is, as this idea advances, undergoing change of the most essential sort, is slowly getting 'overturned,' as they angrily say, which in the sense of being gradually turned over and having its vertex set where its base used to be, is indisputably true, and means a 'revolution' such as never was before, or at least since letters and recorded history existed among us never was. The great Galileo, or numerous small Galileos, have appeared in our spiritual world too, and are making known to us that the sun stands still; that as for the sun and stars and eternal immensities, they do not move at all, and indeed have something else to do than dance round the like of us and our paltry little dog-hutch of a dwelling place; that it is we and our dog-hutch that are moving all this while, giving rise to such phenomena; and that if we would ever be wise about our situation we must now attend to that fact. I would fain sometimes write a book about all that, and try to make it plain to everybody. But alas! I find again there is next to nothing to be said about it in words at present—and indeed till lately I had vaguely supposed that everybody understood it, or at least understood me to mean it, which it would appear that they don't at all.

A *word* to express that extensive or universal operation of referring the motion from yourself to the object you look at, or *vice versá?* Is there none?

A notable tendency of the human being in case of mutual motions on the part of himself and another object, is to misinterpret the said motion and impute it to the wrong party. Riding in this whirled vehicle, how the hedges seem to be in full gallop on each side of him ; how the woods and houses, and all objects but the fixed blue of heaven, seem to be madly careering at the top of their speed, stormfully waltzing round transient centres, the whole earth gone into menadic enthusiasm, he himself all the while locked into dead quiescence ! And again, if he is really sitting still in his railway carriage at some station when an opposite train is getting under way, his eye informs him at once that *he* is at length setting out and leaving his poor friends in a stagnant state. How often does he commit this error ? It is only in exceptional cases, when helps are expressly provided, that he avoids it and judges right of the matter.

It is very notable of the outward eye, and would be insupportable, did not the experience of each man incessantly correct it for him, in the common businesses and locomotions of this world. In the uncommon locomotion it is not so capable of correction. During how many ages and æons, for example, did not the sun and the moon and the stars go all swashing in their tremendously rapid revolution every twenty-four hours round this little indolent earth of ours, and were evidently *seen* to do it by all creatures, till at length the Galileo appeared, and the Newtons in the rear of him. The experience necessary to correct that erroneous impression of the eyesight was not so easy of attainment. No. It lay far apart from the common businesses, and was of a kind that quite escaped the duller eye. It was attained nevertheless ; gradually got together in the requisite quantity ; promulgated, too, in spite of impediments, holy offices, and such like ; and is now the general property of the world, and only the horses and oxen cannot profit by it. These are notable facts of the outward eyesight and the history of its progress in surveying this material world.

But now, will the favourable reader permit me to suggest to him a fact which, though it has long been present to the consciousness of here and there a meditative individual, has not, perhaps, struck the favourable reader hitherto—that with the inward eyesight and the spiritual universe there is always, and has always, been the same game going on. Precisely a similar game, to infer motion of your own when it is the object seen that moves ; and rest of your own with menadic storming of all the gods and demons ; while it is yourself with the devilish and divine impulses that you have, that are going at express train speed ! I say the Galileo of this, many small Galileos of this, have appeared some time ago—having at length likewise collected (with what infinitely greater labour, sorrow, and endurance than your material Galileo needed) the experience necessary for correcting such illusions of the *inner* eyesight in its turn—a crowning discovery, as I sometimes call it, the essence and summary of all the sad struggles and wrestlings of these last three centuries. No man that reflects need be admonished what a pregnant discovery this is; how it is the discovery of discoveries, and as men become more and more sensible of it will remodel the whole world for us in a most blessed and surprising manner. Such continents of sordid delirium (for it is really growing now very sordid) will vanish like a foul Walpurgis night at the first streaks of dawn. Do but consider it. The delirious dancing of the universe is stilled, but the universe itself (what scepticism did not suspect) is still all there. God, heaven, hell, are none of them annihilated for us, any more than the material woods and houses. Nothing that was divine, sublime, demonic, beautiful, or terrible is in the least abolished for us as the poor pre-Galileo fancied it might be; only their mad dancing has ceased, and they are all reduced to dignified composure; any madness that was in it being recognised as our own henceforth.

What continents of error, world-devouring armies of illusions and of foul realities that have their too true habitation and too sad function among such, will disappear at last wholly from our field of vision, and leave a serener veritable world for us. Scavengerism, which under Chadwick makes such progress in the material streets and beneath them, will alarmingly but beneficently reign in the spiritual fields and thoroughfares; and deluges of spiritual water, which is light, which is clear, pious vision and conviction, will have washed our inner world clean too with truly celestial results for us. Oh, my friend, I advise thee awake to that fact, now discovered of the inner eyesight, as it was long since of the outer, that not the sun and the stars are so rapidly dashing round; nor the woods and distant steeples and country mansions are deliriously dancing and waltzing round accidental centres: that it is thyself, and thy little dog-hole of a planet or dwelling-place, that are doing it merely.

It was God, I suppose, that made the Jewish people and gave them their hook-noses, obstinate characters, and all the other gifts, faculties, tendencies, and equipments they were launched upon the world with. No doubt about that in any quarter. These were the general outfit of the Jews, given them by God

and none else whatever. And now, if in the sedulous use of said
equipments, faculties, and general outfit, with such opportunities
as then were, the Jew people did in the course of ages work out
for themselves a set of convictions about this universe which were
undeniable to them, and of practices grounded thereon which
were felt to be salutary and imperative upon them, were not the
Jew people bound at their peril temporal and eternal to cherish
such convictions and observe said practices with whatever strictest
punctuality was possible, and to be supremely thankful that they
had achieved such a possession ? I fancy they would do all this
with a punctuality and devoutness and sacred rigour in exact proportion to the quantity of obstinate human method, piety, persistence, or of that Jewhood and manhood, and general worth and
wisdom, that were in them ; for which be they honoured as Jews
and men.   And if now they please to call all this by the highest
names in their vocabulary, and think silently, and reverently
speak of it, as promulgated by their great Jehovah and Creator
for them, where was the harm for the time being? Was it not
intrinsically true that their and our unnameable Creator *had* revealed it to them ? having given them the outfit of faculties, character, and situation for discerning and believing the same? Poor
souls ! they fancied their railway carriage (going really at a great
rate, I think, and with a terrible noise through the country) was
perfectly motionless, and that they at least saw the landscape, discerned what landscape there was dancing and waltzing round
them.   Their error was the common one incidental to all passengers and movers through this world—except those overloaded busy
eating individuals that make their transit sleeping. Yes : fall well
asleep ; you will not think the landscape waltzes ; you will see no
landscape, but in their dim vastness the turbid whirlpools of your
own indigestions and nightmare dreams. You will be troubled
with no *mis*conceptions of a Godhood, Providence, Judgment Day,
eternal soul of night, or other sublimity in this world.   Looking
into your own digestive apparatus when sleep has melted it into
the immense, you snore quietly and are free from all that.

So far Carlyle had written, and then threw it aside as
unsatisfactory, as not adequately expressing his meaning,
and therefore not to be proceeded with.   But a very intelligible meaning shines through it ; and when I told him
that I had found and read it, he said that it contained his

real conviction, a conviction that lay at the bottom of all his thoughts about man and man's doings in this world. A sense lay upon him that this particular truth was one which he was specially called on to insist upon, yet he could never get it completely accomplished. On another loose sheet of rejected MS. I find the same idea stated somewhat differently :—

Singular what difficulty I have in getting my poor message delivered to the world in this epoch : things I imperatively need still to say.

1. That all history is a Bible—a thing stated in words by me more than once, and adopted in a sentimental way ; but nobody can I bring fairly into it, nobody persuade to take it up practically as a *fact.*

2. Part of the 'grand Unintelligible,' that we are now learning spiritually too—that the earth *turns,* not the sun and heavenly spheres. One day the spiritual astronomers will find that *this* is the infinitely greater miracle. The universe is not an orrery, theological or other, but a universe ; and instead of paltry theologic brass spindles for axis, &c., has laws of gravitation, laws of attraction and repulsion ; is not a Ptolemaic but a Newtonian universe. As Humboldt's 'Cosmos' to a fable of children, so will the new world be in comparison with what the old one was, &c.

3. And flowing out of this, that the work of genius is not *fiction* but fact. How dead are all people to that truth, recognising it in word merely, not in deed at all ! Histories of Europe ! Our own history ! Eheu ! If we had any vivacity of soul and could get the old Hebrew spectacles off our nose, should we run to Judæa or Houndsditch to look at the doings of the Supreme ? Who conquered anarchy and chained it everywhere under their feet ? Not the Jews with their morbid imaginations and foolish sheepskin Targums. The Norse with their steel swords guided by fresh valiant hearts and clear veracious understanding, it was *they* and not the Jews. The supreme splendour will be seen *there,* I should imagine, not in Palestine or Houndsditch any more. Man of genius to interpret history ! After interpreting the Greeks and Romans for a thousand years, let us now try our own a little. (How clear this has been to myself for a long while !) Not one soul, I believe, has yet taken it into him. Universities founded

by monk ages are not fit at all for this age. 'Learn to read Greek, to read Latin'! You cannot be *saved* (religiously speaking too) with those languages. What of reason there *was* in that! Beautiful loyalty to the ancients Dante and Virgil, *il duca mio.* Beautiful truly so far as it goes! But the superfœtation is now grown perilous, deadly, horrible, if you could see it!

Old piety was wont to say that God's judgments tracked the footsteps of the criminal; that all violation of the eternal laws, done in the deepest recesses or on the conspicuous high places of the world, was absolutely certain of its punishment. You could do no evil, you could do no good, but a god would repay it to you. It was as certain as that when you shot an arrow from the earth, gravitation would bring it back to the earth. The all-embracing law of right and wrong was as inflexible, as sure and exact, as that of gravitation. Furies with their serpent hair and infernal maddening torches followed Orestes who had murdered his mother. In the still deeper soul of modern Christendom there hung the tremendous image of a Doomsday—*Dies iræ, dies illa*—when the All-just, without mercy now, with only terrific accuracy now, would judge the quick and the dead, and to each soul measure out the reward of his deeds done in the body—eternal Heaven to the good, to the bad eternal Hell. The Moslem too, and generally the Oriental peoples, who are of a more religious nature, have conceived it so, and taken it, not as a conceit, but as a terrible fact, and have studiously founded, or studiously tried to found, their practical existence upon the same.

My friend, it well behoves us to reflect how true essentially all this still is: that it continues, and will continue, fundamentally a fact in all essential particulars—its certainty, I say its infallible certainty, its absolute justness, and all the other particulars, the eternity itself included. He that has with his eyes and soul looked into nature from any point—and not merely into distracted theological, metaphysical, modern philosophical, or other cobweb representations of nature at second hand—will find this true, that only the vesture of it is changed for us; that the essence of it cannot change at all. Banish all miracles from it. Do not name the name of God; it is still true.

Once more it is in religion with us, as in astronomy—we know now that the earth moves. But it has not annihilated the stars for us; it has infinitely exalted and expanded the stars and universe. Once it seemed evident the sun did daily rise in the east;

the big sun—a sun-god—did travel for us, driving his chariot over the crystal floor all days : at any rate the sun *went*. Now we find it is only the earth that goes. So too all mythologies, religious conceptions, &c., we begin to discover, are the necessary products of man's godmade mind.

I need add little to these two fragments, save to repeat that they are the key to Carlyle's mind; that the thought which they contain, although nowhere more articulately written out, governed all his judgments of men and things. In this faith he had 'trampled down his own spiritual dragons.' In this faith he interpreted human history, which history witnessed in turn to the truth of his convictions. He saw that now as much as ever the fate of nations depended not on their material development, but, as had been said in the Bible, and among all serious peoples, on the moral virtues, courage, veracity, purity, justice, and good sense. Nations where these were honoured prospered and became strong; nations which professed well with their lips, while their hearts were set on wealth and pleasure, were overtaken, as truly in modern Europe as in ancient Palestine, by the judgment of God.

'I should not have known what to make of this world at all,' Carlyle once said to me, 'if it had not been for the French Revolution.'

This might be enough to say on Carlyle's religion; but there is one aspect of religion on which everyone who thinks at all will wish to know his opinion. What room could there be for prayer in such a scheme of belief as his? In one form or other it has been a universal difficulty. How should ignorant man presume to attempt to influence the will of his Creator, who by the necessity of his nature cannot change, and must and will on all occasions and to all persons do what is just and right?

Reason cannot meet the objection. Yet nevertheless men of the highest powers have prayed and continue to pray. I am permitted to publish the following letters, which show what Carlyle thought about it in 1870. And as he thought in 1870, he thought in 1828. His mind when it was once made up never wavered, never even varied.

From George A. Duncan to Thomas Carlyle.

4 Eyre Place, Edinburgh : June 4, 1870.

Honoured Sir,—I am a stranger to you, but my grandfather, Dr. Henry Duncan, of Ruthwell, was not, and it is a good deal on that ground that I rest my plea for addressing you. Of all the things I possess there is none I value more than a copy of your translation of 'Meister's Apprenticeship,' presented to my grandfather by you, and bearing on its fly-leaf these to me thrice precious words :—' To the Rev. Dr. Duncan, from his grateful and affectionate friend T. Carlyle.' I show it to all my friends with the utmost pride. But I have another plea. I was one of those Edinburgh students to whom, as a father to his sons, you addressed words which I have read over at least six times, and mean, while I live, to remember and obey. I have still one plea more. You know that in this country, when people are perplexed or in doubt, they go to their minister for counsel : you are my minister, my only minister, my honoured and trusted teacher, and to you I, having for more than a year back ceased to believe as my fathers believed in matters of religion, and being now an inquirer in that field, come for light on the subject of prayer. There are repeated expressions in your works which convince me that in some form or other you believe in prayer, and the fact that the wisest men, Luther, Knox, Cromwell, and that greater Man whose servants they were, were pre-eminently men of prayer, is at variance with the thought which still forces itself upon me, that to attempt to change the Will of Him who is Best and Wisest (and what is prayer, if it is not that?) is in the last degree absurd. The only right prayer, it seems to me, is 'Thy will be done ; ' and that is a needless one, for God's will shall assuredly be done at any rate. Is it too much to hope that you will kindly write me a few lines throwing light on this subject? I have read Goethe's ' Confessions of a Fair Saint,' and also what you say with regard to Cromwell's prayers, but still I have not been able to arrive at a conviction. Lest these remarks should seem to you intolerably shallow, I must inform you that I am only twenty.

Would it interest you in any measure to read some letters written by you to Mr. Robert Mitchell when this old century was in its teens, and thus recall from your own beloved past a thousand persons, thoughts, and scenes and schemes bygone ? Mr. M. left my grand-uncle, Mr. Craig, one of his trustees, and among the papers which thus fell into Mr. Craig's hands were several letters from you to Mr. Mitchell. Mr. C.'s daughters lately gave them to one of my sisters, and I believe that if you expressed the slightest wish to see them, I should be able to persuade her to let me send them to you, though she guards them very jealously.

Believe me, yours ever gratefully,

GEO. A. DUNCAN.

Thomas Carlyle to George A. Duncan.

Chelsea : June 9, 1870.

Dear Sir,—You need no apology for addressing me ; your letter itself is of amiable ingenuous character ; pleasant and interesting to me in no common degree. I am sorry only that I cannot set at rest, or settle into clearness, your doubts on that important subject. What I myself practically, in a half-articulate way, believe on it I will try to express for you.

First, then, as to your objection of setting up *our* poor wish or will in opposition to the will of the Eternal, I have not the least word to say in contradiction of it. And this seems to close, and does, in a sense though not perhaps in all senses, close the question of our prayers being *granted,* or what is called ' heard ;' but that is not the whole question.

For, on the other hand, prayer is and remains always a native and deepest impulse of the soul of man ; and correctly gone about, is of the very highest benefit (nay, one might say, indispensability) to every man aiming morally high in this world. No prayer no *religion,* or at least only a *dumb* and lamed one ! Prayer is a turning of one's soul, in heroic reverence, in infinite desire and *endeavour,* towards the Highest, the All-Excellent, Omnipotent, Supreme. The modern Hero, therefore, ought *not* to give up praying, as he has latterly all but done.

Words of prayer, in this epoch, I know hardly any. But the act of prayer, in great moments, I believe to be still possible ; and that one should gratefully accept such moments, and count them blest, when they come, if come they do—which latter is a most rigorous preliminary question with us in all cases. ' *Can* I *pray*

in this moment' (much as I may *wish* to do so)? 'If not, then
NO!' I can at least stand silent, inquiring, and *not* blasphemously
lie in this Presence!

On the whole, Silence is the one safe form of prayer known to
me, in this poor sordid era—though there are ejaculatory words
too which occasionally rise on one, with a felt propriety and veracity; words very welcome in such case! Prayer is the aspira-
tion of our poor struggling heavy-laden soul towards its Eternal
Father; and, with or without words, ought *not* to become impossible, nor, I persuade myself, need it ever. Loyal sons and subjects *can* approach the King's throne who have no 'request' to
make there, except that they may continue loyal. Cannot they?

This is all I can say to you, my good young friend; and even
this, on my part and on yours, is perhaps too much. Silence,
silence! 'The Highest cannot be spoken of in words,' says
Goethe. Nothing so desecrates mankind as their continual bab-
bling, both about the speakable and the unspeakable, in this bad
time!

Your grandfather was the amiablest and kindliest of men; to me
pretty much a *unique* in those young years, the one cultivated man
whom I could feel myself permitted to call *friend* as well. Never
can I forget that Ruthwell Manse, and the beautiful souls (your
grandmother, your grand-aunts, and others) who then made it
bright to me. All vanished now, all vanished!

Please tell me *whose* son you are—not George John's, I think,
but Wallace's, whom I can remember only as a grave boy? Also
whether bonny little 'Barbara Duncan' is still living; or indeed
if she ever lived to be your aunt? I have some sad notion No.
I will not trouble you about the Mitchell letters: I wrote many
letters to the good Mitchell; but I fear now they were all of a
foolish type, fitter to burn than to read at present. Tell me also,
if you like, a little more about yourself, your pursuits and endeavours, your intended course in the world. You perceive I expect
from you one more letter at least, though it is doubtful whether I
can *answer* any more, for *reasons* you may *see* sufficiently!

Believe me, dear Sir,

Yours with sincere good wishes,

T. CARLYLE.

CHAPTER II.

A.D. 1828.   ÆT. 33.

I HAVE already described Craigenputtock as the dreariest
spot in all the British dominions. The nearest cottage is
more than a mile from it; the elevation, 700 feet above
the sea, stunts the trees and limits the garden produce to
the hardiest vegetables. The house is gaunt and hungry-
looking. It stands with the scanty fields attached as an
island in a sea of morass. The landscape is unredeemed
either by grace or grandeur, mere undulating hills of
grass and heather, with peat bogs in the hollows between
them. The belts of firs which now relieve the eye and
furnish some kind of shelter were scarcely planted when
the Carlyles were in possession. No wonder Mrs. Carlyle
shuddered at the thought of making her home in so stern
a solitude, delicate as she was, with a weak chest, and
with the fatal nervous disorder of which she eventually
died already beginning to show itself. Yet so it was to
be. She had seen the place in March for the first time in
her life, and then, probably, it had looked its very worst.
But in May, when they came to settle, the aspect would
have scarcely been mended. The spring is late in Scotland; on the high moors the trees are still bare. The
fields are scarcely coloured with the first shoots of green,
and winter lingers in the lengthening days as if unwilling
to relax its grasp. To Mrs. Carlyle herself the adventure
might well seem desperate. She concealed the extent of
her anxiety from her husband, though not entirely from
others. Jeffrey especially felt serious alarm. He feared

not without reason that Carlyle was too much occupied with his own thoughts to be trusted in such a situation with the charge of a delicate and high-spirited woman, who would not spare herself in the hard duties of her situation.

The decision had been made, however, and was not to be reconsidered. Jeffrey could only hope that the exile to Siberia would be of short duration. When the furniture at Comely Bank was packed and despatched, he invited Mr. and Mrs. Carlyle to stay with him in Moray Place, while the carts were on the road. After two days they followed, and in the last week of May they were set down at the door of the house which was now to be their home. The one bright feature in the situation to Carlyle was the continual presence of his brother at the farm. The cottage in which Alexander Carlyle lived was attached to the premises; and the outdoor establishment of field, stall, and dairy servants was common to both households.

I resume the letters.

To John Carlyle.

Craigenputtock : June 10, 1828.

My dear Jack,—We received your much-longed-for letter two days ago before leaving Edinburgh in such a scene of chaotic uproar as I had never witnessed, and do earnestly hope I shall never witness again, for the house was full of mats and deal boxes and straw and packthread, and there was a wrapping and a stitching and a hammering and tumbling; and Alick and Jamie came with six carts to take away our goods; and all things were wrenched from their old fixtures, and dispersed and scattered asunder, or united only by a common element of dust and noise. What would the sack of a city be, when the dismantling of a house is such! From all packers and carpenters, and flittings by night or day, Good Lord deliver us.

I have waited here above two weeks in the vain hope that some calmness would supervene. But painters and joiners still desecrate every corner of our dwelling, and I write in the midst of confusion worse confounded as better than not writing at all.

We have arrived at Craigenputtock and found much done, but still much to do; we must still rush and run with carts and saddlehorses to Dumfries every second day, and rejoice when we return if the course of events have left us a bed to sleep on. However, by the strength of men's heads and arms a mighty improvement is and will be accomplished, and one day we calculate a quiet house must stand dry and clean for us amid this wilderness; and the philosopher will hoe his potatoes in peace on his own soil, and none to make him afraid. Had we come hither out of whim one might have sickened and grown melancholy over such an outlook; but we came only in search of food and raiment, and will not start at straws. Away then with *Unmuth und Verdruss!* Man is born to trouble and toil as the sparks fly upwards. Let him toil, therefore, as his best is, and make no noise about the matter. Is the day wearisome, dusty, and full of *midges* that the galled limbs are like to fail?

> Ein guter Abend kommt heran,
> Wenn ich den ganzen Tag gethan. . . .

Next evening, after the arrival of your letter, I wrote to Messrs. Black and Young, booksellers, London (of the 'Foreign Review'), directing them to pay twenty out of forty pounds which they had ordered me to draw on them for, into the hands of Messrs. Ransome & Co. to be paid to the Baron von Eichthal at Munich.[1] I hope the money may have reached you by this time. I sent these booksellers a long paper on Goethe for their next still unprinted number; the forty pounds was for an essay on his 'Helena.' I meant to send them another piece (on the life of Heyne) for this number; but where is the cunning that could write a paper here in the midst of uncreated night? But I am getting very sick, and must leave you till after dinner, and go *stick* some rows of peas which are already flourishing in our new garden.

. . . Alas! Jack, there is no sticking of peas for me at this hour, the cutting-tools being all in active operation elsewhere; so I sit down to talk with you again, still *impransus*, though in better health than I was an hour ago. Indeed, I have been in considerably better health ever since I came hither, and found my red chestnut Irish doctor (though ill) saddled, waiting for me in his stall. By degrees I do think I shall grow as sound as another

---

[1] With whom John Carlyle was then living.

man; and then, when the German doctor is settled within sight of
me at Dumfries,[1] and we see him twice a week, and all is fixed on
its own footing, will not times be brighter than they have been
with us?   One blessing we have always to be thankful for—unity
and brotherly love, which makes us, though a struggling, still a
united family—and are we not all spared together in this wonderful existence still to hope as we struggle?   Let us ever be grateful to the Giver of all good, and struggle onward in the path He
directs.   Some traces of our presence may also be left behind us
in this pilgrimage of life, some grains added to the great pyramid
of human endeavour.   What more has man to wish for?

Of the Craig o' Putta I cannot yet rightly speak till we have
seen what adjustment matters will assume.   Hitherto, to say
truth, all prospers as well as we could have hoped.   The house
stands heightened and white with rough cast, a light hewn porch
in front and canns on the chimney-heads; and within it all seems
firm and sound.   During summer, as we calculate, it will dry, and
the smoke we have reason to believe is now pretty well subdued,
so that on this side some satisfaction is to be looked for.   We appear also to have been rather lucky in our servants.   An active maid
came with us from Edinburgh.   A dairywoman, also of good omen,
comes to us to-morrow from Thornhill; and a good-humoured
slut of a byre-woman was retained after half a year's previous trial.
Then we have two sufficient farming men and a bonneted strip-
ling skilful in sheep, from this glen.   Alick himself is an active
little fellow as ever bent ——, and though careworn is diligent,
hearty, and compliant.   He lives in his little room, which is still
but half-furnished like the rest of the house.[2]   Mary has been
visiting at Scotsbrig, and is now learning to sew at Dumfries.
Jane the lesser (Jean) has taken her place here and furnishes butter and *afterings* (*jibbings*)[3] for tea, though we are still in terrible
want of a cheeseboard, and by the blessing of Heaven shall get
one to-morrow afternoon.   Jane (the greater) is surveying all
things, proving all things, that she may hold fast to what is good.
She watches over her joiners and painters with an eye like any
hawk's, from which nothing crooked, unplumb or otherwise irregular can hide itself a moment.   And then, to crown our felicity,

[1] John Carlyle's present intention.
[2] Not yet in occupation of his own cottage.
[3] Annandale expressions, meaning—what?   The explanatory word itself
requires explaining.

we have two fowls hatching in the wood, a duck with twelve eggs, and a hen with (if I mistake not) eleven, from which, for they are properly fed and cared for, great things are expected. Nay, it was but these three nights ago that we slew a Highland stot and salted him in a barrel, and his puddings even now adorn the kitchen ceiling.

From Edinburgh or other peopled quarters of the world I have yet heard nothing. We left Edward Irving there preaching like a Boanerges, with (as Henry Inglis very naively remarked) the town divided about him, 'one party thinking that he was quite mad, another that he was an entire humbug.' For my own share I would not be intolerant of any so worthy a man; but I cannot help thinking that if Irving is on the road to truth, it is no straight one. We had a visit from him, and positively there does seem a touch of extreme exaltation in him. I do not think he will go altogether mad, yet what else he will do I cannot so well conjecture. Cant and enthusiasm are strangely commingled in him. He preaches in steamboats and all open places, wears clothes of an antique cut (his waistcoat has flaps or tails midway down the thigh) and in place of ordinary salutation bids 'the Lord bless you.' I hear some faint rumour of his out-heroding Herod since we left the North, but we have not yet got our newspaper, and so know nothing positive. So 'the *Laurt* bless HIM!' for the present, and if you pass through London on your return, you are engaged to go and see him, and, I think he said, 'abide with him' or 'tarry with him' on your way.

The last two nights we spent in Edinburgh were spent—where think you? In the house of Francis Jeffrey, surely one of the kindest little men I have ever in my life met with. He and his household (wife and daughter) have positively engaged to come and pay us a visit here this very summer! I am to write him an article on Burns as well as on Tasso. But alas, alas! all writing is as yet far from my hand. Walter Scott I did not see because he was in London; nor hear of, perhaps because he was a busy or uncourteous man, so I left his Goethe medals to be given him by Jeffrey.[1] Lockhart had written a kind of 'Life of Burns,' and men in general were making another uproar about Burns. It is this book, a trivial one enough, which I am to *pretend* reviewing. Further, except continued abuse of Leigh Hunt for his 'Lord

---

[1] They had been originally entrusted to Wilson. How they had been passed to Jeffrey I do not know.

Byron, and some of his Contemporaries,' there seemed no news in the literary world, or rather universe; for was there ever such a world as it has grown?

Be steady and active and of good cheer, my dear Doctor, and come home and live beside us, and let us all be as happy as we can.

I am ever, your true brother,

T. CARLYLE.

The carpenters and plasterers were at last dismissed. Craigenputtock became tolerable, if not yet 'cosmic,' and as soon as all was quiet again, Carlyle settled himself to work.[1] Tasso was abandoned, or at least postponed, but

---

[1] It was now that the 'bread' problem had to be encountered, of which Miss Jewsbury speaks in her 'Recollections of Mrs. Carlyle.' Carlyle could not eat such bread as the Craigenputtock servants could bake for him, or as could be bought at Dumfries, and Mrs. Carlyle had to make it herself. Miss Smith, an accomplished lady living at Carlisle, has kindly sent me a letter in which the story is characteristically told by Mrs. Carlyle herself. It is dated January 11, 1857—after an interval of nearly thirty years. Mrs. Carlyle writes :—

'So many talents are wasted, so many enthusiasms turned to smoke, so many lives split for want of a little patience and endurance, for want of understanding and laying to heart what you have so well expressed in your verses—the meaning of *the Present*—for want of recognising that it is not the greatness or littleness of "the duty nearest hand," but the spirit in which one does it, that makes one's doing noble or mean. I can't think how people who have any natural ambition and any sense of power in them escape going *mad* in a world like this without the recognition of that. I know I was very near mad when I found it out for myself (as one has to find out for oneself everything that is to be of any real practical use to one).

'Shall I tell you how it came into my head? Perhaps it may be of comfort to you in similar moments of fatigue and disgust. I had gone with my husband to live on a little estate of *peat bog* that had descended to me all the way down from John Welsh the Covenanter, who married a daughter of John Knox. *That* didn't, I am ashamed to say, make me feel Craigenputtock a whit less of a peat bog, and a most dreary, untoward place to live at. In fact, it was sixteen miles distant on every side from all the conveniences of life, shops, and even post office. Further, we were very *poor*, and further and worst, being an only child, and brought up to "great prospects," I was sublimely ignorant of every branch of useful knowledge, though a capital Latin scholar, and very fair mathematician ! ! It behoved me in these astonishing circumstances to learn to sew ! Husbands, I was shocked to find, wore their stockings into holes, and were always losing buttons, and *I* was expected to "look to all that ; " also it behoved me to learn to *cook !* no capable servant

the article on Burns was written—not so ungraciously, so
far as regarded Lockhart, as the epithet 'trivial' which
had been applied to his book might have foreboded. But
it is rather on Burns himself than on his biographer's account of him that Carlyle's attention was concentrated. It
is one of the very best of his essays, and was composed
with an evidently peculiar interest, because the outward
circumstances of Burns's life, his origin, his early sur-
roundings, his situation as a man of genius born in a farmhouse not many miles distant, among the same people and
the same associations as were so familiar to himself, could
not fail to make him think often of himself while he was
writing about his countryman. How this article was judged
by the contemporary critics will be presently seen. For

choosing to live at such an out-of-the-way place, and my husband having bad
digestion, which complicated my difficulties dreadfully. The *bread*, above all,
brought from Dumfries, "soured on his stomach" (oh Heaven!), and it was
plainly my duty as a Christian wife to bake at home. So I sent for Cobbett's
Cottage Economy, and fell to work at a loaf of bread. But knowing nothing
about the process of fermentation or the heat of ovens, it came to pass that
my loaf got put into the oven at the time that myself ought to have been put
into bed; and I remained the only person not asleep in a house in the middle of
a desert. One o'clock struck, and then two, and then three; and still I was sitting there in an immense solitude, my whole body aching with weariness, my
heart aching with a sense of forlornness and *degradation*. That I, who had been
so petted at home, whose comfort had been studied by everybody in the house,
who had never been required to *do* anything but *cultivate my mind*, should
have to pass all those hours of the night in watching *a loaf of bread*—which
mightn't turn out bread after all! Such thoughts maddened me, till I laid down
my head on the table and sobbed aloud. It was then that somehow the idea
of Benvenuto Cellini sitting up all night watching his Perseus in the furnace
came into my head, and suddenly I asked myself: "After all, in the sight of
the Upper Powers, what is the mighty difference between a statue of Perseus
and a loaf of bread, so that each be the thing one's hand has found to do?
The man's determined will, his energy, his patience, his resource, were the
really admirable things of which his statue of Perseus was the mere chance
expression. If he had been a woman living at Craigenputtock, with a dyspeptic husband, sixteen miles from a baker, and he a bad one, all these same
qualities would have come out more fitly in a *good* loaf of bread.

'I cannot express what consolation this germ of an idea spread over my un-
congenial life during the years we lived at that savage place, where my two
immediate predecessors had gone *mad*, and the third had taken to *drink*.'

himself, it is too plain that before he came to the end of it the pastoral simplicities of the moorland had not cured Carlyle of his humours and hypochondrias. He had expected that change of scene would enable him to fling off his shadow. His shadow remained sticking to him; and the poor place where he had cast his lot had as usual to bear the blame of his disappointment. In his diary there stands a note: 'Finished a paper on Burns, September 16, 1828, at this Devil's Den, Craigenputtock.'

Meanwhile, though he complained of hearing little from the world outside, his friends had not forgotten him. Letters came by the carrier from Dumfries, and the Saturday's post was the event of the week. Jeffrey especially was affectionate and assiduous. He reproached Carlyle for not writing to him, complained of being so soon forgotten, and evidently wished to keep his friend as close to him as possible. The papers on German literature had brought a pamphlet upon Jeffrey about Kant, from 'some horrid German blockhead;' but he was patient under the affliction and forgave the cause. King's College had been set on foot in London on orthodox principles, under the patronage of the Duke of Wellington and the bishops. He offered to recommend Carlyle to them as Professor of Mysticism; although mysticism itself he said he should like less than ever if it turned such a man as Carlyle into a morbid misanthrope, which seemed to be its present effect. Sir Walter had received his medals and had acknowledged them; had spoken of Goethe as his master, and had said civil things of Carlyle, which was more than he had deserved. Jeffrey cautioned Carlyle to be careful of the delicate companion who had been trusted to him; offered his services in any direction in which he could be of use, and throughout, and almost weekly, sent to one or other of the 'hermits' some note or letter, short or long, but always sparkling, airy, and honestly affectionate. I am sorry that I am not at liberty to print these letters *in extenso;* for they would show that Jeffrey had a genuine regard and admiration for Carlyle, which was never completely appreciated. It was impossible from their relative positions that there should not be at least an appearance of patronage on Jeffrey's part. The reader has probably discovered that Carlyle was proud, and proud men never wholly forgive those to whom they feel themselves obliged.

Late in the summer there came a letter from the young Charles Buller, now grown to intellectual manhood, and thinking about entering public life. He and his old tutor had not forgotten each other. Carlyle had watched him through Cambridge, and had written to caution him against certain forms of Liberal opinion towards which Mrs. Strachey had seen with alarm that her brilliant nephew was tending. Buller replies:—

To Thomas Carlyle.

August 31, 1828.

I can hardly say I feel sorry for your disappointment respecting St. Andrews and the London University, since you seem to have been utterly careless of success. The former I suppose went almost solely by ministerial influence ; and as my father has not quite arrived at the degree of Toryism and baseness which would make a man support the Duke of Wellington's Government, he could hardly have done any good in that way. You have, I see, left Edinburgh. Which and where is the awfully cacophonious place where you have taken up your residence ? I would venture to hint that you have kept a perplexing silence respecting the posture of your present life.

I see the London University allows people to give lectures in some manner of connection with them without being appointed by them. Suppose you were to propose to give lectures on German literature and philosophy, I should think you would get an innumerable quantity of pupils. I do not know whether the new ' King's College' is closed to all teachers by M.A.'s and Reverends. If not, I should think you might possibly stand a good chance of getting some appointment there, and it would certainly be a great thing to have one person in that establishment who knows anything beyond that slender and antique lore which the two venerable Universities of Oxford and Cambridge impart to their *élèves*. But I only mention this, for I am utterly ignorant whether this new King's College is to teach anything beyond loyalty and Church of Englandarianism, or to have any teachers except a Greek and Latin lecturer, and perhaps one in Divinity to explain the Catechism. But if you think it worth while I would obtain information from the Bishop of Llandaff, who is the best of the people who have anything to do with it.

We forwarded your letter to Mrs. Strachey, who I dare say will not have acknowledged it, because she has just had the misfortune of—a tenth child. We have some expectation of seeing Miss Kirkpatrick soon, but she is in great trouble. Her brother William, perhaps you already know, died in May after a lingering and painful illness. His poor young wife has gone mad, and Kitty, after all this, has been involved in a very wearisome and distressing dispute with Mrs. Kirkpatrick's sister respecting the care of her brother's children.

And now I refer once more to what you said in your letter to me about myself. You seem to hope that my Utilitarianism and blankness in religion will not last long. If they are wrong, that is, not a true conclusion of my reason, I hope that I may abandon them, and that soon. But I have adopted Utilitarianism because I think it affords the best explanation of men's opinions on morals, and because on it may be built, I think, the best framework on which we may form and instruct the natural feelings of men to do that which produces peace and good will among them.

I think, moreover, that the doctrines of the Utilitarians, whether promulgated under that name or under others, have already done no little good in shaming the world out of some of its worst theories of right and wrong respecting most important matters of practice. That many of the Utilitarians are grossly intolerant I am very ready to admit. But is not this the invariable concomitant (except in the very first geniuses) of zeal for the truth? and especially so when men have, like the Utilitarians, to keep their new principles by main force of logic against the intolerance of the stupid champions of orthodoxy, and the general disfavour even of the better and wiser part of the community?

With regard to my blankness in religion—you call by a mild name a set of opinions to which men usually attach a name that burns worse than Inquisitor's fire and faggot—I have fixed myself in that, because I have not yet found that faith which I could believe, and none among the creeds of this world that I could *wish* to be true. I could picture to myself a bright creed truly ; but to think that it could be real because it was pretty would be childish indeed.

But my steed awaits me.

Believe me, ever yours sincerely,
CHARLES BULLER.

July this year had been intensely hot. Jeffrey had complained of being stifled in the courts, and for the moment had actually envied his friends their cool mountain breezes. The heat had been followed in August by rain. It had been 'the wettest, warmest summer ever known.' Alexander Carlyle had been living hitherto with his brother, the cottage which he was to occupy with one of his sisters not being yet ready. The storms had delayed the masons ; while the article on Burns was being written the premises were still littered with dirt, and Carlyle's impatience with small misfortunes perhaps had inspired the unpleasant epithet of Devil's Den with which he had already christened his home. He appears to have remained, however, in a—for him—tolerable humour.

To John Carlyle.

August 25, 1828.

In this mansion we have had a battle like that of St. George and the Dragon. Neither are we yet conquerors. Smoke and wet and chaos. The first we have subdued ; the last two we are subduing. May the Lord keep all Christian men from flitting.

As to literature, which also is bread-making, I have done nothing since Whitsunday but a shortish paper on Heyne [1] for the 'Foreign Review,' which will appear in No. 4. A long article on Goethe is just publishing in No. 3, [2] which has been, for want of cash, I believe, exceedingly delayed ; and at this very date I am very busy, and third part done, with a 'fair, full, and free' essay on Burns for the 'Edinburgh Review.' None can say how bilious I am, and

---

[1] *Miscellanies*, vol. ii. p. 75.   [2] *Ibid.*, vol. i. p. 233.

am like to be; but I have begun to ride daily on Larry,[1] and so Jeffrey shall have his article at the appointed time. That wonderful little man is expected here very soon with *Weib und Kind.* He takes no little interest in us, writes often, and half hates, half loves me with the utmost sincerity. Nay, he even offers me in the coolest, lightest manner the use of his purse, and evidently rather wishes I would use it. *Proh Deûm atque hominum fidem!* This from a Scotchman and a lawyer! Jane is in considerable trepidation getting the house fully equipped for these august visitors. Surely I think she will succeed. Nay, already we are very smart. Here is a drawing-room with Goethe's picture in it, and a piano, and the finest papering on the walls; and I write even now behind it, in my own little library, *out* of which truly I can see nothing but a barn-roof, tree tops, and empty hay-carts, and under it perhaps a stagnant midden, cock with hens, overfed or else dazed with wet and starvation; but *within* which I may see a clear fire (of peats and Sanquhar coals), with my desk and books and every accoutrement I need in fairest order. Shame befall me if I ought to complain, except it be of my own stupidity and pusillanimity. Unhappily we still want a front door road, and the lawn is mostly a quagmire.

Several weeks ago I had a long letter from Goethe[2] enclosing another from Dr. Eckermann, his secretary, full of commendations and congratulations about my criticism of his 'Helena.' I ought to have written to him long ago, but cannot and must not, till I have done with Burns. If you pass within any manageable distance of Weimar you will surely wait on this sage man. Seriously, I venerate such a person considerably more not only than any king or emperor, but than any man that handles never so expertly the tools of kings and emperors. *Sein Excellenz* already knows you by name, and will welcome you in his choicest mood.

Did you hear of the horrible accident at Kirkcaldy? Irving was going to preach there, and the kirk fell and killed eight and twenty persons. 'What think'st a he means,' said my father, 'gawn up and down the country tevelling and screeching like a wild bear?' Heaven only knows completely. Walter Welsh wonders they do not 'lay him up.' I add no more.

Your brother,   T. Carlyle.

---

[1] The Irish horse of 'genius,' who had thrown him at Hoddam Hill.

[2] I find no copy of this letter. The original appears to be lost among the rest.

The Jeffreys were to have come in September, while the weather was still fine, but they had gone first to the western Highlands, and their visit was put off till the next month. Meanwhile the article on Burns had been sent off, and before the appearance of the visitors at Craigenputtock a sharp altercation had commenced between the editor and his contributor on certain portions of it, which was not easily ended. On the article itself the world has pronounced a more than favourable verdict. Goethe considered it so excellent that he translated long passages from it, and published them in his collected works;[1] but, as Goethe had observed about Schiller, contemporaries always stumble at first over the writings of an original man. The novelty seems like presumption. The editor of the 'Edinburgh Review' found the article long and diffuse, though he did not deny that 'it contained much beauty and felicity of diction.' He insisted that it must be cut down— cut down perhaps to half its dimensions. He was vexed with Carlyle for standing, as he supposed, in his own light, misusing his talents and throwing away his prospects. He took the opportunity of reading him a general lecture.

'I suppose,' he said, 'that you will treat me as something worse than an ass when I say that I am firmly persuaded the great source of your extravagance, and of all that makes your writings intolerable to many and ridiculous to not a few, is not so much any real peculiarity of opinions, as an unlucky ambition to appear more original than you are, or the humbler and still more delusive hope of converting our English intellects to the creed of Germany and being the apostle of another Reformation. I wish to God I could persuade you to fling away these affectations, and be contented to write like your famous countrymen of all ages: as long at least as you write to

[1] Goethe's *Works*, vol. xxxiii. pp. 181 *et seq.*

your countrymen and for them. The nationality for which you commend Burns so highly might teach you, I think, that there are nobler tasks for a man like you than to vamp up the vulgar dreams of these Dousterswivels you are so anxious to cram down our throats ; but which I venture to predict no good judge among us will swallow, and the nation at large speedily reject with loathing.'

So spoke the great literary authority of the day. The adventurous Prince who would win the golden water on the mountain's crest is always assailed by cries that he is a fool and must turn back, from the enchanted stones which litter the track on which he is ascending. They too have once gone on the same quest. They have wanted faith, and are become blocks of rock echoing commonplaces ; and if the Prince turns his head to listen to them, he too becomes as they. Jeffrey tried to sweeten his admonitions by compliments on the article upon Goethe ; but here too he soon fell to scolding. 'Though I admire,' he said, 'the talent of your paper, I am more and more convinced of the utter fallacy of your opinions and the grossness of your idolatry. I predict too, with full and calm assurance, that your cause is hopeless, and that England never will admire, nor indeed endure, your German divinities. It thinks better and more of them indeed than it ever will again. Your eloquence and ingenuity a little mask their dull extravagance and tiresome presumption. As soon as they appear in their own persons everybody will laugh. I am anxious to save you from this *fœda superstitio.* The only harm it has yet done you is to make you a little verbose and prone to exaggeration. There are strong symptoms of both in your Burns. I have tried to staunch the first, but the latter is in the grain, and we must just risk the wonder and the ridicule it may bring on us.'

This was not merely the protest of an editor, but the

reproach of a sincere friend. Jeffrey ardently desired to recommend Carlyle and to help him forward in the world. For Carlyle's own sake, and still more for the sake of his young and delicate relative, he was vexed and irritated that he should have buried himself at Craigenputtock. He imagined, and in a certain sense with justice, that Carlyle looked on himself as the apostle of a new faith (to a clever man of the world the most absurd and provoking of illusions), which the solitude of the moors only tended to encourage.

With October the promised visit was accomplished. How he came with Mrs. Jeffrey and his daughter, how the big carriage stood wondering how it had got there in the rough farm-yard, how Carlyle and he rode about the country, with what astonishment he learnt that his dinner had been cooked for him by his hostess's own hands, how he delighted them all in the evenings with his brilliant anecdotes and mimicries—all this has been told elsewhere and need not be repeated. Those two days were a sunny island in the general dreariness, an Indian summer before winter cut the Carlyles off from the outside world and wrapped them round with snow and desolation. During the greater part of the Jeffreys' stay controverted subjects were successfully avoided. But Carlyle's talk had none the less provoked Jeffrey. He himself, with a spiritual creed which sat easy on him, believed nevertheless that it was the business of a sensible man to make his way in the world, use his faculties to practical purposes, and provide for those who were dependent upon him. He saw his friend given over as he supposed to a self-delusion which approached near to foolish vanity, to have fallen in love with clouds like Ixion, and to be begetting chimæras which he imagined to be divine truths. All this to a clear practical intelligence like that of Jeffrey was mere non-sense, and on the last night of his stay he ended a long argument in a tone of severe reproach for which he felt himself afterwards obliged to apologise. His excuse, if excuse was needed, was a genuine anxiety for Carlyle's welfare, and an equal alarm for his wife, whose delicacy, like enough, her husband was too much occupied with his own thoughts to consider sufficiently. 'I cannot bring myself to think,' he said in a letter which he wrote after he had left them, 'that either you or Mrs. Carlyle are naturally placed at Craigenputtock; and though I know and reverence the feelings which have led you to fix there for the present, I must hope it will not be long necessary to obey them in that retreat. I dare not advise, and do not even know very well what to suggest to a mind so constituted as yours; but I shall be proud to give you my views upon anything that occurs to yourself, and pray understand that few things in this world can give me more gratification than being able to be of any serious use to you. Take care of the fair creature who has trusted herself so entirely to you. Do not let her ride about in the wet, nor expose herself to the wintry winds that will by-and-by visit your lofty retreat; and think seriously of taking shelter in Moray Place[1] for a month or two, and in the meantime be gay and playful and foolish with her, at least as often as you require her to be wise and heroic with you. You have no *mission* upon earth, whatever you may fancy, half so important as to be innocently happy—and all that is good for you of poetic feeling and sympathy with majestic nature will come of its own ac-cord without your straining after it. That is my creed, and right or wrong I am sure it is both a simpler and a humbler one than yours.'

The trouble with the article on Burns was not over. Jeffrey, as editor, had to consider the taste of the great

[1] Jeffrey's house in Edinburgh.

Liberal party in literature and politics, and to disciples of
Bentham, as indeed to the average reader of any political
persuasion, Carlyle's views were neither welcome nor intelligible.   When the proof sheets came, he found 'the first
part cut all into shreds—the body of a quadruped with the
head of a bird, a man shortened by cutting out his thighs
and fixing the knee-caps on the hips.'   Carlyle refused to
let it appear 'in such a horrid shape.'   He replaced the
most important passages, and returned the sheets with an
intimation that the paper might be cancelled, but should
not be mutilated.   Few editors would have been so forbearing as Jeffrey when so audaciously defied.   He complained, but he acquiesced.   He admitted that the article
would do the Review credit, though it would be called
tedious and sprawling by people of weight whose mouths
he could have stopped.   He had wished to be of use to
Carlyle by keeping out of sight in the Review his mannerism and affectation ; but if Carlyle persisted he might have
his way.

Carlyle was touched ; such kindness was more than he
had looked for.   The proud self-assertion was followed by
humility and almost penitence, and the gentle tone in
which he wrote conquered Jeffrey in turn.   Jeffrey said
that he admired and approved of Carlyle's letter to him in
all aspects.   'The candour and sweet blood' which was
shown in it deserved the highest praise; and, as the dying
pagan said in the play, 'If these are Christian virtues I am
a Christian,' so Jeffrey, hating as he did what he called
Carlyle's mysticism, was ready to exclaim, if these were
mystic virtues he was mystic.   'But your virtues are your
own,' he said, 'and you possess them not in consequence of
your mysticism, but in spite of it.   You shall have anything you like.   I cannot chaffer with such a man, or do
anything to vex him; and you shall write mysticism for

me if it will not be otherwise, and I will print it too at all
hazards with very few and temperate corrections.   I think
you have a great deal of eloquence and talent, and might do
considerable things if —— But no matter ;. I will not tire
of you ; after all, I believe there are many more things as
to which we agree than about which we differ, and the
difference is not radical, but formal chiefly.'

CHAPTER III.

A.D. 1829.   ÆT. 34.

So the winter settled down over Craigenputtock. The
weekly cart struggled up when possible from Dumfries
with letters and parcels, but storms and rain made the
communications more and more difficult. Old James Carlyle came over from Scotsbrig for a week after the Jeffreys
went, an Edinburgh friend followed for three days more,
and after that few faces save those of their own household
were seen at the Carlyles' door. Happily for him he was
fully employed. The 'Foreign Review' and the 'Edinburgh' gave him as much work as he could do. He had
little need of money; Scotsbrig supplied him with wheat
flour and oatmeal, and the farm with milk and eggs and
hams and poultry. There was little that needed buying
save tea and sugar and tobacco; and his finances (for his
articles were long and handsomely paid for) promised for
a time to be on an easy footing in spite of the constant expenses of his brother John at Munich. There were two
horses in the stable—Larry, the Irish horse of 'genius,'
and Harry, Mrs. Carlyle's pony.[1] In fine weather they

---

[1] Carlyle told me a story of these two horses, illustrative of the sense of
humour in animals. I cannot date it either by day or year, and therefore I
give it in a note. They had a vicious old sow, who was the tyrant and the
terror of the farm-yard. One day Carlyle was smoking his pipe outside his
front door, when he heard shrieks of rage and agony combined from the back
of the house. He went round to see what was the matter. A deep drain had
been opened across the yard, the bottom of which was stiff clay. Into this
by some unlucky curiosity the sow had been tempted to descend, and being
there found a difficulty in getting out. The horses were loose. The pony

occasionally rode or walked together. But the occasions grew rarer and rarer. Carlyle was essentially solitary. He went out in all weathers, indifferent to wet and, in spite of his imagined ill-health, impervious to cold. But he preferred to be alone with his thoughts, and Mrs. Carlyle was left at home to keep the house in proper order. She by education, and he by temperament, liked everything to be well kept and trim. He was extremely dainty about his food. He did not care for delicacies, but cleanliness and perfect cookery of common things he always insisted on, and if the porridge was smoked, or the bread heavy, or the butter less than perfect, or a plate or a dish ill-washed, he was entirely intolerable. Thus the necessary imperfections of Scotch farm-servant girls had to be supplemented by Mrs. Carlyle herself. She baked the bread, she dressed the dinner or saw it dressed, she cleaned the rooms. Among her other accomplishments she had to learn to milk the cows, in case the byre-woman should be out of the way, for fresh milk was the most essential article of Carlyle's diet. Nay, it might happen that she had to black the grates to the proper polish, or even scour the floors while Carlyle looked on encouragingly with his pipe. In addition to this she had charge of dairy and poultry ; not herself necessarily making butter or killing fowls, but directing what was to be done and seeing that it was done properly. Her department, in short, was the whole establishment. This winter she was tolerably well, and as long as her health lasted she complained of nothing. Her one object was to keep Carlyle contented, to prevent him from being fretted by any petty annoyance,

saw the opportunity—the sow was struggling to extricate herself. The pony stood over her, and at each effort cuffed her back again with a stroke of the fore hoof. The sow was screaming more from fury than pain. Larry stood by watching the performance and smiling approval, nodding his head every time that the beast was knocked back into the clay, with (as Carlyle declared) the most obvious and exquisite perception of the nature of the situation.

and prevent him also from knowing with how much labour to herself his own comfort was secured.

Thus the months passed on pleasantly. The 'tempests,' about which Jeffrey had been so anxious, howled over the moors, but did not much affect them. Carlyle's letters were written in fair spirits. The Devil's Den had become a tolerable home. Mrs. Carlyle, it seems, when she could spare time, galloped down alone to Templand (15 miles) to see her mother.

To John Carlyle.

Craigenputtock: November 26, 1828.

This house, bating some outskirt things, which must be left till spring, is really substantial, comfortable, and even half elegant. I sit here in my little library and laugh at the howling tempests, for there are green curtains and a clear fire and papered walls. The 'old kitchen' also is as tight a dining room as you would wish for me, and has a black clean barred grate, at which, when filled with Sanquhar coals, you might roast Boreas himself. The good wife too is happy and contented with me and her solitude, which I believe is not to be equalled out of Sahara itself. You cannot figure the stillness of these moors in a November drizzle. Nevertheless I walk often under cloud of night, in good Ecclefechan clogs, down as far as Carstammon Burn, sometimes to Sandy Wells, conversing with the void heaven in the most pleasant fashion. Besides Jane also has a pony now which can canter to perfection even by the side of Larry. To-morrow she is going over to Templand with it, and it is by her that I send this letter. Grace, our servant, a tight tidy careful sharp-tempered woman, is the only other inmate of the house.

I write hard all day, and then Jane and I, both learning Spanish for the last month, read a chapter of 'Don Quixote' between dinner and tea, and are already half through the first volume and eager to persevere. After tea I sometimes write again, being dreadfully slow at the business, and then generally go over to Alick and Mary and smoke my last pipe with them; and so I end the day, having done little good, perhaps, but almost no ill that I could help to any creature of God's.

So pass our days, except that sometimes I stroll with my axe or bill in the plantations, and when I am not writing I am reading.

We had Henry Inglis here for three days, and our father for a week lately, both of whom seemed highly contented with this wonderful Craig. Alick and Mary, you already understand, live in their own cottage, or rather double farmhouse, for were it once dried it will be the bieldest, tightest mansion of its sort within some miles of it. They have two man-servants and two maid-servants, are fattening, or merely boarding, quantities of black cattle, have almost a dozen pigs, and plenty of weak corn, and about eighty cartloads of potatoes, to say nothing of turnip acres, to feed them with. Alick is about thatching a cattle shed, long since built (of dry stones), down near the moor, and we have had roadsmen for many weeks gravelling the front of this door (a most marked improvement), making us a proper road to it, and thoroughly repairing the old road. Thus you see chaos is rolling himself back from us by degrees, and all winter we are to have stone-diking, and planting, and draining (if I can write for the cash), till by-and-by I think this hermitage will positively become a very tolerable place. For the rest we drink tea together every Sunday night and live in good brotherhood, having no neighbours that do not wish us well.

As to my writing, it is only at present a most despicable 'article' entitled 'German Playwrights,' with which I expect to be done in a week.

Next I mean to write one on Novalis, and probably a larger one on Voltaire. Some day these roads will be made and sky-lights mended, and all tight and pargetted, and I shall have leisure to cease reviewing, and try to give work for reviewing.

Our news, beyond our own household, are mostly of a sombre cast. James Anderson, the young Laird of Straquhar, our kind neighbour and acquaintance, died after two days' illness a few weeks ago. John Grier, of the Grove, is gone to his long home. He also died suddenly, but like a just man, and with entire composure. Is not this world a mystery, and grand with terror as well as beauty?[1] My letter, you will see, ends in sable, like the life of man. My own thoughts grow graver every day I live.

When Carlyle was in good spirits, his wife had a pleasant time with him. 'Ill to live wi',' impatient, irritable

---

[1] In a previous letter Carlyle, speaking of another death, says : 'Oh God, it is a fearful world, this we live in, a film spread over bottomless abysses, into which no eye has pierced.' The same expression occurs in the *French Revolution.* The image had already impressed itself into his mind.

over little things, that he always was ; but he was charming, too ; no conversation in my experience ever equalled
his ; and unless the evil spirit had possession of him, even
his invectives when they burst out piled themselves into
metaphors so extravagant that they ended in convulsions
of laughter with his whole body and mind, and then all
was well again. Their Spanish studies together were delightful to both. His writing was growing better and
better. She—the most watchful and severest of critics,—
who never praised where praise was not deserved, was
happy in the fulfilment of her prophecies, and her hardest
work was a delight to her when she could spare her husband's mind an anxiety or his stomach an indigestion. At
Christmas she had a holiday, going down to her mother
and grandfather at Templand. But while away among
her own people her heart was on the Craig. This is one
of the letters which Carlyle himself annotated, in the sad
days when she was lost to him for ever.

To Thomas Carlyle.

Templand : December 30, 1828.

Goody, Goody, dear Goody,—You said you would weary, and I
do hope in my heart you are wearying. It will be so sweet to
make it all up to you in kisses when I return. You will *take me*
and hear all my bits of experiences, and your heart will beat when
you find how I have longed to return to you. Darling, dearest,
loveliest, 'The Lord bless you.' [1] I think of you every hour,
every moment. I love you and admire you, like—like anything.
My own Good-Good. But to get away on Sunday was not in my
power : my mother argued, entreated, and finally *grat* (wept). I
held out on the ground of having appointed Alick to meet me at
church ; but that was untenable. John Kerr [2] could be sent off at
break of day to tell that I could not come. I urged that the
household would find themselves destitute of every Christian
comfoart, unless I were home before Wednesday. That could be

[1] 'Poor Edward Irving's practice and locution, suspect of being somewhat
too solemn ! T. C.'
[2] The Templand man-servant.

taken care of by sending anything that was wanted from here.
Tea, sugar, butchers' meat, everything was at my service. Well,
but I wanted, I said, to be your *first-foot* on New Year's Day. I
might be gratified in this also. She would hire a post-chaise and
take me over for that day on condition I returned at night!

In short, she had a remedy ready for everything but death, and
I could not without seeming very unkind and ungracious, refuse
to stay longer than I proposed. So I write this letter 'with my
own hand' [Ed. Irving] that you may not be disappointed from
day to day; but prepare to welcome me 'in your choicest mood'
on Sunday. If the day is at all tolerable, perhaps Alick or you
will meet me at church. Mrs. Crichton, of Dabton, was very pressing that you and I should spend some days with them just now,
'when their house was full of company.' But I assured her it
would be losing labour to ask you. However, by way of consolation, I have agreed to 'refresh' a party for her with my presence
on Friday, and held out some hope that you would visit them at
your leisure. 'I am sure the kindness of those people ——' 'The
Lord bless them!'[1]

Dearest, I wonder if you are getting any victual. There must
be cocks at least, and the chickens will surely have laid their eggs.
I have many an anxious thought about you; and I wonder if you
sleep at nights, or if you are wandering about—on, on—smoking
and killing mice. Oh, if I was there I could put my arms so close
about your neck, and hush you into the softest sleep you have had
since I went away. Good night. Dream of me.

I am ever,
Your own GOODY.

The first year of Craigenputtock thus drew to an end.
The storms of December were succeeded by frost, and the
moors were bound fast in ice. Carlyle continued as busy
as ever at what he called 'the despicable craft of reviewing,' but doing his very best with it. No slop-work ever
dropped from his pen. He never wrote down a word
which he had not weighed, or a sentence which he had
not assured himself contained a truth. Every one of the
articles composed on this bare hill-top has come to be reprinted unaltered, and most of them have a calmness too

---

[1] Irving.

often absent from his later writings. Handsome pay, as I said, came in, but not more than was needed. Brother John was a constant expense; and even in the 'Dunscore wilderness' life was impossible without money. 'Alas!' Carlyle said, 'for the days when Diogenes could fit up his tub, and let the "literary world" and all the other worlds except the only true one within his own soul wag hither and thither at discretion.'

Voltaire was now his subject. His mind was already turning with an unconscious fascination towards the French Revolution. He had perceived it to be the most note-worthy phenomenon of modern times. It was interesting to him, as an illustration of his conviction that untruthful-ness and injustice were as surely followed by divine retribu-tion as the idolatries and tyrannies of Biblical Egypt and Assyria; that the Power which men professed on Sundays to believe in was a living Power, the most real, the most tremendous of all facts. France had rejected the Reforma-tion. Truth had been offered her in the shape of light, and she would not have it, and it was now to come to her as lightning. She had murdered her prophets. She had received instead of them the scoffing Encyclopædists. Yet with these transcendental or 'mystic' notions in his head, Carlyle could write about the most worldly of all men of genius, as himself a man of the world. He meets Voltaire on his own ground, follows him into his private history with sympathising amusement; falls into no fits of horror over his opinions or his immoralities; but regards them as the natural outcome of the circumstances of the time. In Voltaire he sees the representative Frenchman of the age, whose function was to burn up unrealities, out of the ashes of which some more healthy verdure might eventually spring. He could not reverence Voltaire, but he could not hate him. How could he hate a man who had fought man-fully against injustice in high places, and had himself many a time in private done kind and generous actions? To Carlyle, Voltaire was no apostle charged with any divine message of positive truth. Even in his crusade against what he believed to be false, Voltaire was not animated with a high and noble indignation. He was simply an instrument of destruction, enjoying his work with the pleasure of some mocking imp, yet preparing the way for the tremendous conflagration which was impending. There is, of course, audible in this article a deep undertone of feeling. Yet the language of it is free from everything like excited rhetoric. In the earlier part of his career Carlyle sympathised with and expected more from the distinctive functions of revolution than he was able to do after longer experience. ' I thought,' he once said to me, ' that it was the abolition of rubbish. I find it has been only the kindling of a dunghill. The dry straw on the outside burns off; but the huge damp rotting mass remains where it was.'

Thinking on these momentous subjects, Carlyle took his nightly walks on the frozen moor, the ground crisp under his feet, the stars shining over his head, and the hills of Dunscore (for advantage had been taken of the dryness of the air) ' gleaming like Strombolis or Etnas with the burning of heath.' ' Craigenputtock otherwise silent, solitary as Tadmore in the wilderness; yet the infinite vault still over it, and the earth a little ship of space in which he was sailing, and man everywhere in his Maker's eye and hand.'

The new year perhaps did not bring many letters; for Carlyle's friends were still few, and his intimate friends who would write on such occasions were very few. One letter, however, could not fail to come from the faithful Jeffrey, who sent, as a New Year greeting, ' kind thoughts and good wishes,' with a laughing lecture against ' dogmatism,' and ' the desperate darkness of audacious mysticism.' From this Jeffrey passed to moralising on human life and things in general. Edinburgh and the whole of Britain had been shaken by the Burke and Hare business. With the light touch, half jesting and half serious, which is the charm of Jeffrey's style, he spoke of himself as living in fear of fever and dissection, yet not less gaily, less carelessly than usual. Men, he said, were naturally predestinarians, and ran their risks patiently because they could not avoid them. The pestilent and murdering angels had passed him so far, and he was grateful for his escape. Carlyle had been reading 'Don Quixote,' and in writing to Jeffrey had alluded to it, contrasting old times with new. Jeffrey protested against Carlyle's damnable heresy, insisting that there were plenty of shabby fellows whining over petty aches and finding life irksome in the age and country of Cervantes, and that in the Britain of George IV. there were stout-hearted, bright-spirited men who bore up against captivity and worse ills as cheerily as he did. He invited Carlyle to come and stay with him in Edinburgh, and shake off his sickly fancies. They might furnish swelling themes for eloquence, but were out of date and never convinced anybody; and as for Carlyle's notion that a man ought to have *a right creed as to his relations with the universe*, he would never persuade anyone that the regulation of life was such a laborious business as he would make it, or that it was not better to go lightly through it *with the first creed that came to hand*, than spend the better half of it in an anxious verification of its articles. It would matter less if Carlyle was but amusing himself with paradoxes, but he was 'so dreadfully in earnest.' He was neutralising half the fame and all the use of his talents, and keeping aloof from him most of the men who were fittest for his society.

Never had Jeffrey written to Carlyle with more warmth. The provocation to which he confessed was but the overflowing of good will to which his friend's views prevented him from giving the effect which he desired. The good will, though perfectly genuine, was not entirely disinterested. Carlyle's essays had drawn the notice of the distinguished band of men who were then the chief contributors to the 'Edinburgh Review.' They had recognised that he had extraordinary talents; that if he could be brought to his senses and would subscribe the articles of the Whig faith, he might be an invaluable recruit to the great party of Reform. Jeffrey himself was about to retire from the editorship of the 'Edinburgh Review,' and to become Dean of the Faculty. His advice, though not decisive, would be of weight in the choice of his successor, and he had seriously thought of recommending Carlyle. Brougham, Macaulay, Sydney Smith would all have more or less to be consulted; and perhaps the political chiefs as well; yet if his friend would only be amenable, burn his Goethe, renounce his mysticism, and let his talents and virtues have fair play, Jeffrey must have thought that the objections in those quarters would not be insurmountable.

So was Carlyle tempted in his hermitage, like another St. Anthony, by the spirit of this world, and in a more seductive dress than that in which it assailed the Christian saint. There was no situation in the empire more attractive to literary ambition than the editorship of the 'Edinburgh Review' in those its palmy days of glory and power. To have been even thought of for such an office implied that the attention of the Reform leaders had been drawn to him; and that if not in this way, yet in some others, he might, if he pleased, be advanced to some lucrative and honourable office. The difficulty was not on their side, it was on his. The way which they called heresy he called truth, and the kind, honest, but seducing angel assailed him in vain.

Carlyle, though in the 'Reminiscences of Lord Jeffrey' he has acknowledged a general wish on Jeffrey's part to

serve him, which was thwarted by his own persistency,
has passed over without mention this particular instance
of it. He never mentioned it even in conversation to
myself. But the fact was so. Jeffrey is himself the witness. The publishers of the 'Review' came down to Edinburgh to consult with him. Carlyle was not actually proposed. The prudent and cautious views of the Longmans,
and Jeffrey's wish to spare Carlyle the mortification of being rejected, prevented his pretensions from being brought
directly under discussion. But the inflexibility and independence of Carlyle's character were the chief, perhaps the only obstacles. Jeffrey was bitterly disappointed.
The person selected was Macvey Napier, the editor of the
'Encyclopædia,' 'a safe man at all events.' Jeffrey, writing to Carlyle, could not hide his mortification. ' It was
with mixed sorrow and anger,' he said, that he saw his
friend renouncing his natural titles to distinction for such
fantastical idolatry. The folly of his own fair cousin's an-
cestors, who threw away their money in improving and
adorning Craigenputtock, was but a faint type of Carlyle's. But he could not help him ; he would pray for him
if it would do any good.

A further effect of the change of editorship was that it
threatened at first the close of Carlyle's connection with
the 'Review,' even as a contributor. Jeffrey continued to
edit till the middle of 1829, and so long as he was in the
chair Carlyle's help was still solicited. The Voltaire had
been written for the 'Edinburgh,' if the 'Edinburgh'
would have it, and a corresponding article was in contemplation upon Johnson, Voltaire's direct antithesis. Neither
of these subjects pleased Jeffrey. Carlyle, he thought,
perhaps in this case with some want of judgment, could
have nothing new to say on either of them. But as the
time of his withdrawal drew near he begged hard for a
parting contribution for his last number. The Voltaire

would have answered well for him, but he did not even
ask to look at it. On any other subject Carlyle might
write what he pleased ; mysticism of the worst kind should
not be rejected. He was really ambitious, he said, of having a morsel of mysticism. He was going to take advantage of his approaching abdication by plaguing Brougham
with an attack on Utilitarianism ; and it was but reasonable that he should use the same retreat from responsibility in encouraging Carlyle to commit a fresh outrage on
the rational part of his readers. Any topic would serve as
a text. Jeffrey suggested 'Vivian Grey' or 'Pelham.'
'Vivian Grey' he considered better than the best novel
which any German had ever written. Carlyle proposed
Southey, but Macaulay had forestalled him. In the end
Carlyle wrote the 'Signs of the Times,' the first of the
essays in which he brought out his views of the condition of modern English society—a most signal outrage indeed, if that was what Jeffrey wanted, on 'the Philosophy of Progress' which was preached so continuously from
the Edinburgh pulpit. He gave Jeffrey full warning of
what was coming. Jeffrey only encouraged him with visibly malicious amusement. But the cautious character
which he ascribed to Napier made it probable that this
article might be his last in that periodical.

Of outward incidents meanwhile the Craigenputtock
history was almost entirely destitute. The year 1829
rolled by without interruption to the tranquil routine of
daily life. John Carlyle came home from Germany and
became sometimes his brother's guest till a situation as
doctor could be found for him. Carlyle himself wrote and
rode and planted potatoes. His wife's faculty for spreading grace about her had extended to the outside premises,
and behind the shelter of the trees she had raised a rose
garden. An old but strong and convenient gig was added
to the establishment. When an article was finished Car-

lyle allowed himself a fortnight's holiday: he and Mrs. Carlyle driving off with Larry either to Templand or to Scotsbrig; the pipe and tobacco duly arranged under cover on the inner side of the splashboard. The Jeffreys passed through Dumfries in the summer. Their friends from the Craig drove down to see them, and were even meditating afterwards an expedition in the same style throughout England as far as Cornwall.

Carlyle was full of thoughts on the great social questions of the day. He wished to see with his own eyes the actual condition of the people of England, as they lived in their own homes. The plan had to be abandoned for want of means, but he had set his own heart upon it, and Mrs. Carlyle would have been glad too of a change from a solitude which was growing intolerably oppressive. Carlyle's ill humours had not come back, but he was occupied and indifferent. There is a letter from his wife to old Mrs. Carlyle at Scotsbrig, undated, but belonging evidently to March of this year, in which she complains of the loneliness. 'Carlyle,' she says, 'never asks me to go with *him*, never even looks as if he desired my company.'

One visitor, however, came to Craigenputtock in the summer whose visit was more than welcome. Margaret, the eldest of Carlyle's sisters, had the superiority of mind and talent which belonged to her brother, and she had along with it an instinctive delicacy and nobleness of nature which had overcome the disadvantages of her education. She had become a most striking and interesting woman, but unhappily along with it she had shown symptoms of consumption. In the preceding autumn the family had been seriously alarmed about her. She had been ill all through the winter, but she had rallied with the return of warm weather. The cough ceased, the colour came back to her cheeks, she was thought to have recovered entirely, and in June or July she rode over with her

brother John from Scotsbrig to Craigenputtock, picking
up on the way a precious letter which was waiting at
Dumfries post office.

I remember (Carlyle writes) one beautiful summer evening,
1829, as I lounged out of doors smoking my evening pipe, silent
in the great silence, the woods and hill tops all gilt with the flaming splendour of a summer sun just about to set, there came a
rustle and a sound of hoofs into the little bending avenue on my
left (sun was behind the house and me), and the minute after
brother John and Margaret direct from Scotsbrig, fresh and handsome, as their little horses ambled up, one of the gladdest sights
and surprises to me. 'Mag, dear Mag, once more.' [1]   John had
found a letter from Goethe for me at the post-office, Dumfries.
This, having sent them in doors, I read in my old posture and
place, pure white the fine big sheet itself, still purer the noble
meaning all in it, as if mutely pointing to eternity—letter fit to be
read in such a place and time.[2]   Our dear Mag stayed some
couple of weeks or more (made me a nice buff-coloured cotton
waiscoat, I remember).   She was quietly cheerful, and complained of nothing; but my darling, with her quick eye, had noticed too well (as she then whispered to me) that the recovery was
only superficial, and that worse might be ahead.   It was the last
visit Margaret ever made.

Nothing more of special moment happened this year.
Life went on as usual; but the autumn brought anxieties
of more than one description.   The letters that remain are
few, for his wife and his brother Alexander, to whom he
wrote most confidentially, were both at Craigenputtock, and
his brother John also was for several months with him.
He was trying to produce something better than review
articles, and was engaged busily with an intended history
of German literature, for which he had collected a large
quantity of books.   But John Carlyle, who was naturally
listless, had to be stimulated to exertion, and was sent to
London to look for employment.   Employment would not

[1] The account is taken from the *Reminiscences*. The concluding words are
inserted from a letter.

[2] I discover no trace of this letter. Perhaps it may yet be found.

come; perhaps was less assiduously looked for than it
might have been. The expense of his maintenance fell
on Carlyle, and the reviews were the only source to which
he could look. More articles therefore had to be produced
if a market could be found for them. Jeffrey, constant in
his friendship, consulted the new editor of the 'Edinburgh,' and various subjects were suggested and thought
over. Carlyle proposed Napoleon, but another contributor was in the way. Jeffrey was in favor of Wycliffe,
Luther, or 'the Philosophy of the Reformation.' Napier
thought a striking article might be written on some poetical subject; but when Jeffrey hinted to him some of Carlyle's views on those topics, and how contemptuously he
regarded all the modern English singers, the new editor
'shuddered at the massacre of the innocents to which he
had dreamt of exciting him.' Still, for himself, Jeffrey
thought that if Carlyle was in a relenting mood, and
wished to exalt or mystify the world by a fine rhapsody
on the divine art, he might be encouraged to try it.

Liking Jeffrey as Carlyle did, he was puzzled at so
much interest being shown in him. He called it a mystery. Jeffrey humorously caught up the word, and accepted it as the highest compliment which Carlyle could
pay. In a humbler sense, however, he was content to
think it natural that one man of a kind heart should feel
attracted towards another, and that signal purity and lofti-
ness of character, joined to great talents and something of
a romantic history, should excite interest and respect.

Jeffrey's anxiety to be of use did not end in recommendations to Napier. He knew how the Carlyles were
situated in money matters. He knew that they were
poor, and that their poverty had risen from a voluntary
surrender of means which were properly their own, but
which they would not touch while Mrs. Welsh was alive.
He knew also that Carlyle had educated and was still sup-

porting his brother out of his own slender earnings. He saw, as he supposed, a man of real brilliancy and genius weighed down and prevented from doing justice to himself by a drudgery which deprived him of the use of his more commanding talents; and with a generosity the merit of which was only exceeded by the delicacy with which the offer was made, he proposed that Carlyle should accept a small annuity from him. Here again I regret that I am forbidden to print the admirable letter in which Jeffrey conveyed his desire, to which Carlyle in his own mention of this transaction has done but scanty justice. The whole matter he said should be an entire secret between them. He would tell no one—not even his wife. He bade Carlyle remember that he too would have been richer if he had not been himself a giver where there was less demand upon his liberality. He ought not to wish for a monopoly of generosity, and if he was really a religious man he must do as he would be done to; nor, he added, would he have made the offer did he not feel that in similar circumstances he would have freely accepted it himself. To show his confidence he enclosed 50*l*., which he expected Carlyle to keep, and desired only to hear in reply that they had both done right.

Carlyle was grateful, but he was proud. He did not at the time, or perhaps ever, entirely misconstrue the spirit in which Jeffrey had volunteered to assist him; but it is hard, perhaps it is impossible, for a man to receive pecuniary help, or even the offer of pecuniary help, from a person who is not his relation without some sense that he is in a position of inferiority; and there is force in the objection to accepting favours which Carlyle thus describes, looking back over forty years:—

Jeffrey generously offered to confer on me an annuity of 100*l*., which annual sum had it fallen on me from the clouds would have been of very high convenience at the time, but which I could not for a moment have dreamt of accepting as gift or sub-ventionary help from any fellow-mortal. It was at once in my handsomest, gratefullest, but brief and conclusive way declined from Jeffrey. 'Republican equality,' the silently fixed law of human society at present : each man to live on his own resources, and have an equality of economics with every other man ; danger-ous, and not possible except through cowardice or folly to depart from said clear rule till perhaps a better era rise on us again.

From a letter written at the time there appears through his genuine gratitude a faint but perceptible tinge of wounded feeling.

Do but think of Jeffery (he wrote to his brother, who was really the cause that he was in difficulties). A letter was lying here from him offering in the daintiest style to settle a hundred a year on unworthy me. I have just sent the meekest, friendliest, but most emphatic refusal for this and all coming times. Do not mention this, for you see it has never gone beyond the length of a flourish of rhetoric, and is scarcely fit to mention. Only when-ever we think of our Dean of the Faculty let us conceive him as a *multum in parvo* that does credit to Scotland and humanity.

If anyone thinks that Carlyle was deficient in gratitude, let him remember that gratitude is but one of many feel-ings which are equally legitimate and reputable. The gentleman commoner at Pembroke College meant only kindness when he left the boots at Johnson's door ; but Johnson, so far from being grateful, flung the boots out of the window, and has been praised by all mankind for it.

From his brother himself Carlyle was careful to con-ceal the scanty state to which his resources were reduced. From his notebook I find that at one time in 1830 he had but five pounds left with which to face the world. Yet he still wrote cheerfully, and remittances were still sent, with no word except of kind exhortation to exertion.

To John Carlyle, London.

Craigenputtock : February 11, 1830.

Your last letter, dear brother, though but of a sable texture, gave me more real satisfaction than any you had written. It exhibits

you in a figure of decided action, which after so many weeks of
storm-bound inactivity we all heartily longed and prayed to see you
in.   Spite of all difficulties, and these are too many and too heavy,
I now doubt not a moment that you will find yourself a settlement and ultimately prosper there.   But you are now at the pinch
of the game, Jack, and must *not* falter.   Now or never!   Oh, my
dear brother, do not loiter, do not linger, trusting to the chapter of
chances and help from other men.   Know and feel that you are
still there yourself ; *one* heart and head that will never desert your
interests.   I know the many difficulties and hesitations, how
wretched you are while others only fancy you sluggish.   But,
thank Heaven, you are now afoot, fairly diligent and intent.   What
way it is in you to make you will make ; and already I can well
believe you are far happier ; for evil, as Jean Paul truly says, is
like a nightmare—the instant you begin to *stir* yourself it is already gone.

   Meanwhile do not fret yourself over much ; a period of proba-
tion and adventure is appointed for most men, is good for all men.
For your friends especially—and testifying by deeds your affection to them—give yourself *no* sorrow.   There is not a friend you
have, Jack, who doubts for an instant of your affection ; neither is
their wish with regard to you to see you rich and famous, but
to see you self-collected, diligent, and wise, steering your way
manfully through this existence, resolutely and with clear heart
as beseems a man, as beseems *such* a man.   Whether you ride in
carriages and drink Tokay, and have crowds to follow after you,
or only walk in Scotch clogs like the rest of us, is a matter—so
you *do* walk—of far smaller moment.   'Stout heart to a stay brae'
then, my brave boy!   There is nothing in the world to frighten a
clear heart.   They can refuse you guinea fees, but the godlike
privilege of alleviating wretchedness, of feeling that you are a
true man, let the whole host of gigmen say to it what they will,
no power on earth, or what is under it, can take from you.   Oh
then, my brother, up and be doing !   Be my real stout brother as
of old, and I will take you to my heart and name you proudly,
though in the world's eye you were the lowest of the low.   What
charm is in a name ? Physician, surgeon, apothecary—all but
quack—is honourable.   There are plenty of poor to practise on.
If you gain but twenty shillings during the first half year do not
despair.   As for the poor ten pounds you get from me, you are
heartily welcome to it thrice over.   My only grief is that in the

present posture of affairs I can furnish nothing more. The Blacks
have not so much as paid me yet. However, times will not always
be so bad, and while I have help to give depend on it as your own.

Your affectionate brother,

T. C.

The Fates this winter were doing their very worst to
Carlyle. His wife had escaped harm from the first season
at Craigenputtock, but was not to be let off so easily a
second time. All went well till the close of December; a
fat goose had been killed for the new year's feast; when
the snow fell and the frost came, and she caught a violent
sore-throat, which threatened to end in diphtheria. There
was no doctor nearer than Dumfries, and the road from
the valley was hardly passable. Mrs. Welsh struggled up
from Templand through the snow-drifts; care and nursing kept the enemy off, and the immediate danger in a few
days was over; but the shock had left behind it a sense of
insecurity, and the unsuitableness of such a home for so
frail a frame became more than ever apparent. The old
father at Scotsbrig fell ill, too, this January and showed
signs of breaking, and beside the illness of those dear to
him, the repose of the country was startled by more than
one frightful tragedy. The death of a Craigenputtock
neighbour affected Carlyle much.

Rob Clerk of Craigmony (he wrote to his brother John) had
been drinking at Minny hire, perhaps the day you were departing.
He tumbled off his chair with a groan, gave a snort or two on the
floor, and was by his companions reckoned to be dead drunk. At
their convenient leisure they hoisted him and his boy, also drunk,
into the cart, which Johnny McCawe's 'lassie' (happily sober)
drove home under cloud of night to his aunt. Rob spoke none,
moved none, and his aunt carried him in on her back and laid him
on the bed, and after hours of sedulous ministering discovered
him to be—dead! Rob was once a man that could have tuned
markets with his own purse, and he would not 'taste' in those
days. But he failed in trade twice; since then has led a strange

wet and dry existence, drunk in all corners of Britain from Sussex to Sutherland, and *so* found his end at length. Is it not a wild world this? Who made it? who governs it? who gets good of it? Without faith I think a man were forced to be an atheist.

The next letter, one of the very few which Carlyle ever addressed to a public journal, explains itself.

To the Editor of the 'Dumfries and Galloway Courier.'

April 12, 1830.

Mr. Editor,—Some time last autumn a 'fatal accident' stood recorded in the newspapers, of a young man having come by his death at a place called Knockhill, near Ecclefechan, in this county, under somewhat singular circumstances. The young man, it appeared, had been engaged in some courtship with one of the maid-servants of the house; had come that night to see her in the fashion common, or indeed universal, with men of his station in that quarter, was overheard by the butler, was challenged, pursued, and, refusing to answer any interrogatory, but hastening only to escape, was shot dead by him on the spot. No man who has lived three weeks in the south of Scotland can be ignorant that such visits occur nightly everywhere, and have occurred from time immemorial. It is a custom by many blamed, by some applauded. In the romantic spirit sometimes displayed in it; in the long journeyings and wistful waitings for an interview; in the faithfulness with which the rustic wooer at all hazards keeps his secret which is also another's, Dr. Currie traces among our peasants some resemblance to the gallantry of a Spanish Cavalier. In company with the butler so fatally watchful on this occasion were two men to have assisted him in any defence, in any seizure. Whether he knew the individual fugitive, then within some feet of his gun, is uncertain; that he guessed his errand there is scarcely so. Enough the poor young man who had refused to speak fell to the ground exclaiming only, Oh, lasses, lasses!" and in a few instants was no more.

> Ready or not ready, no delay!
> On to his Judge's bar he must away.

Last week I looked over your circuit intelligence with some anxiety to see how this case had been disposed of, but unfortunately without effect. There was no notice of it there. Interesting trials enough we have had, trials for attempting to shoot rabbits, for writing marriage lines, for stealing a pair of breeches; but for the 'shedder of blood' there was no trial. To none of his Majesty's justiciars, it would seem, has any hint of that transaction been communicated. Whether it was ever so much as glanced at, much less thoroughly sifted by any official personage, high or low, appears not from the record—nowhere the smallest whisper of it.

May I ask in the name of all that is wonderful how this has been? Is it lawful, then, to put to death any individual whom you may find flirting with your maid after ten at night? Nay, is it *so* lawful that no inquiry can be needed on the subject; but the whole matter may be hushed up into insignificance, with a few bows or shrugs? If we have an Act of Parliament to that purport it is well; only let us understand clearly how it runs. May any British subject, the poorest cotter, keep his loaded gun for our rural Celadons, and shoot them with less ceremony than he dare do snipes? Or is it only men possessing certain 'ploughgates of land' that enjoy such a privilege? If so, might not it be well that they were bound to take out some licence or game certificate first?

Of your Public Prosecutor I know not even the name. The master of that Knockhill mansion, the unhappy creature his servant, are, if possible, still more unknown to me. Hatred of them, love of them, fear or hope of them, have I none. Neither say I, nor know I, whether in that act the wretched homicide did right or did wrong. But in the name of God, let all official courtesies and hole and corner work be far from us when 'man's blood' is on our floor! Let the light in on it, the clear eye of public inquiry, or the spot will blacken there for ever. Let the law with its fifteen good men and true speak forth an open verdict, that the muttered curses of a whole district may cease.

Vox.

CHAPTER IV.

THE outward life of a man of letters is in his works. But in his works he shows only so much of himself as he considers that the world will be benefited or interested by seeing; or rather, if he is true artist he does not show his own self at all. The more excellent the thing produced, the more it resembles a work of nature in which the creation is alone perceived, while the creating hand is hidden in mystery. Homer and Shakespeare are the greatest of poets, but of the men Homer and Shakespeare we know next to nothing. 'The blind old bard of Chio's rocky isle' has been even criticised out of existence, and ingenious inquirers have been found to maintain that the Stratford player furnished but a convenient name, and that the true authors of 'Henry IV.' or 'Hamlet,' were Queen Elizabeth's courtiers and statesmen.

Men of genius do not care to hang their hearts upon their sleeve for daws to peck at; yet if they have left anywhere their written conversations with themselves, if they have opened a door into the laboratory where the creative force can be seen in its operation, and the man himself can be made known to us as he appeared in undress and in his own eyes, the public who are interested in his writings may count it as a piece of rare good fortune. No man who has any vital force in him ever lies to himself. He may assume a disguise to others; but the first condition of success is that he be true to his own soul and has looked his own capacities and his own faults fairly in the face. I have already given some extracts from Carlyle's Journal. The entries are irregular, sometimes with a blank of several years. For 1829 and 1830 it is unusually ample, and that the story may not be interrupted I place before the reader collectively the picture which it gives of Carlyle's mind. Some incidents are alluded to which have still to be related. The reader will learn what he may find wanting in the chapter which will follow.

EXTRACTS FROM A DIARY KEPT AT CRAIGENPUTTOCK.
1829—1830.

February, 1829.—Has the mind its cycles and seasons like nature, varying from the fermentation of *werden* to the clearness of *seyn,* and this again and again, so that the history of a man is like the history of the world he lives in? In my own case I have traced two or three such vicissitudes. At present, if I mistake not, there is some such thing at hand for me.

Above all things I should like *to know England;* the essence of social life in this same little island of ours. But how? No one that I speak to can throw light on it; not he that has worked and lived in the midst of it for half a century. The blind following the blind! Yet each cries out, 'What glorious sunshine we have!' The 'old literature' only half contents me. It is ore and not metal. I have not even a *history* of the country half precise enough. With Scotland it is little better. To me there is nothing poetical in Scotland but its religion. Perhaps because I know nothing else so well. England, with its old chivalry, art, and 'creature comfort,' looks beautiful, but only as a cloud country, the distinctive features of which are all melted into one gay sunny mass of hues. After all we are a world 'within ourselves,' a 'self-contained house.'

The English have never had an artist except in poetry : no musician ; no painter. Purcell (was he a native?) and Hogarth are not exceptions, or only such as confirm the rule.

He who would understand England must understand her Church—for that is half of the whole matter. Am I not conscious of a prejudice on that side? Does not the very sight of a shovel hat in some degree indispose me to the wearer thereof? Shut up my heart against him? This must be looked into. Without love there is no knowledge.

Do I not also partly despise, partly hate, the aristocracy of Scotland? I fear I do, though under cover. This too should be remedied. On the whole I know little of the Scottish gentleman, and more than enough of the Scottish *gigman*. All are not mere rent-gatherers and game-preservers.

Have the Scottish gentry lost their national character of late years, and become mere danglers in the train of the wealthier English? Scott has seen certain characters among them of which I hitherto have not heard of any existing specimen.

Is the true Scotchman the peasant and yeoman; chiefly the former?

Shall we actually go and drive through England, to see it? Mail coaches are a mere mockery.

A national character, that is, the description of one, tends to realise itself, as some prophecies have produced their own fulfilment. Tell a man that he is brave, and you help him to become so. The national character hangs like a pattern in every head; each sensibly or insensibly shapes himself thereby, and feels pleased when he can in any manner realise it.

Is the characteristic strength of England its love of justice, its deep-seated universally active sense of fair play? On many points it seems to be a very stupid people; but seldom a hide-bound, bigoted, altogether unmanageable and unaddressable people.

The Scotch have more enthusiasm and more consideration; that is, at once more sail and ballast. They seem to have a *deeper* and *richer* character as a nation. The old Scottish music, our songs, are a highly distinctive feature.

Read Novalis' 'Schriften' for the second time some weeks ago, and wrote a review of them. A strange mystic unfathomable book, but full of matter for most earnest meditation. What is to become (next) of the world and the sciences thereof? Rather, what is to become of *thee* and thy sciences? Thou longest to *act* among thy fellow men, and canst yet scarcely *breathe* among them.

Friedrich Schlegel dead at Dresden on the 9th of January. Poor Schlegel, what a toilsome seeking was thine! Thou knowest now whether thou hast found—or thou carest not for knowing!

What am I to say of Voltaire? His name has stood at the top of a sheet for three days and no other word! Writing is a dreadful labour, yet not so dreadful as *idleness*.

Every living man is a visible mystery; he walks between two eternities and two infinitudes. Were we not blind as moles we should value our humanity at ∞, and our rank, influence, &c. (the trappings of our humanity) at 0. Say I am a man, and you say all. Whether king or tinker is a mere appendix.—'Very true, Mr. Carlyle, but then——' we must believe truth and practice error?

Pray that your eyes be opened, that you may *see* what *is* before them! The whole world is built, as it were, on light and glory— only our *spiritual* eye must discern it; to the bodily eye Self is as a perpetual *blinder*, and we see nothing but darkness and contradiction.

Luther, says Melanchthon, would often, though in robust health, go about for *four days* eating and drinking—nothing! 'Vidi continuis quatuor diebus, cum quidem recte valeret, prorsus nihil edentem aut bibentem. Vidi sæpe alias multis diebus quotidie exiguo pane et halece contentum esse.' Content for many days with a little piece of bread and herring. *O tempora! O mores!*

Luther's character appears to me the most worth discussing of all modern men's. He is, to say it in a word, a great man in every sense; has the soul at once of a conqueror and a poet. His attachment to music is to me a very interesting circumstance; it was the channel for many of his finest emotions, for which words, even words of prayer, were but an ineffectual exponent. Is it true that he did leave Wittenberg for Worms with nothing but his Bible and his flute? There is no scene in European history so splendid and significant. I have long had a sort of notion to write some life or characteristic of Luther. A picture of the public thought in those days, and of this strong lofty mind overturning and new moulding it, would be a fine affair in many senses. It would require immense research. Alas! alas! when are we to have another Luther? Such men are needed from century to century; there seldom has been more need of one than now.

Wrote a paper on Voltaire for the 'Foreign Review.' It appears to have given some, very slight, satisfaction; pieces of it breathe afar off the right spirit of composition. When shall I attain to write wholly *in that spirit?*

Paper on Novalis for F. R. just published. Written last January amid the frosts. Generally poor. Novalis is an anti-mechanist—a deep man—the most perfect of modern spirit-seers. I thank him for somewhat.

August 5, 1829.—Also just finished an article on the 'Signs of the Times' for the 'Edinburgh Review,' as Jeffrey's last speech. Bad in general, but the best I could make it under such incubus influences.

Every age appears surprising and full of vicissitudes to those that live therein—as indeed it is and must be—vicissitudes from nothingness to existence; and from the tumultuous wonders of existence forward to the still wonders of death.

Politics are not our life—which is the practice and contemplation of goodness—but only the *house* wherein that life is led. Sad duty that lies on us to *parget* and continually repair our houses, saddest of all when it becomes our sole duty.

An institution, a law of any kind, may became a *deserted* edifice; the walls standing, no life going on within but that of bats, owls, and unclean creatures. It will then be pulled down if it stand interrupting any thoroughfare. If it do not so stand, people may leave it alone till a grove of natural wood grow round it; and no eye but that of the adventurous antiquarian may know of its existence, such a tangle of *brush* is to be struggled through before it can be come at and viewed.

All language but that concerning *sensual* objects is or has been figurative. Prodigious influence of metaphors! Never saw into it till lately; a truly useful and philosophical work would be a good 'Essay on Metaphors.'

Begin to think more seriously of discussing Martin Luther. The only inspiration I know of is that of genius. It was, is, and will always be of a divine character.

Wonderful universe! Were our eyes but opened, what a 'secret' were it that we daily see and handle without heed!

Understanding is to reason as the talent of a beaver (which can build houses, and uses its tail for a trowel) to the genius of a prophet and poet. Reason is all but extinct in this age; it can never be altogether extinguished.

'Das Seligseyn ist um eine Ewigkeit älter als das Verdammt-seyn.'—JEAN PAUL.

'The mixture of those things by speech which by nature are divided is the mother of all error.'—HOOKER.

Error of political economists about improving waste lands as compared with manufacturing. The manufacture is worn and *done*. The machine itself dies. The improved land remains an addition to the estate *for ever*. What is the amount of this error? I see not, but reckon it something considerable.

Is it true that of all quacks that ever quacked (boasting themselves to be somebody) in any age of the world, the political economists of this age are, for their intrinsic size, the loudest? Mercy on us, what a quack-quacking; and their egg, even if *not* a wind one, is of value simply one halfpenny.

Their whole philosophy (!) is an arithmetical computation performed in words; requires, therefore, the intellect, not of Socrates or Shakespeare, but of Cocker or Dilworth. Even if this were right—which it scarcely ever is, for they miss this or the other item, do as they will, and must return to practice and take the low *posteriori* road after all—the question of money-making, even of national money-making, is not a high but a low one; as they treat it, among the highest. Could they tell us how wealth is and should be *distributed*, it were something; but they do not attempt it.

Political philosophy ? Political philosophy should be a scientific revelation of the whole secret mechanism whereby men cohere together in society ; should tell us what is meant by 'country' (*patria*), by what causes men are happy, moral, religious, or the contrary. Instead of all which it tells us how 'flannel jackets' are exchanged for 'pork hams,' and speaks much about 'the land last taken into cultivation.' They are the hodmen of the intellectual edifice, who have got upon the wall and will insist on building as if they were masons.

The Utilitarians are the 'crowning mercy' of this age, the summit (now first appearing to view) of a mass of tendencies which stretch downwards and spread sidewards over the whole intellect and morals of the time. By-and-by the clouds will disperse, and we shall see it all in dead nakedness and brutishness; our Utilitarians will pass away with a great noise. You think not ? Can the reason of man be trodden under foot for ever by his sense ? Can the brute in us prevail for ever over the angel ?

The Devil has his elect.

'Pero digan lo que quisieren los historiadores ; que desnudo naci, desnudo mi hallo, ni pierdo ni gano, aunque por verme puesto in libros y andar por ese mundo de mano en mano, no se me da un trigo, que digan de mi todo lo que quisieren,' says Sancho.—'Quixote,' iv. 117.

January 14, 1830.—Does it seem hard to thee that thou shouldst toil in dulness, sickness, isolation ? Whose lot is not even thus ? Toil then, and *tais-toi.*

Either I am degenerating into a *caput mortuum*, and shall never think another reasonable thought ; or some new and deeper view of the world is about to arise in me. Pray heaven the latter ! It is dreadful to live without vision. When there is no light the people perish.

With considerable sincerity I can pray at this moment, 'Grant me, O Father, enough of wisdom to live well ; prosperity to live easily grant me or not, as Thou seest best.' A poor, faint *prayer* as such, yet surely a kind of wish, as indeed it has generally been with me ; and now a kind of comfort to feel it still in my otherwise too withered heart.

I am a 'dismembered limb,' and feel it again too deeply. Was I ever other? Stand to it tightly, man, and do thy utmost. Thou hast little or no hold on the world; promotion will never reach thee, nor true fellowship with any active body of men; but hast thou not still a hold on thyself? *Ja, beym Himmel!*

Religion, as Novalis thinks, is a social thing. Without a church there can be little or no religion. The action of mind on mind is mystical, infinite; religion, worship can hardly (perhaps not at all) support itself without this aid. The derivation of *Schwär-merey* indicates some notion of this in the Germans. To *schwär-men* (to be enthusiastic) means, says Coleridge, to *swarm*, to crowd together and excite one another.

What is the English of all quarrels that have been, are, or can be, between man and man? Simply this. Sir, you are taking more than your share of pleasure in this world, something from *my* share; and by the gods you shall not—nay, I will fight you rather. Alas! and the whole lot to be divided is such a beggarly account of empty boxes, truly a 'feast of shells,' not eggs, for the yolks have all been blown out of them. Not enough to fill half a stomach, and the whole human species famishing to be at them. Better we should say to our brother, 'Take it, poor fellow, take that larger share which I reckon mine, and which thou so wantest; take it with a blessing. Would to Heaven I had but enough for thee!' This is the moral of the Christian religion; how easy to write, how *hard* to practise.

I have now almost done with the Germans. Having seized their opinions, I must turn me to inquire *how* true are they? That truth is in them no lover of truth will doubt; but how much? And after all one needs an intellectual scheme (or ground plan of the universe) drawn with one's own instruments. I think I have got rid of materialism. Matter no longer seems to me so ancient, so unsubduable, so *certain* and palpable as mind. *I* am mind; whether matter or not I know not, and can not. Glimpses into the spiritual universe I have sometimes had (about the true nature of religion), the possibility after all of supernatural (really natural) influences. Would they could but stay with me, and ripen into a perfect view.

Miracle? What is a miracle? Can there be a thing more mi-

raculous than any other thing? I myself am a standing wonder.
It is the inspiration of the Almighty that giveth us understanding.

What is poetry? Do I really love poetry? I sometimes fancy
almost not. The jingle of maudlin persons with their mere (even
genuine) sensibility is unspeakably fatiguing to me. My greatly
most delightful reading is where some Goethe musically *teaches*
me. Nay, any fact relating especially to man is still valuable and
pleasing. My memory, which was one of the best, has failed sadly
of late years (principally the last two) ; yet not so much by defect
in the faculty, I should say, as by want of earnestness in using it.
I attend to few things as I was wont ; few things have any interest
for me. I live in a sort of waking dream. Doubtful it is in the
highest degree whether ever I shall make men hear my voice to
any purpose or not. Certain only that I shall be a *failure* if I do
not, and unhappy ; nay, unhappy enough (that is, with suffering
enough) even if I do. My own talent I cannot in the remotest
degree attempt at estimating. Something superior often does
seem to lie in me, and hitherto the world has been very kind ; but
many things inferior also ; so that I can strike no balance. Hang
it, try and leave this *Grübeln*. *What we have done* is the only mirror
that can show us what we *are*. One great desideratum in every
society is a man to hold his peace.

> Oh Time, how thou fliest ;
> False heart, how thou liest ;
> Leave chattering and fretting,
> Betake thee to doing and getting.

April 17.—Got dreadfully ill on with a most tremendous speculation on history, intended first as an introduction to my German
work, then found at last that it would not do there, and so cut it
out after finishing it, and gave it to my wife. I carry less weight
now, and skim more smoothly along. Why cannot I write books
(of that kind) as I write letters? They are and will be of only
temporary use.

Francis Jeffrey the other week offered me a hundred a year,
having learned that this sum met my yearly wants. He did it
neatly enough, and I had no doubt of his sincerity. What a state
of society is this in which a man would rather be shot through
the heart twenty times than do both himself and his neighbour a
real ease. How separate pride from the natural necessary feeling
of self? It is ill to do, yet may be done. On the whole I have

been somewhat in the wrong about 'independence;' man is not independent of his brother. Twenty men united in love can accomplish much that to two thousand isolated men were impossible. Know this, and know also that thou hast a power of thy own, and standest with a Heaven above even *Thee*. And so *im Teufel's Namen*, get to thy work then.

June 8.—Am about beginning the second volume of that German Lit. History; dreadfully lazy to start. I know and feel that it will be a trivial insignificant book, do what I can; yet the writing of it sickens me and inflames my nerves as if it were a poem! Were I done with this, I will endeavour to *compile* no more.

Is not the Christian religion, is not every truly vital interest of mankind (?), a thing that *grows?* Like some Nile whose springs are indeed hidden, but whose full flood, bringing gladness and fertility from its mysterious mountains, is seen and welcomed by all.

Received about four weeks ago a strange letter from some Saint Simonians at Paris, grounded on my little 'Signs of the Times.'[1] These people have strange notions, not without a large spicing of truth, and are themselves among the *Signs*. I shall feel curious to know what becomes of them. *La classe la plus pauvre* is evidently in the way of rising from its present deepest abasement. In time it is likely the world will be better divided, and he that has the toil of ploughing will have the first cut at the reaping. A man with 200,000*l.* a year eats the whole fruit of 6666 men's labour through a year; for you can get a stout spadesman to work and maintain himself for the sum of 30*l.* Thus we have private individuals whose wages are equal to the wages of seven or eight thousand other individuals. What do those highly beneficed individuals *do* to society for their wages?—*Kill partridges.* CAN this last? No, by the soul that is in man it cannot, and will not, and shall not!

Our political economists should collect statistical *facts;* such as, 'What is the lowest sum a man can live on in various countries? What is the highest he gets to live on? How many people work with their hands? How many with their heads? How many not at all? and innumerable such. What all want to know

---

[1] Just appeared in the *Edinburgh Review*, and reprinted in the *Miscellanies*.

is the condition of our fellow men; and strange to say it is the thing least of all understood, or to be understood as matters go. The present 'science' of political economy requires far less intellect than successful bellows mending; and perhaps does less good, if we deduct all the evil it brings us. Though young it already carries marks of decrepitude—a speedy and soft death to it.

You see two men fronting each other. One sits dressed in red cloth, the other stands dressed in threadbare blue; the first says to the other, 'Be hanged and anatomised!' and it is forthwith put in execution, till Number Two is a skeleton. Whence comes it? These men have no *physical hold* of each other; they are not in contact. Each of the bailiffs, &c., is included in his own *skin*, and not hooked to any other. The reason is, *Man is a spirit.* Invisible influences run through *Society*, and make it a mysterious whole full of life and inscrutable activities and capabilities. Our individual existence is mystery; our social, still more.

Nothing can act but where it is? True—if you will—only *where is it?* Is not the distant, the dead, whom I love and sorrow for HERE, in the genuine spiritual sense, as really as the table I now write on? Space is a mode of our sense, so is time (this I only half understand); *we* are—we know not what—light sparkles floating in the æther of the Divinity! So that this solid world after all is but an air-image; our *me* is the only reality, and all is godlike or God.

Thou wilt have no mystery and mysticism; wilt live in the daylight (rushlight?) of truth, and see thy world and understand it? Nay, thou wilt laugh at all that believe in a mystery; to whom the universe is an oracle and temple, as well as a kitchen and cattle-stall? *Armer Teufel!* Doth not thy cow calve, doth not thy bull gender? Nay, peradventure, dost not thou thyself gender? Explain me that, or do one of two things: retire into private places with thy foolish cackle; or, what were better, give it up and weep, not that the world is mean and disenchanted and prosaic, but that thou art vain and blind.

Is anything more wonderful than another, if you consider it maturely? *I* have *seen* no men rise from the dead; I have seen some thousands rise from *nothing*. I have not force to fly into the sun, but I *have* force to lift my hand, which is equally strange.

Wonder is the basis of worship; the reign of wonder is peren-

nial, indestructible ; only at certain stages (as the present) it is
(for some short season) *in partibus infidelium.*

August, 1830.—What is a man if you look at him with the mere
logical sense, with the understanding? A pitiful hungry biped
that wears breeches. Often when I read of pompous ceremonials,
drawing-room levées, and coronations, on a sudden the *clothes* fly
off the whole party in my fancy, and they stand there straddling in
a half ludicrous, half horrid condition!

September 7.—Yesterday I received tidings that my project of
cutting up that thrice wretched 'History of German Literature'
into review articles, and so realising *something* for my year's work,
will *not* take effect. The ' course of Providence' (nay, sometimes
I almost feel that there *is* such a thing even for *me*) seems guiding
my steps into new regions ; the question is coming more and more
towards a decision. Canst thou, there as thou art, accomplish
aught good and true ; or art thou to die miserably as a vain pre-
tender? It is above a year since I wrote one sentence that came
from the right place ; since I did one action that seemed to be
really worthy. The want of money is a comparatively insignificant
affair; were I doing well otherwise, I could most readily consent
to go destitute and suffer all sorts of things. On the whole I am
a——. But tush!

The moral nature of a man is not a composite factitious concern, but lies in the very heart of his being, as his very self of
selves. The first alleviation to irremediable pain is some conviction that it has been merited, that it comes from the All-just—
from God.

What am I but a sort of ghost? Men rise as apparitions from
the bosom of night, and after grinning, squeaking, gibbering some
space, return thither. The earth they stand on is bottomless ; the
vault of their sky is infinitude ; the life-*time* is encompassed with
eternity. O wonder! And they buy cattle or seats in Parliament,
and drink coarser or finer fermented liquors, as if all this were a
city that had foundations.

I have strange glimpses of the power of spiritual union, of association among men of like object. Therein lies the true element
of religion. It is a truly supernatural climate. All wondrous
things, from a Pennenden Heath or Penny-a-week Purgatory So-

ciety, to the foundation of a Christianity, or the (now obsolete) exercise of magic, take their rise here. Men work godlike miracles thereby, and the horridest abominations. Society is a wonder of wonders, and politics (in the right sense far, very far, from the common one) is the noblest science. *Cor ne edito!* Up and be doing! Hast thou not the strangest, grandest of all talents committed to thee, namely, LIFE itself? O heaven! And it is momentarily rusting and wasting, if thou use it not. Up and be doing! and pray (if thou but can) to the unseen Author of all thy strength to guide thee and aid thee; to give thee, if not victory and possession, unwearied activity and *Entsagen.*

Is not every thought properly an inspiration? Or how is one thing more inspired than another? Much in this.

Why should politeness be peculiar to the rich and well born? Is not every man *alive*, and is not every man infinitely venerable to every other? 'There is but one temple in the universe,' says Novalis, 'and that is the body of man.'

Franz von Sickingen was one of the noblest men of the Reformation period. He defended Ulrich von Hutten, warred against perfidious Würtemberg, was the terror of evildoers, the praise of whoso did well. Hutten and he read Luther together: light rising in darkness! He also stood by Götz von Berlichingen, and now walks in poetry. But why I mention him here is his transcendent good breeding. He was at feud with his superior the Bishop of Triers, and besieged by him, and violently defending himself against injustice at the moment when he received his death wound. His castle was surrendered; Triers and others approached the brave man, over whose countenance the last paleness was already spreading: he took off his cap to Triers, there as he lay in that stern agony. What a picture!

Nulla dies sine lineâ. Eheu, eheu! Yesterday accordingly I wrote a thing in dactyls, entitled the 'Wandering Spirits,' which now fills and then filled me with 'detestation and abhorrence.' No matter—to-day I must do the like. *Nulla dies sine lineâ.* To the persevering, they say, all things are possible. Possible or impossible, I have no other implement for trying.

Last night I sat up very late reading Scott's 'History of Scot-

land.' An amusing narrative, clear, precise, and I suppose accurate : but no more a history of Scotland than I am Pope of Rome.
A series of palace intrigues and butcheries and battles, little more
important than those of Donnybrook Fair; all the while that
Scotland, quite unnoticed, is holding on her course in industry, in
arts, in culture, as if 'Langside' and 'Clean-the-Causeway' had
remained unfought. Strange that a man should think that he
was writing the history of a nation while he is chronicling the
amours of a wanton young woman called queen, and a sulky booby
recommended to kingship for his fine limbs, and then blown up
with gunpowder for his ill behaviour! Good heaven! let them
fondle and pout and bicker *ad libitum :* what has God's fair creation and man's immortal destiny to do with them and their trade?

One inference I have drawn from Scott: that the people in
those old days had a singular talent for nicknames : King *Toom-
Tabard*, *Bell-the-Cat* (less meritorious), the *Foul Raid*, the *Round-
about Raid*, *Clean-the-Causeway*, the *Tulchan* Prelates, &c. &c.
Apparently there was more humour in the national mind than
now.

For the rest the 'Scottish History' looks like that of a gipsy
encampment—industry of the rudest, largely broken by sheer
indolence ; smoke, sluttishness, hunger, scab and—blood. Happily, as hinted, Scotland herself *was not there.*

Lastly, it is noteworthy that the nobles of the country have
maintained a quite despicable behaviour from the times of Wallace downwards. A selfish, ferocious, famishing, unprincipled
set of hyænas, from whom at no time and in no way has the country derived any benefit. The day is coming when these our modern hyænas (though *toothless*, still mischievous and greedy beyond
limit) will (quietly I hope) *be paid off : Canaille fainéante, que
faites-vous là ?* Down with your double-barrels ; take spades, if
ye can do no better, and work or die.

The quantity of pain thou feelest is indicative of the quantity
of life, of talent thou hast : a stone feels no pain. (Is that a fact?)

September 9.—Wrote a fractionlet of verse entitled 'The Bee-
tle'[1] (a real incident on Glaisters Moor), which, alas! must stand
for the *linea*, both of Tuesday and Wednesday. To-day I am to
try I know not what. Greater clearness will arrive. I make far

---

[1] *Miscellanies*, vol. i., Appendix II., No. 6.

most progress when I *walk*, on solitary roads—of which there are enough here.

Last night came a whole bundle of 'Fraser's Magazines,' &c.: two little papers by my brother in them, some fables by me ; and on the whole such a hurly-burly of rhodomontade, punch, loyalty, and Saturnalian Toryism as eye hath not seen. This out-Black-woods Blackwood. Nevertheless, the thing has its meaning—a kind of wild popular lower comedy, of which John Wilson is the inventor. It may perhaps (for it seems well adapted to the age) carry down his name to other times, as his most remarkable achievement. All the magazines (except the 'New Monthly') seem to aim at it ; a certain quickness, fluency of banter, not excluding sharp insight, and Merry Andrew drollery, and even humour, are available here ; however, the grand requisite seems to be im-pudence, and a fearless committing of yourself to talk in your drink. *Literature* has *nothing* to do with this ; but printing has ; and printing is now no more the peculiar symbol and livery of lit-erature than writing was in Gutenberg's day.

Great actions are sometimes historically barren ; smallest ac-tions have taken root in the moral soil and grown like banana for-ests to cover whole quarters of the world. Aristotle's philoso-phy and the Sermon on the Mount (and both too had *fair trial*), the 'Mécanique Céleste' and the 'Sorrows of Werter,' Alexander's expedition, and that of Paul the Apostle of the Gentiles! Of these, however, Werter is half a *gourd*, and only by its huge *de-cidua* (to be used as manure) will fertilise the future. So, too, with the rest; all are *deciduous*, and must at last make manure, only at longer dates. Yet of some the root also (?) seems to be undying.

What are Schiller and Goethe if you try them in that way? As yet it is too soon to try them. No true effort *can* be lost.

One thing we see : the moral nature of man is deeper than his intellectual ; things planted down into the former may grow as if for ever ; the latter as a kind of drift mould produces only an-nuals. What is Jesus Christ's significance? *Altogether moral.* What is Jeremy Bentham's significance? Altogether intellectual, logical. I name him as the representative of a class important only for their numbers, intrinsically wearisome, almost pitiable and pitiful. Logic is their sole foundation, no other even recognised as possible; wherefore their system is a *machine* and cannot *grow* or endure; but after thrashing for a little (and doing good service that way) must thrash itself to pieces and be made fuel. Alas, poor England! stupid, purblind, pudding-eating England! Bentham with his *Mills* grinding thee out morality; and some Macaulay, also be-aproned and a grinder, testing it, and decrying it,[1] because—it is not his own Whig established Quern-morality—I mean that the Utilitarians *have* logical machinery, and do grind fiercely and potently, *on their own foundation;* whereas the Whigs have no foundation, but must stick up their handmills, or even pepper mills, on what fixture they can come at, and then grind as it pleases Heaven. The Whigs are amateurs, the Radicals are guild-brethren.

The sin of this age is dilettantism; the Whigs and all 'moderate Tories' are the grand dilettanti. I begin to feel less and less patience for them. This is no world where a man should stand trimming his whiskers, looking on at work or touching it with the point of a gloved finger. *Man sollte greifen zu!* There is more hope of an atheist utilitarian, of a superstitious ultra (Tory), than of such a lukewarm withered mongrel. He would not believe though one rose from the dead. He is wedded to idols—let him alone.

September, about the 28th.[2]—Rain! rain! rain! The crops all lying tattered, scattered, and unripe; the winter's bread still under the soaking clouds! God pity the poor!

It was a wise regulation which ordained that certain days and times should be set apart for seclusion and meditation—whether as fasts or not may reasonably admit of doubt; the business being to get *out* of the body to philosophise. But on the whole there is a deep significance in SILENCE. Were a man forced for a length of time but to *hold his peace,* it were in most cases an incalculable benefit to his insight. Thought works in silence, so does virtue. One might erect statues to Silence. I sometimes think it were good for me, who after all cannot err much in loquacity here, did I impose on myself at set times the duty of not speaking for a day. What folly would one avoid did the tongue lie quiet till the mind had finished and was calling for utterance. Not only our good

---

[1] Macaulay's Essay on James Mill.
[2] Even a regular count of days was lost at Craigenputtock.

thoughts, but our good purposes also, are frittered asunder, and dissipated by unseasonable speaking of them. Words, the strangest product of our nature, are also the most potent. Beware of speaking. Speech is human, silence is divine, yet also brutish and dead : therefore we must learn both arts ; they are both difficult. Flower roots *hidden* under soil. Bees working in darkness, &c. The soul, too, in silence. Let not thy left hand know what thy right hand doeth. Indeed, secresy is the element of all goodness ; every virtue, every beauty is mysterious. I hardly understand even the surface of this. . . .

October 28.—Written a strange piece 'On Clothes.'[1] Know not what will come of it.

> Gutes Pferd
> Ist's Hafer's werth (myself ? November 24).

Received the 'ornamented Schiller' from Goethe, and wondered not a little to see poor old Craigenputtock engraved at Frankfort-on-the-Main. If I become anything, it will look well; if I become nothing, a piece of kind dotage (on his part). Sent away the 'Clothes,' of which I could make a kind of book, but cannot afford it. Have still the book *in petto* (?), but in the most chaotic shape.

The Whigs in office, and Baron Brougham Lord Chancellor! Haystacks and cornstacks burning over all the south and middle of England! Where will it end? Revolution on the back of revolution for a century yet? Religion, the cement of *society*, is not here : we can have no permanent beneficent arrangement of affairs.

Not that we want *no* aristocracy, but that we want a *true* one. While the many work with their hands, let the few work with their heads and hearts, *honestly*, and not with a shameless villany pretend to work, or even openly steal. Were the landlords all hanged and their estates given to the poor, we should be (economically) much happier perhaps for the space of thirty years. But the population would be doubled then ; and again the hunger of the unthrifty would burn the granary of the industrious. Alas! that there is no Church, and as yet no apparent possibility of one.

The divine right of squires is equal to the divine right of kings,

---

[1] First sketch of *Sartor Resartus*, intended for a review article.

and not superior? A word has made them, and a word can unmake them.

I have no *property* in anything whatsoever; except, perhaps (if
I am a virtuous man) in my own free will. Of my body I have
only a life rent; of all that is without my skin only an accidental
possession, so long as I can keep it. Vain man! Are the stars
thine because thou lookest on them? Is that piece of earth thine
because thou hast eaten of its fruits? Thy proudest palace what
is it but a tent : pitched not indeed for days but for years? The
earth is *the Lord's*. Remember this, and seek other duties than
game preserving, wouldst thou not be an interloper, sturdy beggar,
and even thief.

> Faules Pferd
> Keines Hafers werth.

The labourer is worthy of his hire, and the idler of his also,
namely, of starvation.

Byron we call 'a dandy of sorrows and acquainted with grief.'
That is a brief definition of him.

What *is* art and poetry? Is the beautiful really higher than
the good? A higher *form* thereof? Thus were a poet not only
a priest, but a high priest.

When Goethe and Schiller say or insinuate that art is higher
than religion, do they mean perhaps this? That whereas religion
represents (what is the essence of truth for man) the good as *infinitely* (the word is emphatic) different from the evil, but sets
them in a state of hostility (as in heaven and hell), art likewise
admits and inculcates this quite infinite difference, but *without*
hostility, with peacefulness, like the difference of two poles which
cannot coalesce yet do not quarrel—nay, should not quarrel, for
both are essential to the whole. In this way is Goethe's morality
to be considered as a *higher* (apart from its comprehensiveness,
nay, universality) than has hitherto been promulgated? *Sehr
einseitig!* Yet perhaps there is a glimpse of the truth here.

Examine by logic the import of thy life and of all lives. What
is it? A making of meal into manure, and of manure into meal.
To the *cui bono* there is no answer from logic.

December 29, 1830.—The old year just expiring; one of the most worthless years I have spent for a long time. *Durch eigne und anderer Schuld!* But words are worse than nothing. To thy *review* (Taylor's 'Hist. Survey'). Is it the most despicable of work? Yet is it not too good for *thee?* Oh, I care not for poverty, little even for disgrace, nothing at all for want of renown. But the horrible feeling is when I cease my own struggle, lose the consciousness of my own strength, and become positively quite worldly and wicked.

In the paths of fortune (fortune!) I have made no advancement since last year; but, on the contrary (owing chiefly to that German Literary History one way and another), considerably retrograded. No matter: had I but progressed in the other better path! But alas, alas! howsoever, *pocas palabras! I* am still here.

Bist *Du* glücklich, Du Gute, dass Du unter der Erde bist? Wo stehst Du? Liebst Du mich noch? God is the God of the dead as well as of the living. The dead as the living are—where *He wills.*

This Taylor is a wretched atheist and Philistine. It is *my* duty (perhaps) to put the flock whom he professes to lead on their guard. Let me do it *well!*

February 7, 1831.—Finished the review of *Taylor* some three weeks ago, and sent it off. It is worth little, and only partially in a right spirit.

Sent to Jack to liberate my 'Teufelsdröckh' from editorial durance in London, and am seriously thinking to make a book of it. The thing is not right—not *art;* yet perhaps a nearer approach to art than I have yet made. We ought to try. I want to get it done, and then translate 'Faust,' as I have partially promised to Goethe. Through 'Teufelsdröckh' I am yet far from seeing my way; nevertheless materials are partly forthcoming.

No sense from the 'Foreign Quarterly Review;' have nearly determined on opening a correspondence on the matter of that everlasting MS.[1] with Bowring of the 'Westminster.' Could write also a paper on the Saint Simonians. One too on Dr. Johnson, for Napier. Such are the financial aspects. *N.B. I have some five pounds to front the world with*—and expect no more for months. Jack, too, is in the neap tide. Hand to the oar.

---

[1] German Literature.

All Europe is in a state of disturbance, of revolution. About this very time they may be debating the question of British 'Reform' in London. The Parliament opened last week. Our news of it expected on Wednesday. The times are big with change. Will *one* century of constant fluctuation serve us, or shall we need two? Their Parliamentary reforms and all that are of small moment; a beginning (of good and evil), nothing more. The whole frame of society is rotten, and must go for fuel wood—and where is the new frame to come from? I know not, and no man knows.

The only sovereigns of the world in these days are the literary men (were there any such in Britain)—the prophets. It is always a theocracy: the king has to be anointed by the priest; and now the priest, the Goethe for example, will not, cannot consecrate the existing king who therefore is a usurper, and reigns only by sufferance. What were the bet that King William were the last of that profession in Britain, and Queen Victoria never troubled with the sceptre at all? Mighty odds: yet nevertheless not infinite; for what thing is certain now? No mortal cares twopence for any king, or obeys any king except through *compulsion;* and society is not a ship of war. Its government cannot always be a press-gang.

What are the episcopal dignitaries saying to it? Who knows but Edward Irving may not yet be a bishop! They will clutch round them for help, and unmuzzle all manner of bull-dogs when the thief is at the gate. Bull-dogs with teeth. The generality have no teeth in that kennel.

Kings *do* reign by divine right, or not at all. The king that were God-appointed would be an emblem of God and could *demand* all obedience from us. But where is that king? The *best man,* could we find him, were he. Tell us, tell us, O ye codifiers and statists and economists, how we shall find him and raise him to the throne: or else admit that the science of polity is worse than unknown to you.

Earl *(Jarl—Yärl),* count, duke, knight, &c., are all titles derived from *fighting.* The honour-titles in a future time will derive themselves from *knowing* and well-*doing.* They will also be conferred with more deliberation and by better judges. This is a prophecy of mine.

God is above us, else the future of the world were well-nigh desperate. Go where we may, the deep *heaven* will be round us.

Jeffrey is Lord-Advocate and M.P. Sobbed and shrieked at taking office, like a bride going to be married. I wish him altogether well, but reckon he is on the wrong course; Whiggism, I believe, is all but for ever done. Away with Dilettantism and Machiavellism, though we should get atheism and Sansculottism in their room! The latter are at least substantial things, and do not build on a continued wilful falsehood. But oh! but oh! where is Teufelsdröckh all this while? The south-west is busy thawing off that horrible snowstorm. Time rests not—thou only art idle. To pen! to pen!

'Benvenuto Cellini' a very worthy book; gives more insight into Italy than fifty Leo Tenths would do. A remarkable man Benvenuto, and in a remarkable scene. Religion and art with ferocity and sensuality; polished respect with stormful independence; faithfully obedient subjects to popes who are not hierarchs but plain scoundrels! Life was far sunnier and richer then; but a time of change, loudly called for, was advancing, and but lately has reached its crisis. Goethe's essay on Benvenuto quite excellent.

Pope's 'Homer's Odyssey,' surely a very false, and though ingenious and talented, yet bad translation. The old epics are great because they (musically) show us the *whole world* of those old days. A modern epic that did.the like would be equally admired, and for us far more admirable. But where is the genius that can write it? Patience! patience! he will be here one of these centuries.

Is Homer or Shakespeare the greater genius? It were hard to say. Shakespeare's world is the more complex, the more spiritual, and perhaps his mastery over it was equally complete. ' *We are such stuff* as dreams are made of.' There is the basis of a whole poetic universe. To that mind all forms and figures of men and things would become ideal.

What is a *whole?* or how specially *does* a poem differ from prose? Ask not a definition of it in words, which can hardly express common logic correctly. Study to create in thyself a *feeling* of it; like so much else it cannot be made clear, hardly even to thy thought (?).

I see some vague outline of what a *whole* is: also how an individual delineation may be 'informed with the Infinite;' may appear hanging in the universe of time and space (partly) : in which case is it a poem and a whole? Therefore are the true heroic poems of these times to be written with the *ink of science?* Were a correct philosophic biography of a man (meaning by philosophic *all* that the name can include) the only method of celebrating him? The true history (had we any such, or even generally any dream of such) the true epic poem? I partly begin to surmise so. What after all is the true proportion of St. Matthew to Homer—of the Crucifixion to the fall of Troy?

On the whole I wish I could define to myself the true relation of moral genius to poetic genius; of religion to poetry. Are they one and the same—different forms of the same ; and if so, which is to stand higher, the Beautiful or the Good? Schiller and Goethe seem to say the former, as if it included the latter, and might supersede it : how truly I can never well see. Meanwhile that the *faculties* always go together seems clear. It is a gross calumny on human nature to say that there ever was a mind of surpassing talent that did not also surpass in *capability* of virtue ; and *vice versá.* Nevertheless, in both cases there are female geniuses too, minds that admire and receive, but can hardly create. I have observed that in these also the taste for religion and for poetry go together. The most wonderful words I ever heard of being uttered by man are those in the four Evangelists by Jesus of Nazareth. Their intellectual talent is hardly inferior to their moral. On this subject, if I live, I hope to have much to say.

And so ends my first note-book after nigh eight years, here at Craigenputtock, at my *own* hearth, and though amid trouble and dispiritment enough, yet with better outlooks than I had then. My outward world is not much better (yes it is, though I have far less money), but my inward *is,* and I can promise myself never to be *so* miserable again. Farewell, ye that have fallen asleep since then; farewell, though distant, perhaps near me ! Welcome the good and evil that is to come, through which God assist me to struggle wisely. What have I to look back on? Little or nothing. What forward to? My own small sickly force amid wild enough whirlpools ! The more diligently apply it then. Νὺξ ἔρχεται.

CHAPTER V.

A. D. 1830.   ÆT. 35.

IT appears from the journal that early in 1830 Carlyle
had advanced so far with his History of German Literature that he was hoping soon to see it published and off
his hands.   A first sketch of 'Teufelsdröckh'—the egg out
of which 'Sartor Resartus' was to grow—had been offered
without result to London magazine editors.   Proposals
were made to him for a Life of Goethe.   But on Goethe
he had said all that for the present he wished to say.
Luther was hanging before him as the subject which he
wantèd next to grapple, could he but find the means of
doing it.   But the preliminary reading necessary for such
a work was wide and varied.   The books required were
not to be had at Craigenputtock; and if the literary history could once be finished, and any moderate sum of
money realised upon it, he meditated spending six months
in Germany, taking Mrs. Carlyle with him, to collect materials.   He had great hopes of what he could do with
Luther.   An editor had offered to bring it out in parts in
a magazine, but Carlyle would not hear of this.

I rather believe (he said) that when I write that book of the
great German lion, it shall be the best book I have ever written,
and go forth, I think, on its own legs.   Do you know we are actually talking of spending the next winter in Weimar, and preparing all the raw material of a *right Luther* there at the fountain-
head—that is, of course, if I can get the history done and have
the cash.

Jeffrey started at the idea of the winter at Weimar—at

least for Mrs. Carlyle—and suggested that if it was carried out she should be left in his charge at Edinburgh.
He was inclined, he said, to be jealous of the possible influence of Goethe, who had half bewitched her at a distance—unless indeed the spell was broken by the personal
presence of him. But Jeffrey's fears were unnecessary.
There was no Weimar possible for Carlyle, and no Life of
Luther. The unfortunate 'German Literature' could not
find a publisher who would so much as look at it. Boyd,
who had brought out the volumes of 'German Romance,'
wrote that he would be proud to publish for Carlyle upon
almost any other subject except German Literature. He
knew that in this department Carlyle was superior to any
other author of the day, but the work proposed was not
calculated to interest the British public. Everyone of the
books about German literature had been failures, most of
them ruinous failures. The feeling in the public mind
was that everything German was especially to be avoided,
and with the highest esteem for Carlyle's talent he dared
not make him an offer. Even cut up into articles he still
found no one anxious to take it. There was still another
hope. Carlyle's various essays had been greatly noticed
and admired. An adventurous bookseller might perhaps
be found who would bid for a collected edition of them.
The suggestion took no effect however. The 'Teufelsdröckh' had to be sent back from London, having created
nothing but astonished dislike. Nothing was to be done
therefore but to remain at Craigenputtock and work on,
hoping for better times. Fresh articles were written, a
second on Jean Paul, a slight one on Madame de Staël,
with the first of the two essays on history which are published in the 'Miscellanies.' He was thus able to live, but
not so far as money was concerned to overtake the time
which he had spent over his unsaleable book; his finances
remained sadly straitened, and he needed all his energy to

fight on against discouragement. One bright gleam of comfort came to him from Weimar in the summer of this year. Communication had been kept up constantly with Goethe since the Comely Bank time. In the winter 1829–30, Mrs. Carlyle, writing to her mother-in-law at Scotsbrig, says :

Carlyle is over head and ears in business to-night writing letters to all the four winds. There is a box to be despatched for Goethe containing all manner of curiosities, the most precious of which is a lock of my hair. There is also a smart Highland bonnet for his daughter-in-law, accompanied by a nice little piece of poetry professing to be written by me, but in truth I did not write a word of it.

> Scotland prides her in the bonnet blue
> That brooks no stain in love or war ;
> Be it on Ottilie's head a token true
> Of Scottish love to kind Weimar.

Goethe's answer reached Craigenputtock about June.[1]

[1] Das werthe Schatzkästlein, nachdem es durch den strengsten Winter vom Continent lange abgehalten worden, ist endlich um die Hälfte März glücklich angelangt.

Um von seinem Gehalt zu sprechen, erwähne zuerst die unschätzbare Locke, die man wohl mit dem theuren Haupte verbunden möchte gesehen haben, die aber hier einzeln erblickt mich fast erschreckt hätte. Der Gegensatz war zu auffallend ; denn ich brauchte meinen Schädel nicht zu berühren um zu wissen dass daselbst nur Stoppeln sich hervorthun ; es war mir nicht nöthig vor dem Spiegel zu treten, um zu erfahren dass eine lange Zeitreise ihnen ein missfarbiges Ansehen gegeben. Die Unmöglichkeit der verlangten Erwiederung fiel mir aufs Herz, und nöthigte mich zu Gedanken deren man sich zu entschlagen pflegt. Am Ende aber blieb mir doch nichts übrig als mich an der Vorstellung zu begnügen : eine solche Gabe sey dankbarlichst ohne Hoffnung irgend einer genügenden Gegengabe anzunehmen. Sie soll auch heilig in der ihrer würdigen Brieftasche aufbewahrt bleiben, und nur das Liebenswürdigste ihr zugesellt werden.

Der schottische elegante Turban hat, wie ich versichern darf, zu manchem Vergnüglichen Gelegenheit gegeben. Seit vielen Jahren werden wir von den Einwohnern der drey Königreiche besucht, welche gern eine Zeit lang bey uns verweilen und gute Gesellschaft geniessen mögen. Hierunter befinden sich zwar weniger Schotten, doch kann es nicht fehlen dass nicht noch das Andenken an einen solchen Landsmann sich in einem schönen Herzen so lebendig finde, um die National-Prachtmütze, die Distel mit eingeschlossen, als einen wünschenswerthesten Schmuck anzusehen ; und die gütige Senderinn hätte

To Thomas Carlyle.

The precious casket, after having been long detained from the Continent through the most severe winter, has at last safely arrived towards the middle of March. With regard to its contents, I mention first the inestimable lock of hair, which one would have wished to have seen together with the dear head, but which as here seen by itself had almost frightened me. The contrast was too

sich gewiss gefreut das lieblichste Gesicht von der Welt darunter hervorgucken zu sehen. Ottilie aber dankt zum allerverbindlichsten, und wird, sobald unsere Trauertage vorüber sind, damit glorreich aufzutreten nicht ermangeln.

Lassen Sie mich nun eine nächste Gegensendung ankündigen, welche zum Juni als der günstigsten Jahreszeit sich wohl wird zusammengefunden haben. Sie erhalten :—

1. Das Exemplar Ihres übersetzten Schiller, geschmückt mit den Bildern Ihrer ländlichen Wohnung (by day and night!), begleitet von einigen *Bogen* in meiner Art, wodurch ich zugleich dem Büchlein offnen Eingang zu verschaffen, besonders aber die Communication beyder Länder und Literaturen lebhafter zu erregen trachte. Ich wünsche dass diese nach Kenntniss des Publicums angewandten Mittel Ihnen nicht misfallen, auch der Gebrauch, den ich von Stellen unserer Correspondenz gemacht, nicht als Indiscretion möge gedeutet werden. Wenn ich mich in jüngeren Jahren von dergleichen Mittheilungen durchaus gehütet, so ziemt es dem höhern Alter auch solche Wege nicht zu verschmähen. Die günstige Aufnahme des Schillerischen Briefwechsels gab mir eigentlich hiezu Anlass und Muth.

Ferner finden Sie beygelegt :—

2. Die vier noch fehlende Bände gedachter Briefe. Mögen Sie Ihnen als Zauberwagen zu Dienste stehen, um sich in der damaligen Zeit in unsere Mitte zu versetzen, wo es eine unbedingte Strebsamkeit galt, wo niemand zu fordern dachte und nur zu verdienen bemüht war. Ich habe mir die vielen Jahre her den Sinn, das Gefühl jener Tage zu erhalten gesucht und hoffe es soll mir fernerhin gelingen.

3. Eine fünfte Sendung meiner Werke liegt sodann bey, worin sich wohl manches unterhaltende, unterrichtende, belehrende, brauchbar anzuwendende finden wird. Man gestehe zu dass es auch Ideal-Utilitarier gebe, und es sollte mir sehr zur Freude gereichen, wenn ich mich darunter zählen dürfte. Noch eine Lieferung, dann ist vorerst das beabsichtigte Ganze vollbracht, dessen Abschluss zu erleben ich mir kaum zu hoffen erlaubte. Nachträge giebt es noch hinreichend. Meine Papiere sind in guter Ordnung.

4. Ein Exemplar meiner Farbenlehre und der dazu gehörigen Tafeln soll auch beygfügt werden; ich wünsche, dass Sie den zweyten, als den *historischen* Theil, zuerst lesen. Sie sehen da die Sache herankommen, stocken, sich aufklären und wieder verdüstern. Sodann aber ein Bestreben nach neuem Lichte ohne allgemeinen Erfolg. Alsdann würde die erste Hälfte des ersten Theils, als die *didactische* Abtheilung, eine allgemeine Vorstellung geben wie ich die Sache angegriffen wünsche. Freylich ist ohne Anschauung der Experimente hier nicht durchzukommen; wie Sie es mit der *polemischen* Ab-

striking, for there was no need for my touching my skull in order to know that stubbles only would show themselves there. It was not necessary for me to stand before the looking-glass in order to know that the long passage of time had imparted to my hair a discoloured appearance. The impossibility of the asked-for return troubled my heart, and drove me to thoughts which one is wont to put aside. In the end, however, nothing remained to me but to be satisfied with the thought that such a gift must be gratefully accepted, without the hope of any sufficient return. It shall remain sacredly kept, in a pocket-book worthy of it, and only the most loved shall ever bear it company.

The elegant Scotch turban has, as I may assure you, been the occasion of much enjoyment. For many years we have had visits from the inhabitants of the three kingdoms, who like to stay with us for a time and enjoy good society. Though there are fewer Scots among them, it cannot be but that the memory of one such countryman should be so vivid in some one beautiful heart *here* as to make it look on that splendid national head-dress, including the thistle, as a most desirable ornament. The kind sender would, no doubt, have been delighted to see the most charming face in the world looking out from under it. Ottilie sends her most grateful thanks, and will not fail, as soon as our mourning is over, to make a glorious appearance in it.

Let me now in return announce to you an approaching despatch, which I hope to have put together by June, as the most favourable time of the year. You receive :—

1st. The copy of your translated Schiller, adorned with the

theilung halten wollen und können, wird sich alsdann ergeben. Ist es mir möglich, so lege besonders für Sie ein einleitendes Wort bey.

5. Sagen Sie mir etwas zunächst wie Sie die Deutsche Literatur bey den Ihrigen einleiten wollen ; ich eröffne Ihnen gern meine Gedanken über die Folge der Epochen. Man braucht nicht überall ausführlich zu seyn : gut aber ist's auf-manches vorübergehende Interessante wenigstens hinzudeuten, um zu zeigen dass man es kennt.

Dr. Eckermann macht mit meinen Sohn eine Reise gegen Süden und bedauert, nicht wie er gewünscht hatte, diesmal beyhülflich syn zu können. Ich werde gern, wie obgesagt, seine Stelle vertreten. Diesen Sommer bleib ich zu Hause und sehe bis Michael Geschäfte genug vor mir.

Gedenken Sie mit Ihrer lieben Gattinn unserer zum besten und empfangen wiederholten herzlichen Dank für die schöne Sendung.

Treu angehörig,
J. W. Goethe.

Weimar, den 13. April, 1830.

pictures of your country home (by day and night), accompanied by some sheets in my own style, whereby I try to gain a ready entrance for the little book, and more especially to infuse greater life into the intercourse of the two countries and literatures. I hope that the means which I have employed according to my knowledge of the public may not displease you, and that the use which I have made of some passages of our correspondence may not be taken as an indiscretion. Though in my earlier years I have carefully abstained from such communications, it behoves a more advanced age not to despise even such ways. It was really the favourable reception of my correspondence with Schiller which gave me the impulse and courage for it. Further, you will find added—

2nd. The four volumes, still wanting, of those letters. May they serve as a magic chariot to transport you into our midst at that period, when we thought of nothing but striving, where no one thought of asking for rewards, but was only anxious to deserve them. I have tried for these many years to keep alive the sense and the feeling of those days. I hope I shall succeed in this for the future also.

3rd. A fifth copy of my works is also there, in which I hope may be found many things amusing, instructive, improving, and fit for use. Let it be admitted that there exist ideal utilitarians also, and it would give me much pleasure if I might count myself among them. Still one number, and I shall have finished the whole of what I intended for the present, and the completion of which I hardly allowed myself to hope I should see. Supplements there are plenty, and my papers are in good order.

4th. A copy of my ' Treatise on Colour,' with the tables belonging to it, shall also be added ; and I wish you to read the second, as the *historical* part, first. You see how the subject arose, how it came to a standstill, how it grew clear, and how it became dark again ; then a striving after new light, without a general success. Afterwards, the first half of the first part, being the *didactic* section, would give a general idea how I wish to see the subject taken up. Only without seeing the experiments, it is impossible to get on here. You will then see what you wish and are able to do with the *polemical* portion. If it is possible I shall add an introductory word especially for you.

5th. Please to tell me first how you wish to introduce German literature among your people. I shall then open my thoughts to you on the succession of the epochs. It is not necessary to be very exhaustive everywhere, but it is well to point at least to many things which had a passing interest, in order to show that one knows them. Dr. Eckermann is making a journey with my son, southwards, and regrets that this time he is not able to be useful as he had wished. I should gladly, as I said just now, take his place. I shall stay at home this summer, and until Michaelmas have plenty of work before me.

May you and your dear wife keep us in best remembrance, and receive once more my hearty thanks for the beautiful presents.

Sincerely yours,
J. W. GOETHE.

Weimar : April 13, 1830.

Attached to the letter to Carlyle were a few additional lines on the request of Mrs. Carlyle for a lock of his hair, to which he had been unable to accede. The original remains preserved among her treasures, the only autograph of Goethe which I have succeeded in finding.[1]

An incomparable black ringlet demands a few more words from me. I have to say with real regret that the desired exchange is, alas! impossible. Short and miscoloured, and robbed of all its grace, old age must be content if the inner man can still throw out a flower or two when the outward bloom has departed. I would gladly find a substitute, but as yet I have not succeeded. My fairest greetings to the admirable wife. I trust the box has arrived safe. G.

Goethe had already spoken of his inability to comply in his first letter. This little note was perhaps intended for the *surrogat* which he had been vainly looking for ; as an autograph which Mrs. Carlyle might keep for herself.

---

[1] Eine unvergleichliche schwarze Haarlocke veranlasst mich noch ein Blättchen beyzulegen, und mit wahrhaftem Bedauern zu bemerken dass die verlangte Erwiederungleider unmöglich ist. Kurz und missfarbig, alles Schmuckes entbehrend, muss das Alter sich begnügen wenn sich dem Innern noch irgend eine Blüthe aufthut, indem die Aeussere verschwunden ist. Ich sinne schon auf irgend ein Surrogat ; ein solches zu finden hat mir aber noch nicht glücken wollen. Meine schönsten Grüsse der würdigen Gattinn.

Möge das Kästchen glücklich angekommen seyn.

G.

If the box came at the time which he intended, the pleasure which it must have given was soon clouded. The journal alludes to the death of the most dearly loved of all Carlyle's sisters. The Carlyles as a family were passionately attached to each other. Margaret Carlyle's apparent recovery was as delusive as her sister-in-law had feared. In the winter she fell ill again ; in the spring she was carried to Dumfries in the desperate hope that medical care might save her. Carlyle has written nothing more affecting than the account of her end in the ' Reminiscences of Irving.' A letter written at the time to his brother, if wanting the mellow beauty which the scene had assumed in his memory, is even more impressive from the greater fulness of detail.

To John Carlyle.

Craigenputtock : June 29, 1830.

It was on Monday night when Alick took leave of our sister. On Tuesday, if I remember rightly, she felt ' better,' but was evidently fast growing weaker. In the afternoon it was pretty evident to everyone that she was far gone. The doctor, who was unwearied in his assiduities, formed a worse opinion at every new examination. All hope of a complete cure had vanished some days before. Our mother asked her in the afternoon if she thought herself dying. She answered, ' I dinna ken, mother, but I never was so sick in my life.' To a subsequent question about her hopes of a future world, she replied briefly, but in terms that were comfortable to her parents. It was about eight at night when John Currie was despatched to go and seek a horse and proceed hither ; where, as you already know, he arrived about midnight. By this time the sick-room was filled with sympathising relatives. The minister, Mr. Clyde, also came and feelingly addressed her. She recognised everyone, was calm, clear as she had ever been ; sometimes spoke in whispers, directing little services to be done to her ; once asked where Mary was, who had gone out for a moment. Twice she asked for the ' drops,' I believe that ' mixture ' I spoke of. The first time, our mother, who now cared chiefly for her soul's weal, and that sense and recollection might be given her in that stern hour, answered dissuasively, but said if she asked for them a second time they should be given her. Some hours before, our mother had begged her forgiveness if she had ever done her anything wrong; to which the dying one answered, 'Oh no, no, mother, never, never,' earnestly, yet quietly, and without tears. About a quarter-past ten she asked again for the drink (or drops, which were taken in water), and took the glass which Mary also held in her own hand. She whispered to Mary, 'Pour up,' swallowed about half the liquid, threw her head on the pillow, looking out with her usual look ; but her eyes quickly grew bright and intense, the breath broke into long sighs, and in about two minutes a slight quiver in the under lip gave token that the fight was fought and the wearied spirit at its goal. I saw her in the winding-sheet about six o'clock, beautiful in death, and kissed her pale brow, not without warm tears which I could not check. About mid-day, when she was laid in the coffin, I saw her face once more for the last time.

Our mother behaved in what I must call an heroic manner. Seeing that the hour was now come, she cast herself and her child on God's hand, and endeavoured heartily to say, 'His will be done.' Since then she has been calmer than any of us could have hoped—almost the calmest of us. No doubt the arrow still sticks in her heart, and natural sorrow must have its course ; but I trust she seeks and finds the only true balm, howsoever named, by which man's woe can be healed and made blessed to him.

Thus, dear brother, has our eldest and best sister been taken from us, mercifully, as you said, though sorrowfully, having been spared much suffering, and carried in clear possession of her sense and steadfastness through that last solemn trial. We all wept sore for her as you have done and now do, but will endeavour to weep no more. I have often thought she had attained all in life that life could give her—a just, true, meekly invincible completed character, which I and so many others, by far more ambitious paths, seek for in vain. She was in some points, I may say deliberately, superior to any woman I have ever seen. Her simple clearness of head and heart, her perfect fairness, and quiet, unpretending, brief decisiveness in thought, word, and act (for in all these she was remarkable) made up so true and brave a spirit as, in that unaffected guise, we shall hardly look upon again. She might have been wife to a Scottish martyr, and spoken stern truths to the ear of tyrants, had she been called to that work. As it is, she sleeps in a pure grave, and our peasant maiden to us who knew her is more than a king's daughter. Let us for ever remember her and love her, but cease from henceforth to mourn for her. She was mercifully dealt with—called away when her heart if not unwounded was yet unseared and fresh, amidst pain and heaviness it is true, but not in any agony or without some peaceful train of hope enlightening her to the end. The little current of her existence flowed onward like a Scottish brook through green simple fields. Neither was it caught into the great ocean over chasms and grim cataracts, but gently and as among thick clouds whereon hovered a rainbow.

I might tell you something of the funeral arrangements, and how the loss has left the rest of us. Early on Tuesday our mother and Mary set off for Scotsbrig in one of Alick's carts which happened to be there. A coffin was speedily got ready, with burial litter, &c.; and it was agreed that Alick and I should attend the body down to Scotsbrig next day, where it was to lie till Saturday, the day of the funeral. All Wednesday these things kept him and me incessantly busy; the poor Alick was sick to the heart, and cried more that day than I had ever seen him do in his life. At night I had to return hither and seek Jenny. I was the messenger of heavy and unexpected tidings. Jane too insisted on going with us; so next morning (Thursday) we set out hence, Jenny and I in a gig, Jane riding behind us. At Dumfries, where Alick had remained to watch all night, we found Jacob with a hearse. About two o'clock we moved off, the gig close following the hearse, Jane and Alick riding behind us. We reached Scotsbrig about six. Poor Robert Crow was dreadfully affected. He waked every night, spoke earnestly and largely on the subject of the deceased, and by his honesty and sensibility and pure sincere religious bearing endeared himself to everyone. On Saturday about half-past one the procession moved away. Our mother stood like a priestess in the door, tearless when all were weeping. Our father and Alick went in the gig. The former, ill in health, looked resolute, austere, and to trivial condolers and advisers almost indignant. The coffin was lowered into a very deep grave on the east side of our headstone in the Ecclefechan churchyard, and the mourners, a numerous company, separated; W. Graham and a few others accompanying us home to that stupid horrid ceremony, a funeral tea, which in our case was speedily transacted.

Yesterday morning we set out on our return. It had been settled that Mary was to stay yonder for a fortnight or ten days, our mother and Jenny to come hither. I drove the former in the gig; Jenny came in a cart with Bretton. We settled various accounts, &c., at Dumfries, and arrived here about eleven, all well. Mother had a good sleep, and is pretty well in health. She talked of returning to the Sacrament. Our father was complaining much, and evidently suffering somewhat severely. His appetite is bad. He has a cold, coughs a little, and is in bad spirits when left to himself. I bought him some paregoric, but he was breathless, dispirited, and could not eat. We hope the good weather would mend him would it come. The rest of us are well. God bless you, dear brother.   T. CARLYLE.

We are all sad and dull (he wrote a fortnight later) about her that is laid in the earth. I dream of her almost nightly, and feel not indeed sorrow, for what is life but a continual dying? Yet a strange obstruction and haunting remembrance. Let us banish all this, for it is profitless and foolish.

> Thy quiet goodness, spirit pure and brave,
>   What boots it now with tears to tell ;
> The path to rest lies through the grave :
>   Loved sister, take our long farewell.

We shall meet again, too, if God will. If He will *not*, then better we should not meet.

From the ' Journal ' I add a few more words.

On the 22nd of June my sister Margaret died at Dumfries, whither she had been removed exactly a week before for medical help. It was a Thursday night, about ten minutes past ten. Alick and I were roused by express about midnight, and we arrived there about four. That solstice night, with its singing birds and sad thoughts, I shall never forget. She was interred next Saturday at Ecclefechan. I reckoned her the best of all my sisters—in some respects the best woman I had ever seen.

> Whom bring ye to the still dwelling ?
> 'Tis a tired playmate whom we bring you ;
> Let her rest in your still dwelling
> Till the songs of her heavenly sisters awaken her.

And so let me betake myself again with what energy I can to the commencement of my task. Work is for the living, rest is for the dead.

Margaret Carlyle sleeps in Ecclefechan churchyard. Her father followed soon, and was laid beside her. Then after him, but not for many years, the pious, tender, original, beautiful-minded mother. John Carlyle was the next of their children who rejoined them, and next he of whom I am now writing: The world and the world's business scatter families to the four winds, but they collect again in death. Alick lies far off in a Canadian resting-place ; but in his last illness, when the memory wanders, he too had travelled in spirit back to Annandale and the old days when his brother was at college, and with the films of the last struggle closing over his eyes he asked anxiously if 'Tom was come back from Edinburgh.'

The loss of this sister weighed heavily on Carlyle's spirits, and the disappointment about his book fretted him on the side to which he might naturally have turned to seek relief in work. Goethe's steady encouragement was of course inspiriting, but it brought no grist to the mill, and the problem of how he was to live was becoming extremely serious. Conscious though he was of exceptional powers, which the most grudging of his critics could not refuse to acknowledge, he was discovering to his cost that they were not marketable. He could not throw his thoughts into a shape for which the Sosii of the day would give him money. He had tried poetry, but his verse was cramped and unmelodious. He had tried to write stories, but his convictions were too intense for fiction. The 'dreadful earnestness' of which Jeffrey complained was again in his way, and he could have as little written an entertaining novel as St. Paul or St. John. His entire faculty—intellect and imagination alike—was directed upon the sternest problems of human life. It was not possible for him, like his friend at Craigcrook, to take up with the first creed that came to hand and make the best of it. He required something which he could really believe. Thus his thoughts refused to move in any common groove. He had himself to form the taste by which he could be appreciated, and when he spoke his words provoked the same antagonism which every original thinker is inevitably condemned to encounter—antagonism first in the form of wonder, and when the wonder ceased of irritation and angry enmity. He taught like one that had authority—a tone which men naturally resent, and must resent, till the teacher has made his pretensions good. Every element was absent from his writing which would command popularity, the quality to which book-sellers and review editors are obliged to look if they would live themselves. Carlyle's articles were magnetic enough, but with the magnetism which repelled, not which at-tracted. His faith in himself and in his own purposes never wavered; but it was becoming a subject of serious doubt to him whether he could make a living, even the humblest, by literature. The fair promises of the last year at Comely Bank had clouded over; instead of invita-tions to write, he was receiving cold answers to his own proposals. Editors, who had perhaps resented his haughty style, were making him 'feel the difference,' neglecting to pay him even for the articles which had been accepted and put in type. His brother John, finding also patients who would pay slow in sending for him, and not willing to give his services gratuitously, was thinking that he too would become a man of letters, and earn his bread by writing for magazines. Carlyle warned him off so dan-gerous an enterprise with the most impressive earnestness.

To John Carlyle.

Craigenputtock: August 6, 1830.

I sympathise in your reluctance to enter on the practice of medicine, or indeed of any professional duty; well understanding the difficulties that lie at the porch of all and threaten the solitary adventurer. Neither can I be surprised at your hankering after a literary life, so congenial as I have often heard you hint it would be to your tastes. Nevertheless it *would* greatly astonish me if beyond mere preliminary reveries these feelings produced any influence on your conduct. The voice of all experience seems to be in favour of a profession. You sail there as under convoy in the middle of a fleet, and have a thousandfold chance of reaching port. Neither is it Happy Islands and halcyon seas alone that you miss, for literature is thickly strewed with cold Russian Nova Zemblas, where you shiver and despair in loneliness; nay often, as in the case of this 'Literary History of Germany,' you anchor on some slumbering whale and it ducks under and leaves you spinning in the eddies. To my mind nothing justifies me for having adopted the trade of literature, except the remembrance that I had no other but these two—that of a schoolmaster or that of a priest: in the one case with the fair prospect of speedy maceration and starvation; in the other of *perjury*, which is infinitely worse. As it is, I look confidently forward to a life of poverty, toil, and dispiritment, so long as I remain on this earth, and hope only that God will grant me patience and strength to struggle onwards through the midst of it, working out his will as I best can in this lonely clay-pit where I am set to dig. The pitifullest of all resources is complaining, which accordingly I strive not to practice : only let these things be known for my brother's warning, that he may order his life better than I could do mine.

For the rest I pretend not to thwart your own judgment, which ought to be mature enough for much deeper considerations; neither would I check these overflowings of discouragement, poured as they naturally should be into a brother's ear; but after all that is come and gone I expect to learn that your medical talent, sought over all Europe, and indisputably the most honourable a man can have, is no longer to be hidden in a napkin, still less to be thrown away into the lumber-room; but to come forth into the light of day for your own profit and that of your fellow men.

Tell me, therefore, dear Jack, that you are in your own lodging resolute, compacted, girt for the fight, at least endeavouring to do your true duty. Now, as ever I have predicted that success was certain for you, my sole fear is that such wavering and waiting at the pool may in the end settle into a habit of fluctuation and irresolution far enough from your natural character ; a fear which of course every new week spent in drifting to and fro tends to strengthen.

Fear nothing, Jack. Men are but poor spindle-shanked whiffling *wonners*, when you clutch them through the mass of drapery they wear. To throw plenty of them over the house-ridge were no such feat for a right fellow. Neither is their favour, their envy, their admiration, or anything else the poor devils can give or withhold, our life or our death. Nay, the worst we and they fear is but a bugbear, a hollow shadow, which if you grasp it and smite it dissolves into air. March boldly up to it and to them; strong and still like the stars, 'Ohne Hast doch ohne Rast.'[1] There is a soul in some men yet, even yet, and God's sky is above us, and God's commandment is in us—

> Und wenn die Welt voll Teufel wär',
> Und wollt' uns gar verschlingen,
> So fürchten wir uns nicht so sehr :
> Es muss uns doch gelingen.[2]

Up and be doing. Be my brother and life companion, not in word and feeling only, but in deepest deed !

With regard to that manuscript of the Literary History of Germany, get it out of ——'s claws if you have not as I trust already done so. To which now add an article on Schiller that Fraser has, that he talked of giving to some magazine or other, but that I desire to have the privilege of giving or retaining myself, being minded, as I said already, to have no more business transactions with that gentleman. Get the two MSS. therefore, dear Jack, and wrap them up tightly till I send for them. The Schiller by-and-by I intend for the 'Foreign Quarterly Review.'[3] About the history I wrote to Gleig,[4] Colburn's editor of some 'Library of General Knowledge,' three weeks ago, and again to-day, having received no answer. Fraser offered to negotiate for me there in a letter he sent me last week, but he need not mingle further in the matter, I think. If I do not hear in a week I shall decide for myself, and cut Gleig as I have done other editors, and try some different method of realising a pound or two. Get you the MSS. in the first place. Tait, to whom I wrote, declines. I am now got

[1] Without haste, yet without rest.
[2] From Luther's Hymn.
[3] It was, however, published after all in *Fraser's Magazine*, and stands now in the third volume of the *Miscellanies*.
[4] Afterwards the well-known Chaplain-General.

as far as Luther, and if I can get no bookseller I will stop short there, and for the present slit it up into review articles, and publish it that way.[1] Magazine Fraser has never offered me a doit for Richter's critique, and not even printed it at all. If you can get any cash from the fellow it will come in fine stead just now, when I have above 200*l.* worth of writing returned on my hands, and no Fortunatus' hat close by. Adieu, Jack. We are poor men, but nothing worse.

Your brother,

T. CARLYLE.

To a proud gifted man it was no pleasant thing to chaffer with publishers and dun for payments, which were withheld perhaps to bend the spirit of their too independent contributor. Carlyle bore his humiliation better than might have been expected. Indeed, as a rule, all serious trials he endured as nobly as man could do. When his temper failed it was when some metaphorical gnat was buzzing in his ear. John Carlyle succeeded in extorting the few pounds that were owing from Fraser.

To John Carlyle.

Craigenputtock : August 21, 1830.

In returning from Scotsbrig this day week, whither I had gone on the Thursday before, I found your letter lying safe for me at Dumfries, and in spite of its valuable enclosure only bearing single postage. That last circumstance was an error on the part of his Majesty which it did not strike me in the least to rectify. We hear that Providence is a rich provider, and truly in my case I may thankfully say so. Many are the times when some seasonable supply in time of need has arrived when it was not in the least looked for. I was not by any means quite out of money when your bank paper came to hand ; but I saw clearly the likelihood, or rather the necessity, of such an event, which now by this 'sea-

---

[1] Partially accomplished in the following years, after many difficulties. The Nibelungen Lied appeared in the *Westminster Review*, and Early German Literature in the *Foreign Quarterly*. These essays, which are still the best upon their special subjects which exist in the English language, are specimens of the book which could find no publisher. They too are in the third volume of the *Miscellanies*.

sonable interposition' is put off to a safer distance.   Pity that
poor fellows should hang so much on cash!   But it is the general
lot, and whether it be ten pounds or ten thousand that would relieve us, the case is all the same, and the tie that binds us equally
mean.   If I had money to carry me up and down the world in
search of good men and fellow-labourers with whom to hold communion, and heat myself into clearer activity, I should think myself happier; but in the mean time I have *myself* here for better
or worse; and who knows but my imprisonment in these moors,
sulkily as I may sometimes take it, is really for my good?   If I
have any right strength it will.   If not, then what is the matter
whether I sink or swim?   Oh that I had but a little real wisdom ;
then would all things work beautifully together for the best ends.
Meanwhile the Dunscore Patmos is simply the place where of all
others in the known world I can live *cheapest*, which in the case of
a man living by literature, with little saleable talent, and who
would very fain not prove a liar and a scoundrel, this is a momentous point.   So let us abide here and work, or at least rest and be
thankful.

I am happy to tell you that if this Literary History is not finished, it is now at least concluded.   On Tuesday last I had a very
short note from Captain, or rather Curate ———, which had been
twice requested from him, stating that he found 'the publishers
averse,' chiefly on the score of terms (which terms I had never
hinted at), and indicating that he himself was averse chiefly on
the score of size, as *one* volume would have suited the Library better.   Further, it appeared from this note that the Reverend Editor
was in all human probability a cold-hearted, shabbyish, dandy parson and lieutenant, who, being disappointed that I would not work
for him at low wages, and any kind of work, wished to have nothing more to do with me, in which implied wish I could not but
heartily, though sorrowfully, coincide, so that nothing remains for
you but to send me back that ill-starred MS. as soon as you can,
that I may consign it to its ultimate distinction.

Assure Fraser that I feel no shadow of spleen against him, but
a true sentiment of friendship and regret at all the trouble he has
had.   For your satisfaction understand I am positively glad this
intolerable business is done, nay, glad that it is done in this way
rather than another.   What part of the MS. I can split into review
articles I will serve in that way ; for the present leaving the whole
narrative complete down to Luther, to serve as an Introduction to

my various essays on German Literature, in the compass of which essays (had I one or two more, for example Luther, Lessing, Herder) there already lies the best History of German Literature that I can easily write ; and so were there a flourishing prophetic and circumspective essay appended by way of conclusion, we had a very fair *Geschichte*, or at least a *zur Geschichte*, all lying cut and dry, which can be published at any time if it is wanted ; if not in my lifetime, then in some other, till which consummation it will lie here eating no bread. And so for all things, my brother, let us be thankful. I will work no more in 'Libraries,' or, if I can help it, in compilation. If my writing cannot be sold, it shall at least have been written out of my own heart. Also henceforth I will endeavour to be my own editor, having now arrived at the years for it. Nay, in the Devil's name, have I not a kail garden here that will grow potatoes and onions? The highest of men have often not had so much.

Too much of your sheet is already filled with my own concerns. At Scotsbrig, as I must tell you, matters wore a more tolerable aspect than I anticipated. Our mother was as well as usual, rather better, having been out at hay-making. Our father was still weak and somewhat dispirited, but as far as I could see he had no disease working on him, save loss of appetite and the general feebleness belonging to those years he has now arrived at. He sits most of the day, reading miscellaneously enough, wanders sometimes among the labourers, or even does little jobs himself. He seemed much quieter and better tempered.

Alick has written that he cannot keep this farm longer than Whitsunday, finding it a ruinous concern. Let Mrs. Welsh arrange the rest herself. Alick knows not well what he is to turn him to. Other farms might be had, but it is a ticklish business taking farms at present. Poor outlook there, nothing but loss and embarrassment. I often calculate that the land is all let some thirty per cent. too high ; and that before it can be reduced the whole existing race of farmers must be ruined : that is, the whole agricultural tools (which are capital) broken in pieces and burnt in the landlords' fire, to warm his pointers with.

Ach Gott! The time is sick and out of joint. The perversities and mismanagements, moral and physical, of this best-of-all stage of society are rising to a head ; and one day, see it who may, the whole concern will be blown up to Heaven, and fall thence to Tartarus, and a new and fairer era will rise in its room. Since the time of Nero and Jesus Christ there is no record of such embarrassments and crying, or, what is still worse, silent abominations. But the day, as we said, *will* come; for God is still in Heaven, whether Henry Brougham and Jeremiah Bentham know it or not; and the gig, and gigmania [1] must rot or start into thousand shivers, and bury itself in the ditch, that *Man* may have clean roadway towards the goal whither through all ages he is tending. *Fiat, fiat!*

Make my kindest compliments to my old friend your landlord,[2] whose like, take him for all in all, I have not yet looked upon. Tell him that none more honestly desires his welfare. Oh were I but joined to such a man! Would the Scotch Kirk but expel him, and his own better genius lead him far away from all Apocalypses, and prophetic and theologic chimæras, utterly unworthy of such a head, to see the world as it here lies visible, and is, that we might fight together for God's *true* cause even to the death! With one such man I feel as if I could defy the earth. But patience! patience! I shall find one, perhaps. At all events, courage! courage! What have we to look for but toil and trouble? What drivellers are we to whimper when it comes, and not front it, and triumph over it.

God for ever bless you, dear brother.

Heartily yours,

T. CARLYLE.

[1] Allusion to Thurtell's trial: 'I always thought him a respectable man.' 'What do you mean by respectable?' 'He kept a gig.'
[2] Irving, who had taken John Carlyle to live with him.

CHAPTER VI.

TRIALS had fallen sharply on Carlyle, entirely, as Jeffrey had said, through his own generosity. He had advanced 240*l.* in the education and support of his brother John. He had found the capital to stock the farm at Craigenputtock, and his brother Alick thus had received from him half as much more—small sums, as rich men estimate such matters, but wrung out by Carlyle as from the rock by desperate labour, and spared out of his own and his wife's necessities. John (perhaps ultimately Alexander, but of this I am not sure) honourably repaid his share of this debt in the better days which were coming to him, many years before fortune looked more kindly on Carlyle himself. But as yet John Carlyle was struggling almost penniless in London. Alick's farming at Craigenputtock, which Carlyle had once rashly thought of undertaking for himself, had proved a disastrous failure, and was now to be abandoned.[1] The pleasant family party there had to be broken up, and his brother was to lose the companionship which softened the dreariness of his solitude. Alick

---

[1] Carlyle, however, had brought his genius to bear on the cultivation in a single instance, though he could not save the farm. A field at Craigenputtock was made useless by a crop of nettles which covered the whole of it. They had been mowed down many times, but only grew the thicker; and to root them out would have been a serious expense. It struck Carlyle that all plants were exhausted by the effort of flowering and seeding, and if an injury would ever prove mortal to the nettle it would be at that particular crisis. He watched the field till the seed was almost ripe, then mowed it once more, and with complete success. So at least he described the experiment to me. Gardeners will know if the success was accidental or was due to some other cause.

Carlyle had the family gift of humour. His letters show
that had he been educated he too might have grown into
something remarkable. Alick could laugh with all his
heart and make others laugh. His departure changed the
character of the whole scene. Carlyle himself grew discontented. An impatient Radicalism rings through his
remarks on the things which were going on round him.
The political world was shaken by the three glorious days
in Paris. England, following the example, was agitating
for Reform, and a universal and increasing distress flung
its ominous shadow over the whole working community.
Reports of it all, leaking in through chance visitors, local
newspapers, or letters of friends, combined with his own
and his brother's indifferent and almost hopeless prospects,
tended too naturally to encourage his gloomy tendencies.
Ever on the watch to be of use to him, the warm-hearted
Jeffrey was again at hand to seduce him into conformity
with the dominant Liberal ways of thinking; that in the
approaching storm he might at least open a road for himself to his own personal advancement. In August Jeffrey
pressed his two friends in his most winning language to
visit him at Craigcrook. Carlyle, he said, was doing nothing, and could employ himself no better than to come
down with his blooming Eve out of his 'blasted Paradise,'
and seek shelter in the lower world. To Mrs. Carlyle he
promised roses and a blue sea, and broad shadows stretching over the fields. He said that he felt as if destined
to do them real service, and could now succeed at last.
Carlyle would not be persuaded; so in September the Jeffreys came again unlooked for to Craigenputtock. Carlyle
was with his family at Scotsbrig.

Returning (he said, Sept. 18, 1830) late in the evening from a
long ride, I found an express from Dumfries that the Jeffreys
would be all at Craigenputtock that night. Of the riding and
running, the scouring and scraping and Caleb Balderstone arrang-

ing my unfortunate but shifty and invincible Goody must have had, I say nothing. Enough, she is the cleverest of housewives, and might put innumerable *blues* to shame. I set out next morning, and on arriving here actually found the Dean of the Faculty with his adherents, sitting comfortably in a house swept and garnished awaiting my arrival. Of the *shine* itself I have room for no description. It all went prosperously on, and yesterday morning they set out homewards, reducing us instantly to our own more *commodious farthing rushlight,* which is our usual illumination. The worthy Dean is not very well, and I fear not very happy. We all like him better than we did. He is the most sparkling, pleasant little fellow I ever saw in my life.

How brilliant Jeffrey was, how he delighted them all with his anecdotes, his mockeries, and his mimicries, Carlyle has amply confessed; and he has acknowledged the serious excellence which lay behind the light exterior. It was on this occasion that he sent the 50*l.* to Hazlitt which came too late and found poor Hazlitt dying. It was on this occasion that he renewed his generous offer to lift Carlyle for a time over his difficulties out of his own purse, and when he could not prevail, promised to help John Carlyle in London, give him introductions, and if possible launch him in his profession. He charged himself with the Literary History, carried it off with him, and undertook to recommend it to Longman. From all this Jeffrey had nothing to gain: it was but the expression of hearty good will to Carlyle himself for his own sake and for the sake of his wife, in whom he had at least an equal interest. He wrote to her as cousin: what the exact relationship was I know not; but it was near enough, as he thought, to give him a right to watch over her welfare; and the thought of Carlyle persisting, in the face of imminent ruin, in what to him appeared a vain hallucination, and the thought still more of this delicate woman degraded to the duties of the mistress of a farmhouse, and obliged to face another winter in so frightful a climate, was simply horrible to him. She had not concealed from him that she was not happy at Craigenputtock; and the longer he reflected upon it the more out of humour he became with the obstinate philosopher who had doomed her to live there under such conditions.

It is evident from his letters that he held Carlyle to be gravely responsible. He respected many sides of his character, but he looked on him as under the influence of a curious but most reprehensible vanity, which would not and could not land him anywhere but in poverty and disappointment, while all the time the world was ready and eager to open its arms and lavish its liberality upon him if he would but consent to walk in its ways and be like other men. In this humour nothing that Carlyle did would please him. He quarrelled with the 'Literary History.' He disliked the views in it; he found fault with the style. After reading it, he had to say that he did not see how he could be of use in the obstetrical department to which he had aspired in its behalf.

> Hang them! (said Carlyle bitterly, as one disappointment trod on the heels of another), hang them! I have a book in me that will cause ears to tingle, and one day out it must and will issue. In this valley of the shadow of magazine editors we shall not always linger. Courage! Not hope—for she was always a liar—but courage! courage!

An account of Jeffrey's visit is inserted in the Journal. Carlyle was evidently trying to think as well as he could about his *great* friend, and was not altogether succeeding.

> The Jeffreys were here for about a week. Very good and interesting beyond wont was our worthy Dean. He is growing old, and seems dispirited and partly unhappy. The fairest cloak has its wrong side where the seams and straggling stitches afflict the eye! Envy no man. *Nescis quo urit.* Thou knowest not where the shoe pinches.
>
> Jeffrey's essential talent sometimes seems to me to have been that of a Goldoni, some comic dramatist, not without a touch of

fine lyrical pathos. He is the best mimic in the lowest and highest senses I ever saw. All matters that have come before him he has taken up in little dainty comprehensible forms ; chiefly logical— for he is a Scotchman and a lawyer—and encircled with sparkles of conversational wit or *persiflage;* yet with deeper study he would have found poetical forms for them, and his *persiflage* might have incorporated itself with the love and pure human feeling that dwells deeply in him. This last is his highest strength, though he himself hardly knows the significance of it; he is one of the most loving men alive ; has a true kindness not of blood and habit only, but of soul and spirit. He cannot *do* without being loved. He is in the highest degree social; and in defect of this *gregarious;* which last condition he in these bad times has for the most part had to content himself withal. Every way indeed he has fallen on evil days : the prose spirit of the world—to which world his kindliness draws him so strongly and so closely—has choked up and all but withered the better poetic spirit he derived from nature. Whatever is highest he entertains, like other Whigs, only as an ornament, as an appendage. The great business of man he, intellectually, considers, as a wordling does, *to be happy.* I have heard him say, 'If folly were the happiest I would be a fool.' Yet his daily life belies this doctrine, and says—' Though goodness were the most wretched, I would be good.'

In conversation he is brilliant, or rather sparkling, lively, kind, willing either to speak or listen, and above all men I have ever seen ready and copious, on the whole exceedingly pleasant in light talk—yet alas! light, light, too light. He will talk of nothing *earnestly,* though his look sometimes betrays an earnest feeling. He starts contradictions in such cases, and argues, argues. Neither is his arguing like that of a thinker, but of the advocate—victory, not truth. A right *terræ filius* would feel irresistibly disposed to wash him away. He is not a strong man in any shape, but nimble and tough.

He stands midway between God and Mammon, and his preaching through life has been an attempt to reconcile them. Hence his popularity—a thing easily accountable when one looks at the world and at him, but little honourable to either. Literature! poetry! Except by a dim indestructible instinct which he has never dared to avow, yet being a true poet in his way could never eradicate, he knows not what they mean. A true newspaper critic on the great scale ; no priest, but a concionator.

Yet on the whole he is about the *best man* I ever saw. Sometimes I think he will abjure the devil if he live, and become a pure light. Already he is a most tricksy, dainty, beautiful little spirit. I have seen gleams on the face and eyes of the man that let you look into a higher country. God bless him! These jottings are as sincere as I could write them; yet too dim and inaccurately compacted. I see the nail, but have not here hit it on the head.

Meanwhile, and in the midst of Jeffrey's animadversions, Carlyle himself was about to take a higher flight. He 'had a book in him which would cause ears to tingle.' Out of his discontent, out of his impatience with the hard circumstances which crossed, thwarted, and pressed him, there was growing in his mind 'Sartor Resartus.' He had thoughts fermenting in him which were struggling to be uttered. He had something real to say about the world and man's position in it to which, could it but find fit expression, he knew that attention must be paid. The 'clothes philosophy,' which had perhaps been all which his first sketch contained, gave him the necessary form. His own history, inward and outward, furnished substance; some slight invention being all that was needed to disguise his literal individuality; and in the autumn of the year he set himself down passionately to work. Fast as he could throw his ideas upon paper the material grew upon him. The origin of the book is still traceable in the half fused, tumultuous condition in which the metal was poured into the mould. With all his efforts in calmer times to give it artistic harmony he could never fully succeed. 'There are but a few pages in it,' he said to me, 'which are rightly done.' It is well perhaps that he did not succeed. The incompleteness of the smelting shows all the more the actual condition of his mind. If defective as a work of art, 'Sartor' is for that very reason a revelation of Carlyle's individuality.

The idea had first struck him when on a visit with Mrs.

Carlyle at Templand. Customs, institutions, religious creeds, what were they but *clothes* in which human creatures covered their native nakedness, and enabled men themselves to live harmoniously and decently together? Clothes, dress, changed with the times; they grew old, they were elaborate, they were simple; they varied with fashion or habit of life; they were the outward indicators of the inward and spiritual nature. The analogy gave the freest scope and play for the wilfullest and wildest humour. The Teufelsdröckh, which we have seen seeking in vain for admission into London magazines, was but a first rude draft. Parts of this perhaps survive as they were originally written in the opening chapters. The single article, when it was returned to him, first expanded into two; *then* he determined to make a book of it, into which he could project his entire self. The 'Foreign Quarterly' continued good to him. He could count on an occasional place in 'Fraser.' The part already written of his 'Literary History,' slit into separate articles, would keep him alive till the book was finished. He had been well paid for his 'Life of Schiller.' If the execution corresponded to the conception, that 'Sartor' would be ten times better.

On the 19th of October he described what he was about to his brother. 'I am leading the stillest life, musing amidst the pale sunshine, or rude winds of October Tirl the Trees, when I go walking in this almost ghastly solitude, and for the rest writing with impetuosity. I think it not impossible that I may see you this winter in London. I mean to come whenever I can spare the money, that I may look about me among men for a little. What I am writing at is the strangest of all things. A very singular piece, I assure you. It glances from heaven to earth and back again, in a strange satirical frenzy, whether fine or not remains to be seen.'

Near the same date he writes to his mother :—

The wife and I are very quiet here, and accustoming ourselves
as fast as we can to the stillness of winter which is fast coming on.
These are the greyest and most silent days I ever saw. My besom,
as I sweep up the withered leaves, might be heard at a furlong's
distance. The woods are getting very parti-coloured; the old
trees quite bare. All witnesses that another year has travelled
away. What good and evil has it brought us? May God sanctify
them both to every one of us! I study not to get too *wae;* but
often I think of many solemn and sad things, which indeed I do
not wish to forget. We are all in God's hand; otherwise this
world, which is not wholly a valley of the shadow of death, were
too frightful. Why should we fear? Let us hope. We are in the
place of hope. Our life is a hope. But far better than all rea-
sonings for cheerfulness is the diligence I use in following my
daily business. For the last three weeks I have been writing my
task-work again, and get along wonderfully well. What it is to be
I cannot yet tell—whether a book or a string of magazine articles.
We hope the former; but in either case it may be worth something.

'Sartor' was indeed a free-flowing torrent, the outburst-
ing of emotions which as yet had found no escape. The
discontent which in a lower shape was rushing into French
Revolutions, Reform Bills, Emancipation Acts, Socialism,
and Bristol riots and rick burnings, had driven Carlyle into
far deeper inquiries—inquiries into the how and why of
these convulsions of the surface. The Hebrew spiritual
robes he conceived were no longer suitable, and that this
had something to do with it. The Hebrew clothes had
become 'old clothes'—not the fresh wrought garments
adapted to man's real wants, but sold at second-hand, and
gaping at all their seams. Radical also politically Carlyle
was at this time. The constitution of society, as he looked
at it, was unjust from end to end. The workers were
starving; the idle were revelling in luxury. Radicalism,
as he understood it, meant the return of Astræa—an approach to equity in the apportionment of good and evil in

this world ; and on.the intellectual side, if not encouragement of truth, at least the withdrawal of exclusive public
support of what was not true, or only partially true. He
did then actually suppose that the Reform Bill meant
something of that kind ; that it was a genuine effort of
honourable men to clear the air of imposture. He had not
realised, what life afterwards taught him, that the work
of centuries was not to be accomplished by a single political change, and that the Reform Bill was but a singeing
of the dungheap. Even then he was no believer in the
miraculous effects to be expected from an extended suf-
frage. He knew well enough that the welfare of the State,
like the welfare of everything else, required that the wise
and good should govern, and the unwise and selfish should
be governed ; that of all methods of discovering and pro-
moting your wise man the voice of a mob was the least
promising, and that if Reform meant only liberty, and the
abolition of all authority, just or unjust, we might be
worse off perhaps than we were already. But he was impatient and restless ; stung no doubt by resentment at the
alternative offered to himself either to become a humbug
or to be beaten from the field by starvation ; and the
memorable epitaph on Count Zaehdarm and his achievements in this world showed in what direction his intellectual passions were running.

It seems that when Jeffrey was at Craigenputtock Carlyle must have opened his mind to him on these matters,
and still more fully in some letter afterwards. Jeffrey,
who was a Whig of the Whigs, who believed in liberty,
but by liberty meant the right of every man to do as he
pleased with his own as long as he did not interfere with
his neighbour, had been made seriously angry. Mysticism
was a pardonable illusion, provoking enough while it lasted,
but likely to clear off, as the morning mist when the sun
rises higher above the horizon ; but these political views,

taken up especially by a man so determined and so passionately in earnest as Carlyle, were another thing, and an infinitely more dangerous thing. Reform within moderate limits was well enough, but these new opinions if they led to anything must lead to revolution. Jeffrey believed that they were wild and impracticable ; that if ever misguided missionaries of sedition could by eloquence and resolute persistence persuade the multitude to adopt notions subversive of the rights of property, the result could only be universal ruin. His regard and even esteem for Carlyle seem to have sensibly diminished from this time. He half feared him for the mischief which he might do, half gave him up as beyond help—at least as beyond help from himself. He continued friendly. He was still willing to help Carlyle within the limits which his conscience allowed, but from this moment the desire to push him forward in the politico-literary world cooled down or altogether ceased.

He tried the effect, however, of one more lecture, the traces of which are visible in 'Sartor.' He had a horror of Radicalism, he said. It was nothing but the old feud against property, made formidable by the intelligence and conceit of those who had none. . . . Carlyle's views either meant the destruction of the right of property altogether, and the establishment of a universal co-operative system—and this no one in his senses could contemplate— or they were nonsense. Anything short of the abolition of property, sumptuary laws, limitation of the accumulation of fortunes, compulsory charity, or redivision of land, would not make the poor better off, but would make all poor ; would lead to the destruction of all luxury, elegance, art, and intellectual culture, and reduce men to a set of savages scrambling for animal subsistence. The institution of property brought some evils with it, and a revolting spectacle of inequality. But to touch it would entail evils still greater ; for though the poor suffered, their lot was only what the lot of the great mass of mankind must necessarily be under every conceivable condition. They would escape the pain of seeing others better off than they were, but they would be no better off themselves, while they would lose the mental improvement which to a certain extent spread downwards through society as long as culture existed anywhere, and at the same time the hope and chance of rising to a higher level, which was itself enjoyment even if it were never realised. Rich men after all spent most of their income on the poor. Except a small waste of food on their servants and horses, they were mere distributors among frugal and industrious workmen.

If Carlyle meant to be a politician, Jeffrey begged him to set about it modestly and patiently, and submit to study the questions a little under those who had studied them longer. If he was a Radical, why did he keep two horses himself, producing nothing and consuming the food of six human creatures, that his own diaphragm might be healthily agitated? Riding-horses interfered with the subsistence of men five hundred times more than the unfortunate partridges.[1] So again Carlyle had adopted the Radical objections to machinery. Jeffrey inquired if he meant to burn carts and ploughs—nay, even spades too, for spades were but machines? Perhaps he would end by only allowing men to work with *one* hand,[2] that the available work might employ a larger number of persons. Yet for such aims as these Carlyle thought a Radical insurrection justifiable and its success to be desired. The very first enactments of a successful revolution would be in this spirit: the overseers of the poor would be ordered to give twelve or twenty shillings to every man who could

---

[1] See the Zaehdarm Epitaph.

[2] A curiously accurate prophecy on Jeffrey's part, not as regarded Carlyle, but as to the necessary tendency of the unionist theory.

not, or said he could not, earn as much by the labour to which he had been accustomed.

Speculations on these and kindred subjects are found scattered up and down in 'Sartor.' Jeffrey was crediting Carlyle with extravagances which it is impossible that even in his then bitter humour he could have seriously entertained. He was far enough from desiring insurrection, although a conviction did lay at the very bottom of his mind that incurably unjust societies would find in insurrection and conflagration their natural consummation and end. But it is likely that he talked with fierce exaggeration on such subjects. He always did talk so. It is likely, too, that he had come to some hasty conclusions on the intractable problems of social life, and believed changes to be possible and useful which fuller knowledge of mankind showed him to be dreams. Before a just allotment of wages in this world could be arrived at—just payment according to real desert—he perceived at last that mankind must be themselves made just, and that such a transformation is no work of a political revolution. Carlyle too had been attracted to the St. Simonians. He had even in a letter to Goethe expressed some interest and hope in them ; and the wise old man had warned him off from the dangerous illusion. 'Von der Société St. Simonien bitte Dich fern zu halten,' Goethe had said. 'From the Society of the St. Simonians I entreat you to hold yourself clear.' [1] Jeffrey's practical sense had probably suggested difficulties to Carlyle which he had overlooked ; and Goethe carried more weight with him than Jeffrey. 'Sartor' may have been improved by their remonstrances ; yet there lie in it the germs of all Carlyle's future teaching—a clear statement of problems of the gravest import, which cry for a solution, which insist on a solution, yet on

[1] This sentence alone survives of Goethe's letter on the occasion, extracted in one of Carlyle's own.

which political economy and Whig political philosophy
fail utterly to throw the slightest light. I will mention
one to which Carlyle to his latest hour was continually returning. Jeffrey was a Malthusian. He had a horror
and dread of over-population. ' Sartor' answers him with
a scorn which recalls Swift's famous suggestion of a remedy for the distresses of Ireland.

The old Spartans had a wiser method, and went out and hunted
down their Helots, and speared and spitted them, when they
grew too numerous. With our improved fashions of hunting,
now, after the invention of firearms and standing armies, how
much easier were such a hunt. Perhaps in the most thickly
peopled countries some three days annually might suffice to shoot
all the able-bodied paupers that had accumulated within the
year. Let Government think of this. The expense were trifling;
the very carcases would pay it. Have them salted and barrelled.
Could you not victual therewith, if not army and navy, yet richly
such infirm paupers, in workhouses and elsewhere, as enlightened
charity, dreading no evil of them, might see good to keep alive?

And yet there must be something wrong. A full-formed horse
will in any market bring from twenty to two hundred friedrichs
d'or. Such is his worth to the world. A full-formed man is not
only worth nothing to the world, but the world could afford him
a good round sum would he simply engage to go and hang himself. Nevertheless, which of the two was the more cunningly devised article, even as an engine? Good heavens! a white European man, standing on his two legs, with his two five-fingered
hands at his shacklebones, and miraculous head on his shoulders,
is worth, I should say, from fifty to a hundred horses!

What portion of this inconsiderable terraqueous globe have ye
actually tilled and delved till it will grow no more? How thick
stands your population in the pampas and savannas of America,
round ancient Carthage and in the interior of Africa, on both
slopes of the Atlantic chain, in the central platform of Asia, in
Spain, Greece, Turkey, Crim Tartary, and the Curragh of Kildare?
One man in one year, as I have understood it, if you lend him
earth, will feed himself and nine others. Alas! where are now
the Hengsts and Alarics of our still growing, still expanding
Europe, who when their home is grown too narrow will enlist, and

like fire-pillars guide onwards those superfluous masses of indomitable living valour, equipped not now with the battle-axe and war-chariot, but with the steam-engine and ploughshare? Where are they? Preserving their game!

When Carlyle published his views on 'the Nigger question,' his friends on both sides of the Atlantic were astonished and outraged. Yet the thought in that pamphlet and the thought in 'Sartor' is precisely the same. When a man can be taught to work and made to work, he has a distinct value in the world appreciable by money like the value of a horse. In the state of liberty where he belongs to nobody, and his industry cannot be calculated upon, he makes his father poorer when he is born. Slavery might be a bad system, but under it a child was worth at least as much as a foal, and the master was interested in rearing it. Abolish slavery and substitute anarchy in the place of it, and the parents, themselves hardly able to keep body and soul together, will bless God when a timely fever relieves them of a troublesome charge.

This fact, for fact it is, still waits for elucidation, and I often heard Carlyle refer to it; yet he was always able to see 'the other side.' No Hengst or Alaric had risen in the fifty years which had passed since he had written 'Sartor;' yet not long before his death he was talking to me of America and of the success with which the surplus population of Europe had been carried across the sea and distributed over that enormous continent. Frederick himself, he said, could not have done it better, even with absolute power and unlimited resources, than it had 'done itself' by the mere action of unfettered liberty.

CHAPTER VII.

A CHANGE meanwhile came over the face of English politics. Lord Grey became Prime Minister, and Brougham Chancellor, and all Britain was wild over Reform and the coming millennium. Jeffrey went into Parliament and was rewarded for his long services by being taken into the new Government as Lord Advocate. Of course he had to remove to London, and his letters, which henceforward were addressed chiefly to Mrs. Carlyle, were filled with accounts of Cabinet meetings, dinners, Parliamentary speeches—all for the present going merry as a marriage bell. Carlyle at Craigenputtock continued steady to his work. His money difficulties seemed likely to mend a little. Napier was overcoming his terror, and might perhaps take articles again from him for the 'Edinburgh.' The new 'Westminster' was open to him. The 'Foreign Quarterly' had not deserted him, and between them and 'Fraser' he might still find room enough at his disposal. The Literary History was cut up as had been proposed; the best parts of it were published in the coming year in the form of Essays, and now constitute the greater part of the third volume of the 'Miscellanies.' A second paper on Schiller, and another on Jean Paul, both of which had been for some time seeking in vain for an editor who would take them, were admitted into the 'Foreign Review' and 'Fraser.' Sufficient money was thus ultimately obtained to secure the household from starvation. But some months passed before these arrangements could be completed, and

'Sartor' had to go on with the prospect still gloomy in the extreme. Irving had seen and glanced over the first sketch of it when it was in London, and had sent a favourable opinion. Carlyle himself, notwithstanding his work, found time for letters to his brother, who was still hankering after literature.

To John Carlyle.

Craigenputtock: February 26, 1831.

Till Wednesday I am preparing 'Reineke' and various little etceteras, after which I purpose seriously inclining heart and hand to the finishing of 'Teufelsdröckh'—if indeed it be finishable. How could you remember Irving's criticism so well? Tell him it was quite like himself; he said all that was friendly, flattering, and encouraging, yet with the *right* faults kindly indicated—a true picture painted *couleur de rose.* I will make the attempt. And now, dear Jack, as to the last fraction of the letter; a word about you. Sorry am I to see your supplies running so low, and so little outlook for bettering them : yet what advice to give you ? I have said a thousand times when you could not believe me, that the trade of literature was worse as a trade than that of honest street sweeping; that I know not how a man without some degree of prostitution could live by it, unless indeed he were situated like me, and could live upon potatoes and point if need were—as indeed need has been, is, and will be, with better men than me. If the angels have any humour I am sure they laughed heartily to-day, as I myself have repeatedly done, to see Alick setting off with twelve pence of copper, a long roll like a pencase, the whole disposable capital of both our households. I realised six, he six, so he was enabled to go. I was for keeping three, but he looked wistfully, and I gave him them with loud laughter. He had borrowed all our money and did *not* get payments last Wednesday, but surely will on Monday. . . . I could also prove that a life of scribbling is the worst conceivable for cultivating thought, which is the noblest, and the only noble thing in us. Your ideas never get root, cannot be sown, but are ground down from day to day. Oh that I heard of any medicine for your practising, were it only on the lower animals. However, patience—courage. The time is coming—dear Jack, keep a stout heart; I think I notice in you a considerable improvement since you left us; a far more manly bearing. Never despond. If you see no feasible method of ever fairly attempting to get professional employment in London, why then I think I would leave London. Do not fall into straits. Do not involve yourself in debt. Come out of it. Come *hither*. Share our provisions, such as the good God gives us—our roof and our welcome, and we will consider which way you are next to try it. Above all hide nothing from me, and I will hide it from the Scotsbrig people whenever you bid me.

And so God bless you, dear brother. Fear nothing but behaving unwisely.

T. CARLYLE.

Alick Carlyle was to leave Craigenputtock at Whitsuntide, a neighbouring grazier having offered the full rent for the farm, which Alick was unable to afford. Where he was to go and what was to become of him was the great family anxiety.

Little things (said Carlyle) are great to little men, to little man; for what was the Moscow expedition to Napoleon but the offering also for a new and larger farm whereon to till? and this too was but a mere clout of a farm compared with the great farm whose name is *Time*, or the quite boundless freehold which is called Eternity. Let us feel our bits of anxieties therefore, and make our bits of efforts, and think no shame of them.

Both brothers were virtually thrown upon his hands, while he seemingly was scarce able to take care of himself and his wife. When Alick was gone he and she would be left 'literally *unter vier Augen*, alone among the whinstone deserts; within fifteen miles not one creature they could so much as speak to,' and 'Sartor' was to be written under such conditions. Another winter at Craigenputtock in absolute solitude was a prospect too formidable to be faced. They calculated that with the utmost economy they might have 50*l.* in hand by the end of the summer, 'Teufelsdröckh' could by that time be finished. Mrs. Carlyle could stay and take care of Craigenputtock, while Carlyle himself would visit 'the great beehive and wasp's

nest of London,' find a publisher for his book, and then
see whether there was any other outlook for him. If none
offered, there was still a resource behind, suggested perhaps
by the first success of Irving and advised by Charles Buller.

I have half a mind (he wrote to John, warning him at the same
time to be secret about it) to start when I come there, if the
ground promise well, and deliver a dozen lectures in my own Annandale accent with my own God-created brain and heart, to such
audience as will gather round me, on some section or aspect of
this strange life in this strange era, of which my soul, like Eliphaz
the Temanite's, is getting fuller and fuller. Does there seem to
thee any propriety in a man that has organs of speech and even
some semblance of understanding and sincerity sitting for ever,
mute as a milestone, while quacks of every colour are quacking as
with lungs of brass? True, I have no pulpit; but as I once said,
cannot any man make him a pulpit simply by inverting the nearest tub? And what are your Whigs, and Lord Advocates, and
Lord Chancellors, and the whole host of unspeakably gabbling
parliamenteers and pulpiteers and pamphleteers, if a man suspect
that there is fire enough in his belly to burn up the entire creation of such? These all build on mechanism; one spark of dy-
namism, of inspiration, were it in the poorest soul, is stronger
than they all.

As for the Whig Ministry with whom Jeffrey might appear to
connect me, I partly see two things: first, that they will have
nothing in any shape to do with me, did I show them the virtue
of a Paul; nay, the more virtue the less chance, for virtue is the
will to choose the good, not tool-usefulness, to forge at the expe-
dient: secondly, that they, the Whigs, except perhaps Brougham
and his implements, will not endure. The latter, indeed, I should
wonder little to see one day a second Cromwell. He is the cun-
ningest and the strongest man in England now, as I construe him,
and with no better principle than a Napoleon has—a worship and
self-devotion to power. God be thanked that I had nothing to do
with his University and its committees. So that Providence
seems saying to me, 'Thou wilt never find pulpit, were it but a
rhetoric chair, provided for thee. Invert thy tub, and speak if
thou hast aught to say.'

Keep this inviolably secret, and know meanwhile that if I can
raise 50*l.* at the right season, to London I will certainly come.

John Carlyle on his own account needed fresh admonition. Patients he could hear of none. The magazine editors were inclining for his name's sake to listen to him. Carlyle's feeling about it was like that of the rich man in torment.

To John Carlyle.

Craigenputtock : March 27, 1831.

I am clear for your straining every sinew simply to get *medical employment,* whether as assistant surgeon or in *any* other honest capacity. Without any doubt as the world now stands your safety lies there. Neither are you so destitute of friends and influence that on any given reasonable plan a considerable force of help could not be brought to bear. There are several, of weight, that would on more than one ground rejoice to do their best for you. Your world of London lies too dim before me for specification in this matter. Towards this, however, all your endeavours ought doubtless to be directed. Think and scheme and inquire, or rather continue to do so : once foiled is nothing like final defeat. So long as life is in a man there is strength in him. *Ein anderes Mal wollen wir unsere Sache besser machen*—' the next time we will manage our affairs better '—this was Fritz's *Wahlspruch;* and in this place of hope, where indeed there is nothing for us but hope, every brave man in reverses says the like.

For your success with the ' New Monthly,' or even with Napier, I care little, except so far as it might enable you to continue longer in London on the outlook. In other respects I am nearly sure failure would even be for your good. Periodical writing is, as I have often said, simply the worst of all existing employments. No mortal that had another noble art, the noblest with but one single exception, but would turn from it with abhorrence and cleave with his whole heart to the other. I am of opinion that you have a talent in you, perhaps far deeper than you yourself have often suspected ; but also that it will never come to growth in that way. Incessant scribbling is inevitable death to thought. What can grow in the soil of that mind which must all be riddled monthly to see if there are any grains in it that will sell ? A hack that contents himself with gathering any offal of novelty or the like, and simply spreads this out on a stand and begs the passengers to buy it, may flourish in such craft ; an honest man, much more a man of any original talent, cannot. Thoughts fall on us, as I said, like seed. This you will find to be true. It is time only and silence that can ripen them. So convinced am I of the dangerous, precarious, and on the whole despicable and ungainly nature of a life by scribbling in any shape, that I am resolved to investigate again whether even I am for ever doomed to it.

I will not leave literature; neither should you leave it. Nay, had I but two potatoes in the world, and one true idea, I should hold it my duty to part with one potato for paper and ink, and live upon the other till I got it written. To such extremities may a *mere* man of letters be brought in Britain at present; but no wise *you*, who have another footing, and can live in a steady genial climate till experience have evoked into purity what is in you—*then* to be spoken with authority in the ears of all.

Such lesson, my dear brother, had you to learn in London before even the right effort could begin. It is a real satisfaction that, however bitterly you are learning or have learnt it, henceforth your face and force are turned in the true direction. If not to-day, then to-morrow you must and will advance prosperously and triumph. Forward, then, *festen Muth's und frohen Sinn's*, and God be with you. Fear nothing; *die Zeit bringt Rosen*.

Of public matters I could write much; but, greatly as the spectacle of these times—a whole world quitting its old anchorage and venturing into new untried seas with little science of sailing aboard—solicits one's attention, they do not interest either of us chiefly. I have signed no petition; nay, I know not whether, had I the power by speaking a word to delay that consummation or hasten it, I would speak the word. It is a thing I have either longed for passionately or with confidence carelessly predicted any time these fifteen years. If I with any zeal approve of it now, it is simply on the ground of this incontrovertible aphorism which the state of all the industrious in these quarters too lamentably confirms—

> Hungry guts and empty purse
> May be better, can't be worse.

There is no logic yet discovered that can get behind this. Yes, in God's name, *let* us try it the other way. Jane ' salutes you with greetings and sisterly blessings.' [1] Adieu, dear Jack, *für jetzt*.

Ever your brother,

T. CARLYLE.

[1] Phrase of Edward Irving's.

In this period of 'potatoes and point' and 'farthing rushlights' for illumination after dark, the reader may be anxious to know how Mrs. Carlyle was getting on. Little can be said about this, for Carlyle tells next to nothing of her save in sad letters to Jeffrey, the nature of which, for they have not been preserved, can only be conjectured from Jeffrey's replies to them. We are left pretty much to guess her condition; and of guesses, the fewer that are ventured the better. Here, however, is one letter of her own inquiring after a servant for her mother—one of the collection which Carlyle has himself made, and has attached notes and preface to it.

To Miss Jean Carlyle, Scotsbrig.

[Betty Smail, mother of the two servant girls treated of here, was a dependant and cottager at Scotsbrig, come of very honest farmer people, though now reduced. She was herself a hardy, striving, noteworthy, lithe body, stood a great deal of sorrow and world-contradiction well, and died, still at Scotsbrig, very deaf, and latterly gone quite blind, age about ninety, only last year (1868), or the year before. Her girl Jean did not go, I think. Both these poor girls died in their mother's lifetime: one, probably Jean, soon after this of sudden fever; the other still more tragically of some *neuralgic* accident—suicide, thought not to be voluntary, hardly two weeks before my own great loss. Ah me!—T. C.]

Craigenputtock: Spring, 1831.

My dearest Jean,—I was meaning to write you a long letter by Alick, but I have been in bed all day with a headache, and am risen so confused and dull that for your sake as well as my own I shall keep my speculations—news I have none—till another opportunity, merely despatching in a few words a small piece of business I have to trouble you with, which will not wait.

My mother is wanting a woman at next term to take charge of her few cattle, work out, and assist at the washings. Not wishing to hire one out of Thornhill, she has requested me to look about for her, and would have liked Betty Smail, whom I formerly recommended, provided she had been leaving the Andersons. But I was happy to find (having been the means of placing there) that she is not leaving them, and continues to give great satisfaction by her honest, careful, obliging character. Miss Anderson happened to mention to Betty that I had been inquiring about her for my mother, when she suggested that her sister Jean, who is out of a place, might possibly answer. You know this Jean. Is she still disengaged ? would she be willing to come? and do you think she would be fit for the place ?

That you may be better able to form a judgment in the matter, I must tell you my mother has already *one* Jean, who is a *favourite* of some standing ; and you know there is not houseroom at Templand for *two* favourites at once.

The present Jean maintains her ground partly by good service, partly by *wheedling*. To get the good-will of her mistress, and so have a comfortable life, the new comer, besides the usual requisites in a byre-woman, should possess the art of wheedling in a still higher degree,[1] or she should be an obtuse, imperturbable character that would take 'the good the gods provided,' and for the rest 'jouk until the jaw gaed by,' would go on honestly milking her cows and ' clatting ' her byre 'in maiden meditation fancy free,' till under a change of ministry, which always comes at last, she might find herself suddenly promoted in her turn.

Now all this is very ill-natured, and you will mind it only so far as you see sense in it. It means simply that if Jean Smail be a very sensitive or quarrelsome character, and at the same time without *tact*, she would not be likely to prosper. Send me word by Alick what you think. I need hardly add that a servant who *pleases* could not possibly find a better place.

Tell your mother, with my love, that the hen she has sent to be *eaten* has laid the first egg of our whole stock.

God bless you. More next time, as the Doctor says.

Ever affectionately yours,

JANE W. CARLYLE.

Meanwhile the affairs of the poor Doctor were coming to extremity. Excellent advice might be given from Craigenputtock ; but advice now was all that could be af-

---

[1] ' Truish—emphatic for business' sake.—T. C.'

forded. Even his magazine articles, for which he had
been rebuked for writing, could not be sold after all. It
was time clearly for a *deus ex machinâ* to appear and
help him. Happily there was a *deus* in London able and
willing to do it in the shape of Jeffrey. Though he had
failed in inducing Carlyle to accept pecuniary help from
him, he could not be prevented from assisting his brother,
and giving him or lending him some subvention till something better could be arranged. Here, too, Carlyle's pride
took alarm. It was pain and humiliation to him that any
member of his family should subsist on the bounty of a
stranger. He had a just horror of debt. The unlucky
John himself fell in for bitter observations upon his indolence. John, he said, should come down to Scotland and
live with him. There was shelter for him and food
enough, such as it was. He did not choose that a brother
of his should be degraded by accepting obligations. But
this time Jeffrey refused to listen. It might be very wrong,
he admitted, for a man to sit waiting by the pool till an angel stirred the water, but it was not necessarily right therefore that because he could not immediately find employment in his profession, he should renounce his chances and
sit down to eat potatoes and read German at Craigenputtock. He had no disposition to throw away money without a prospect of doing good with it, but he knew no better use to which it could be put than in floating an industrious man over the shoals into a fair way of doing good
for himself. Even towards Carlyle, angry as he had been,
his genuine kindness obliged him to relent. If only he
would not be so impracticable and so arrogant! If only
he could be persuaded that he was not an inspired being,
and destined to be the founder of a new religion! But a
solitary life and a bad stomach had so spoilt him, all but
the heart, that he despaired of being able to mend him.

Jeffrey was so evidently sincere that even Carlyle could

object no longer on his brother's account. 'My pride,' he said, ' were true pride—savage, satanic, and utterly damnable—if it offered any opposition to such a project when my own brother and his future happiness was concerned.' Jeffrey did not mean to confine himself to immediate assistance with his purse. He was determined to find, if possible, some active work for John. Nothing could be done immediately, for he was obliged to leave London on election business. Help in money at least was to be given as soon as he returned; Carlyle using the interval for another admonition.

Consider your situation (he wrote to his brother on the 8th of May) with unprejudiced, fearless mind, listening no moment to the syren melodies of hope, which are only melodies of sloth, but taking cold prudence and calculation with you at every step. *Nimm Dich zusammen.* Gather yourself up. Feel your feet upon the rock before you rest, not upon the quicksand, where resting will but engulph you deeper. In your calculations, too, I would have you throw out literature altogether. Indeed, I rather believe it were for your good if you quite burnt your magazine pen and devoted yourself exclusively and wholly to medicine, and nothing but medicine. Magazine work is below street-sweeping as a trade. Even I, who have no other, am determined to try by all methods whether it is not possible to abandon it.

At Craigenputtock the most desperate pinch was not yet over. One slip of the Literary History came out in the April number of the 'Edinburgh' in the form of a review of Taylor's 'Historic Survey of German Poetry,'[1] but payment for it was delayed or forgotten. Meanwhile the farm-horses had been sold. Old Larry, doing double duty on the road and in the cart, had laid himself down and died—died from overwork. So clever was Larry, so humorous, that it was as if the last human friend had been taken away. The pony had been parted with also, though it was recovered afterwards; and before payment

[1] *Miscellanies*, vol. iii.

came from Napier for the article they were in real extremity. Alick by his four years of occupation was out of pocket 300*l.* These were the saddest days which Carlyle had ever known.

The summer came, and the Dunscore moors grew beautiful in the dry warm season. 'So pure was the air, the foliage, the herbage, and everything round him,' that he said, if Arcadianly given, he 'might fancy the yellow buttercups were asphodel, and the whole scene a portion of Hades—some outskirt of the Elysian Fields, the very perfection of solitude.' Between the softness of the scene and the apparent hopelessness of his prospects, Carlyle's own heart seems for a moment to have failed. He wrote to Jeffrey in extreme depression, as if he felt he had lost the game, and that there was nothing for it but to turn cynic and live and die in silence. The letter I have not seen, and I do not know whether it has been preserved, but Jeffrey's answer shows what the tone of it must have been. 'The cynic tub,' 'the primitive lot of man,' Jeffrey frankly called an unseemly and unworthy romance. If Carlyle did not care for himself, he ought to think of his young and delicate wife, whose great heart and willing martyrdom would make the sacrifice more agonising in the end. It was not necessary. He should have aid— effective aid; and if he pleased he might repay it some day ten times over. Something should be found for him to do neither unglorious nor unprofitable. He was fit for many things, and there were more tasks in the world fit for him than he was willing to believe. He complimented him on his last article in the 'Edinburgh.' Empson had praised it warmly. Macaulay and several others, who had laughed at his 'Signs of the Times,' had been struck with its force and originality. If he would but give himself fair play, if he could but believe that men might differ from him without being in damnable error, he would make his way to the front without difficulty. If Jeffrey had been the most tender of brothers he could not have written more kindly. Carlyle if one of the proudest was also one of the humblest of mortals. He replied, 'that he was ready to work at any honest thing whatsoever;' 'that he did not see that literature could support an honest man otherwise than *à la* Diogenes.' 'In this fashion he meant to experiment if nothing else could be found, which however through all channels of investigation he was minded to try for.'

It is not easy to see precisely what kind of employment Jeffrey had really in view for Carlyle. At one time no doubt he had thought of recommending him strongly to the Government. At another he had confessedly thought of him as his own successor on the 'Edinburgh Review.' But he had been frightened at Carlyle's Radicalism. He had been offended at his arrogance. Perhaps he thought that it indicated fundamental unsoundness of mind. He little conjectured that the person for whom he was concerning himself was really one of the most remarkable men in Europe, destined to make a deeper impression upon his contemporaries than any thinker then alive. This was not to be expected; but it must be supposed that he was wishing rather to try the sincerity of Carlyle's professions than that he was really serious in what he now suggested. He gave a list of possible situations: a clerkship at the Excise or the Board of Longitude or the Record Office, or a librarianship at the British Museum, or some secretaryship in a merchant's house of business. He asked him which of these he would detest the least, that he might know before he applied for it.

Poor Carlyle ! It was a bitter draught which was being commended to his lips. But he was very meek; he answered that he would gratefully accept any one of them : but even such posts as these he thought in his despondency to be beyond his reach. He was like the pilgrim in the valley of humiliation. 'I do not expect,' he told his mother, 'that he will be able to accomplish anything for me. I must even get through life *without a trade*, always in poverty, as far better men have done. Our want is the want of faith. Jesus of Nazareth was not poor, though he had not where to lay his head. Socrates was rich enough. I have a deep, irrevocable, all-comprehending Ernulphus curse to read upon Gigmanity : that is the Baal worship of our time.'

Though brought down so low, he could not entirely love the hand which had made him feel where he stood in the world's estimation. His unwillingness that John should accept money from Jeffrey was not removed.

To John Carlyle.

Craigenputtock : July 7, 1831.

Help towards work I would solicit from any reasonable man. Mere pecuniary help for its own sake is a thing one should always be cautious of accepting. Few are worthy to give it, still fewer capable of worthily receiving it. Such is the way of the time we live in. Meanwhile, relax not your own efforts for a moment. Think, project, investigate. You are like a soul struggling towards birth ; the skilfullest accoucheur (pardon the horrible figure) can but help the process. Here, too, the Cæsarean operation, as I have seen, is oftenest fatal to the fœtus. In short, Jack, there lie the rudiments of a most sufficient man and doctor in thee : but wise *will* must first body them forth. Oh, I know the thrice-cursed state you are in—hopeless grim death-defying thoughts ; a world shut against you by inexpugnable walls. Rough it out ; toil it out ; other way of making a *man* have I never seen. One day you will see it all to have been needed, and your highest, properly your only blessing.

I must not take all your encomiums about my scriptorial genius. Nevertheless, I am coming up to look about me, and if possible even to establish myself in London. This place is as good as done ; not even the last advantage, that of living in any pecuniary sufficiency, for I never was as poor. Naso,[1] the blockhead, has

---

[1] Napier, of the *Edinburgh Review.*

neither paid me nor written to me. But we are in no strait. I shall even raise the wind for a London voyage without much difficulty. I can write to Naso, if he will not to me. I have some thoughts of cutting him and his calcined *caput mortuum*—dead men's ashes of Whiggism—at any rate. But fair and soft. I now see through Teufel, write at him literally night and day, yet cannot be done within—say fifteen days. Then I should like to have a week's rest, for I am somewhat in the inflammatory vein. As to the Teufel itself, whereof 122 solid pages lie written off, and some 40 above half ready are to follow, I cannot pretend to prophecy. My humour is of the stoical sort as concerns it. Sometimes I think it goodish, at other times bad; at most times the best I can make it here. A strange book all men will admit it to be. Partially intended to be a true book I know it to be. It shall be printed if there is a possibility. You anticipate me in the suggestion of lodgings. There must I live, and nowhere as a guest. *Dreitägiger Gast wird eine Last.* A guest after three days is a burden. Have you no little bedroom even where you are; and one little parlour would serve us both. I care about nothing but a bed where I can sleep. That is to say, where are no bugs and no noises about midnight; for I am pretty invincible when once fairly sealed. The horrors of nerves are somewhat laid in me, I think; yet the memory of them is frightfully vivid. For the rest, my visit to London is antigigmanic from heart to skin. The venerable old man (Goethe) sends me ten days ago the noblest letter I ever read.[1] Scarcely could I read it without tears. Let me die the death of the righteous; let my last end be like his. Goethe is well and serene. Another box on the way hither. We all salute you.

T. C.

The picture of Carlyle's condition—poor, almost without hope, the companions which had made the charm of his solitude—his brother Alick, his horse Larry—all gone or going, the place itself disenchanted—has now a peculiar interest, for it was under these conditions that 'Sartor Resartus' was composed. A wild sorrow sounds through its sentences like the wind over the strings of an æolian harp. Pride, too, at intervals fiercely defiant, yet yielding

---

[1] Not to be found.

to the inevitable, as if the stern lesson had done its work. Carlyle's pride needed breaking. His reluctance to allow his brother to accept help from Jeffrey had only plunged him into worse perplexities. John had borrowed money, hoping that his articles would enable him to repay it. The articles had not been accepted, and the hope had proved a quicksand. Other friends were willing to lend what was required, but he would take nothing more; and the only resource left was to draw again upon Carlyle's almost exhausted funds.

To John Carlyle.

Craigenputtock : July 12, 1831.

I wrote last Thursday under cover to the Lord Advocate, which letter you have before this received. However, not knowing the right address, I was obliged to address the M.P. at 'London,' so that some delay may have occurred. Alick and I [1] were down at the kirk on Sunday. I went for the first time these many months, on account of the Irish collection : and there your letter was lying which demands a quite instantaneous reply. I regretted greatly that no device of mine could take effect sooner than to-night; but as if it had been some relief, I made ready another letter for your behoof (of which anon) that very night, and have had it lying here sealed ever since. It was a letter to Bowring, requesting him to pay the Nibelungen article [2] forthwith into your hands. I did this as courteously as possible, and imagine he will not fail. However, a day or two may elapse ; and in the meantime you have nothing. Had I been at Dumfries I would have got a Bank of England note ; but there is none such here : we have not even a better than this of *one* pound, though I tried to borrow a *five* in vain. So you must receive it as our poor *non plus ultra*. Take it to William Hamilton in Cheapside. Say your brother was sending you money, and requested that he would give you a sovereign for this. If Bowring do not send before it is done, I think you may call on him. I suppose there will be three sheets, and their pay is only ten guineas. Take off it what you have need of till I come.

---

[1] Alick Carlyle, unable to find another farm or occupation, had come back for a time, and was living in a small room in the yard at Craigenputtock.

[2] I.e., the money due for it.

Write also a word on the papers to say how it is,[1] and how you are. I have had you little out of my head since Sunday last.

Shocking as your situation is, however, we all here agree that it is more hopeful than we have ever yet had clear argument to think it. Thank God you have done no wrong. Your conscience is free, and *you yourself* are there. We all reckon that your conduct in that matter of Jeffrey's 20*l.* was entitled to be called *heroic.* Sooner or later, my dear brother, it must have come to this, namely, that your own miscellaneous industry could not support you in London, and that you ceased to borrow, better, we say, now than never. Bear up; front it bravely. There are friendly eyes upon you, and hearts praying for you. Were we once together it will be peremptorily necessary to consider how the land lies and what is to be done. In all situations (out of Tophet) there is a *duty,* and our highest blessedness lies in doing it. I know not whether Jeffrey may be able to do anything for you. He speaks to me rather more hopefully than he seems to have done to you.

I shall study to be with you about the beginning of August. I have written as you suggested to Napier for a note to Longman, also for payment of what he owes me. I am struggling forward with Dreck, sick enough, but not in bad heart. I think the world will no wise be enraptured with this medicinal *Devil's-dung;* that the critical republic will cackle vituperatively, or perhaps maintain total silence—*à la bonne heure!* It was the best I had in me. What God has given me, that the Devil shall not take away. Be of good cheer, my brother. Behave wisely, and continue to trust in God. No doubt *He* sent you hither to work out His will. It is man's mission and blessedness could he but rightly walk in it. Write to me. Trust in me.

Ever your brother,

T. CARLYLE.

Once more on the 17th of the same month—

I am labouring at Teufel with considerable impetuosity, and calculate that, unless accidents intervene, I may be actually ready to get under way at the end of the month. But there will not be a minute to lose. I sometimes think the book *will* prove a kind of medicinal *assafœtida* for the pudding stomach of England, and produce new secretions there. *Jacta est alea!* I will speak out

[1] The Carlyles communicated with one another by cipher on newspapers, to save postage.

what is in me, though far harder chances threatened. I have no
other trade, no other strength or portion in this earth. Be it so.
Hourly you come into my head, sitting in your lone cabin in that
human chaos with *mehr als ein Schilling* and bread and water for
your dinner ; and I cannot say but I respect you more and love
you more than ever I did. Courage ! Courage ! *Tapferkeit*, ' deliberate valour' is God's highest gift, and comes not without trial
to any. Times will mend ; or, if times never mend, then in the
Devil's name let them stay as they are, or grow worse, and *we* will
mend. I know but one true wretchedness—the want of work
(want of wages is comparatively trifling), which want, however, in
such a world as this planet of ours *cannot* be permanent unless we
continue blind therein. I must to my Dreck, for the hours go.
Gott mit Dir !

It was a sad, stern time to these struggling brothers ;
and it is with a feeling like what the Scots mean by *wae*
that one reads the letters that Jeffrey was writing during
the worst of it to Mrs. Carlyle. He had done what he was
allowed to do. Perhaps he thought they understood their
own matters best; and it was not easy to thrust his services on so proud a person as Mrs. Carlyle's husband, when
they were treated so cavalierly ; but he did not choose to
let the correspondence fall, and to her he continued to
write lightly and brilliantly on London gaieties and his
own exploits in the House of Commons. The tone of
these letters must have been out of harmony with the
heavy hearts at Craigenputtock, but he was still acting as
a real friend and remained on the watch for opportunities
to be of use, if not to Carlyle himself, yet at least to his
brother.

So July ran out and ' Sartor ' was finished, and Carlyle
prepared to start, with the MS. and the yet unpublished
sections of the Literary History in his portmanteau, to find
a publisher for one or both of them ; to find also, if possible, some humble employment to which his past work
might have recommended him ; to launch himself, at any

rate, into the great world, and light on something among its floating possibilities to save him from drowning, which of late had seemed likely to be his fate. With Craigenputtock as a home he believed that he had finally done. The farm which was to have helped him to subsist had proved a failure, and had passed to strangers. Living retired in those remote moorlands, he had experienced too painfully that from articles in reviews he could count on no regular revenue, while the labour lost in the writing led to nothing. Work of such a kind, if it was to be profitable, must become an intellectual prostitution ; and to escape from this was the chief object of his London journey. He had so far swallowed his pride as to accept after all a loan of 50*l.* from Jeffrey for his expenses. The sums due to him would provide food and lodging during his stay. Such hopes as he still may have entertained of the realisation of his old dream of making a mark in the world lay in the MS. of 'Sartor.' 'It is a work of genius, dear,' Mrs. Carlyle said to him as she finished the last page— she whose judgment was unerring, who flattered no one, and least of all her husband. A work of genius ! Yes ; but of genius so original that a conventional world, measuring by established rules, could not fail to regard it as a monster. Originality, from the necessity of its nature, offends at its first appearance. Certain ways of acting, thinking, and speaking are in possession of the field and claim to be the only legitimate ways. A man of genius strikes into a road of his own, and the first estimate of such a man has been, is, and always will be, unfavourable. Carlyle knew that he had done his best, and he knew the worth of it. He had yet to learn how hard a battle still lay ahead of him before that worth could be recognised by others. Jeffrey compared him to Parson Adams going to seek his fortune with his manuscript in his pocket. Charles Buller, more hopeful, foretold gold and glory. Jeffrey, at any rate, had made it possible for him to go; and, let it be added, John Carlyle, notwithstanding his struggles to avoid obligations, had been forced to accept pecuniary help from the same kind hand.

Night before going (he wrote in 1866), how I still remember it! I was lying on my back on the sofa in the drawing room. She sitting by the table late at night, packing all done, I suppose. Her words had a guise of sport, but were profoundly plaintive in meaning. 'About to part; and who knows for how long, and what may have come in the interim.' This was her thought, and she was evidently much out of spirits. 'Courage, dear—only for a month,' I would say to her in some form or other. I went next morning early, Alick driving; embarked at Glencaple Quay. Voyage as far as Liverpool still vivid to me. The rest, till arrival in London, gone—mostly extinct.

CHAPTER VIII.

A.D. 1831. ÆT. 36.

Extracts from Carlyle's Note Book, begun in London 1831.

August 4th.—Left Craigenputtock and my kind little wife, Alick driving me, at two o'clock in the morning. Shipped at Glencapel; hazy day; saw Esbie in the steerage; talked mysticism with him during six weary hours we had to stay at Whitehaven. Reimbarkment there amidst bellowing and tumult and fiddling unutterable, all like a spectral vision. 'She is not there.' St. Bees Head. Man with the nose. Sleep in the steamboat cabin : confusion worse confounded. Morning views of Cheshire—the Rock, Liverpool, and steamboats.

August 5th, 9.30 in the morning.—Land at Liverpool; all abed at Maryland Street.[1] Boy Alick[2] accompanies me over Liverpool. Exchange, dome : dim view there. Dust, toil, cotton bags, hampers, repairing ships, disloading stones. Carson a hash : melancholy body of the name of Sloan. Wifekin's assiduity in caring for me.

August 6th (Saturday).—Taken to one Johnstone, a frenchified Lockerby man, who leads me to Change. Place in 'Independent Tally Ho,' Sir! See George Johnstone, surgeon, whom I had unearthed the night before. Patient of his. He dines with us. Walk on the Terrace, near the Cemetery. Have seen the steam coaches in the morning. Liverpool a dismembered aggregate of streets and sand-pits. Market! hubbub!

August 8th.—Go out to find Esbie. He calls on me. Confused family dinner; ditto tea. G. Johnstone again; talk; to bed.

August 9th.—Off on Monday morning. Shipped through the Mersey; coached through Eastham, Chester, Overton (in Wales),

---

[1] Liverpool home of Mrs. Carlyle's uncle John,—the uncle who was made bankrupt through a fraudulent partner, and afterwards paid all his creditors in full.

[2] John's son.

Ellesmere, Shrewsbury, Wolverhampton, Birmingham ; attempt at tea there. Discover, not without laughter, the villany of the Liverpool coach bookers. Henley-in-Arden. Stratford-on-Avon (horses lost there). Get to sleep. Oxford at three in the morning. Out again there ; chill but pleasant. Henley, Maidenhead, &c. Arrive, full of sulphur, at White Horse Cellar, Piccadilly. Dismount at the Regent Circus, and am wheeled (not whirled) hither [1] about half-past ten. Poor Jack waiting all the while at the Angel, Islington. Talk together when he returns ; dine at an eating-house among Frenchmen, one of whom ceases eating to hear me talk of the St. Simonians. Leave my card at the Lord Advocate's, with promise to call next morning. Sulphurous enough.

These extracts supply the lost places in Carlyle's memory, and serve as a frame into which to fit the following letter to his wife. The intense affection which he felt for her is visible in every line.

To Mrs. Carlyle, Craigenputtock.

6 Woburn Buildings, Tavistock Square : August 11, 1831.

Dearest and Wife,—I have got a frank for you and will write from the heart whatever is in the heart. A blessing it was that you made me give such a promise ; for I feel that an hour's speech in speaking with my own will do me infinite good. It is very sweet in the midst of this soul-confusing phantasmagoria to know that I have a fixed possession elsewhere ; that my own Jeannie is thinking of me, loving me ; that her heart is no dream like all the rest of it. Oh love me, my dearest—always love me. I am richer with thee than the whole world could make me otherwise.

But to be practical. Expect no connected or even intelligible narrative of all the chaotic sights, sounds, movements, countermovements I have experienced since your lips parted from mine on our threshold—still less of all the higher chaotic feelings that have danced their wild torch dance within me. For the present I must content myself, like Sir William Hamilton, with ' stating a fact or two.' Understand then, Goodykin, that after infinite confusion, I arrived at Liverpool about eight o'clock on the morning

---

[1] To 6 Woburn Buildings, Tavistock Square—the house of George Irving, Edward Irving's brother, where John Carlyle lodged.

after I left you, quite sleepless, and but for your dinner (which I parted with a certain 'Esbie,' whom Alick knows well, whom I found in the boat and preached mysticism to for six hours), quite victual-less. The Maryland Street people [1] were not up, but soon rose and received me well. Delightful it was to get into a room and—have my face washed; and then on opening my trunk to find everywhere traces of my good 'coagitor's' [2] care and love. The very jujube box with its worsted and darning needle did not escape me; it was so beautiful I could almost have cried over it. Heaven reward thee, my clear-headed, warm-hearted, dearest little Screamikin!

John Welsh was the same substantial, honest fellow whom we have always known him: he and I got along, as we always do, beautifully together.

The Auntie was loud, talkative, argumentative, infinitely bustling, but also very assiduous in showing me kindness. To make a long tale short, I left them on Sunday morning at half-past seven with many blessings and two cups of sufficient coffee, which the good housewife would not be prevented from making me at that early hour.

Which last hospitality I may well say was doubly blest; for it so turned out this was the only refection I received till my arrival in London on the following day about ten o'clock! I must except a penny loaf snatched from the landlady of an inn in Shropshire; and a cup of hot sugar and water (as the whole time proved only fifteen minutes), for which I had the pleasure of paying half-a-crown in the village of Birmingham. How all this happened, and I was sent circulating over the whole West of England, set my watch by the Shrewsbury clock, and saw portions of Wales, and had the delightfulest drive, only no victual, or knowledge by what route I was bound—all this depended on the art of the Liverpool coach agents, at which, villanous as it was, I could not help laughing, when, after leaving Birmingham, I came to see into the mystery. There are men in Liverpool who will *book* you to go by any coach you like, and to enter London at any place and hour *you* like, and then send you thither by any coach or combination of coaches *they* like. I was booked for a certain imaginary 'Tally Ho,' went by seven successive vehicles none of which had that name, and entered London three hours later and by quite the op-

---

[1] Mr. John Welsh and his family.
[2] His wife. Somebody's pronunciation of 'coadjutor.'

posite side than I had appointed John to wait at. Sulphurous enough. However, I have now had sleep and am well. The only mischief done *was the breaking of the eggs*, which, however, the warehouseman has now made good again. So do not grieve thyself, dearest. The broken eggs are dearer to me than the whole ones would have been. There is a pathos in them, and I love Jeannie more.

With little difficulty I conveyed myself and luggage to Jack's old lodgings, and there learnt his actual address at no great distance, and, to my astonishment, in the upper floor of George Irving's house, who also lets lodgings. It is a very beautiful sitting-room, an immense bedroom above (and John sleeps with George), for which we are to pay 25*s*. weekly. Quiet and airy, and among known people. All is right in this respect.

The first day I did little; yet walked over to the Duke's,[1] found him out, and left my card with a promise for next morning. It is between two and three miles from this. On arriving there I was asked my name and then instantly ushered in and welcomed in their choicest mood by the whole family. Mrs. Jeffrey was as kind as ever; Charlotte too came simpering in and looked as if she would let me live. The Advocate retired and re-entered with your picture, which was shown round; for little I could have *grat* over it. After a time by some movements I got the company dispersed, and the Advocate by himself, and began to take counsel with him about 'Teufelsdröckh.' He thought Murray, in spite of the Radicalism, would be the better publisher; to him accordingly he gave me a line, saying that I was a genius and would likely become eminent; further, that he (Jeffrey) would like well to confer with him about that book. I directly set off with this to Albemarle Street; found Murray out; returned afterwards and found him in, gave an outline of the book, at which the Arimaspian smiled, stated also that I had nothing else to do here but the getting of it published, and was above all anxious that his decision should be given soon. He answered that he would begin this very afternoon, and that on Wednesday next he would give me an answer. I then went off; despatched my 'Teufelsdröckh' with *your* tape round him. Of the probable issue I can form no conjecture: only Murray seemed to know me, and I dare say is very anxious to keep well with Ministers, so will risk what he dares.

[1] Jeffrey's house in Jermyn Street.

Napier's letter is also come, with a note to Rees, which I think I shall perhaps not deliver (perhaps, too, I may) till after next Wednesday.

Badams called here an hour after I came : he brought his wife next day. I was out, but saw them in the evening. She is a good woman, and good-looking, whom I think you will like. *He* is in no good way, I doubt; yet not without hope. I have also seen Mrs. Montagu ; talked longer with her than I shall speedily do again, for she seems to me embittered and exasperated ; and what have I to do with her quarrels? Jack she seems positively to have cut, because he would not turn with her in a day from a transcendental apotheosis of Badams to excommunication. All things go round and round. For me, as I told her, I would continue to love all parties and pity all, and hate or quarrel with none.

Jack stands *glowering o'er me*, as you know is his wont. Tell Alick all my news ; read him the letter (so much of it as you can read), and give to everyone my kindest brotherly love.

August 15.

Your kind precious letter came to me on Friday like a cup of water in the hot desert. It is all like yourself : so clear, precise, loving, and true to the death. I *see* poor Craigenputtock through it, and the best little Goodykin sitting there, hourly meditating on me and watching my return. Oh, I am very rich were I without a penny in the world! But the Herzen's Goody must not fret herself and torment her poor sick head. I will be back to her ; not an hour will I lose. Heaven knows the sun shines not on the spot that could be pleasant to me where she were not. So be of comfort, my Jeannie, and with thy own sweet orderly spirit make calmness out of confusion, and the dawn (as it does in some climates) to shine through the whole night till it be morning, and the sun once more embraces his fair kind earth. For the rest, thou canst not be too 'Theresa-like ;' [1] it is this very fidelity to practical nature that makes the charm of the picture. . . .

I am getting a little more composed in this whirlpool, and can tell you better how it whirls.

On Friday morning, the day after I wrote, Jack walked down with me to Longmans, and I delivered Napier's note to a staid, cautious, business-like man, who read it with an approving smile,

---

[1] Theresa, in *Wilhelm Meister.*

listened to my description of the 'German Literary History' with
the same smile in a *fixed* state, and then (like a barbarian as he
was) 'declined the article.' He was polite as possible, but seemed
determined on risking *nothing*. If Murray fail me (as Wednesday
will probably show), I have calculated that it will be hardly worth
while to offer these people Dreck, but that I must try some other
course with him. *I hope not at all*, therefore hardly think that
Murray will accept (so lucky were it), and am already looking out
what I can for other resources in the worst issue. Dreck
shall be printed if a man in London will do it; if not with, then
without, 'fee or reward.' I even conjecture still that this is the
time for him : everybody I see participates in the feeling that
society is nigh done; that she is a Phœnix perhaps not so many
conjecture. I agree with my prophetess in thinking that some
young adventurous bookseller were the hopefullest. We shall see
soon.

Saturday morning I wrote to Goethe (with kindest love from
you too); also to Charles Buller and to Fraser (notifying my
presence), then off for Shooter's Hill some ten miles away, where
we arrived in time for dinner. Strachey is as alert as ever. In
his poor lady I had room to mark the doings of time. She wore a
sad secluded look; I learnt she had been for three years violently
dyspeptical. Our recognition was franker on my part than on
hers; only her eyes spoke of gladness; nay, she seemed to have a
kind of fear of me, and in a little *special* conversation I had it all
to myself. She inquired kindly for you, whom I described as one
that she would like, *a hater of lies*, to begin with. Poor Julia
Strachey! She is like a flower frozen among ice, and now contented with such soil : a hitherto unnoticed girl had rushed up to
a woman, and in the long black locks I noticed a streak of grey.
Fleeting time! Here too might I partly discern that *my* place
was changed, though still (not?) *empty*. A 'female friend,' skilled,
it is said, in the Greek tragedians (*credat Apella*), was there, brim
full of intolerant Church of Englandism—a little grey-eyed, ill-bred,
fat button of a creature (very like a certain white sempstress in Ecclefechan) : with her in the course of the evening I was provoked
for one moment, so pert was she, to run tilt, and I fear transfix her.
Strachey was beginning a hoarse laugh, but suddenly checked
himself, as a landlord should : and little Button went off to bed
without good-night, but was blithe again next morning. That *such*
should be the only friend of such! Let not us, dear Jeannie, com-

plain of solitude. I have still *you*, with really a priceless talent
for silence, as Mrs. S. too has. I say priceless, for this Button
wants it wholly, and thereby I felt would have driven me in three
days to blank despair.

The orator was at Leamington when I arrived. He only returned
Saturday night, has already been up here to see me, and left a
message that he would be at home all day. From all I can see,
Irving seems to have taken his part: is forgotten by the intellectual
classes, but still flourishes as a green bay-tree (or rather green
cabbage-tree) among the fanatical classes, whose ornament and
beacon he is. Strangely enough it is all fashioned among these
people : a certain everlasting *truth*, ever new truth, reveals itself
in them, but with a *body* of mere froth and soap-suds and other
the like ephemeral impurities. Yet I love the man, and can
trustfully take counsel of him. His wife I saw some nights ago—
leaner, clearer-complexioned, I should say clearer-hearted also, and
clearer-headed, but, alas ! *very* straitlaced, and living in the *suds*
element.

I forced myself out this morning to go and breakfast with the
Advocate, and was there before anyone was up. Charlotte the
younger and the elder received me in their choicest mood. In
the midst of breakfast a side door opened, and the poor Duke looked
in in his night-gown (for they have made the back drawing-room
into a bed-room) to ask for me, and with the old quizzicality in
his little face declared, ' Why, Charley, I've got the cholera, I believe.' He called me afterwards into his bed-room to ask how I
was progressing, thought it likely that Murray would publish at
some time or other, spoke of John, asked for your health, and what
I had prescribed for you. Letters arriving, I got your frank and
withdrew, straitly charged to return. I am to take tea this evening at Badams's, where Godwin is promised.

Wednesday, August 17.

I left off on the eve of seeing Irving and taking tea with Godwin. The first object I accomplished. Irving, with his huge
fleece of now grizzled hair, was eager to talk with me and see me
often. I was with him last night, and being quite in his neighbourhood (within three minutes), shall take frequent opportunities
of seeing him. He is bent on our coming to London, of which I
myself can yet say nothing. Some vague schemes of settling within some miles of it (as at Enfield, where Badams is to live) are

hovering about me, which I will overhaul and see through. It will all depend on this, can I get work here and money for it to keep any sort of house ? which question is yet far from answered or answerable. However, I hope, and fear not.

Next came Godwin. Did you not grudge me that pleasure, now ? At least, mourn that you were not there with me ? Grudge not, mourn not, dearest Jeannie ; it was the most unutterable stupidity ever enacted on this earth. We went, Jack and I, to the huge Frenchwoman Mrs. Kenny's (once Mrs. Holcroft), Badams's mother-in-law, a sort of more masculine *Aurelia* ('Wilhelm Meister'), who lives, moves, and has her being among plays, operas, dilettantes, and playwrights. Badams and his wife had not returned from the country, but in a few minutes came. Mrs. Godwin already sate gossiping in the dusk—an old woman of no significance ; by-and-by dropped in various playwrightesses and play-wrights, whom I did not even look at ; shortly before candles Godwin himself (who had been drinking *good* green tea by his own hearth before stirring out). He is a bald, bushy-browed, thick, hoary, hale little figure, taciturn enough, and speaking when he does speak with a certain *epigrammatic* spirit, wherein, except a little shrewdness, there is nothing but the most commonplace character. (I should have added that he wears spectacles, has full grey eyes, a very large blunt characterless nose, and ditto chin.) By degrees I hitched myself near him, and was beginning to open him and to open on him, for he had stared twice at me, when suddenly enough began a speaking of French among the Kennys and Badamsinas (for they are all French-English), and presently Godwin was summoned off to—take a hand at whist ! *I* had already flatly declined. There did the philosopher sit, and a swarm of noisy children, chattering women, noisy dilettantes round him ; and two women literally crashing hoarse thunder out of a piano (for it was louder than an iron forge) under pretext of its being music by Rossini. I thought of my own piano, and the far different fingering it got ; looked sometimes not without sorrow at the long-nosed whist-player, and in the space of an hour (seeing supper about to be laid in another room) took myself away.

Next morning (Tuesday) I went to Bowring's. Figure to yourself a thin man about my height and bent at the *middle* into an angle of 150°, the *back* quite straight, with large grey eyes, a huge turn-up nose with straight nostrils to the very point, and large projecting close-shut mouth : figure such a one walking restlessly about the room (for he had been thrown out of a gig, and was in pain), frank of speech, vivid, emphatic, and *verständig*. Such is the Radical Doctor. We talked copiously, he utterly utilitarian and Radical, I utterly mystical and Radical; and parted about noon with a standing invitation on his part to come again, and promise to introduce me to the 'Examiner' editor (Fonblanque); and a certain trust on my part and disposition to cultivate further acquaintance. He named several booksellers whom I might apply to in case Murray baulked me, as I calculate he is but too like to do.

Wednesday morning I put on clean raiment (nothing but the white trowsers are wearable here for the heat, and I have still only two pairs), and drawing myself a chart on a slip of paper, started off to Albemarle Street according to bargain. The dog of a bookseller gone to the country. I leave my card with remonstrances and inquiries when? The clerk talks of 'Mr. Murray writing to you sir?' I will call again to-morrow morning and make Mr. M. speak to me, I hope. . . .

Thursday.—I went to the House of Commons last night and found at the door a Speaker's order awaiting me from the Duke. It is a pretty apartment that of theirs; far smaller than I expected,[1] hardly larger than some drawing-rooms you have seen, with some four ranges of benches rising high behind each other like pews in a church gallery, an oval open space in the middle, at the farther extremity of which sits the Speaker in what seemed a kind of press (like our wardrobe, only oaken); opposite him is the door. A very narrow gallery runs all round atop for reporters, strangers, &c. I was seated on the ground floor below this. Althorp spoke, a thick, large, broad-whiskered, farmer-looking man; Hume also, a powdered, clean, burly fellow; and Wetherell, a beetle-browed, sagacious, quizzical old gentleman; then Davies, a Roman-nosed dandy, whom I left *jannering*, having left it all in some three-quarters of an hour. O'Connell came and spoke to an individual before me. You would call him a well-doing country shopkeeper, with a bottle-green frock or great coat, and brown scratch wig. I quitted them with the highest contempt; our poor Duke, or any known face, I could not see.

This morning I returned to Albemarle Street; the bookseller was first denied to me, then showed his broad one-eyed face, and with fair speeches signified that his family were all ill, and he had

[1] The old house, before the fire.

been called into the country ; and my manuscript—lay still un-
opened ! I reminded him not without emphasis of the engagement made, and how I had nothing else to do here but see that
matter brought to an end, to all which he pleaded hard in extenu-
ation, and for two or three days' further allowance. I made him
name a new day : ' Saturday *first ;* ' then I am to return and learn
how the matter stands. He is said to be noted for procrastination,
but also for honourableness, even munificence. My prospects
apart from him are not brilliant ; however, loss of time is the
worst of all losses ; he shall not keep me dancing round him very
long, go how it may. Of the Duke I would gladly take counsel ;
but find no opportunity to speak—a visit profits almost nothing.
Happily, however, I can take counsel of *myself*.

I am to dine with Drummond the banker to-morrow, an admirer
of mine whom I have never seen. On Saturday with Allan Cunningham. These are my outlooks for the present.

August 22.

My dearest little Comforter,—Your dear kind letter arrived that
Thursday night, though not till late—with the very latest of the
' Twopennies,' I think ; which invaluable class of men keep travelling here all day from eight in the morning till ten at night.
My blessings on thee, little Goody, for the kind news thou send-
est ! It is all a living picture, and the dear Screamikin artist
standing in the middle of it, both acting it and drawing it for my
sake. I saw your half-insane beer-barrel of a Fyffe,[1] and the
midges all buzzing round him in the sultry morning ; the racket of
the Macturk chaise, your rushing forth to the post-office, your
eager devouring of my letter, and all the rest of it, in which, alas !
the headache and the two hours of sleep did not escape me. Compose thyself, my darling ; we *shall* not be separated, come of it
what may. And how should we do, think'st thou, with an eternal
separation ? O God, it is fearful ! fearful ! But is not a little
temporary separation like this needful to manifest what *daily*
mercy is in our lot which otherwise we might forget, or esteem as
a thing of course ? Understand, however, once more that I have
yet taken up with no other woman. Nay, many as I see—light
air-forms tripping it in satin along the streets, or plumed amazons
curbing their palfreys in the park with pomp and circumstance

[1] A Haddington doctor, one of Miss Welsh's many suitors before her marriage.

enough—there has no one yet fronted me whom even to look at I would exchange with my own. *Ach Gott!* there is not such a one extant. Yes, as proud as I am grown (for the more the Devil pecks at me, the more vehemently do I wring his nose), and standing on a kind of basis which I feel to be of adamant, I perceive that of all women my own Jeannie is the wife for me; that in her true bosom (once she were a mystic) a man's head is worthy to lie. Be a mystic, dearest; that is, stand with me on this everlasting basis, and keep thy arms around me : through life I fear nothing.

But I must proceed with my journal of life in London. My narrative must have finished on Thursday night about five o'clock. Jack and I went out to walk and make calls after that; found no one at home but Mrs. Badams, who was nigh weeping when she spoke to us of her husband. Poor thing, she has a ticklish game to play; for Badams seems to me to be hovering on the verge of ruin—uncertain as yet whether he will turn back, or only plunge down, down. I tell all this in one word : he is in the habit of daily drinking brandy till his head gets confused. He began this accursed practice not many months ago for the sake of an intolerable headache he had, and which brandy (then nauseous enough to him) was wont to cure; but now I suspect the nauseousness has ceased, and the brandy is chiefly coveted because it yields stupefaction. His volition seems gone, or quite dormant; his *gig* has broken down with him all to shivers, at full speed.[1]

With the Montagus I have somewhat less sympathy. It seems still uncertain whether they will lose anything by him,[2] and their ferocity (except from Basil) is quite transcendental. On the whole my original impression of that 'noble lady' was the true one. * * * * * * * * * * * She goes upon words—words. I called once more and left my card, and shall continue at rare intervals to do the like; but for trust or friendship it is now more clearly than ever a chimæra. I smiled (better than the Duke did) at her offer of 'giving you money' to come hither. *Jane Welsh Carlyle* a taker of money in this era of the gigmen! *Nimmer und nimmermehr.* *

Tush ! it is all stuff and fudge and fiddle-faddle, of which I begin to grow aweary. Oh no, my dearest; we will have no meet-

---

[1] Badams—once one of Carlyle's truest and most useful friends—died miserably soon after.

[2] Badams had led them into some speculation which had not been successful.

ings that we cannot purchase for ourselves. We shall meet; nay, perhaps, ere long thou shalt see London and thy husband in it, on earnings of our own. From all which the practical inference is, 'let us endeavour to clear our minds of cant.'

Friday I spent with Irving in the *animali parlanti* region of the *supernatural*. Understand, ladykin, that the 'gift of tongues' is here also (chiefly among the women), and a positive belief that God is still working miracles in the Church—by hysterics. Nay, guess my astonishment when I learned that poor Dow of Irongray[1] is a wonder-worker and speaker with tongues, and had actually 'cast out a devil' (which however returned again in a week) between you and Dumfries! I gave my widest stare; but it is quite indubitable. His autograph letter was read to me, detailing all that the '*Laart*' had done for him. Poor fellow! it was four days after his wife's death. I was very wae for him, and not a little shocked. Irving hauled me off to Lincoln's Inn Fields to hear my double (Mr. Scott), where I sate directly behind a speakeress with tongues, who unhappily, however, did not perform till after I was gone. My double is more like 'Maitland,' the cotton-eared, I hope, than me; a thin, black-complexioned, vehement man, earnest, clear, and narrow as a tailor's listing. For a stricken hour did he sit expounding in the most superannuated dialect (of *Chroist* and so forth), yet with great heartiness the meaning of that one word *Entsagen*. The good Irving looked at me wistfully, for he knows I cannot take miracles in; yet he looks so piteously, as if he implored me to believe. Oh dear! oh dear! was the Devil ever busier than now, when the supernatural must either depart from the world, or reappear there like a chapter of Hamilton's 'Diseases of Females'?

At night I fondly trusted that we had done with the miraculous; but no, Henry Drummond too is a believer in it. This Drummond, who inhabits a splendid mansion in the west, proved to be a very striking man. Taller and leaner than I, but erect as a plummet, with a high-carried, quick, penetrating head, some five-and-forty years of age, a singular mixture of all things—of the saint, the wit, the philosopher—swimming, if I mistake not, in an element of dandyism. His dinner was dandiacal in the extreme: a meagre series of pretentious kickshaws, on which no hungry jaw could satisfactorily bite, flunkies on all hands, yet I had to ask four times before I could get a morsel of bread. His wife has had

[1] A Craigenputtock neighbour.

'twenty miscarriages,' and looks pitiful enough. Besides her we were five : Spencer Percival, Member of the House (of Stupids, called of Commons) ; Tudor, a Welshman, editor of the 'Morning Watch ; ' our host, Irving, and I. They were all prophetical, Toryish, ultra-religious. I emitted, notwithstanding, floods of Teufelsdröckhist Radicalism, which seemed to fill them with *ween-der* and amazement, but was not ill received, and indeed refused to be gainsayed. We parted with friendliest indifference, and shall all be happy to meet again, and to part again. This Drummond, who is a great pamphleteer, has 'quoted' me often, it seems, &c. He is also a most munificent and beneficent man—as his friends say.

On Saturday morning I set out for Albemarle Street. Murray, as usual, was not in ; but an answer lay for me—my poor 'Teufels-dröckh,' wrapped in new paper, with a letter stuck under the packthread. I took it with a silent fury and walked off. The letter said he regretted exceedingly, &c. ; all his literary friends were out of town ; he himself occupied with a sick family in the country ; that he had conceived the finest hopes, &c. In short, that 'Teufelsdröckh' had never been looked into ; but that if I would let him keep it for a month, he would *then* be able to say a word, and by God's blessing a favourable one.

I walked on through Regent Street and looked in upon James Fraser, the bookseller. We got to talk about 'Teufelsdröckh,' when, after much hithering and thithering about the black state of trade, &c., it turned out that honest James would publish the book for me on this principle : if I would give *him* a sum not exceeding 150*l.* sterling ! ' I think you had better wait a little,' said an Edinburgh advocate to me since, when he heard of this proposal. 'Yes,' I answered, 'it is my purpose to wait to the end of eternity for it.' ' But the public will not buy books.' ' The public has done the wisest thing it could, and ought never more to buy what they call books.'

Spurning at destiny, yet in the mildest terms taking leave of Fraser, I strode through the streets carrying Teufelsdröckh openly in my hand. I took a pipe and a glass of water, and counsel with myself. I was bilious and sad, and thought of my dear Jeannie, for whom also were these struggles. Having rested a little, I set out again to the Longmans, to hear what they had to say. The German Literary History having soon been despatched, I describe Teufelsdröckh, bargain that they are to look at it themselves, and send it back again in two days : that is to-morrow. They are honest, rugged, punctual-looking people, and will keep their word, but the chance of declining seems to me a hundred to one. *A la bonne heure!* I have a problem which *is* possible : either to get Dreck printed, or to ascertain that I *cannot,* and so tie him up and come home with him. So fear nothing, love. I care not a doit for the worst ; and thou too hast the heart of a heroine—art worthy of me were I the highest of heroes. Nay, my persuasion that Teufelsdröckh is in his place and his time here, grows stronger the more I see of London and its philosophy. The doctrine of the Phœnix, of Natural Supernaturalism, and the whole Clothes Philosophy (be it but well stated) is exactly what all intelligent men are wanting.

Sunday morning had a snip of a note from Empson. Walked over to Jermyn Street ; saw the Duke ; had to tell him openly (or not at all) how it stood with my manuscript ; felt clear and sharp as a war weapon, for the world was not brotherly to me. The Charlottes were at church. I consulted the Duke about Napier ; found my own idea confirmed that he was anxious enough to have me write, but afraid lest I committed him ; so that 'agreeing about subjects' would be the difficulty. Jeffrey asked to see my MS. when the Longmans had done with it : he would look through it and see what he could *talk* to Murray concerning it. I gladly consented ; and thus for a while the matter rests. Murray is clearly the man if he will ; only I have lost ten days by him already, for he might have told me what he did finally tell in one day.

Carlyle, little sanguine as he was, had a right to be surprised at the difficulty of finding a publisher for his book. Seven years before he had received a hundred pounds for his 'Life of Schiller.' It had been successful in England. It had been translated into German under the eye of Goethe himself. 'Sartor' Carlyle reckoned to be at least three times as good, and no one seemed inclined to look at it.

Meanwhile, on another side of his affairs the prospect unexpectedly brightened. His brother had been the heaviest of his anxieties. A great lady, 'the Countess of Clare,' was going abroad and required a travelling physician. Jeffrey heard of it, and with more real practical kindness than Carlyle in his impatience had been inclined to credit him with, successfully recommended John Carlyle to her. The arrangements were swiftly concluded. The struggling, penniless John was lifted at once into a situation of responsibility and security, with a salary which placed him far beyond need of further help, and promised to enable him to repay at no distant time both his debt to Jeffrey, and all the money which Carlyle had laid out for him. Here was more than compensation for the other disappointments. Not only Carlyle had no longer to feel that he must divide his poor earnings to provide for his brother's wants in London, but he could look without anxiety on his own situation. He even thought himself permitted, instead of returning to Craigenputtock, to propose that Mrs. Carlyle should join him in London without the help of Mrs. Montagu. He was making friends; he was being talked about as a new phenomenon of a consequence as yet unknown. Review and magazine editors were recovering heart, and again seeking his assistance. He could write his articles as well in a London lodging as in the snowy solitudes of Dunscore, while he could look about him and weigh at more leisure the possibilities of finally removing thither. He wrote to propose it, and awaited his wife's decision. Meanwhile his letters continue his story.

To Mrs. Carlyle, Scotsbrig.

London : August 26, 1831.

My dear Mother,—As Jack proposes writing to my father, doubtless he will mention the good tidings he has to tell, namely, of an appointment to be travelling physician to a lady of great rank, the Countess of Clare, with a salary of 300 guineas a year, all travelling expenses included. This is the work of the Lord Advocate, Jeffrey, and is looked on by everyone as a piece of real good fortune. For yourself, my dear mother, I know how you dislike foreign voyaging, and that all your maternal fears will be awakened by this arrangement. However, you too will reflect that anything in honesty is better than forced *idleness*, which was poor

Doil's [1] condition here ; also you may take my word for it that the
dangers of such a course of travel are altogether trifling—not
equal to those of walking the London streets, and running, every
time you cross, lest coaches break a limb of you. The lady herself is an invalid, and must journey with every convenience.
Italy, whither they are bound, is the finest of climates ; and the
sailing part of it is simply of three hours' continuance—in whole,
twenty-five miles. I have seen some people who know the Countess, and all give her a good character. She is young (perhaps
thirty-three), courteous, and has behaved in this transaction with
great liberality. Jack also is much more prudent and manly in
his ways than he was ; so that I think there is a fair prospect of
his even doing the poor lady some good, and getting into a friendly
relation to her, which also may eventually do himself much good.
Something mysterious there is in the condition of this high personage. She was married some years ago, and shortly after that
event she parted from her husband (they say by her own determination), the nearest friends know not for what reason ; and now
she lives in a sort of widowhood (her husband is Governor of
Bombay, and said to be 'a very good sort of man'), so that being farther in ill-health she is probably unhappy enough, and has
need of good counsel every way.

The business of the book proceeds but crabbedly. The whole
English world I find has ceased to read books, which, as I often
say to the booksellers, is the wisest thing the English world could
do, considering what wretched froth it has been dosed with for
many years, under the false title of 'books.' Every mind is en-
grossed with political questions, and in a more earnest mood than
to put up with such stuff as has been called literature. Meanwhile, though I cannot but rejoice in this state of public opinion,
yet the consequences to myself are far from favourable. The present, too, I find, is the deadest part of the whole year for business, so that every way the matter moves heavily, and I require to
have my own shoulder at it always or it would not move at all.
Hitherto I have made no approximation to a bargain, except finding that man after man will not *act*, and only at best demands
'time for consideration,' which, except in very limited measure, I
cannot afford to give him. The MS. is at present in Jeffrey's
hands, whence I expect to receive it in some two days with a favourable, or at worst an unfavourable judgment—in either of which

[1] Family nickname of John Carlyle.

cases I shall find out what to do. Little money, I think, will be had for my work, but I will have it printed if there be a man in London that will do it, even without payment to myself. If there be no such man, why then what is to be done but tie a piece of good *skeenyie* about my papers, stick the whole in my pocket, and march home again with it, where at least potatoes and onions are to be had, and I can wait till better times. Nay, in any case I find that either in possession or pretty certain expectation, I am otherwise worth almost 100*l.* of cash ; so that while the whinstone house stands on the moor, what care I for one of them, or for all of them with the arch-Enemy at their head ?

Of any permanent settlement here there is as yet nothing definite to be said. I see many persons here, some of them kind and influential, almost all of them ignorant enough, and in need of a teacher ; but no offer that can be laid hold of presents itself or fixedly promises itself. This also I will see through. If God who made me and keeps me alive have work for me here, then here must I pitch my tent ; if not, then elsewhere, still under his kind sky, under his all-seeing eye, to me alike where. I am rather resolute sometimes, not without a touch of grimness, but never timid or discouraged ; indeed, generally quite quiet and cheerful. If I see no way of getting home soôn, I have some thoughts of bringing Jane up hither, for she must be very lonely where she is. We shall see.

Thus, my dear mother, does it stand with us. I write you all this to satisfy your anxieties. Be of good cheer ; trust for us, as for all things, in the Giver of good, who will order *all* things *well.* Assure my father of my entire love ; and say that I hope to tell him many things when I return.

My kindest love to all, not forgetting Jean or any of the girls. God keep you and all of them. That is ever my heart's prayer. Many times, too, does *she* that is not now with us [1] revisit my thoughts : inexpressibly sad, inexpressibly mild ; but I mourn not. I rather rejoice that *she* is now safe in the land of eternity, not in the troublous, ever-shifting land of time and of dreams. Oh, often I think that she is *with* me in my heart whispering to me to bear and forbear even as she did, to endure to the end, and then we shall meet *again* and part no more. Even as God will be it !

I conclude mournfully but not unhappily. Shall not the Great Father wipe away the tears from all eyes ? Again and again I

[1] His sister Margaret.

say, let us trust in Him and Him only. Let us ever live in hope, in faith! God bless you all!

I am, dear mother, your affectionate son,

T. Carlyle.

To Mrs. Carlyle, Craigenputtock.

August 29.

Dearest Wife,—This is Monday, and I have already, taking no counsel with flesh and blood, discharged two little duties : first gone and seen Empson (whom I had heretofore missed) *before* breakfast ; second, arranged my washerwoman's goods, and made an invoice thereof that she may call for them, which duty it were my dear Goody's part to do were I not for a time Goodyless ; so that now at noontide I can sit down with a clear conscience, and talk heartily and heartsomely with my own child about all things and about nothing, as is my wont and my delight. Thus in this spectre crowded desert I have a living person whose heart I can clasp to mine, and so feel that I too am alive. Do you not love me better than ever now? I feel in my own soul that thou dost and must. Therefore let us never mourn over this little separation which is but to make the reunion more blessed and entire.

Your two letters are here in due season, like angels (angel means heavenly *messenger*) from a far country. The first, as I prophesied, lay waiting for me at my return ; the second I found lying on the Duke's table on Saturday, and snatched it up and read it in the hubbub of Piccadilly so soon as I could tear myself out into the solitude of crowds. Bless thee, my darling! I could almost wish thee the pain of a ride to Dumfries weekly for the sake of such a letter. But *had* you actually to faint all the way up? Heaven forbid! And the 'disease' on that fair face—how is it? If no better, never mind ; I swear that it shall and will get better, or if it do not, that I will love you more than ever while it lasts. Will that make amends? It is no vain parade of rhetoric ; it is a serious *fact :* my love for you does not depend on looks, and defies old age and decay, and, I can prophesy, will grow stronger the longer we live and toil together. Yes, Jeannie, though I have brought you into rough, rugged conditions, I feel that I have saved you : as Gigmaness you could not have lived ; as woman and wife you need but to see your duties in order to do them, and to say from the heart, It is good for me to be here. So keep thy arms round me, and be my own prophetess and second self, and fear nothing, let the Devil do his worst. Poor Elizabeth![1] I fear, as you fear, that it is not well with her. Nevertheless, who knows the issues of life and death? Let us hope the best. Above all, do not you be a coward. I love you for your *bravery*, and because you have the heart of a valiant woman. Oh, my darling, is it conceivable that we should live divided in this unfriendly scene? Crown me with all laurels that ever decorated man's brow: were it other than the bitterest of mockeries if *she* who had struggled with me were not there to share it?

But I must check this lyrical tendency. Of history there is little to be told. Slowly, slowly does the business of poor Dreck get along, let me push it as I may. Heaven bless my own prophetess, who has from the first prophesied only good of it. Yes, good will come of it; for it was honestly meant, and the best we could do. Meanwhile do but mark how sluggishly it loiters.

Yesterday I returned (to Jermyn Street), found the family coach at the door, and all in the act of drawing on gloves to go out, except the Duke, with whom, after some gabblement with the others, I had the unwonted satisfaction of a private conversation—for ten minutes. Inquiring for Teufelsdröckh, as I was privileged to do, the critic professed that he had 'honestly read' twenty-eight pages of it (surprising feat); that he objected to the dilatoriness of the introductory part (as *we* both did also), and very much admired the scene of the sleeping city; further, that he would write to Murray that very day,[2] as I gather from Empson he has since done, to appoint a meeting with him, and if possible attain some finish with that individual at least. He (Jeffrey) would look through the book further in the interim, &c. &c.

Patience, patience! Hard times I said, dearest, for literary men. Nevertheless, let us take them as they come. Nay, Allan Cunningham advises me that it were almost 'madness' to press forward a literary work at this so inauspicious season and not to wait for a while—which, nevertheless, I cannot listen to. Why wait? *Rusticus expectat;* besides, Dreck must be *printed* as the first condition. Whether we get any money for him, or how much, is a quite secondary question. I have nothing for it but to *try*— try to the uttermost—and in the villanous interval of expectation to explore this wild, immeasurable chaos, and ascertain whether I can build aught in it. Such remains my outlook hitherto. Jeff-

---

[1] I do not know to whom this refers.

[2] Longman, after looking through the MS., had civilly declined it.

rey and I also spoke about the 'place under Government.' *Davon wird Nichts*, 'All filled up;' 'Applicants;' 'Economical Ministry,' &c. &c.—all which the Devil is welcome to, if he like. *Aide-toi, le ciel t'aidera.* I think of these things with considerable composure, at times with a certain silent ferocity. 'That *my* wife should walk on foot!' Yet, is she not my wife, and shall I not love her the more that she shares evil with me as if it were good? Let us fear nothing. I have the strength of 20,000 Cockneys while thou art with me. Let hard come to hard as it will; we will study to be ready for it. . . .

Of all the deplorables and despicables of this city and time the saddest are the 'literary men.' *Infandum! Infandum!* It makes my heart sick and wae. Except Churchill, and perhaps chiefly because he liked *me*, I have hardly found a man of common sense or common honesty. They are the Devil's own vermin, whom the Devil in his good time will snare and successively eat. The creature —— called again; the most insignificant *haddock* in nature— a dirty, greasy cockney apprentice, altogether empty, and non-extant except for one or two metaphysical quibbles (about every law*r* of nature being an idea*r* of the mind, &c.), and the completest outfit of innocent blank self-conceit I ever in life chanced to witness. He is a blown bladder, wherein no substance is to be sought. And yet a curious figure, intrinsically *small*, small; yet with a *touch* of geniality which far apart from Coleridge and cockneyism might have made him a small *reality*. God be with him! He was almost as wearisome as ——, and *very much detached*, as it struck me; knew nothing of men or things more than a sucking dove, at the same time looked out with an occasional gleam of geniality in his eyes; seemed even to like me, though I had barbarously enough entreated him.

The more comfortable was it to meet Empson this morning, in whom I at least found *sanity*, and what I have all along had to dispense with, the bearing of at least a *gentleman*. I am glad I went to Empson—went through two miles of tumultuous streets; found Empson in the solitude of the Temple, reading a newspaper in a flannel nightgown (which reminded me of Goody's, for it had a *belt*, only it was twice as large); a tall, broad, thin man, with wrinkled face, baldish head, and large mild melancholy dreamy blue eyes under bushy brows. He has a defect in his *trachea*, and can only mumble in speech, which he does with great copiousness in a very kindly style, confused enough, at the same time

listening with the profoundest attention and toleration to whatever you offer in reply. He is, as I thought, on the threshold of
mysticism, but I think will go deeper. Probably enough one
might grow to like such a man ; at all events I will try, and so I
think will you ; with your mother (were she more cultivated, or he
more ignorant) he were the man according to God's heart. Of
young Mill (the Spirit of the Age man) he speaks very highly, as
of a converted Utilitarian who is studying German ; so we are all
to meet, along with a certain Mrs. Austin, a young Germanist and
mutual intercessor (between Mill and Empson), and breakfast
some day in the Templar's lodgings. *Quod felix faustumque sit !*
It does my soul good to meet a true soul. Poor inexperienced
Glen is the only phenomenon of that sort I have yet seen here,
but I will riddle creation till I find more. Thus before your arrival (if such be our decision) I may perhaps have a little pleasant
circle to present you to, for of the *old* there is very *little* to be made ;
Irving alone stands true, and he (poor fellow !) is working miracles, while the Montagus, Stracheys, &c., have mostly, I fear,
drifted quite to leeward.

About your journey to London I myself know not what to say.
The persuasion grows more and more upon me that we should
spend the winter here. Say, Goody, would it not be pleasant to
THEE ? Tell me distinctly ; and yet I already know it would, but
that (as beseems a good wife) you subordinate your wishes to the
common good, and will not even speak of them. Well, but here
in this lodging we live actually (Jack and I) for some two guineas
a week ; or suppose in the winter season, and with many little
gracefulnesses which Goody would superadd, it cost *us* two—three
guineas : what then ? It is little more than we used to spend in
Edinburgh including rent ; and we can thoroughly investigate
London. I cannot promise you the comforts of our own poor
Craig ; yet it is a handsome lodging, and with purely honest people. Our drawing-room (for such it is) will be of the coldest, I
doubt ; but coals are not so very dear, and the female mind can
devise thicker clothes. How then ? shall it be decided on ? We
have to go somewhither : why not come *hither*, where my part of
the going is already finished ? Thyself shalt say it. Use thy
prophetic gift. If it answer yes, then will I strive to obey.

To the Same.

September 4.

Thursday was the wettest of wet days, even till after bedtime ;

the first day wherein I did not once stir out (except after dark to Irving's, who was not at home). Highgate and Coleridge were not to be thought of. After reading Goody's letter, I sate diligently over my proof-sheets—the day unvisited by any adventure except a little message from Mrs. Austin.

On Friday Jack and I walked over to the House of Lords; saw the Chancellor sitting between two Lords (two are necessary : one of them Earl Ferrers, son of him that was hanged, and the ugliest man extant, very like David Laing), a considerable handful of listeners and loiterers, and the poor little darling (Jeffrey) with a grey wig on it, and queer coatie with bugles or buttons on the cuffs, snapping away and speaking there in a foreign country among entire strangers. The fat Rutherford sate also within the ring, with Dr. Lushington (the divorcer) and certain of the clerk species. I declare I was partly touched with something of human feeling. However, our little darling seemed as gleg as ever; the '*trachea*' in moderate order; and was telling his story like a little king of elves. The Chancellor is a very particularly ignoble-looking man; a face not unlike your uncle Robert's, but stonier, and with a deeper, more restless, more dangerous eye ; *nothing* but business in his face—no ray of genius, and even a considerable tincture of insincerity. He was yawning awfully, with an occasional twitching up of the corners of the upper lip and point of the nose. A politician truly and *nothing* more. Learning that the Duke's speech would not end for two hours, I willingly took myself away.

After dinner came your letter, which I read twice; then had tea (black tea of my own) ; then off to the Austins, where I knew there would be green tea, which I had privately determined not to have. The Frau Austin herself was as loving as ever—a true Germanised spiritual *screamikin*. We were five of a party : her husband, a lean grey-headed painful-looking man, with large earnest timid eyes and a clanging metallic voice, that at great length set forth Utilitarianism *steeped* in German metaphysics, not dissolved therein ; a very worthy sort of limited man and professor of law. Secondly, a Frenchman, of no importance whatever, for he uttered not a word except some compliments in his own tongue. Thirdly, John Mill, ' Spirit-of-the-Age.' The other two you know already. This young Mill, I fancy and hope, is ' a *baying* you can love.' A slender, rather tall and elegant youth, with small clear Roman-nosed face, two small earnestly-smiling eyes ; modest, remarkably gifted with precision of utterance, enthusiastic, yet lucid, calm ; not a great, yet distinctly a gifted and amiable youth. We had almost four hours of the best talk I have mingled in for long. The youth walked home with me almost to the door ; seemed to profess, almost as plainly as modesty would allow, that he had been converted by the head of the Mystic School, to whom personally he testified very hearty-looking regard. Empson did not appear (having caught cold, or something of that sort), but by letter (while we were together) engaged Mill and me to breakfast with him on Tuesday. I met poor Empson to-day riding towards Holborn, the large melancholy eyes of the man turned downwards, so that he did not observe me. On the whole, Goodykin, these rudiments of a mystic school (better than I anticipated here) are by far the most cheering phenomenon I see in London. Good will come of it. Let us wait and see in what way.

At the Duke's this morning, where I found Rutherford and Jayme Relish, the Galloway stot, who stared at me as if minded to gore, or afraid of being gored, till I bowed. I was led by his lordship into a private room, and there indulged with ten minutes' private talk on the subject of 'Teufelsdröckh.' The short of it is this : Murray will print a short edition (750 copies) of Dreck on the half-profits system (that is, I getting *nothing*, but also giving nothing) ; after which the sole copyright of the book is to be mine ; which offer he makes, partly out of love to 'your lordship ;' chiefly from 'my great opinion of the originality,' &c. A poorish offer, Goody, yet perhaps after all the best I shall get. Better considerably than *my* giving 150*l.* for the frolic of having written such a work ! I mean to set off to-morrow morning to Colburn and Bentley (whom Fraser has prepared for me), and ascertain whether they will pay me *anything* for a first edition. Unless they say about 100*l.* I will prefer Murray. Murray *wished* me to try everywhere. You shall hear to-morrow how I speed, and then prophesy upon it.

I have this day written off to Napier to say that I have an article on *Luther* ready to write, and ask whether he will have it. Fifty pounds will be highly useful (thank God, not yet quite indispensable), and I can gain it handsomely in this way. These, dearest, are all my news. It is all very wooden, and would be dull to anyone but her it is written for. She will not think it dull, but interesting as the Epistle of a Paul to the church which is at Craig o' Putto.

Monday, 4 o'clock.—I was at Colburn's about eleven. After wait-

ing a weary hour in the Bentleian apartments saw a muddy character enter, to whom I explained myself and Dreck.[1] The muddy
man uttered the common cant of compliments, hinted at the sole
object of publishers being money, the difference between talent
and popularity, &c. &c. The purport will be that we shall have
nothing to do with one another. So much I could gather partly
from the muddy man. I shall go over and see Murray to-morrow
morning, and if he will put his hand to the plough and get on
with the printing forthwith, I mean to close with him and have
done. The offer is not so bad : 750 copies for the task of publish-
ing poor Dreck, and the rest of him *our own*. If he do not succeed, how could I ask any man to do more? If he do, then we
have opening for another bargain. Let us hope nothing, Goody ;
then we fear nothing. By one or the other means our poor little
pot *will* keep boiling, and shall, though the Devil himself said
nay.

Anticipating slightly, I may finish here the adventures
of 'Sartor' or Dreck, and for the present have done with
it. Murray at Jeffrey's instance had agreed to take the
book on the terms which Carlyle mentioned—not, however, particularly willingly. Jeffrey himself, who had
good practical knowledge of such things, thought that it
'was too much of the nature of a rhapsody to command
success or respectful attention.' Murray perhaps rather
wished to attach to himself a young man of unquestionable genius, whose works might be profitable hereafter,
than expected much from this immediate enterprise. He
decided to run the risk, however. The MS. was sent to
the printer, and a page was set in type for consideration,
when poor Murray, already repenting of what he had done,
heard that while he was hesitating 'Sartor' had been offered
to Longman, and had been declined by him. He snatched
at the escape, and tried to end his bargain. He professed
to think, and perhaps he really thought, that he had been
treated unfairly. The correspondence that ensued must
have made Murray more and more wonder what strange

---

[1] Neither Colburn nor Bentley in person, as appeared after.

being he was in contact with, and may be preserved as a curiosity.

To Thomas Carlyle, Esq.

Ramsgate : September 17.

Dear Sir,—Your conversation with me respecting the publication of your MS. led me to infer that you had given me the preference, and certainly not that you had already submitted it to the greatest publishers in London, who had declined to engage in it. Under these circumstances it will be necessary for me also to get it read by some literary friend before I can in justice to myself engage in the printing of it.

I am, dear Sir,

Your faithful servant,

JOHN MURRAY.

The apparent reflection on a want of sincerity in Carlyle was not altogether generous on Murray's part, but perhaps only too natural.

Carlyle answers :—

To John Murray, Esq.

Sir,—I am this moment favoured with your note of the 17th from Ramsgate, and beg to say in reply—

First, that your idea derived from conversation with me of my giving you the preference to all other publishers was perfectly correct : I had heard you described as a man of honour, frankness, and even generosity, and knew you to have the best and widest connections; on which grounds I might well say and can still well say that a transaction with you would please me better than a similar one with any other member of the trade.

Secondly, that your information of my having submitted my manuscript to the greatest publishers in London, if you mean thereby that after it first came out of your hands it lay two days in those of Messrs. Longman and Rees, and was from them delivered over to the Lord Advocate, is also perfectly correct. If you mean anything else, incorrect.

Thirdly, that if you wish the bargain which I had understood myself to have made with you unmade, you have only to cause your printer who is now working on my manuscript to return the same without danger or delay, and consider the business as finished.

To Thomas Carlyle.

Albemarle Street : Wednesday.

My dear Sir,—Had I been informed that during the interval in which I had returned the MS. to you it had been offered to Messrs. Longman and sent back after remaining with them two days, I certainly should have requested permission to have had it left to me for perusal before I determined upon its publication, and I only wish to be placed in the same position as I should have been had I been previously informed of that fact.

I am, my dear Sir,

Your obliged servant,

JOHN MURRAY.

Rough Draft of Reply.

Sir,—Though I cannot well discover what damage or alteration my MS. has sustained by passing through the hands of Messrs. Longman and Rees, I with great readiness enter into your views, and shall cheerfully release you from all engagement or shadow of engagement with me in regard to it, the rather as it seems reasonable for me to expect some higher remuneration for a work that has caused me so much effort, were it once fairly examined. Such remuneration as was talked of between *us* can, I believe, at all times be procured.

Perhaps you could now fix some date at which I might look for your decision on a quite new negotiation, if you incline to engage in such. I shall then see whether the limited extent of my time will still allow me to wait yours.

If not, pray have the goodness to cause my papers to be returned with the least possible delay.

The result was the letter from the 'bookseller,' enclosing the critical communication from his literary adviser, which Carlyle with pardonable malice attached as an Appendix to 'Sartor' when it was ultimately published, and which has been thus preserved as a singular evidence of critical fallibility. But neither is Murray to be blamed in the matter nor his critic. Their business was to ascertain whether the book, if published, would pay for the printing; and it was quite certain, both that the taste which

could appreciate Carlyle did nôt exist till he himself
created it, and that to 'Sartor,' beautiful and brilliant as
it now seems, the world would then have remained blind.
Carlyle himself, proud, scornful, knowing if no one else
knew the value of the estimate 'of the gentleman in the
highest class of men of letters' who had been consulted
in the matter, judged Murray after his fashion far too
harshly. In a letter to his wife he says:—

The printing of 'Teufelsdröckh,' which I announced as commencing, and even sent you a specimen of, has altogether stopped,
and Murray's bargain with me has burst into air. The man behaved like a pig, and was speared, not perhaps without art; Jack
and I at least laughed that night *à gorge déployée* at the answer I
wrote his base *glare* of a letter : he has written again in much po-
liter style, and I shall answer him, as McLeod advised my grandfather's people, 'sharp but mannerly.' The truth of the matter
is now clear enough ; Dreck cannot be disposed of in London at
this time. Whether he lie in my trunk or in a bookseller's cof-
fer seems partly indifferent. Neither, on the whole, do I know
whether it is not better that we have stopped for the present.
Money I was to have none; author's vanity embarked on that
bottom I have almost none ; nay, some time or other that the book
can be *so* disposed of it is certain enough.

Carlyle was not alone in his contempt for the existing
literary taste. Macvey Napier, to whom he had expressed
an opinion that the public had been for some time 'fed
with froth,' and was getting tired of it, agreed that 'he
saw no indication in that vast body of any appetite for
solid aliments.' Nay, he added (and the words deserve
to be remarked), 'I am thoroughly convinced that were
another Gibbon to appear and produce another such work
as the "Decline and Fall," the half of an impression of
750 copies would be left to load the shelves of its publisher.'

The article on Luther which Carlyle had offered for the
'Edinburgh' could not get itself accepted. Napier recog-

nised that Luther was a noble subject, but he could not spare space for the effective treatment of it. He recommended instead a review of Thomas Hope's book on Man ; and Carlyle, accepting the change, made Hope the text for the paper which he called ' Characteristics.' This essay, more profound and far-reaching even than ' Sartor,' was written in these autumn weeks in London.

CHAPTER IX.

MRS. CARLYLE had entered eagerly into the scheme for joining her husband in London. Six weeks' solitude at Craigenputtock, with strangers now in occupation of the farm, had tried even her fortitude beyond her strength, and Alick and Jean Carlyle had gone from Scotsbrig to take care of her.

To Mrs. Carlyle, Scotsbrig.

Craigenputtock : September, 1831.

A thousand thanks, my dear kind mother, for sending Jean and Alick to my rescue. If some such mercy had not been vouchsafed me I think I must soon have worked myself into a fever or other violent disorder; for my talent for fancying things, which is quite as great as your own, had so entirely got the upper hand of me that I could neither sleep by night nor rest by day. I have slept more, since they came and have kept me from falling into dreams, than I had done for a fortnight before.

I have news, if you have not heard it already, more joyful to me, I suspect, than to you : I am going to my husband, and as soon as I can get ready for leaving. Now do not grieve that he is not to return so soon as we expected. I am sure it is for his good, and, therefore, for all our goods. Here he was getting more and more unhappy, more and more dissatisfied with the world and himself. I *durst* not have counselled him to such a step; but whenever he proposed it himself, I cordially approved. But I will tell you all about this and other matters when I come and see you all again before I set out.

Carlyle wants me to bring some butter, oatmeal, &c., which are not to be got good in London for love or money, and without the smallest remorse I apply to you to help me. I *have* some butter of our own cows; but as it has been salted in small quantities, sometimes in warm weather and by my own hands, which are not the most expert, I am afraid it will not be good enough; at all rates, inferior to the Scotsbrig thing.

Jean is going with me to Templand to-day, as a sort of protection against my mother's agitations. Next week she will help me to pack.

Your affectionate
JANE W. CARLYLE.

Carlyle, meanwhile, continued his account of himself in his letters. Napier had not then written conclusively about his article, and he was restless.

To Mrs. Carlyle, Craigenputtock.

London : September 11.

My days flow rather uselessly along. If Naso do not write soon I will seek some other ta>k, were it the meanest. No one can force you to be idle, but only yourself. Neither is the world *shut* against anyone; but it is HE that is shut. God grant us some little touch of wisdom; let Fate turn up what card she likes, so we can play it well. I feel as if I had yet much to suffer, but also something to do. Do thou help me, my little woman; thou art worthy of that destiny, and perhaps it is appointed thee. These are fearful times, yet is there greatness in them. Now is the hour when he that feels himself a man should stand forth and prove himself such. Oh, could I but live in the light of that holy purpose and keep it ever present before me, I were happy—too happy!

Meanwhile, unfortunately for these many months, and now as formerly, I am rather wicked. Alas! Why should I dwell in the element of contempt and indignation, not rather in that of patience and love? I was reading in Luther's 'Tischreden,' and absolutely felt ashamed. What have I suffered? What did he suffer? One should actually, as Irving advises, 'pray to the Lord,' did one but know how to do it. The *best* worship, however, is stout working. *Frisch zu!*

I have not seen the Duke for a week. I acknowledge in myself a certain despicable tendency to think crabbedly of the poor Duke: a quite vulgar feeling it is. Merely as if he were not kind enough to *me*. Is he not kinder than most other men are? Shame on me! Out of various motives, among which love is not wholly wanting, he really wishes to do me good. Are not all others of his order indifferent to me? Should not he be at all times *more* and not *less?* Yet his path is not my path, nor are his thoughts my thoughts. It is more and more clear to me that we shall never do any good together. Let him come and sit with you in that 'flowerpot tub,' if he like; let us do him what kindness we can, which is not much, and stand ever with kind looks in that direction, yet always, too, on our side of the Strand. Frivolous gigmanity *cannot* unite itself to our stern destiny; let it pass by on the other side. But oh, my dear Jeannie, do help me to be a little softer, to be a little merciful to *all* men, even gigmen. Why should a man, though bilious, never so 'nervous,' impoverished, bugbitten, and bedevilled, let Satan have dominion over him? Save me, save me, my Goody! It is on this side that I am threatened; nevertheless we *will* prevail, I tell thee : by God's grace we will and shall.

September 14.

On Monday night I walked round from putting in your letter and borrowed me the last 'Quarterly Review,' to read the article there on the Saint Simonians, by Southey; it is an altogether miserable article, written in the spirit not of a philosopher but of a parish precentor. He knows what they are *not*, so far at least as the Thirty-nine Articles go; but nothing whatsoever of what they *are*. 'My brother, I say unto thee, thou art a poor creature.' The rest of the 'Review' is also despicable enough—blind, shovel-hatted, hysterically lachrymose. Lockhart, it seems, edits it out of Roxburghshire, rusticating by some 'burn' in that country. Tuesday night John Mill came in and sate talking with me till near eleven—a fine clear enthusiast, who will one day come to something; yet to nothing poetical, I think : his fancy is not rich; furthermore, he cannot *laugh* with any compass. You will like Mill. Glen [1] is a man of greatly more natural material; but hitherto he is like a blind Cyclops, *ill* educated, yet capable of good education; he may perhaps reap great profit from us.

Edward Irving is graver than usual, yet has still the old faculty of laughter; on the whole, a true sufficient kind of man, very anxious to have me stay here, where 'in two years or so' I should not

---

[1] 'Glen, who was mentioned before, was a young graduate of Glasgow studying law in London, of very considerable though utterly confused talent. Ultimately went mad, and was boarded in a farmhouse near Craigenputtock, within reach of us, where in seven or eight years he died.—T. C.'

fail to find some appointment. What I lament is that such a mind should not be in the van, but wilfully standing in the rear, bringing up the tagrag and bobtail, however well he do it. 'Miracles' are the commonest things in the world here. Irving said to Glen, '*When* I work miracles.' He and I have never fastened upon that topic yet, but by-and-by he shall hear my whole mind on it, for he deserves such confidence.

I gave your compliments to Empson, who received them with wreathed smiles and mumbles of heartiest welcome. I think you will like him—a bushy-faced kind-looking creature with most melancholy short-sighted eyes. He is from Lincolnshire ; walks much, I take it, with women, men being too harsh and còntradictory with him. He was sitting in yellow nightgown, without neckcloth, shaggy enough, and writing with his whole might for Naso (Napier).

Of Macaulay I hear nothing very good—a sophistical, rhetorical, ambitious young man of talent ; 'set in there,' as Mill said, ' to make flash speeches, and he makes them.' It seems to me of small consequence whether we meet at all.

To Mrs. Carlyle, Scotsbrig.

September 19, 1831.

My dear Mother,—. . . Jane will have told you how languidly everything proceeds with me—how the 'people are all out of town,' everything stagnating because of this Reform Bill, the book trade in particular nearly altogether at a standstill, and lastly, how I, as the best thing I could do, have been obliged to give my poor book away (that is, the first edition of it),[1] and am even glad to see it printed on these terms. This is not very flattering news of the encouragement for men of my craft ; nevertheless, I study to say with as much cheerfulness as I can, *Be it so !* The Giver of all Good has enabled me to write the thing, and also to do *without* any pay for it : the pay would have been wasted away and flitted out of the bit as other pay does ; but if there stand any truth recorded there, *it* will not 'flit.' Nay, if there be even no truth (as where is the man that can say with confidence the inspiration of the Almighty has given *me* understanding), yet it was the nearest approach to such that I could make ; and so in God's name let it take its fortune in the world, and sink or swim

---

[1] This was written a day or two before the final collapse with Murray.

as the All-disposer orders. There remains for ever the maxim, 'In all thy ways acknowledge Him.'

I am earnestly expecting Jane, that some sort of establishment may be formed here, where we can spend the winter with more regularity and composure than I have hitherto enjoyed. Then we can look about us over this whirlpool, and I, in the meantime, shall most probably write some considerable essay for the 'Edinburgh Review,' that so, when we return, *Mall* may not be altogether out of *shafts.* Of any permanent appointment here I as yet see, with my own eyes, not the slightest outlook ; neither, indeed, is my heart set on such, for I feel that the King's palace with all it holds would in good truth do little for me ; and the prayer I ever endeavour to make is, 'Show me my duty, and enable me to do it.' If my duty be to endure a life of poverty and what 'light afflictions' attend on it, this also will not terrify me.

Meanwhile, I am not without my comforts ; one of the greatest of which is to have found various well-disposed men, most of them young men, who can feel a sort of scholarship towards me. My poor performances in the writing way are better known here than I expected ; clearly enough, also, there *is* want of instruction and light in this mirk midnight of human affairs ; such want as probably for eighteen hundred years there has not been. If *I* have any light to give them, let me give it ; if none, then what is to be done but seek for it, and hold my peace till I find it.

To Mrs. Carlyle, Liverpool.[1]

London : September 23.

My poor Goody,—All yesterday my thoughts were with thee in thy lone voyage, which now I pray the great Giver of Good may have terminated prosperously. Never before did I so well understand my mother's anxious forecasting ways. I felt that my best possession was trusted to the false sea, and all my cares for it could avail nothing. Do not wait a moment in writing. I shall have no peace till I know that you are safe. Meanwhile, in truth there is no use in tormenting myself ; the weather, here at least, was good. I struggle while I can to believe that it has all passed without accident, and that you are now resting in comparative safety in your uncle's house among friends.

Of rest I can well understand you have need enough. I grieve

---

[1] His wife had gone by water from Annan to her uncle's house at Liverpool : from thence to proceed by coach to London.

to think how harassed you have been of late, all which, I fear, has acted badly on your health ; these bustlings and tossings to and fro are far too rough work for you. I can see, by your two last letters especially, that it is not well with you ; your heart is, as it were, choked up, if not depressed. You are agitated and provoked, which is almost the worse way of the two. Alas ! and I have no soft Aladdin's Palace here to bid you hasten and take repose in. Nothing but a noisy, untoward lodging-house, and no better shelter than my own bosom. Yet is not this the best of all shelters for you ? the only safe place in this wide world ? Thank God, this still is yours, and I can receive you there without distrust, and wrap you close with the solacements of a true heart's love. Hasten thither, then, my own wife. Betide what may, we will not despair, were the world never so unfriendly. *We* are indivisible, and will help each other to endure its evils, nay to conquer them.

Mrs. Carlyle arrived in London on the first of October, a good deal shattered by the journey and the charge of the miscellaneous cargo of luggage which she had brought with her : oatmeal, hams, butter, &c., supplied by the generous Scotsbrig to lighten the expense of the London winter. George Irving's lodgings, being found to contain bugs, were exchanged for others. John Carlyle departed with Lady Clare for Italy. Carlyle and his wife quartered themselves at Ampton Street, turning out of Gray's Inn Road, where they had two comfortable rooms in the house of an excellent family named Miles, who belonged to Irving's congregation. Here friends came to see them : Mill, Empson, later on Leigh Hunt, drawn by the article on Hope ('Characteristics') which Carlyle was now assiduously writing, Jeffrey, and afterwards many more, the Carlyles going out into society, and reconnoitring literary London. Mrs. Carlyle in her way was as brilliant as her husband was in his own ; she attracting every one, he wondered at as a prodigy, which the world was yet uncertain whether it was to love or execrate.

Carlyle's 'Journal' tells us generally what was passing

within him and round him, how London affected him, &c. His and Mrs. Carlyle's letters fill out the picture.

Extracts from Journal.

October 10.—Wife -arrived ten days ago. We here quietly enough in 4 Ampton Street, and the world jogging on at the old rate. Jack must be by this time in Paris. 'Teufelsdröckh,' after various perplexed destinies, returned to me, and now lying safe in his box. The book contents me little; yet perhaps there is material in it; in any case, I did my best.

The Reform Bill lost (on Saturday morning at six o'clock) by a majority of forty-one. The politicians will have it the people must *rise.* The people will do nothing half so foolish—for the present. London seems altogether quiet. Here they are afraid of Scotland, in Scotland of us.

On Saturday saw Sir James Mackintosh (at Jeffrey's), and looked at and listened to him, though without speech. A broadish, middle-sized, grey-headed man, well-dressed, and with a plain courteous bearing; grey intelligent (unhealthy yellow-whited) eyes, in which plays a dash of cautious vivacity (uncertain whether fear or latent ire), triangular unmeaning nose, business mouth and chin; on the whole, a sensible official air, not without a due spicing of hypocrisy and something of pedantry, both no doubt involuntary. The man is a Whig philosopher and politician, such as the time yields, our best of that sort, which will soon be extinct. He was talking mysteriously with other 'Hon. Members' about 'what was to be done'—something *à la* Dogberry the thing looked to me, though I deny not that it is a serious conjuncture, only believe that change has some chance to be for the better, and so see it all with composure.

Meanwhile, *what* was the true duty of a man? Were it to stand utterly aloof from politics (not ephemeral only, for that of course, but generally from all speculation about social systems, &c.), or is not perhaps the very want of this time an infinite want of Governors, of knowledge how to govern itself? Canst thou in any measure spread abroad reverence over the hearts of men? That were a far higher task than *any* other. Is it to be done by art? or are men's minds as yet shut to art, and open only at best to oratory? not fit for a *Meister*, but *only for a better and better Teufelsdröckh?* *Think and be silent.*

Mary Wollstonecraft's 'Life of Godwin.' An Ariel imprisoned in a brickbat! It is a real tragedy and of the deepest. Sublimely virtuous endowment; in practice, misfortune, suffering, death . . . by destiny, and also by desert. An English Mignon; Godwin an honest boor that loves her, but cannot guide or save her.

Strange tendency everywhere noticeable to speculate on *men*, not on *man*. Another branch of the mechanical temper. Vain hope to make mankind happy by politics! You *cannot* drill a regiment of knaves into a regiment of honest men, enregiment and organise them as cunningly as you will. Give us the honest men, and the well-ordered regiment comes of itself. Reform one man —reform thy own inner man; it is more than scheming out reforms for a nation.

John told me of having seen in Holborn a man walking steadily along with some six baskets all piled above each other, his name and address written in large characters on each, so that he exhibited a statue of some twelve feet, and so by the six separate announcements had his existence sufficiently proclaimed. The trade of this man was basket-making; but he had found it needful to study a quite new trade—that of walking with six baskets on his head in a crowded street.

In like manner Colburn and Bentley, the booksellers, are known to expend ten thousand pounds annually on what they call advertising, more commonly called *puffing*. Puffing (which is simply the *second* trade, like that of basket-carrying) flourishes in all countries; but London is the true scene of it, having this one quality beyond all other cities—a quite immeasurable size. It is rich also, stupid, and ignorant beyond example; thus in all respects the true Goshen of quacks.

Every man I meet with mourns over this state of matters; no one thinks it remediable. You must do as the others do, or they will get the start of you or tread you under foot. 'All true, Mr. Carlyle BUT': I say, 'All true, Mr. Carlyle AND.' The first beginning of a remedy is that some *one* believe a remedy possible; believe that if he cannot live by truth, then he can *die* by it. Dost *thou* believe it? Then is the new era begun!

How men are hurried here ; how they are hunted and terrifically chased into double-quick speed ; so that in self-defence they *must not* stay to look at one another ! Miserable is the scandal-mongery and evil speaking of the country population : more frightful still the total ignorance and mutual heedlessness of these poor souls in populous city pent. ' Each passes on quick, transient, regarding not the other or his woes.' Each must button himself together, and take no thought (not even for evil) of his neighbour. There in their little cells, divided by partitions of brick or board, they sit strangers, unknowing, unknown, like passengers in some huge ship ; each within his own cabin. Alas ! and the ship is life ; and the voyage is from eternity to eternity.

Everywhere there is the most crying want of *government*, a true all-ruining anarchy. No one has any *knowledge* of London, in which he lives. It is a huge aggregate of little systems, each of which is again a small anarchy, the members of which do not *work* together, but *scramble* against each other. The soul (what can be properly called the soul) lies dead in the bosom of man ; starting out in mad, ghastly night-walkings—*e.g.* the gift of tongues. Ignorance eclipses all things with its owlet wings. Man walks he knows not whither ; walks and wanders till he walks into the jaws of death, and is then devoured. Nevertheless, *God is in it.* Here, even here, is the revelation of the Infinite in the Finite ; a majestic poem (tragic, comic, or epic), couldst thou but read it or recite it ! Watch it then ; study it ; catch the secret of it ; and proclaim the same in such accent as is given thee. Alas ! the spirit is willing, but the flesh is weak.

On Thursday night last (this is Monday), the 28th of October, dined with Fonblanque, editor of the 'Examiner.' An honourable Radical ; might be something better. London bred. Limited by education more than by nature. Something metallic in the tone of his voice (like that of Professor Austin). For the rest, a tall, loose, lank-haired, wrinkly, wintry, vehement-looking flail of a man. I reckon him the best of the fourth estate now extant in Britain. Shall see him again.

Allan Cunningham with us last night. Jane calls him a genuine Dumfriesshire mason still ; and adds that it is delightful to see a genuine man of any sort. Allan was, as usual, full of Scottish anecdotic talk. Right by instinct ; has *no* principles or *creed* that I can see, but excellent old Scottish *habits* of character. An interesting man.

Walter Scott left town yesterday on his way to Naples. He is to proceed from Plymouth in a frigate, which the Government have given him a place in. Much run after here, it seems ; but he is old and sick, and cannot enjoy it; has had two shocks of palsy, and seems altogether in a precarious way. To me he is and has been an object of very minor interest for many, many years. The novelwright of his time, its favourite child, and *therefore* an almost worthless one. Yet is there something in his deep recognition of the worth of the past, perhaps better than anything he has *expressed* about it, into which I do not yet fully see. Have never spoken with him (though I might sometimes without great effort) ; and now probably never shall.

What an advantage has the pulpit where you address men already arranged to hear you, and in a vehicle which long use has rendered easy ; how infinitely harder when you have all to create—not the ideas only and the sentiments, but the symbols and the mood of mind ! Nevertheless, in all cases where man addresses man, on his spiritual interests especially, there is a *sacredness*, could we but evolve it, and think and speak in it. Consider better what it is thou meanest by a *symbol ;* how far thou hast insight into the nature thereof.

Is *Art* in the old Greek sense possible for men at this late era? or were not perhaps the founder of a religion our true Homer at present ? The *whole soul* must be illuminated, made harmonious. Shakespeare seems to have had no religion but his poetry.

Where is To-morrow resident even now? Somewhere or somehow it *is*, doubt not of that. On the common theory thou mayest think thyself into madness on this question.

November 2.—How few people speak for Truth's sake, even in its humblest modes ! I return from Enfield, where I have seen Lamb, &c. &c. Not one of that class will tell you a straightforward story or even a credible one about any matter under the sun. All must be packed up into epigrammatic contrasts, startling exaggerations, claptraps that will get a plaudit from the galleries ! I have heard a hundred anecdotes about William Hazlitt for example ; yet cannot by never so much cross-questioning even form to myself the smallest notion of how it really stood with him.

Wearisome, inexpressibly wearisome to me is that sort of clatter; it is not walking (to the end of time you would never advance, for these persons indeed have no WHITHER) ; it is not bounding and frisking in graceful, natural joy; it is dancing—a St. Vitus's dance. Heigh ho! Charles Lamb I sincerely believe to be in some considerable degree insane. A more pitiful, ricketty, gasping, staggering, stammering Tomfool I do not know. He is witty by denying truisms and abjuring good manners. His speech wriggles hither and thither with an incessant painful fluctuation, not an opinion in it, or a fact, or a phrase that you can thank him for— more like a convulsion fit than a natural systole and diastole. Besides, he is now a confirmed, shameless drunkard; *asks* vehemently for gin and water in strangers' houses, tipples till he is utterly mad, and is only not thrown out of doors because he is too much despised for taking such trouble with him. Poor Lamb! Poor England, when such a despicable abortion is named genius! He said there are just two things I regret in England's history : first, that Guy Fawkes' plot did not take effect (there would have been so glorious an *explosion*) ; second, that the Royalists did not hang Milton (then we might have laughed at them), &c. &c. *Armer Teufel!*

Carlyle did not know at this time the tragedy lying behind the life of Charles Lamb, which explained or extenuated his faults. Yet this extravagantly harsh estimate is repeated—scarcely qualified—in a sketch written nearly forty years after.

Among the scrambling miscellany of notables that hovered about us, Leigh Hunt was probably the best, poor Charles Lamb the worst. He was sinking into drink, poor creature ; his fraction of 'humour,' &c., I recognised, and recognised—but never could accept for a great thing, a genuine, but essentially small and cockney thing; and now with gin, &c., superadded, one had to say 'Genius! This is not genius, but diluted insanity. Please remove this!'

The gentle Elia deserved a kinder judgment. Carlyle considered 'humour' to be the characteristic of the highest order of mind. He had heard Lamb extravagantly praised, perhaps, for this particular quality, and he was provoked to find it combined with habits which his own stern Calvinism was unable to tolerate.

To return to the letters:—

To Mrs. Carlyle, Scotsbrig.

4 Ampton Street, Mecklenburgh Square, London :
October 20, 1831.

My dear Mother,—We have nestled down here in our tight little lodging, and are as quiet as we could wish to be. Jane is in better health than she has enjoyed for many months ; I, too, am fully better. We live thriftily, have companions and conversation of the best that can be had ; and except that I cannot honestly tell myself that I am *working* (though I daily make the attempt to work and keep scraffling and feltering), we ought to call ourselves very well off indeed. The people of the house are cleanly, orderly, and seem honest—no noises, no bugs disturb us through the night ; on the whole it is among the best places for *sleep* I have been in, as you may judge by this fact, that more than once we have slept almost ten hours at a stretch—a noble spell of sleeping, of which, however, both of us, so long disturbed and tost about, had need enough. The worst thing about our establishment is its *hamperedness*, which is so much the more sensible to us coming from the desert vastness of the moor at Craigenputtock. I have a sort of feeling as if I were tied up in a *sack* and could not get my fins *stirred*. No doubt this will wear off, for one needs but little room to work profitably in ; my craft especially requires nothing but a chair, a table, and a piece of paper. Were I once fairly heated at my work, I shall not mind what sort of harness I am in. Napier writes to me that he expects a ' striking essay ' from my hand for his next 'Edinburgh Review,' so I must bestir me, for there is little more than a month to work in.

Some of my friends here are talking of possible situations for me, but as yet on no ground that I can fairly see with my own eyes. I let it be known to every one who takes interest in me that I am very desirous to work at *any* honest employment I am acquainted with ; but for the rest, able to hold on my way whether I find other employment or not. If I can earn myself a more liberal livelihood, I hope I shall be thankful for it, and use it as it beseems me ; nay, I would even live in London for the sake of such a blessing ; but if nothing of the kind turn up, as is most likely, then I can also, with all contentment, return to the Whinstone Craig, and rejoice that this city of refuge is left me. Truly thankful ought I to be that the Giver of all Good has imparted to me this highest of all blessings ; light to discern His hand in the confused workings of this evil world ; and to follow fearlessly whithersoever He beckons ! Ever be praised God for it ! I was once the miserablest of all men, but shall not be so any more. On the whole, however, there is work in abundance for me here—men ignorant on all hands of me of what it most concerns them to know ; neither will I turn me from the task of teaching them as it is given me. Had I once investigated the ground fully, I may perhaps lift up my voice so that it shall be heard a little farther than heretofore. But I wish to do nothing rashly, to take no step which I might wish in vain to retrace.

Meanwhile, my book, withdrawn from all bookselling consultations, lies safe in the box, waiting till the book-trade revive before I make a farther attempt. The *Reform Bill,* I suppose, must be disposed of first ; and when that may be I know not, neither, indeed, care. If the world will not have my bit-book, then, of a truth, my bit-book can do without the world. One good thing in the middle of all this stagnation is that we are perfectly peaceable here, though the contrary was by some apprehended. The newspapers will tell you, as their way is, about wars and rumours of wars ; but you need not believe them, or heed them. I see no symptom of revolting among the people, neither do I believe that anything short of hunger will raise them—of which, happily, there is as yet no approach. So keep yourself perfectly easy, my dear mother, and know that we are as safe as we could anywhere be ; nay, at the first stir of 'revolution' cannot we hasten to the *Craig* and sit there and see them revolve it out for their own behoof.

I dare say you have not seen in the newspapers, but will soon see something extraordinary about poor Edward Irving. His friends here are all much grieved about him. For many months he has been puddling and muddling in the midst of certain insane jargonings of hysterical women, and crackbrained enthusiasts, who start up from time to time in public companies, and utter confused stuff, mostly 'Ohs' and 'Ahs,' and absurd interjections about 'the body of Jesus ;' they also pretend to 'work miracles,' and have raised more than one weak bedrid woman, and cured people of 'nerves,' or as they themselves say, 'cast devils out of them.' All which poor Irving is pleased to consider as the 'work

of the Spirit,' and to janner about at great length, as making *his*
church the peculiarly blessed of Heaven, and equal to or greater
than the primitive one at Corinth. This, greatly to my sorrow and
that of many, has gone on privately a good while, with increasing
vigour; but last Sabbath it burst out publicly in the open church;
for one of the 'Prophetesses,' a woman on the verge of derange-
ment, started up in the time of worship, and began to speak with
tongues, and, as the thing was encouraged by Irving, there were
some three or four fresh hands who started up in the evening sermon and began their ragings; whereupon the whole congregation
got into foul uproar, some groaning, some laughing, some shriek-
ing, not a few falling into swoons: more like a Bedlam than a
Christian church. Happily, neither Jane nor I were there, though
we had been the previous day. We had not even heard of it.
When going next evening to call on Irving, we found the house
all decked out for a 'meeting,' (that is, about this same 'speaking
with tongues'), and as we talked a moment with Irving, who had
come down to us, there rose a shriek in the upper story of the
house, and presently he exclaimed, 'There is one prophesying;
come and hear her!' We hesitated to go, but he forced us up
into a back room, and there we could hear the wretched creature
raving like one possessed: *hooing*, and *haing*, and talking *as* sensibly as one would do with a pint of brandy in his stomach, till
after some ten minutes she seemed to grow tired and become silent.
     Nothing so shocking and altogether unspeakably deplorable was
it ever my lot to hear. Poor Jane was on the verge of fainting,
and did not recover the whole night. And now the newspapers
have got wind of it and are groaning loudly over it, and the congregation itself is like to split on the matter; and for poor Irving in any case dark mad times are coming. You need not speak
of all this, at least not be the first to speak of it; most likely it
will be too public. What the final issue for our most worthy, but
most misguided friend may be, I dare not so much as guess.
Could I do anything to save him, it were well my part, but I despair of being able to accomplish anything. I began a letter to
him yesterday, but gave it up as hopeless when I heard that the
newspapers had interfered, for now Irving I reckon *will not* draw
back, lest it should seem fear of men rather than of God. The
unhappy man! Let us nevertheless hope that he is not utterly
lost, but only gone astray for a time. Be thankful also that our
wits are still in some measure left with us.

.   .   .   .

The newspapers call on Irving's people for the honour of Scotland to leave him or muzzle him. The most general hypothesis
is that he is a quack, the milder that he is getting cracked. Poor
George is the man I pity most; he spoke to us of it, almost with
tears in eyes, and earnestly entreated me to deal with his brother,
which, when he comes hither (by appointment on Tuesday), I
partly mean to attempt, though now I fear it will be useless. It
seems likely that all the Loselism of London will be about the
church next Sunday, that his people will quarrel with him; in any
case that troublous times are appointed him. My poor friend!
And yet the punishment was not unjust, that he who believed
without inquiry should now believe against all light, and porten-
tously call upon the world to admire as inspiration what is but a
dancing on the verge of bottomless abysses of madness. I see not
the end of it—who does?

Carlyle did attempt, as he has related in the ' Reminiscences,' and as he tells in his letters, to drag Irving back
from the precipice; but it proved as vain as he had feared;
and all that he could do was but to stand aside and watch
the ruin of his true and noble-minded friend. The last
touch was added to the tragedy by the presence of Mrs.
Carlyle to witness the catastrophe.

Meanwhile London was filling again after the holidays;
and the autumn brought back old faces of other friends
whom Carlyle was glad to see again. The Bullers were
among the earliest arrivals. Charles Buller, then beginning his brief and brilliant career, was an advanced Radical in politics, and equally advanced in matters of speculation. He had not yet found a creed, as he had said,
which he could even wish to believe true. He had a generous scorn of affectation, and did not choose, like many
of his contemporaries, to wear a mask of veiled hypocrisy.
The hen is terrified when the ducklings she has hatched
take to water. Mrs. Buller, indeed, shared her son's feelings and felt no alarm; but her sister, Mrs. Strachey,

who, a good religious woman, was shocked at a freedom less common then than it is now, because it could be less safely avowed, and in despair of help from the professional authorities, to whom she knew that her nephew would not listen, she turned to Carlyle, whose opinions she perhaps imperfectly understood, but of whose piety of heart she was assured.

Carlyle was extremely fond of Charles Buller. He was the only person of distinction or promise of distinction with whom he came in contact that he heartily admired; and he, too, had regretted to see his old pupil rushing off into the ways of agnosticism. Well he knew that no man ever came, or ever could come, to any greatness in this world in irreverent occupation with the mere phenomena of earth. The agnostic doctrines, he once said to me, were to appearance like the finest flour, from which you might expect the most excellent bread; but when you came to feed on it you found it was powdered glass and you had been eating the deadliest poison. What he valued in Buller was his hatred of cant, his frank contempt of insincere professions. But refusal even to appear to conform with opinions which the world holds it decent to profess, is but the clearing of the soil from weeds. Carlyle, without waiting to be urged by Mrs. Strachey, had long been labouring to sow the seeds in Buller of a nobler belief; but a faith which can stand the wear and tear of work cannot be taught like a mathematical problem, and if Carlyle had shown Mrs. Strachey the condition of his own mind, she would scarcely have applied to him for assistance. Buller died before it had been seen to what seed sown such a mind as his might eventually have grown.

Thomas Carlyle to Mrs. Carlyle, Scotsbrig.

November 10, 1831.

. . . .

I feel in some measure getting to my feet again after so long stumbling. Some time ago, I actually began a paper for the 'Edinburgh Review,' at which I am daily working. My hand was sadly out; but by resolute endeavour I feel that it will come in again, and I shall perhaps make a tolerable story of it. So long as I can work it is all well with me: I care for nothing. The only thing I have to struggle against is idleness and falsehood. These are the two Devil's emissaries that, did I give them heed, would work all my woe. A considerable paper of mine came out in the 'Foreign Quarterly Review' (Cochrane's), which, with several other things that you have not yet seen, I hope to show you and get you to read when I return. Cochrane's pay will serve to keep *Mall in shaft* till we turn northward. Meanwhile all goes on as well as we could hope; our lodgings continue very comfortable and very cheap; so that we can *both* live for little more than it used in my last London residence to cost me alone. The people are very cleanly, polite, decent-minded people; they have seen better days, and seem to have a heart above their lot. Both of us sleep well; our health is fully of the old quality: we eat and breathe, and have wherewith to eat and breathe; for honest thinking and honest acting the materials are *everywhere* laid down to one.

Except the printing of my book, or rather the trying for it so long as there seems any good chance, I have no special call at London. Nevertheless, there are many profitable chances for me here; especially many persons with whom I find much encouragement and perhaps improvement in associating. A considerable knot of *young* men in particular I discover here that have had their eyes on me, and wish for insight from me; with these it seems quite possible some good may be done. Among the number was my landlord this morning,[1] a secretary in one of the Government offices, whom I met with for the first time. He had a whole party to meet me: four of the best mannered, most pleasant persons I have for a long time seen: all ingenuous persons 'lying,' what so few do, 'open to light.' The disciple or associate I have most to do with is one John Mill (the son of a Scotchman of eminence), acquainted with the Bullers, &c., who is a great favourite here. It was he that brought about my meeting this morning with my secretary (Taylor) and his friends, whom I hope to see again. Charles Buller also has come to town; he made his appearance here the other day, was in about an hour followed

---

[1] Henry (now Sir Henry) Taylor, with whom he had been at breakfast.

by Mill, and the two made what Jane called 'a pleasant forenoon call of seven hours and a half.' Charles is grown a great tower of a fellow, six feet three in height, a yard in breadth, shows great talent and great natural goodness, which I hope he will by-and-by turn to notable account. I met him and Strachey amid the raw, frosty fog of Piccadilly this morning, and expect to see him some evening soon. Mrs. Strachey is just returned from Devonshire, whence she had written us a very kind and true-looking letter, and we *expect* to see her soon. The Montagus go hovering much about us; but their intercourse is of inferior profit : their whole way of life has a certain hollowness, so that you nowhere find firm bottom. One must try to take the good out of each and keep aloof from the evil that lies everywhere mixed with it.

Irving comes but little in our way; and one does not like to go and seek him in his own house in a whole posse of enthusiasts, ranters, and silly women. He was here once, taking tea, since that work of the 'Tongues' began. I told him with great earnestness my deep-seated, unhesitating conviction that it was *no* special work of the Holy Spirit, or of any spirit, save of that black, frightful, unclean one that dwells in Bedlam. He persists, mildly obstinate, in his course, greatly strengthened therein by his wife, who is reckoned the beginner of it all. What it will all lead to I pretend not to prophesy. I do not think it can spread to any extent even among the vulgar here at this time of day ; only a small knot of ravers now rave in that old worn-out direction. But for Irving himself the consequences frighten me. That he will lose his congregation seems calculated on by his friends ; but perhaps a far darker fear is not out of the question, namely that he may lose his own wits. God guard him from such a consummation! None of you, I am sure, will join in any ill-natured clamours against him. Defend him rather with brotherly charity, and hope always that he will yet be delivered from this real delusion of the Devil.

Jane wanted me to tell you of the 'Examiner' editor,[1] but I have not space here. The poor fellow has been thrown out of a gig, and is tediously lame; so I have not yet seen him here, neither was he at home when I pilgrimed over the other day, but gone to Brighton for sea air. My ideas, therefore, were only formed by candle-light. He is a long, thin, *tawtie*-headed man,

[1] Fonblanque.

with wrinkly, even baggy face, keen, zealous-looking eyes, a sort of well toned, honestly argumentative voice; very much the air of a true-hearted Radical. He was all braced with straps, moving on crutches, and hung together loosely, you would have said, as by *flail-cappins*. However, we got along bravely together, and parted, after arguing and assenting and laughing and mourning at considerable length, with mutual purposes to meet again. I rather like the man; there is far more in him than in most of Radicals; besides, he means *honestly*, and has a real feeling where the shoe pinches, namely, that the grand misery is the condition of the poor classes.

I had much to write about the state of matters here, and to quiet your fears especially about the cholera, which so many torment themselves with. It is in truth a disease of no such terrific quality, only that its effect is sudden, and the people have heard so much about it. Scarcely a year but there is a *typhus fever* in Glasgow or Edinburgh that kills far *more* than the cholera does in like cases. For my part, I am even satisfied that it has reached our coasts (where I have long inevitably expected it), and that now the reality which is measurable will succeed the terror which is unmeasurable, and doing great mischief both to individual peace of mind and all kinds of commercial intercourse. The worst effect here will be that same interruption; thus already the coals which come from Northumberland are beginning to rise. On the whole, however, it is our purpose to run no unnecessary risks; therefore, should the danger really come near us, and the disease break out in London under a shape in any measure formidable, we will *forthwith bundle our gear*, and return to Puttock till it is over. This we have resolved on, so disquiet not yourself, my dear mother; there is no peril for the moment; nay, it is a hundred miles nearer *you* than us. As to *rioting* and all that sort of matter, there is no symptom of it here; neither in case of its actual occurrence have persons like us anything to fear. We are safer here, I take it, than we should be in Dunscore itself. . . . I will write, if aught notable happen, *instantly*. Farewell, dear mother. God bless you all.   T. CARLYLE.

To John Carlyle.

November 13, 1831.

.   .   .   .   .   .

As to Irving, expect little tidings of him. I think I shall henceforth see little of him. His 'gift of tongues' goes on apace. Glen says there was one performing yesterday; but, on the whole, the

Cockneys are too old for such lullabies—they simply think he is gone distracted, or means to 'do' them; and so, having seen it once, come no more back. Edward himself came here about a fortnight ago to tea, and I told him solemnly, with a tone of friendly warning such as he well merited from me, what I thought of that scandalous delusion. He was almost at crying, but remained—as I expected him to remain. It sometimes appears to me the *darkest* fears are actually not groundless in regard to him. God deliver him! If that is not the Devil's own work, then let the Devil lay down the gun.

I know not whether you get any *Galignani's Messenger* or the like, so whether it is worth while to send you any public news. There have been *frightful* riots at Bristol, some hundreds of lives lost, all the public buildings burnt, and many private houses— quite a George Gordon affair—on occasion of Wetherell's arrival there as Recorder, whom unhappily they took that method of convincing that there was *not* 'a reaction' (in regard to Reform). Oh, the unspeakable, blundering, braying, brass-throated, leather-headed fool and fools! If they do not pass that Bill of theirs soon, the country will be a chaos, and 200 Tory lords crying out, Who shall deliver us? The Duke of Northumberland is actually *fortifying* his house here. Other riots there have been at Coventry, at Worcester, &c. Swing also is *as* busy as last winter; all London, all Britain, is organising itself into political unions. Finally, the cholera has actually arrived at Sunderland; a precious outlook! Truly the political aspects of England give even me alarms. A second edition of the French Revolution is distinctly within the range of chances; for there is nowhere any tie remaining among men. Everywhere, in court and cathedral, brazen falsehood now at length stands convicted of a lie, and famishing Ignorance cries, Away with her, away with her! God deliver us. Nay, God will deliver us; for this is His world, not the Devil's. All is perfectly quiet in London hitherto; only great apprehension, swearing-in of constables. Neither is the cholera yet dangerous. It has not spread from Sunderland, where it has now been some ten days. Should the danger grow imminent, we two have determined to fly to Puttock. Meanwhile, I cannot say that twenty choleras and twenty Revolutions ought to terrify one. The crash of the whole solar and stellar systems could only kill you once. 'I have cast away base fear from me for ever,' says Dreck, and he is seldom wholly wrong.

To Mrs. Welsh,[1] Maryland Street, Liverpool.

4 Ampton Street : Tuesday, December, 1831.

My dear Aunt,—When I returned from Enfield, where I had been for a week, I found the box containing the memorials of my heedlessness [2] awaiting me on the top of a cistern outside our staircase window ; and our landlady assured me with the utmost self-complacency that she had done all she could for it in the way of keeping it cool ! She looked rather blank when, after duly commending her care, I informed her it was probably a cloak and shawl, which she might now bring in out of the rain with all despatch. Only to the intellect of a Cockney would a deal box have suggested the exclusive idea of game.

The cloak I got dyed a more sober colour and lined and furred, so as effectually to exclude the cold, no slight conquest of Art over Nature in these days. Some people here have the impudence or ignorance to congratulate me on the agreeable change of climate I have made ; but truly, if my contentment depended mainly on weather, I should wish myself back to our own hill-top without delay. Regarded as a place merely, this noble city is simply the most detestable I ever lived in—one day a ferocious frost, the next a fog so thick you might put it in your pocket ; a Dead Sea of green-coloured filth under foot, and above an atmosphere like one of my uncle's sugar boilers. But, as the French say, *il faut se ranger ;* and so day after day I rush forth with desperate resignation, and even find a sort of sublimity in the infinite horror through which I must make my way, or die of indigestion.

If I am inclined to reflect on the *place*, however (perhaps not without a touch of national prejudice), it is certainly my bounden duty to speak well of the people. Nowhere have I found more worth, more talent, or more kindness ; and I must doubly regret the ill-health I have been suffering under, since it has so curtailed my enjoyment of all this. Nevertheless, though I dare seldom accept an invitation out, I have the pleasantest evenings at home. Scarce a night passes that some acquaintance, new or old, does not drop in at tea ; and then follow such bouts at talking ! Not of our ' Book ' (as my uncle named Carlyle) but of several books.

I have seen most of the literary people here, and, as Edward Irving said after his first interview with Wordsworth, ' I think not of them so highly as I was wont.'

[1] Wife of Mrs. Carlyle's Liverpool uncle.
[2] Things which she had left at Liverpool in passing through.

These people, who have made themselves snug little reputations, and on the strength of such hold up their heads as 'one and somewhat,' are by no means the most distinguished that I meet with either for talent or cultivation; some of them, indeed (Charles Lamb for instance), would not be tolerated in any society out of England. . . .

. . . My kindest love to my uncle and all the weans. Happy New Year and many of them; always the last the best! God bless you all!

Your affectionate

JANE W. CARLYLE.

To Miss Jean Carlyle, Scotsbrig.

4 Ampton Street: December, 1831.

My dear Jean,—You do not write to *me;* but you write, and I am content. The proverb says 'It is not lost that a friend gets;' to which I readily accede, the more readily because a letter with us is always regarded as a common good.

I do not forget you in London, as you predicted. My recollections of all I love are more vivid than at any former period. Often when I have been lying ill here among strangers, it has been my pleasantest thought that there were kind hearts at home to whom my sickness would not be a weariness; to whom I could return out of all this hubbub with affection and trust. Not that I am not kindly used here; from 'the noble lady'[1] down to the mistress of the lodging, I have everywhere found unlooked-for civility, and at least the show of kindness. With the 'noble lady,' however, I may mention my intercourse seems to be dying an easy natural death. Now that we *know* each other, the 'fine en-thu-si-asm' cannot be kept alive without more hypocrisy than one of us at least can bring to bear on it. Mrs. Montagu is an actress. I admire her to a certain extent, but friendship for such a person is out of the question.

Mrs. Austin I have now seen, and like infinitely better. She is coming to tea to-morrow night. If I 'swear everlasting friendship' with any woman here, it will be with her.

But the most interesting acquaintances we have made are the St. Simonians.[2] You may fancy how my heart beat when a card

---

[1] Mrs. Montagu.

[2] 'The St. Simonians, Detrosier, &c., were stirring and conspicuous objects in that epoch, but have now fallen all dark and silent again.—T. C., 1866.'

bearing the name of *Gustave d'Eichthal* was sent up the other day, when I happened to be alone. Our meeting was most cordial; and, as he talks good English, we contrived to carry on a pretty voluble conversation till Carlyle came home and relieved me. He (Gustave) is a creature to love at first sight—so gentle and trustful and earnest-looking, ready to do and suffer all for his faith. A friend accompanies him, whom we had here to-day along with Mill and Detrosier; a stronger, perhaps nobler MAN than Gustave, with whom Carlyle seems to be exceedingly taken. *He* (Duverrier I think they call him) is at first sight ugly : all pitted with the small-pox; but by-and-by you wonder at your first impression, his countenance is so prepossessing and commanding. We hope to see a great deal of these men before we leave London. Both seem to entertain a high respect for Carlyle—as indeed everybody I see does. Glen continues to come a great deal about us; and *blethers* more like a man growing mad than one growing wiser. Carlyle maintains in opposition to me that there is 'method in his madness,' but his idea of the quantity seems daily diminishing.

Of the Irvings we see nothing and hear little good. Carlyle dined at a literary party the other day, where he met Hogg, Lockhart, Galt, Allan Cunningham, &c.

And now God bless you, one and all of you ! My love to everyone.

Your affectionate
JANE W. CARLYLE.

CHAPTER X.

A.D. 1831.   ÆT. 36.

Extracts from Note Book.

November 2.—All the world is in apprehension about the cholera pestilence, which, indeed, seems advancing towards us with a
frightful, slow, unswerving constancy.   For myself I cannot say
that it costs me great suffering ; we are all appointed once to die.
Death is the grand sum total of it all.   Generally, now it seems to
me as if this life were but the inconsiderable portico of man's existence, which afterwards, in new mysterious environment, were to
be-continued without end.   I say, 'seems to me,' for the proof of
it were hard to state by logic ; it is the fruit of faith ; begins to
show itself with more and more decisiveness the instant you have
dared to say, 'Be it *either* way !'   But on the whole our conception of immortality depends on that of *time*, which latter is the
deepest belonging to philosophy, and the one perhaps wherein
modern philosophy has earned its best triumph.   Believe that
properly there *is* no space and no time, how many contradictions
become reconciled.

Sports are all gone from among men; there is now no holiday
either for rich or poor.   Hard toiling, then hard drinking or hard
fox-hunting.   This is not the era of sport, but of martyrdom and
persecution.   Will the new morning never dawn ?   It requires a
certain vigour of the imagination and of the social faculties before
amusement, popular sports, can exist, which vigour at this era is
all but total inanition.   Do but think of the Christmas carols and
games, the Abbots of Unreason, the Maypoles, &c. &c.   Then look
at your Manchesters on Saturdays and Sundays.

'Education' is beyond being so much as despised.   We must
praise it, when it is not *D*education, or an utter annihilation
of what it professes to foster.   The best *educated* man you will

often find to be the artisan, at all rates the man of business. For why? He has put forth his hand and operated on Nature; must actually attain some true insight, or he cannot live. The worst educated man is usually your man of fortune. He has not put forth his hand upon anything except upon his bell rope. Your scholar proper, too, your so-called man of letters, is a thing with clearer vision, through the hundredth part of an eye. A Burns is infinitely better educated than a Byron.

A common persuasion among serious ill-informed persons that the *end of the world* is at hand—Henry Drummond, Edward Irving, and all that class. So it was at the beginning of the Christian era, say rather at the *termination* of the Pagan one. Which is the most ignorant creature of his class even in Britain? Generally speaking the Cockney, the London-bred man. What does the Cockney boy know of the muffin he eats? Simply that a hawker brings it to the door and charges a penny for it. The country youth sees it grow in the fields, in the mill, in the bake-house. Thus of *all* things pertaining to the life of man.

November 4.—To it thou *Taugenichts*. Gird thyself! stir! struggle! forward! forward! thou art bundled up here and tied as in a sack. On, then, as in a sack race, 'Running, not raging.' *Gott sey mir gnädig.*

November 12.—Have been two days as good as idle—hampered, disturbed, quite out of sorts, as it were quite stranded; no tackle left, no tools but my ten fingers, nothing but accidental drift-wood to build even a raft of. 'This is no my ain house.' Art thou aware that no man and no thing, but simply thy own self, can permanently keep this down? Act on that conviction.

How sad and stern is all life to me! Homeless! homeless! would my *task* were *done.* I think I should not care to die; in real earnestness should care very little; this earthly sun has shown me only roads full of mire and thorns. Why cannot I be a kind of artist? Politics are angry, agitating. What have I to do with it? will any Parliamentary Reform ever reform *me?*

This I begin to see, that evil and good are everywhere, like shadow and substance; inseparable (for men), yet not hostile, only opposed. There is considerable significance in this fact, perhaps the *new* moral principle of our era. (How?) It was familiar to Goethe's mind.

November 17.—The nobleness of silence. The highest melody dwells only in silence (the sphere melody, the melody of health); the eye cannot see shadow, cannot see light, but only the two combined. General law of being. Think farther of this.

As it is but a small portion of our thinking that we can articulate into thoughts, so again it is but a small portion, properly only the outer surface of our morality, that we can shape into action, or into express rules of action. Remark farther that it is but the correct coherent shaping of this outward surface, or the incorrect, incoherent, monstrous shaping of it, and no wise the moral force which shaped it, which lies under it, vague, indefinite, unseen, that constitutes what in common speech we call a moral conduct or an immoral. Hence, too, the necessity of tolerance, of insight, in judging of men. For the correctness of that same outer surface may be out of all proportion to the inward depth and quantity; nay, often enough they are in inverse proportion; only in some highly favoured individuals can the great endowment utter itself without irregularity. Thus in great men, with whom inward and as it were latent morality must ever be the root and beginning of greatness, how often do we find a conduct defaced by many a moral impropriety, and have to love them with sorrow? Thus, too, poor Burns must record that almost the only noble-minded men he had ever met with were among the class named Blackguards.

Extremes meet. Perfect morality were no more an object of consciousness than perfect immorality, as pure light cannot any more be seen than pure darkness. The healthy moral nature loves virtue, the unhealthy at best makes love to it.

December 23.—Finished the 'Characteristics' about a week ago; baddish, with a certain beginning of deeper insight in it.

January 13, 1832.—Plenty of magazine editors applying to me, indeed sometimes pestering me. Do not like to break with any, yet must not close with any. Strange state of literature, periodical and other! A man must just lay out his manufacture in one of those old clothes shops and see whether any one will buy it. The *Editor* has little to do with the matter except as commercial broker; he sells it and pays you for it.

Lytton Bulwer has not yet come into sight of me. Is there aught more in him than a dandiacal philosophist? Fear not. Of the infatuated Fraser, with his dog's meat tart of a magazine, what? His pay is certain, and he means honestly, but he is a goose. It was he that sent me Croker's Boswell; am I bound to offer him the (future) article? or were this the rule in such cases; write thy best and the truth. Then publish it where thou canst best. An indubitable rule, but is it rule enough?

Last Friday saw my name in large letters at the 'Athenæum' office in Catherine Street, Strand; hurried on with downcast eyes as if I had seen myself in the pillory. Dilke (to whom I had entrusted Dreck to read it, and see if he could help me with it) asked me for a scrap of writing with my *name.* I could not quite clearly see my way through the business, for he had twice or thrice been civil to me, and I did reckon his 'Athenæum' to be the bad best of literary syllabubs, and thought I might harmlessly say so much; gave him *Faust's curse,* which hung printed there. Inclined now to believe that I did wrong; at least imprudently. Why yield even half a hair's breadth to puffing? Abhor it, utterly divorce it, and kick it to the Devil.

Singular how little wisdom or light of any kind I have met with in London. Do not find a single creature that has communicated an idea to me; at best one or two that can understand an idea. Yet the sight of London works on me strongly. I have not perhaps lost my journey hither.

Hayward of the Temple, a small but active and vivacious 'man of the time,' by a strange impetus takes to me; the first time, they say, he ever did such a thing, being one that lives in a chiar'-oscuro element of which good-humoured contempt is the basis. Dined in his rooms (over Dunning's) with a set of Oxonian Templars, stupid (in part), limited (wholly), conceited. A dirty evening; I at last sunk utterly silent. None of the great personages of letters have come in my way here, and except as sights they are of little moment to me. Jeffrey says he 'praised me to Rogers,' who, &c. &c. It sometimes rather surprises me that his lordship does not think it would be kind to show me the faces of those people. Something discourages or hinders him; what it is I know not, and indeed care not. The Austins, at least the (Lady) Austin, I like; *eine verständige herzhafte Frau.* Empson, a diluted, good-natured, languid *Anempfinder.* The strongest young man, one Macaulay (now in Parliament, as I from the first predicted), an emphatic, hottish, really forcible person, but unhappily without divine idea. Rogers (an elegant, politely malignant old lady, I think) is in town and probably I might see him. Moore is I know not where, a lascivious triviality of great name. Bentham is said to have become a driveller and garrulous old man. Perhaps I will try for a look of him. I have much to see and many things to wind up in London before we leave it.

I went one day searching for Johnson's place of *abode.* Found with difficulty the house in Gough (Goff) Square, where the Dictionary was composed. The landlord, whom Glen and I incidentally inquired of, was just scraping his feet at the door, invited us to walk in, showed us the garret rooms, &c. (of which he seemed to have the obscurest traditions, taking Johnson for a schoolmaster), interested us much; but at length (dog of a fellow) began to hint that he had all these rooms to let as lodgings.

Biography is the only history. Political history as now written and hitherto, with its kings and changes of *tax-gatherers*, is little (very little) more than a mockery of our want. This I see more and *more.*

The world grows to me even more as a magic picture—a true supernatural revelation, infinitely stern, but also infinitely grand. Shall I ever succeed in copying a little therefrom.

January 18.—Came upon Shepherd, the Unitarian parson of Liverpool, yesterday for the first time at Mrs. Austin's. A very large, purfly, flabby man; massive head with long thin grey hair; eyes *both* squinting, both overlapped at the corners by a little roof of a brow, giving him (with his ill-shut mouth) a kind of lazy, good-humoured aspect. For the rest, a Unitarian Radical, clear, steadfast, but every way limited. One rather trivial-looking young lady, and another excessively ill-looking, sat opposite to him, seeming to belong to him. He said Jeffrey did not strike him as 'a very taking man.' Lancashire accent, or some provincial one. Have long known the Unitarians *intus et in cute*, and never got any *good of them*, or any ill.

January 21.—Yesterday sat scribbling some stuff close on the borders of nonsense, about biography as a kind of introduction to 'Johnson.' How is it to be? I see not well; know only that it should be light, and written (by way of experiment) *currente calamo*. I am sickly, not dispirited, yet sad, as is my wont. When did I laugh last? Alas! 'light laughter like heavy money has altogether fled from us.' The reason is, we have *no communion;* company enough, but no fellowship. Time brings roses. Meanwhile, the grand perennial *Communion of Saints* is ever open to us. Enter and worthily comport thyself there.

Nothing in this world is to me more mournful, distressing, and in the end intolerable, than mirth not based on earnestness (for it is false mirth), than wit pretending to be wit, and yet not based on wisdom. Two objects would reduce me to gravity had I the spirits of a Merry Andrew—a death's head and a modern London wit. The besom of destruction should be swept over these people, or else perpetual silence (except when they needed victuals or the like) imposed on them.

In the afternoon Jeffrey, as he is often wont, called in on us; very lively, quick, and light. Chatted about cholera, a subject far more interesting to him than it is to us. Walked with him to Regent Street in hurried assiduous talk. O'Connell I called a real specimen of the almost obsolete species *demagogue*. Why should it be obsolete, this being the very scene for it? Chiefly because we are all dilettantes, and have no heart of faith, even for the coarsest of beliefs. His 'cunning' the sign, as cunning ever is, of a *weak* intellect or a weak character.

Soon after my return home Arthur Buller called with a *mein bester Freund!* A goodish youth, affectionate, at least attached; not so handsome as I had expected, though more so than enough. He walked with me to Fraser's dinner in Regent Street, or rather to the door of Fraser's house, and then took leave, with stipulation of speedy re-meeting. Enter through Fraser's bookshop into a back-room, where sit Allan Cunningham, W. Fraser (the only two known to me personally), James Hogg (in the easy chair of honour), Galt, and one or two nameless persons, patiently waiting for dinner. Lockhart (whom I did not know) requests to be introduced to me—a precise, brief, active person of considerable faculty, which, however, had shaped itself *gigmanically* only. Fond of quizzing, yet not *very* maliciously. Has a broad black brow, indicating force and penetration, but a lower half of face diminishing into the character at best of distinctness, almost of triviality. Rather liked the man, and shall like to meet him again. Galt looks old, is deafish, has the air of a sedate Greenock burgher; mouth indicating sly humour and self-satisfaction; the eyes, old and without lashes, gave me a sort of *wae* interest for him. He wears spectacles, and is hard of hearing; a very large man, and eats and drinks with a certain west country gusto and research. Said little, but that little peaceable, clear, and *gutmüthig*. Wish to see him also again. Hogg is a little red-skinned stiff sack of a body, with quite the common air of an Ettrick shepherd, except that he has a highish though sloping brow (among his yellow grizzled hair), and two clear little beads of blue or grey eyes that sparkle, if not with thought, yet with animation. Behaves himself quite easily and well; speaks Scotch, and mostly narrative absurdity (or even obscenity) therewith. Appears in the mingled character of zany and raree show. All bent on bantering him, especially Lockhart; Hogg walking through it as if unconscious, or almost flattered. His vanity seems to be immense, but also his good-nature. I felt interest for the poor 'herd body,' wondered to see him blown hither from his sheepfolds, and how, quite friendless as he was, he went along cheerful, mirthful, and musical. I do not well understand the man; his significance is perhaps considerable. His poetic talent is authentic, yet his intellect seems of the weakest; his morality also limits itself to the precept 'be not angry.' Is the charm of this poor man chiefly to be found herein, that he *is* a real product of nature, and able to speak naturally, which not one in a thousand is? An 'unconscious talent,' though of the smallest, emphatically *naïve*. Once or twice in singing (for he sung of his own) there was an emphasis in poor Hogg's look—expression of feeling, almost of enthusiasm. The man is a very curious *specimen*. Alas! he is a *man;* yet how few will so much as treat him like a *specimen*, and not like a mere wooden *Punch* or *Judy!* For the rest, our talk was utterly despicable: stupidity, insipidity, even not a little obscenity (in which all save Galt, Fraser, and myself seemed to join) was the only outcome of the night. Literary *men!* They are not worthy to be valets of such. Was a thing said that did not even solicit in mercy to be forgotton? Not so much as the attempt or wish to speak profitably. *Trivialitas trivialitatum, omnia trivialitas!* I went to see, and I saw; and have now said, and mean to be silent, or try if I can speak elsewhere.

Charles Buller entertained as unfavourable an opinion of London magazine writers as Carlyle himself. Mrs.

Strachey's alarm about Buller's theories of life may be corrected by a letter from himself. The Bullers were at this time at Looe, in Cornwall. They came to town in October.

To Thomas Carlyle.

Looe : September 12, 1831.

My dear Friend,—I am very happy to hear from Mrs. Austin that you had called on her, because I was really anxious that you should know so admirable a specimen of the disciples of Bentham and be known to her. But I felt half afraid to introduce you because I did not know how you would get on with—not herself, because she being a Benthamite has taken on herself human form and nature, and is a most delightful specimen of the union of Benthamite opinions and human feelings—but with the more regular Radicals who render the approach to her house dangerous. Conceive how great was my pleasure at learning from her that you had called on her ; that you had come for the purpose of making acquaintance with John Mill ; and that you had met him to your mutual delight. I knew well that to make you esteem one another, nothing was wanting but that you should understand each other. But I did not do sufficient justice to the Catholicism of both of you to feel quite confident that this would be the certain effect of your meeting. In this world of sects people rarely talk to each other for any purpose but to find out the sectarian names which they may fasten on each other ; and if the name but differs, they only spend their time in finding out the various ramifications of each other's dissensions. In names and professed doctrines you and John Mill differ as widely as the poles ; but you may well meet on that point where all clear spirits find each other, the love of truth, which all must attain in their road to truth. To you without any fear I point out John Mill as a true Utilitarian, and as one who does honour to his creed and to his fellow believers ; because it is a creed that in him is without sectarian narrowness or unkindness, because it has not impaired his philosophy or his relish for the beautiful, or repressed any one of those good honest feelings which God gave all men before Bentham made them Utilitarians.

I am delighted at the certain prospect which you hold out to me of seeing you, and of making the acquaintance of Mrs. Carlyle. I shall be delighted to talk once more of old times, and of those which are coming, to tell of what we used to do and think together, and of all that we have done and learned and planned since we have wandered many a weary foot from one another. Thus I shall learn from you what are the outlines of the great work which you are now committing to the judgment of a thoughtless age ; and what manner of life you have been leading in the North, and what kind of one you propose now. I, in my turn, will tell you of some little time well employed, and of much misspent ; of various studies, and creeds, and theories, of many great designs, and of a very small portion of successful fulfilment thereof. I will tell you of my assiduous study of the law, of how the worthy burghers of Liskeard have come to me and offered me a seat for this borough whenever the Reform Bill shall be passed, and of all that I propose to do when I become the most eminent of lawyers and the most furious of demagogues. These matters I promise myself to talk over with you in the city of smoke and season of fog, where I trust I shall meet you in exactly a month.

I rejoice that you think so highly of John Mill. I have just heard from him, and I am happy that he understands and esteems you, as you do him. This is as it should be. I do not see how it matters to one right-minded man in what course the opinions of another fly as long as both spring from the same sacred well of love of truth. I do not believe that you really differ very much in opinion ; sure I am that you will find none of any set of men more deserving to think rightly than John Mill, who thinks deeply and honestly always. He is very different from the herd of creatures whom you have been pestered with in that great mart of conceited folly, where the hawkers of every kind of shallowness and quackery vend their wares in such numbers and with such clamour. This age is the millennium of fools. They have certainly by some means or another obtained a mastery over better men. I do believe that in this land of ours there still exists the good old spirit of industry, and thoughtfulness, and honesty which used to animate our fathers. Yet in literature we are represented by our magazine writers and reviewers (*verbo sit venia*), and annals, and fashionable novels, and fashionable metaphysics and philosophy : and our concerns are managed by the creatures whom you heard gabbling in the House of Commons with a gravity and an ignorance which are not. found combined even in the servants' hall.

I do believe with you that the end of this world of Insipids is

coming. We must kick away the distaff of Omphale and get up
and bestir ourselves to rid the world of monsters. Whether we
shall labour to good purpose, or only show our strength as Her-
cules did in tearing ourselves to pieces, it is not yet given us to
know ; but whenever there is a day of awakening, I trust that all
good men and true will unite against the fools, and take at least
30,000 of them into the valley of salt and slay them.

All other matters I reserve for our meeting, which will certainly
take place before long unless the cholera or such like curse severs
us, or unless the Reform Bill is thrown out, in which case I shall
assuredly remain here with any two or three who may be found to
fight against the 'Rotten-hearted Lords.' But there will be more
than that ; almost as many as there are men.

Adieu ! with my father's and mother's and Arthur's best regards.

Yours sincerely,

CHARLES BULLER.

CHAPTER XI.

A.D. 1832. ÆT. 37.

A GREAT catastrophe was now impending in Carlyle's life. His father had been ailing for more than two years, sometimes recovering a little, then relapsing again; and after each oscillation he had visibly sunk to a lower level. The family anticipated no immediate danger, but he had himself been steadily contemplating the end as fast approaching him, as appears plainly from a small feeble note which had been written on the 21st of September of this year, and remains fastened into his son's note-book, where it is endorsed as ' My father's last letter—perhaps the last thing he ever wrote.'

My dear Son,—I cannot write you a letter, but just tell you that I am a frail old sinner that is very likely never to see you any more in this world. Be that as it may, I could not help telling you that I feel myself gradually drawing towards the hour appointed for all living. And, O God! may that awful change be much at heart with every one of us. May we be daily dying to sin and living to righteousness. And may the God of Jacob be with you and bless you, and keep you in his ways and fear. I add no more, but leave you in his hands and care.

JAMES CARLYLE.

The old man at parting with his son in the summer gave him some money out of a drawer with the peculiar manner which the Scotch call *fey*—the sign of death when a man does something which is unlike himself. Carlyle paid no particular attention to it, however, till the meaning of the unusual action was afterwards made intelligible to him. The reports from Scotsbrig in the autumn and early winter had been more favourable than usual. On the 13th of December Carlyle sent him, evidently without any great misgiving, the last letter which he on his side ever wrote to his father.

My dear Father,—I have long proposed to myself the pleasure of writing you a letter, and must now do it much more hurriedly than I could have wished. I did not mean to undertake it till next week, for at present I am engaged every moment *against time*, finishing an article for the 'Edinburgh Review,' and can expect no respite till after Saturday night. However, our Lord Advocate having called to-day and furnished me with a frank, I embrace the opportunity lest none so good occur afterwards.

Alick informed me in general about ten days ago that you were 'all well.' In the last newspaper[1] stood a word from Jean that she 'would write soon.' I can only pray that she would do so, and hope in the meantime that she may have no worse news to tell me. This weather is very unhealthy—the worst of the whole year; I often think how my mother and you are getting on under it. I hope at least you will take every care, and do not needlessly or needfully expose yourself; it is bad policy to brave the weather, especially for you at this season. I pray you keep much within doors; beware of cold, especially of damp feet. A cup of tea night and morning I should also think a good preventive. But perhaps Jean will be able to inform me that 'all is well;' one of the blessings I ought to be most thankful for, as it is among the most precious for me.

We are struggling forward here as well as we can. My health is not worse than it was wont to be. I think I am even clearer and fresher than when you saw me last. Jane has been complaining somewhat, but is not regularly *sick*. Her cold has left her, and now she has a little occasional cough with weakliness, the like of which is very prevalent here at present. George Irving has been attempting to prescribe for her; she even let him draw a little blood. I rather think, however, that her faith in physicians is somewhat on a level with my own; that she will give them no more of her blood, but trust to exercise, diet, and the return of settled weather.

[1] The family still communicated with one another by hieroglyphics on the newspapers.

I cannot get on with the publishing of my book. Nobody will so much as look at a thing of the sort till this Reform business be done. Nay, I begin to doubt whether I shall at all during the present posture of affairs get my speculation put into print. There is only a limited time that I will consent to wait looking after it. If they *do not* want it, why then let them leave it alone. Either way will do for me; I only want to know which. Meanwhile I am making what little attempts about it seem prudent. If I altogether fail here, I may still have Edinburgh to try in. One way or another, I wish to be at the end of it, and will be so. Our Advocate, who is now quite recovered again and as brisk as a bee, would fain do something useful for me—find me some place or other that would keep me here. I know he has spoken of me to Chancellors and Secretaries of State, and would take all manner of pains; nevertheless I compute simply that the result of it all will be—Nothing; and I still look back to my whinstone fortress among the mountains as the stronghold wherefrom I am to defy the world. I have applications enough for writing, some of them new since I came hither. So long as I can wag the pen there is no fear of me. I also incline to think that something might and perhaps should be done by such as me in the way of lecturing; but not at this time—not under these circumstances. We will wait, and if it seems good try it again. On the whole I always return to this. As the great Guide orders, so be it! While I can say *His will be mine*, there is no power in earth or out of it that can put me to fear.

I could describe our way of life here, which is very simple, had I room. Plenty of people come about us; we go out little to anything like parties, never to dinners; or anywhere willingly except for *profit*. I transact sometimes immense quantities of *talk*—indeed, often talk more than I listen; which course I think of altering. It is and continues a wild wondrous chaotic den of discord, this London. I am often *wae* and awestruck at once to wander along its crowded streets, and see and hear the roaring torrent of men and animals and carriages and waggons, all rushing they know not whence, they know not whither! Nevertheless there *is* a deep divine meaning in it, and God is in the midst of it, had we but eyes to see. Towards two o'clock I am about laying down my pen, to walk till as near dinner (at four) as I like; then comes usually resting stretched on a sofa, with such small talk as may be going till tea; after which, unless some interloper drop in (as happens fully oftener than not), I again open my desk and work till bedtime—about eleven. I have had a tough struggle indeed with this paper; but my hand is now *in* again, and I am doing better. Charles Buller comes now and then about us; a fine honest fellow, among the best we see. There is also one Glen (a young *unhewed* philosopher, a friend of Jack's), and one Mill, a young *hewed* philosopher and partial disciple of mine: both great favourites here. W. Graham, of Barnswark, was in our neighbourhood for three weeks, and will be arriving in Glasgow again about this very night, unless he have struck in by Ecclefechan and home. He is busy with some American patents, and so forth; from which he is sure of a salary for one year, but I think scarcely of anything more. The American Consulship, of which he hoped much, has gone another road. He is fresh and healthy, and I hope will fall in with something. Irving does not come much here; only once since that gift of tongues work began, and we have not been even once with *him*. It was last week that he called. He looked hollow and haggard; thin, grey-whiskered, almost an old man; yet he was composed and affectionate and patient. I could almost have wept over him, and did tell him my mind with all plainness. It seems likely they will take his church from him, and then difficulties of all sorts may multiply on him; but I do not think he will altogether lose his wits—at least not so as to land in Bedlam; and perhaps he may yet see his way through all this, and leave it all behind him. God grant it be so. I have hardly another scrap of room here. I must scrawl my mother a line, and then bid you all good night.

I remain always, my dear Father,

Your affectionate Son,

T. CARLYLE.

John Carlyle was now with Lady Clare at Rome. To him, busy as he was, his brother continued to write with anxious fulness. John Carlyle, with considerable talent, had shown an instability of purpose, for which he received, if he did not require, a steadily sustained stream of admonition.

It was very gratifying to us (Carlyle wrote on the 20th of December) to learn that all went tolerably with you, both as person and as doctor; continue to wish honestly with your whole heart to act rightly, and you will not go far wrong: no other advice is needed, or can be given. I have never despaired, and now I feel more and more certain, of one day seeing you *a man ;* this too in a time like ours when such a result is of all others the hardest to realize. One has to learn the hard lesson of *martyrdom,* and that he has arrived in this earth, not to *receive,* but to *give.* Let him be ready then 'to spend and be spent' for God's cause ; let him, as he needs must, 'set his face like a flint' against all dishonesty and indolence and puffery and quackery and malice and delusion, whereof earth is full, and once for all flatly refuse to do the Devil's work in this which is God's earth, let the issue be simply what it may. 'I must live, Sir,' say many ; to which I answer, 'No, Sir, you need not live ; if your body cannot be kept together without selling your soul, then let the body fall asunder, and the soul be unsold.' In brief, Jack, defy the Devil in all his figures, and spit upon him ; he cannot hurt you.

The good old mother at Scotsbrig was fluttered about her scattered children.

Our mother (wrote one of the sisters) has been healthier than usual this winter, but terribly hadden down wi' anxiety. She told me the other day the first gaet she gaed every morning was to London, then to Italy, then to Craigenputtock,[1] and then to Mary's, and finally began to think them at hame were, maybe, no safer than the rest. When I asked her what she wished me to say to you, she said she had a thousand things to say if she had you here ; 'and thou may tell them, I'm very little fra' them.' You are to pray for us all daily, while separated from one another, that our ways be in God's keeping. You are also to tell the Doctor, when you write, with her love, that he is to read his Bible carefully, and not to forget that God sees him in whatever land he may be.

This message Carlyle duly sent on, and with it the continued diary of his own doings.

To John Carlyle.

I have had such a bout as never man had in finishing a kind of paper for Macvey.[2] I called the thing 'Characteristics,' and despatched it, according to engagement, by the Saturday mail coach.

[1] Where Alexander Carlyle was still staying, without the farm ; having found no other in its place.

[2] Napier, for the *Edinburgh.*

Whether Napier will have it or not is uncertain to me ; but no matter, or only a secondary one, for the thing has some truth in it, and could find vent elsewhere. It is Teufelsdröckh, and preaches from this text : 'The healthy know not of their health, but only the sick.' As to Teufelsdröckh himself, hope has not yet risen for him ; nay, rather, certainly begins to show itself that he has no hope. Glen read the MS. 'with infinite satisfaction ;' John Mill with fears that ' the world would take some time to see what meaning was in it.' 'Perhaps all eternity,' I answered. For the rest we have partially made up our minds here and see the course we have to follow. Preferment there is none to be looked for ; living here by literature is either serving the Devil, or fighting against him at fearful odds ; in lecturing it is also quite clear there could no profitable audience be had as yet, where every lecturer is by nature a quack and tinkling cymbal. So what will remain but to thank God that our whinstone castle is still standing among the mountains ; and return thither to work there, till we can make a new sally. God be thanked, neither my wife nor I am capable of being staggered by any future that the world can proffer. 'From the bosom of eternity shine for us radiant guiding stars.' Nay, our task is essentially high and glorious and happy ; God only give us strength to do it well ! Meanwhile, offers in the literary periodical way come thick enough. Three or four weeks ago Procter wrote to me that E. L. Bulwer had 'some disposition' to employ me in the 'New Monthly Magazine,' of which he is editor, and that it would be advisable for me to call on him ; to which proposal of course there could be no answer, except mild silence—*der Inbegriff aller Harmonieen.* Whereupon in ten days more the mystagogue of the dandiacal body wrote to me a most bland and euphuistically flattering note, soliciting an interview as my ' admirer.' I answered that for some days I was too busy to call, but would when I had leisure, as I yesterday did ; and found him from home. I have also looked into his magazine, and find it polished, sharp, and barren—yet not *al*together—the work as of gig-men, or rather gig-*boys* and whig-boys aiming blindly enough towards something higher: *Ahndungen einer bessern Zeit !* My business being to *see* all men, I will in time look towards the ' Inspired Penman ' once more and ascertain better what his relation to me really is. I have articles in my head, but if Naso (Napier) behave himself he shall have the pick of them.

Napier unexpectedly and even gratefully accepted ' Characteristics.' He confessed that he could not understand it ; but everything which Carlyle wrote, he said, had the indisputable stamp of genius upon it, and was therefore most welcome to the ' Edinburgh Review.' Lytton Bulwer pressed for an article on Frederick the Great ; Hayward was anxious that a final article should be written on Goethe, to punish Wilson for his outrages against the great German in the ' Noctes Ambrosianæ.' Hayward, too, had done Carlyle a still more seasonable service, for he had induced Dr. Lardner to promise to take Carlyle's ' History of German Literature ' for the ' Cabinet Encyclopædia.' The articles on the subject which had already appeared were to form part of it ; some new matter was to be added to round off the story ; and the whole was to be bound up into a *Zur Geschichte*, for which Carlyle was to receive 300*l.* To Hayward then and always he was heartily grateful for this piece of service, though eventually, as will be seen, it came to nothing. These brightening prospects were saddened by the deaths of various eminent persons whom he held in honour. Dr. Becker died of cholera at Berlin, then Hegel· from cholera also ; and still worse, his old friend Mr. Strachey, whom he had met lately in full health, was seized with inflammation of the lungs, and was carried off in a few days.

Worst of all—the worst because entirely unlooked for —came fatal news from Scotsbrig, contained in a sternly tender characteristic note from his sister Jean.

To Thomas Carlyle.

Scotsbrig : January 22, 1832.

My dear Brother,—It is now my painful duty to inform you that our dear father took what we thought was a severe cold last Monday night ; he had great difficulty in breathing, but was always able to sit up most of the day, and sometimes to walk about. Last night he was in the kitchen about six o'clock, but he was evidently turning very fast worse in breathing. He got only one right night's sleep since he turned ill, and had been sometimes insensible, but when one spoke to him he generally recollected himself. But last night he fell into a sort of stupor about ten o'clock, still breathing higher and with greater difficulty. He spoke little to any of us. Seemingly unconscious of what he did, he came over the bedside, and offered up a prayer to Heaven in such accents as it is impossible to forget. He departed almost without a struggle this morning at half-past six. The funeral is to be on Friday ; but my mother says she cannot expect you to be here. However, you must write to her directly. She needs consolation, though she is not unreasonable ; but it was very unexpected. The Doctor durst do nothing. Oh, my dear brother, how often have we written ' all well ! ' I cannot write more at present.

Your affectionate Sister,
JEAN CARLYLE.

Subjoined were these few words :—

It is God that has done it ; be still my dear children.

Your affectionate Mother.

The common theme
Is death of fathers ; reason still hath cried,
From the first corse till he that died to-day,
This must be so ;

yet being so common, it was still 'particular' to Carlyle. The entire family were knit together with an extremely peculiar bond. Their affections, if not limited within their own circle, yet were reserved for one another in their tenderest form. Friendship the Carlyles might have for others ; their love was for those of their own household ; while again, independently of his feeling as a son, Carlyle saw, or believed he saw, in his father personal qualities of the rarest and loftiest kind. Though the old man had no sense of poetry, Carlyle deliberately says that if he had been asked whether his father or Robert Burns had the finest intellect, he could not have answered. Carlyle's style, which has been so much wondered at, was learnt in the Annandale farmhouse; and beyond the intellect there was an inflexible integrity, in word and deed, which Carlyle honoured above all human qualities. The aspect in which he regarded human life, the unalterable conviction that justice and truth are the only bases on which successful conduct, either private or public, can be safely rested, he had derived from his father, and it was the root of all that was great in himself.

Being unable to be present at the funeral, he spent the intervening days in composing the memoir which has been published as the first of his ' Reminiscences.' He was now himself the head of the family, and on him also fell the duty of addressing the remaining members of it on the loss which had befallen them.

As the subject is ' common,' so all that can be said upon it—the sorrows, the consolations, and the hopes—are common also. The greatest genius that ever was born could have nothing new to say about death. Carlyle could but travel along the well-worn road; yet what he wrote is still beautiful, still characteristic, though the subject of it is hackneyed.

London : January 26, 1832.

My dear Mother,—I was downstairs this morning when I heard the postman's knock, and thought it might be a letter from Scotsbrig. Hastening up, I found Jane with the letter open and in tears. The next moment gave me the stern tidings. I had written you yesterday a light hopeful letter, which I could now wish you might not read in these days of darkness. Probably you will receive it just along with this; the first red seal so soon to be again exchanged for a black one. I had a certain misgiving, not seeing Jane's customary ' all well;' and I thought, but did not write (for I strive usually to banish vague fears), ' the pitcher goes often to the well, but it is broken at last.' I did not know that this very evil had actually overtaken us.

As yet I am in no condition to write much. The stroke, all unexpected though not undreaded, as yet painfully crushes my heart together. I have yet hardly had a little relief from tears. And yet it will be a solace to me to speak out with you, to repeat along with you that great saying which, could we lay it rightly to heart, includes all that man can say, 'It is God that has done it.' God supports us all. Yes, my dear mother, it is God has done it ; and our part is reverent submission to His will, and trustful prayers to Him for strength to bear us through every trial.

I could have wished, or I had too confidently hoped, that God had ordered it otherwise ; but what are our wishes and wills ? I trusted that I might have had other glad meetings and pleasant communings with my honoured and honourworthy father in this world, but it was not so appointed. We shall meet no more till we meet in that *other* sphere where God's Presence more immediately is ; the nature of which we know not, only we know that it is God's appointing, and therefore altogether *good.* Nay, already, had we but faith, our father is not parted from *us,* but only withdrawn from our bodily eyes. The dead and the living, as I often repeat to myself, are alike with God. He, fearful and wonderful, yet good and infinitely gracious, encircles alike both them that we see and them that we cannot see. Whoso trusteth in Him has obtained the victory over death ; the King of Terrors is no longer terrible.

Yes, my dear mother, and brothers and sisters, let us see also how mercy has been mingled with our calamity. Death was for a long time ever present to our father's thought ; daily and hourly he seemed meditating on his latter end. The end, too, appears to have been mild as it was speedy ; he parted as gently as most do from this vale of tears ; and, oh ! in his final agony he was enabled to call with his strong voice and strong heart on the God that had made him to have mercy on him ! Which prayer, doubt not one of you, the All-merciful *heard,* and, in such wise as infinite mercy might, gave answer to. And what is the death of one near to us, as I have often thought, but the setting out on a journey an hour before us, which journey we have all to travel ? What is the longest earthly life to the eternity, the endless, the beginningless which encircles it ? The oldest man and the new-born babe are but divided from each other by a single hair's breadth. For myself, I have long continually meditated on death till by God's grace it has grown transparent for me, and holy and great rather than terrific ; till I see that death, what mortals call death, is properly the beginning of life. One other comfort we have to take the bitterness out of our tears—this greatest of all comforts, and properly the only one : that our father was not called away till he had done his work, and done it faithfully. Yes, we can with a holy pride look at our father there where he lies low, and say that his task was well and manfully performed ; the strength that God had given him he put forth in the ways of honesty and well-doing ; no eye will ever see a hollow, deceitful work that *he* did ; the world wants one true man since he was taken away. When we consider his life, through what hardships and obstructions he struggled, and what he became and what he did, there is room for gratitude that God so bore him on. Oh, what were it now to us that he had been a king? now, when the question is not, What *wages* hadst thou for thy work ? but, How was thy work done ?

My dear brothers and sisters, sorrow not, I entreat you—sorrow is profitless and sinful ; but meditate deeply every one of you on this : none of us but started in life with *far* greater advantages than our dear father had ; we will not weep for him, but we will go and do as he has done. Could I write my books as he built his houses, and walk my way so manfully through this shadow world, and leave it with so little blame, it were more than all my hopes. Neither are you, my beloved mother, to let your heart be heavy. Faithfully you toiled by his side, bearing and forbearing as you both could. All that was sinful and of the earth has passed away ; all that was true and holy remains for ever, and the parted shall meet together again with God. *Amen ! so be it !* We, your children, whom you have faithfully cared for, soul and body, and brought up in the nurture and admonition of the Lord, we gather round you in this solemn hour, and say, Be of comfort ! well done, hitherto ; persevere and it shall be well ! We promise here, before God, and the awful yet merciful work of God's hand, that we will continue to love and honour you, as sinful children can. And now, do you pray for us all, and let us all pray in such language as we have for one another, so shall this sore division and parting be the means of a closer union. Let us and everyone know that though this world is full of briars, and we are wounded at every step as we go, and one by one must take farewell and weep bitterly, yet ' there remaineth a *rest* for the people of God.' Yes, for the people of God there remaineth a rest, that rest which in this world they could nowhere find.

And now again I say, do not grieve any one of you beyond what nature forces and you cannot help. Pray to God, if any of you have a voice and utterance; all of you pray always, in secret and silence—if faithful, ye shall be heard openly. I cannot be with you to speak, but read in the Scriptures as I would have done. Read, I especially ask, in Matthew's Gospel, that passion, and death, and farewell blessing and command of Jesus of Nazareth; and see if you can understand and feel what is the ' divine depth of sorrow,' and how even by suffering and sin man is lifted up to God, and in great darkness there shines a light. If you cannot read it aloud in common, then do each of you take his Bible in private and read it for himself. Our business is not to lament, but to improve the lamentable, and make it also peaceably work together for greater good.

I could have wished much to lay my honoured father's head in the grave; yet it could have done no one good save myself only, and I shall not ask for it. Indeed, when I remember, that right would have belonged to John of Cockermouth, to whom I offer in all heartiness my brotherly love. I will be with you in spirit if not in person. I have given orders that *no one* is to be admitted here till after the funeral on Friday. I mean to spend these hours in solemn meditation and self-examination, and thoughts of the Eternal; such seasons of grief are sent us even for that end. God knocks at our heart: the question (is), will we open or not? I shall think every night of the candle burning in that sheeted room, where our dear sister also lately lay. Oh God, be gracious to us, and bring us all one day together in himself! After Friday I return, as you too must, to my worldly work; for that, also, is work appointed us by the heavenly taskmaster. I will write to John to-night or to-morrow. Let me hear from you again as soon as you have composure. I shall hasten all the more homewards for this. For the present, I bid God ever bless you all! Pray for me, my dear mother, and let us all seek consolation *there*.

I am ever, your affectionate,

T. CARLYLE.

The promised letter to his brother was written, and lies before me; but a few sentences only need be extracted from what is essentially a repetition of the last.

Our father's end was happy; he had lived to do all his work, and he did it manfully. His departure, too, was soft and speedy; that last strong cry of his in the death-struggle to God for deliverance, that is one of the things we must remember for ever. Was it not the fit end of a life so true and brave? For a true and brave man, such as there are too few left, I must name my father. If we think what an element he began in, how he with modest unwearied endeavour turned all things to the best, and what a little world of good he had created for himself, we may call his life an honourable, a noble one. In some respects there is perhaps no man like him left. Jane and I were just remarking two days ago that we did not know any man whose spiritual faculties had such a stamp of natural strength. Alas! we knew not that already he was hidden from our eyes. I call such a man, bred up in poor Annandale, with nothing but what the chances of poor Annandale gave him, the true preacher of a gospel of freedom—of what men can do and be. Let his memory be for ever holy to us: let us each in his several sphere go and do likewise.

For myself, death is the most familiar of all thoughts to me—my daily and hourly companion. Death no longer seems terrible; and though the saddest remembrances rise round you, and natural grief will have its course, we can say with our heroic mother: 'It is God that has done it.' Death properly is but a hiding from *us*, from our fleshly organs. The departed are still with us; are not both they and we in the hand of God? A little while and we shall all meet; nay, perhaps see one another again! As God will! He is great; He is also good. There we must leave it, weep and murmur as we will.

I feel, my dear brother, how this stroke must pain you. Speak of it as we may, death is a stern event; yet also a great and sacred one. How holy are the dead! They do rest from their labours, and their works follow them. A whole section of the past seems departed with my father—shut out from me by an impassable barrier. He could tell me about old things, and was wont most graphically to do so when I went to Scotsbrig. Now he will do so no more: it is past, past! The force that dwelt in him had expended itself; he is lost from our eyes in that ocean of time wherein our little islet of existence hangs suspended, ever crumbling in, ever anew bodying itself forth. Fearful and wonderful! Yet let us know that under time lies eternity; if we appear and are (while here) in time and through time, which means change, mortality, we also stand rooted in eternity, where there is no change, no mortality. Be of comfort, then; be of courage! 'The fair flowers of our garland,' said Novalis, 'are dropping off here one by one, to be united again yonder fairer and forever.' Let it be so, please God. His will, not ours, be done!

To Mrs. Carlyle, Scotsbrig.

4 Ampton Street : January 30.

My dear Mother,—I have determined to write you a few lines to-day, my mind, and I trust yours also, being in a state of composure ; though there is specially nothing more to be said, the very sound of my voice will do you good.

Since I wrote last I have been in Scotsbrig more than in London ; the tumult of this chaos has rolled past me as a sound, all empty, with which I had nothing to do. My thought was in the house of mourning, present with you and with the departed. We had excluded *all* external communication from us till the funeral should be passed. I dwelt with my deceased father. Our whole speech and action was of high solemn matters. I walked out alone or with my wife, meditating, peaceably conversing of that great event. I have reason to be very thankful that much composure has been vouchsafed me. I never so saw my honoured father and his earnest, toilsome, manful life as now when he was gone from me ; I never so loved him, and *felt* as if his spirit were still living in me—as if my life was but a continuation of his, and to be led in the same valiant spirit that in a quite other sphere so distinguished him. Be the great Father thanked for His goodness ; chiefly for this, if He have given us any light and faith, to discern and reverence His mysterious ways, and how from the depths of grief itself there rises mildly a holy eternal joy.

Edward Irving on sending up his name was admitted to me on Friday afternoon. His wife was with him. He prayed with us I think about the time they would be in the churchyard. I felt that he meant kindly ; yet cannot say that either his prayer or his conversation worked otherwise on me than disturbingly. I had partly purposed sending for him, but was then thankful I had not done it. His whole mind is getting miserably crippled and weakened ; his insane babble about his tongues and the like were for me like froth to the hungry and thirsty. My father was a *Man*, and should be mourned for like a man. We had to forget our well-meaning visitors, and again take counsel with ourselves, and I trust with the God that dwells in us—were this last done only in *silence.* My father's memory has become very holy to me ; not sorrowful, but great and instructive. I could repeat, though with tears yet with softly resolved heart, ' Blessed are the dead that die in the Lord ; they do rest from their labours, and their works

follow them.' Yes, their *works* are not lost; no grain of truth
that was in them but belongs to eternity and cannot die.

Jane faithfully bore and suffered with me. We spoke much.
I trust that she, too, is one day to 'become perfect through suffering,' and even in this earth to struggle unweariedly towards
perfection as towards the one thing needful. We talked of death
and life, with the significance of each; of the friends we had lost;
of the friends still mercifully left us, and the duties we owed to
them. In our two fathers we found a great similarity with so
much outward difference. Both were *true* men, such as the world
has not many to show now; both faithfully laboured according to
their calling in God's vineyard (which this world is); both are
now in the land of truth and light, while we still toil in that of
falsehood and shadows. A little while, and we too 'shall reap if
we faint not.' Of the other world it seems to me we do know
this, and this only: that it too is God's world; and that for us
and for our buried ones He hath done, and will do, all things *well*.
Let us rest here; it is the anchor of the soul both sure and steadfast; other safety there is none.

To you also, my dear mother, I trust the call has not been
made in vain. I know that you have borne yourself with heroism,
for you have the true strength in you. Sad, doubtless, will your
mood long be—sadder, perhaps, than ours, than mine. Your loss
is the keenest. The companion that had pilgrimed by your side
for seven and thirty years is suddenly called away. Looking on
that hand you now see yourself *alone*. Not alone, dear mother, if
God be with you! Your children also are still round you to bear
up your declining years, to protect and support you, to love you
with the love we owed *both* our parents. Oh, Providence is very
merciful to us!

Neither let any one of us looking back on the departed mourn
uselessly over our faults towards him, as in all things we err and
come short. How holy are the dead! How willingly we take *all*
the blame on ourselves which in life we were so willing to divide!
I say, let us not lament and afflict ourselves over these things.
They were of the earth earthy. Now *he* has done with them;
they do him (nay, except for his own earthly sinfulness, they *did*
him) no evil. Let us remember only, one and all of us, this
truth, and lay it well to heart in our whole conduct: that the living also will one day be dead!

On the whole, it is for the living only that we are called to live

—'to work while it is still to-day.' We will dismiss vain sorrows, and address ourselves with new heart and purer endeavour to the tasks appointed us in life. Forward! forward! Let us *do* more faithfully than ever what yet remains to be done. All else is unprofitable and a wasting of our strength.

We two are purposing to come homeward early in March, and shall most likely come to Scotsbrig first. I have (or found I had already) as good as concluded that bargain about the 'Literary History.' I have a paper on Johnson to write, and many little odds and ends to adjust; after which we seem to have no business to do here, and shall march and leave it for the time. For myself, I fear not the world, or regard it a jot, except as the great task-garden of the Highest; wherein I am called to do *whatever* work the Task-master of men (wise are they that can hear and obey Him) shall please to appoint me. What are its frowns or its favours? What are its difficulties and falsehoods and hollow threatenings to me? With the spirit of my father I will front them and conquer them. Let us fear nothing; only being the slaves of sin and madness: these are the only real slaves.

Jane is out, or she would have sent you her blessing, her affection. She is distinctly growing better, and I hope will have recovered her usual strength ere long. Perhaps she too needed affliction, as which of us does not? Remember us always, as we do you. God ever bless you all.

I remain, dear mother, your affectionate son,

T. CARLYLE.

To John Carlyle, Rome.

4 Ampton Street: February 16, 1832.

. . . I wrote copiously twice to our mother. A letter has since come full of composure and peace. The survivors, our mother in particular, are all well, and knit the closer for this breach among them. Jamie,[1] it seems, as I had partly advised him, makes worship regularly in the household; Alick has promised to do the like in his. John of Cockermouth[2] parted from them at Burnfoot, exhorting them with affectionate tears in his eyes to live all united, as they had heretofore done, and mindful and worthy of the true man whose name they bore. Thus has the scene in mild solemnity closed. When the news first reached me I sat silent some minutes, the word '$\tau\acute{\epsilon}\lambda o s$!' pealing mournfully

[1] The youngest brother.
[2] The half brother. Only son of Mr. James Carlyle's first marriage.

through my heart till tears and sobs gave me relief. Death has long been hourly present with me ; I have long learned to look upon it as properly the beginning of life ; its dark curtain grows more and more transparent ; the departed, I think, are only hidden—they are still here. Both they and we, as I often repeat, 'are with God.' I wrote down in my note-book all that I could remember as remarkable about my father ; his life grew wonderfully clear to me, almost like the first stage of my own. I had great peace and satisfaction in thinking of him. Let us in our wider sphere live worthy of a father so true and so brave ; hope too that in some inscrutable way an eternal re-union is appointed us, for with God nothing is impossible ; at all events, 'that He will do all things well.' Therein lies the anchorage that cannot prove deceitful.

Your last letter seemed to me the best I had ever got from you —perhaps among the best I have ever got from any one. There is so much heartiness and earnestness ; the image of a mind honestly, deeply labouring, in a healthy and genuine position towards nature and men. Continue in that right mood ; strive unweariedly, and all that is yet wanting will be given you. Go on and prosper. *Klarheit, Reinheit, ' Im Ganzen, Guten, Wahren resolut zu leben.'* This is *all* that man wants on earth ; even as of old, 'the one thing needful.' Well do I understand, my dear brother, those thoughts of yours on the Pincian Hill.[1] They tore my inward man in pieces for long years, and literally well nigh put an end to my life, till by Heaven's great grace I got the victory over them—nay, changed them into precious everlasting possessions. I wish you could have read my book [2] at this time, for it turns precisely (in its way) on these very matters ; in the paper ' Characteristics ' also, some of my latest experiences and insights are recorded ; these I still hope you will soon see. Meanwhile be not for a moment discouraged ; for the victory is *certain* if you desire it honestly ; neither imagine that it is by forgetting such high questions that you are to have them answered. Unless one is an animal they cannot be forgotten. This also however is true, that logic will never resolve such things ; the instinct of logic is *to say No.* Remember always that the deepest truth, the truest of all, is actually ' unspeakable,' cannot be argued of, dwells far below the region of articulate demonstration ; it must be felt by trial and indubitable direct experience ; then it is known once and for ever. I wish I could have speech of

[1] Relating to religious difficulties, of the usual kind.
[2] *Sartor Resartus.*

you from time to time; perhaps I might disentangle some things for you. Yet after all the victory must be gained by *oneself.* '*Dir auch gelingt es Dich durchzuarbeiten.*' I will here only mention a practical maxim or two which I have found of chief advantage. First, I would have you know this: that '*doubt* of any sort can only be removed by *action.*' But what to act on? you cry. I answer again in the words of Goethe, 'Do the duty which lies nearest;' do it (not merely pretend to have done it); the next duty will already have become clear to thee. There is great truth here; in fact it i. my opinion, that he who (by whatever means) has ever seen into the *infinite* nature of duty has seen all that costs difficulty. The universe has then become a temple for him, and the divinity and all the divine things thereof will infallibly become revealed. To the same purport is this saying, *die hohe Bedeutung des Entsagens,* once understand *entsagen,* then life *eigentlich beginnt.* You may also meditate on these words, 'the divine depth of sorrow,' 'the sanctuary of sorrow.' To me they have been full of significance. But on the whole, dear brother, study to clear your heart from all selfish *desire,* that *free will* may arise and reign absolute in you. True vision lies in thy *heart;* it is by this that the *eye* sees, or for-ever only fancies that it sees. Do the duty that lies there clear at hand. I must not spend your whole sheet in preaching, and will add only this other precept, which I find more important every day I live. Avoid all idle, untrue talk, as you would the pestilence. It is the curse and all-deforming, all-choking leprosy of these days. For health of *mind* I have the clearest belief that there is no help except in this which I have been inculcating in you: action—religious action. If the mind is cultivated, and cannot take in religion by the old vehicle, a new one must be striven after. In this point of view German literature is quite priceless. I never cease to thank Heaven for such men as Richter, Schiller, Goethe. The latter especially was my evangelist. His works, if you study them with due earnestness, are as the day-spring visiting us in the dark night. Perhaps Lady Clare may profit much by them—only keep away *dilettantism;* sweep it out of being; this is no world for it; this is no revelation of a world for it. Among Goethe's admirers here I find *no* one possessed of almost the smallest feeling of what lies in him. They have eyes but see not, hearts but understand not; as indeed the whole world almost has. Let them go their way, do thou go thine.

CHAPTER XII.

A few weeks only now remained of Carlyle's stay in London. The great change at Scotsbrig recommended, and perhaps required, his presence in Scotland. His brother Alick had finally left Craigenputtock to settle on a farm elsewhere, and the house on the moor could not be left unprotected. In London itself he had nothing further to detain him. He had failed in the object which had chiefly brought him there. 'Sartor Resartus' had to lie unpublished in his desk. On the other hand, he had made new and valuable acquaintances—John Mill, Leigh Hunt, Hayward, Lytton Bulwer—for the first three of whom at least he entertained considerable respect. He had been courted more than ever by magazines. Owing to the effect of his personal presence, he had as much work before him as he was able to undertake, and by Hayward's help Dr. Lardner was likely to accept on favourable terms his 'Literary History.' He had learnt, once for all, that of promotion to any fixed employment there was no hope for him. Literature was and was to be the task of his life. But the doubt of being able to maintain himself honourably by it was apparently removed. His thrifty farmhouse habits made the smallest certain income sufficient for his wants. His wife had parted cheerfully with the luxuries in which she had been bred, and was the most perfect of economical stewardesses. His brother John was now in circumstances to repay the cost of his education, and thus for two years at least he saw his way clearly before him. Some editor-

ship or share of editorship might have been attainable had
he cared to seek such a thing; but the conditions of the
London literary profession disinclined him to any close
connection with it; and he had adjusted his relations with
Napier, Fraser, Lytton Bulwer, and the rest, on terms
more satisfactory to himself than complimentary to them.
With Napier he was on a really pleasant footing. The
'Characteristics' had been published without a word being
altered or omitted. He liked Napier, and excepted him
from his general censures. He was now writing his review of Croker's 'Life of Johnson,' which he had promised Fraser as the last piece of work which he was to do
in London. 'This is the way that I have adjusted myself,' he wrote. 'I say will *you* or your dog's carrion cart
take this article of mine and sell it unchanged? With the
carrion cart itself I have and can have no personal concern.'
'For Fraser I am partly bound as to this piece on Johnson. Bulwer, if he want anything on similar terms, and
I feel unoccupied, shall have it; otherwise not he.' In
such scornful humour he prepared to retreat once more
for another two years to his whinstone castle, and turn
his back on London and the literary world.

My attitude towards literary London, he said in a letter to John
(February 18), is almost exactly what I could wish; great respect,
even love, from some few; much matter of thought given me for
instruction and high edification by the very baseness and ignorance
of the many. I dined at Magazine Fraser's some five weeks ago;
saw Lockhart, Galt, Cunningham, Hogg. Galt has since sent me
a book (new, and worth little); he is a broad gawsie Greenock
man, old-growing, lovable with pity; Lockhart a dandiacal, not
without force, but barren and unfruitful; Hogg, utterly a singing
goose, whom also I pitied and loved. The conversation was about
the basest I ever assisted in. The Scotch here afterwards got up
a brutish thing by way of a 'Burns dinner,' which has since been
called the 'Hogg dinner,' to the number of 500; famished glut-
tony, quackery, and stupidity were the elements of the work,

which has been laughed at much. Enough of literary life. The Montagus live *far* from us ; both Jane and the noble lady seem to have *seen* each other, and found that an interview once in the six weeks was enough. I have been there some thrice since you went. Procter regards me as a proud mystic ; I him (mostly) as a worn-out dud; so we walk on separate roads. The other Montagus are mostly mere *simulacra*, and not edifying ones. Peace be to all such. Of male favourites Mill stands at the top. Jeffrey, from his levity, a good deal lower ; yet he is ever kind and pleasant. I saw Irving yesternight. He is still good-natured and patient, but enveloped in the vain sound of the ' Tongues.' I am glad to think he will not go utterly mad (not madder than a Don Quixote was), but his intellect seems quietly settling into a superstitious *caput mortuum*. He has no longer any opinion to deliver worth listening to on any secular matter. The Chancellor can eject him. It is provided by the original deed of his chapel that the worship there shall be that of the Established Church of Scotland. His managers I know have already consulted Sugden. Whether and how soon they may drive the matter to extremities is not to be guessed. I pity poor Irving, and cannot prophesy of him. His ' Morning Watch,' which he gave me yesternight, is simply the howling of a Bedlamite.

To Alexander Carlyle.

4 Ampton Street : February 19.

. . . .

We are coming home as early as possible in the month of March. We are busy, very busy, and in our usual health ; Jane, though still complaining, rather better than she has long been. I do not think she is to be *strong* again till she has got into her home and native air, which of course will quicken our motions the more.

We have both of us determined to take better care of our health were we once home again; I feel it to be a real point of duty, were it only for the greater quantity and better quality of work which good health enables us to do. We are also minded to try if we cannot be a little more domesticated among the moors of Puttock—to take a greater interest in the people there (who are all immortal creatures, however poor and defaced), and to feel as if the place were a *home* for us. Such as it is, I feel it a great blessing that we have it to go to. For the whole summer and on-wards to winter I already see plenty of *work* before me : how we turn ourselves afterwards need not yet be decided on. I was very glad to learn that you had promised to my mother to keep religion in your house : without religion constantly present in the heart, I see not how a man can live otherwise than unreasonably—than desperately. I think that you do really in heart wish to be a good man ' as the one thing needful ; ' also that you will more and more ' lay aside every weight,' and be found running the race faithfully for the true and only prize of manhood. This is my hope and trust of you, dear brother ; God turn it for both of us more and more into fulfilment. Believe me ever,

Your faithfully affectionate brother,

T. Carlyle

The Carlyles left London on the 25th of March. They returned to Scotland by Liverpool, staying a few days with Mr. Welsh in Maryland Street, and then going on as they had come by the Annan steamer. Mrs. Carlyle suffered frightfully from sea-sickness. She endured the voyage for economy's sake ; but she was in bad health and in worse spirits. The Craigenputtock exile, dreary and disheartening, was again to be taken up ; the prospect of release once more clouded over. Her life was the dreariest of slaveries to household cares and toil. She was without society, except on an occasional visit from a sister-in-law or a rare week or so with her mother at Templand. Carlyle, intensely occupied with his thoughts and his writing, was unable to bear the presence of a second person when busy at his desk. He sat alone, walked alone, generally rode alone. It was necessary for him some time or other in the day to discharge in talk the volume of thought which oppressed him. But it was in vehement soliloquy, to which his wife listened with admiration perhaps, but admiration dulled by the constant repetition of the dose, and without relief or comfort from it. The evenings in London, with the brilliant little circle which had gathered about them, served only to intensify the gloom of the desolate moor, which her nerves, already shattered with illness, were in no condition to encounter. Carlyle observed these symptoms less than he ought to have done. His own health, fiercely as at times he complained of it, was essentially robust. He was doing his own duty with his utmost energy. His wife considered it to be part of hers to conceal from him how hard her own share of the burden had become. Her high principles enabled her to go through with it; but the dreams of intellectual companionship with a man of genius in which she had entered on her marriage had long disappeared; and she settled down into her place again with a heavy heart. Her courage never gave way; but she had a bad time of it. They stayed a fortnight at Scotsbrig, where they heard the news of Goethe's death. At the middle of April they were on the moor once more, and Carlyle was again at his work. The 'Characteristics' and the article on Johnson had been received with the warmest admiration from the increasing circle of young intellectual men who were looking up to him as their teacher, and with wonder and applause from the reading London world. He sat down with fresh heart to new efforts. 'The Death of Goethe' was written immediately on his return for Lytton Bulwer. *Das Mährchen*, 'The Tale,' so called in Germany, as if there were no other fit to be compared with it, was translated for 'Fraser,' with its singular explanatory notes.[1] His great concluding article on Goethe himself, on Goethe's position and meaning in European history, had to be written next for the 'Foreign Quarterly;' another for the 'Edinburgh' on Ebenezer Elliot, the Corn-law Rhymer; and lastly the essay on Diderot, for which he had been collecting materials in London. He had added to his correspondents the new friend John Mill, between whom and himself there had sprung up an ardent attachment.

---

[1] Carlyle told me that he had asked Goethe whether he was right in his interpretation of this story, but that he could never get an answer from him about it.

His letters to Mill are not preserved, but Mill's to him remain. Between Jeffrey and Mrs. Carlyle also the communication began again, Mrs. Carlyle apparently telling her cousin more of her inner state of feeling than she pleased to show to anyone else. Jeffrey had been an almost daily visitor in Ampton Street : he saw and felt for her situation, he regarded himself as, in a sense, her guardian, and he insisted that she should keep him regularly informed of her condition. In London he had observed that she was extremely delicate ; that the prospect of a return to Craigenputtock was intolerable to her. Carlyle's views and Carlyle's actions provoked him more and more. He thought him as visionary as the Astronomer in ' Rasselas,' and confessed that he was irritated at seeing him throwing away his talent and his prospects.

Carlyle, after his reception in London circles, was less than ever inclined to listen to Jeffrey's protests. If in the midst of his speculations he could have spared a moment to study his wife's condition, the state of things at Craigenputtock might have been less satisfactory to him. He was extremely fond of her : more fond, perhaps, of her than of any other living person except his mother. But it was his peculiarity, that if matters were well with himself, it never occurred to him that they could be going ill with anyone else ; and, on the other hand, if he was uncomfortable, he required everybody to be uncomfortable along with him. After a week of restlessness he was at his work in vigorous spirits—especially happy because he found that he could supply Larry's place, and again afford to keep a horse.

Carlyle now takes up his own story.

To Mrs. Carlyle, Scotsbrig.

Craigenputtock : May 2, 1832.

My dear Mother,—We are getting along quite handsomely here, though in the midst of chaos and confusion worse confounded :

Jemmy Aitkin and his man and innumerable oilpots being in full operation. They are painting the dining-room, lobby, and staircase ; and, to avoid such a *slaister* for the future, doing it in oil. We live in the drawing-room meanwhile, and I, for my part, study to ' jook and let the jaw go by,' minding my own business as much as possible, and what is not my own business as little as possible.

Betty Smeal [1] and Mary, of whose safe arrival we were somewhat relieved to hear, would tell you more minutely than my little note how all stood with us a fortnight ago. Jane had sent off to Templand for a maid, but began to regret she had not endeavoured to bargain with the other, who, awkward as she was, seemed faithful and punctual. However, on the Monday a new figure made her appearance ; one ' Nancy ' from Thornhill, a most assiduous, blithe, fond little stump of a body, who will do excellently well. The cow, too, is mending. Jane is far heartier now that she has got to work : to bake ; [2] and, mark this, to *preserve eggs* in lime-water ; so that, as I said, the household stands on a quite tolerable footing.

For a week I felt exceedingly out of my element ; inclined to be wretched and sulky : no work would prosper with me : I had to burn as fast as I wrote. However, by degrees I got *hefted* again, and took obediently to the *gang* and the *gear*. I have got one piece of work done and sent off to London ; the other I have now fairly on the anvil, hot before me, and will soon hammer it out. One that is still in the middle ought not, as you know, to *crow day*. However, I think I can calculate on being pretty well through before this week end ; so that Jane may tell Alick that I shall be *ready for a horse* any time after Wednesday next he likes. I have seen or heard nothing, since his letter, of the Dumfries beast, and will wait now till I be there at any rate, if we are not provided otherwise in the mean time.

This I believe, dear mother, is the main purpose of my letter— that I am to see you again so soon. We will then go through everything by the more convenient method.

I have rooted out a thousand docks with my dock spade, which I find to be an invaluable tool.

Let me pray that I may find you as well as Jane described,

---

[1] A Scotsbrig maid, who had been in charge of Craigenputtock in the winter.

[2] A mistake on Carlyle's part. Mrs. Carlyle had not strength for household work. She did it ; but it permanently broke down her health.

mending the Rackburn road? I add no more but the message of
my wife's true love to one and all of you. My own heart's wishes
are with you always.

I remain, my dear Mother,

Ever your affectionate,

T. CARLYLE.

Jane wishes Jemmy to be on the outlook for a pig for her ; she
would not like to go *beyond* ten shillings, only *wishes* a good one
could be had so, and come up with Alick's cart. I know not
whether the scheme is feasible.—T. C.

To John Carlyle, Naples.

May 22.

We are contented with the appearance of your domestic position, and would fain see further into it. Your noble patient
seems to suffer more than we anticipated. A certain real pity for
her forlorn fortune, so gorgeous outwardly, within so desolate,
comes over me ; one could fancy it no despicable task to struggle
towards rectifying a life wherein are such capabilities of good.
But, alas! how little can be done! Therein, as in so many other
cases, must the patient minister to herself. He whom experience
has not taught innumerable *hard* lessons, will be wretched at the
bottom of Nature's cornucopia ; and some are so dull at taking
up! On the whole, the higher classes of modern Europe, especially of actual England, are true objects of compassion. Be thou
compassionate, patiently faithful, leave no means untried ; work
for thy wages, and it will be well with thee. Those *Herzensergies-
sungen eines Einsamen*, which the late letters abound in, are not
singular to me. The spirit that dwells in them is such as I can
heartily approve of. It is an earnest mind seeking some place of
rest for itself, struggling to get its foot off the quicksand and
fixed on the rock. The only thing I regret or fear is that there
should be so much occupation of the mind upon itself. Turn
outward. Attempt not the impossibility to 'know thyself,' but
solely 'to know what thou canst work at.' This last is a possible
knowledge for every creature, and the only profitable one ; neither
is there any way of attaining it except *trial*, the attempt *to work*.
Attempt honestly ; the result, even if unsuccessful, will be infinitely instructive. I can see, too, you have a great want in your
present otherwise so prosperous condition : you have not anything
like enough *to do*. I dare say many a poor riding apothecary,
with five times your labour and the fifth part of your income, is

happier. Nevertheless, stand to it tightly; every time brings its duty. Think of this, as you are wont, but think of it with a practical intent. All speculation is beginningless and endless. Do not let yourself into *Grübeln*, even in your present state of partial inaction. I well, infinitely too well, know what *Grübeln* is: a wretched sink of darkness, pain, a paralytic fascination. Cover it up; that is to say, neglect it for some outward piece of action; go resolutely forward, you will not heed the precipices that gape on the right hand of you and on the left. Finally, dear brother, 'be alive!' as my Shrewsbury coachman told a Methodist parson; *be alive!* all is included in that. And so, God keep you and me! and make us all happy and honourable to one another, and 'not ashamed to live' (as a voice we have often heard was wont to pray), 'nor afraid to die.' Amen.

I was at Scotsbrig last week, and found them all struggling along, much as of old. Our dear mother holds out well; is in fair health, not more dispirited than almost any one would be under her bereavement, and peaceful, with a high trust in the great Guide of all. We expect her here in about a week, with Alick, who is bringing up the cart with some sort of a horse he was to buy for me. We settled everything at Scotsbrig; the departed had left it all ready for settlement. Your name or mine (as I had myself requested)[1] is not mentioned in the will: it was all between my mother and the other five. Each had to claim some perhaps 120*l.*—each of the five. Our mother has the houses with some 28*l.* yearly during life.

Of ourselves here there is not much new to be said. Jane seemed to grow *very greatly* better when she set foot on her native heath; is now not so well again, but better than in London. I have written two things—a short *Funeral Oration* on Goethe: it is for Bulwer's magazine of June (the 'New Monthly'), and pleases the lady much better than me; then a paper on certain Corn-law Rhymes for Napier, of some twenty-five pages. I am now beginning a far more extensive essay on *Goethe*, for the 'Foreign Quarterly Review.' I am apt to be rather stupid, but do the best I can. Venerable, dear Goethe! but we will not speak a word here. Our pastoral establishment is much like what it was; duller a little

---

[1] Carlyle explains in his journal. He had represented to his father that he and his brother John had received their share of his fortune in their education, and that the rest ought to be divided among those who, by working on the farm, had assisted in earning it.

since Alick went, but also quieter. Our new neighbours have nothing to do with us except little kind offices of business. Articulate speech I hear little, my sole comfort and remedy is work. Work! rather an unnatural state, but not to be altered for the present. With many blessings, too: a kind, true-hearted wife, with whom a true man may share *any* fortune, fresh air, food, and raiment fit for one. The place is even a beautiful place in its kind, and may serve for a workshop as well as another. Let us work then, and be thankful.

The Whig Ministry is all out and gone to the devil, Reform Bill and all. Newspapers will tell you enough. For us here it is little more than a matter of amusement: 'Whoiver's King I'se be soobject.' The country is all in a shriek, but will soon compose itself when it finds that things are—just where they were. Incapable dilettantes and capable knaves—which is worse? Excuse my dulness, dear John. Love me always, and may God bless you.

T. CARLYLE.

P.S. by Mrs. Carlyle:—

My husband says: 'I have written the dullest letter; do take the pen and underline it with something lively!' But alas! dear brother, I have dined—on a peppery pie! and judge whether what he requires be possible: *console-toi.* I will write you a long letter some day, and all out of my own head, as the children say. In the meantime, believe that my affections and heartiest good wishes are with you now and always.

Your sister,

JANE W. C.

Pleasant letters came from London. John Mill, young, ingenuous, and susceptible, had been profoundly impressed by Carlyle. He had an instinct for recognising truth in any form in which it might be presented to him. Charles Buller had foretold that although Mill's and Carlyle's methods of thought were as wide asunder as the poles, they would understand and appreciate each other. They sympathised in a common indignation at the existing condition of society, in a common contempt for the insincere professions with which men were veiling from themselves and from one another their emptiness of spiritual belief;

and neither Mill nor Carlyle as yet realised how far apart
their respective principles would eventually draw them.
The review of Boswell's ' Life of Johnson ' had delighted
Mill. He had read it so often that he could almost repeat it from end to end. He recognised the immense
superiority of intellectual honesty to intellectual power.
He recognised the shallowness and feebleness of modern
thought in the midst of its cant of progress. He professed
himself a humble disciple of Carlyle, eager to be convinced
(which as yet he admitted that he was not) of the greatness of Goethe ; eager to admit with innocent modesty
Carlyle's own superiority to himself.

The letters from Mill were agreeable interludes in the
life at Craigenputtock, pictures of which Carlyle continued
regularly to send to his brother, while he recorded in his
Diary the workings of his own mind.

To John Carlyle, Naples.

Craigenputtock: July 31, 1832.

My dear Brother,—Goodwife Macadam brought us your letter
of the 4th from church with her on Sunday evening. It is the
way the three last have happened to come, so we shall esteem it a
happy omen when our neighbour thinks of getting a sermon. God
be thanked, it is all right. You are well, and have now heard that
we are well. Another letter, sent off through the Advocate by the
Foreign Office, will be already in your hands. We shall henceforth eschew William Fraser as we would the genius of impotence
itself, and trust mainly to the Post, which, though it has loitered,
has never yet absolutely deceived us. I lament for poor Fraser—
a worthy, friendly creature, but whose utter unpunctuality in a
world *built* on time will frustrate every endeavour he may engage
in, except the last—that of quitting life—which will probably be
transacted in *right* season. I am angry, too, as well as sorry ; the
idle losing of letters is a stretch of carelessness to which even the
peasants of Glenessland are superior. Entrust any of them with a
letter, he knows it *must* be attended to. Fraser to all appearance
has also wasted my last letter to Goethe ; at least no message yet
reaches me from Weimar, and I wrote to Eckermann last week on

that hypothesis. Fie, fie, the foolish Fraser! And now, Doctor, taking to ourselves this practical lesson to be for our share in all things doubly and trebly punctual, we will leave the unfortunate man. All is right at last.

Both of us were heartily gratified with your letter. I have the cheering sight before me of a prophecy, often pronounced and asserted, realising itself. Jack is to be a man after all. Your outward relations seem all prosperous and well managed. Your character is unfolding itself into true self-subsistence. In the work appointed you to do you not only seem to work but actually work. For the rest, let us be patient under this delay and separation. Both were perhaps necessary; in any case, if we improve them, will turn to good fruits. I quarrel not with your solitude, nor with anything you do, so it bring yourself contentment and the feeling of profit. This is the best and only *rôle* you can have. Nevertheless, I have always found that companionship with *any* man that will speak out truly his experiences and persuasions (so he have such) was a most precious ingredient in the history of one's life; a thing one turns back to, and finds evermore new meaning in; for indeed this is real, and therefore inexhaustible. God made that man you speak with; all else is more or less theoretical and incomplete. Indeed, in every sense one is but an unhealthy fraction while alone ; only in society with his equals a whole. For which reason it gratifies me that you make acquaintance with Gell and old Squares, the doctor. I could like well to know both of them. Sir W. (*ein Bornirter den man muss gelten lassen*) will make an excellent cicerone ; can tell you all about Troy, too, and who knows what itineraries. Quadri will satirically show you Italian quackery, and how an ardent, hot temperament demeans itself therein. I must also esteem it no small felicity you naturally have : that of associating with a thoroughly courteous society-cultivated woman. No higher piece of art is there in the world. *Schone sie! Verehre sie!* Your whole law lies there. The weak, lovely one will be loved, honoured and protected. Is not in truth a noble woman (noblewoman or not) *Gottes lieblichster Gedanke,* and worth reverencing? Be diligent with your journal. Note everything, let it seem noteworthy or not. Have no eye towards publication, but only towards self enlightenment and pleasant recollection. Publication, if it seems needful, will follow of its own accord. Goethe's Italian travels are a fine model. *Alles rein angeschaut, wie es ist, und seyn muss.* I often figure you in the Toledo street with lemonade-booths and macaroni cook-eries, and loud singing, loud speaking multitudes on the loveliest spot of earth's surface. I here on the Glaisters hillside, in the warm dusk, the wilderness all vapoury and silent except a curlew or two, the great heaven above me, around me only the spirits of the distant, of the dead—all has a preternatural character un-speakably earnest, sad, but nowise wretched. You may tell me, if you like, what German books your lady reads; and on the whole be more and more minute in picturing out to me the current of your natural day. I want to know what clothes you wear, what sort of victual you subsist on.

To turn now the Scottish side of the leaf. I have finished 'Goethe's Works,' and corrected the proof of it since I wrote—a long, desultory, rhapsodic concern of forty-four pages in the 'F. Q. Review.' These are no days for speaking of Goethe. I next went over to Catlinns,[1] and Scotsbrig, leaving Jane at Temp-land (who rued much that she had volunteered to stay behind me). The Catlinns agriculture was all green and prospering. The farmer, with wife and child, had gone over to Brand's of Craighorn, whither I followed them; and, strange enough, was shortly after joined by Jamie and my mother, all engaged that evening to have tea there! Everything was as one could have hoped: crops all excellent, good health, good agreement, good weather. I drove our mother to Annan next forenoon in the clatch, as we call the old gig, which the new grey mare briskly draws along: went and bathed there at the 'back of the hill,' in the very spot where I was near drowned six and twenty years ago, whither I will not return: found Ben Nelson (it was market day); dined with him and talked immeasurably all afternoon, though I had much rather have listened if he had liked.

I was at Annan another bathing day, but missed Ben. However, we chanced to meet on Dodbeck Heights next Wednesday morn-ing as I was returning home: appointed a rendezvous at our inn and then over a thimbleful of brandy and water talked again for the space of two stricken hours. Waugh I now asked for and heard the strangest history. Lying among the pots, forgotten of men, he sees his Aunt Margaret die (poor old Peg!) and himself thereby put in possession of 50*l.* as inheritance. Whereupon, shaving his beard and putting on change of raiment, he walks down to Benson's, and there orders fodder and stall of the best;

---

[1] Alexander Carlyle's new farm.

reigns among the bagmen to heart's content ; shifts after a season
to the King's Arms, Dumfries, and there or in some similar establishment is perhaps even now burning his fifty pound candle to
the socket, and going out in stench ! Saw ever mortal the like ?
The man, Doctor, is once for all deprived of understanding, the
greatest misfortune, properly the only one, that can befall a man.
He hath said to the father of No Work and Darkness, 'Behold I
am thine.' Let me mention here more specially, before quitting
Annandale, that at Scotsbrig all was busy and right ; hay harvest
was at its height the day I came off, and prospering well. Our
mother seemed in better than usual health, was delighted with her
two bathes, and should have (had another) but the clatch failed
and needed repairs. She said after, 'I kenna how many kind
things I wanted to bid (thee say for) me to John ; and thou was
ay gane first.' I said you understood them all, and I constantly
(wrote with) pains about Scotsbrig and her. I am to write thither
this night and send your letter. Alick also I write to : our boy is
going to exchange horses with him for a week (when) we get the
rest of our coals carted. Our newspapers go between these households and sometimes from one to the other ; there is all community we can kept up : frequent messages, constant good wishes.

Since I returned I have been employed translating a little piece
named 'Novelle,' from the fifteenth volume of Goethe, and revis-
ing an old translation of 'THE Mährchen,' with intent to add some
commentary ; and offer both papers to James Fraser. I have an
essay to write on Diderot (for Cochrane), and all his twenty-one oc-
tavos lying here to read first : shall do it, any way, *invitâ Minervâ*,
and may as well begin even now. I have upwards of a hundred
pages to put out of me before winter. Stand to it ? *Nulla dies
sine lineâ.* As to Dreck, he lies here quite calm bound up in
twine. My partial purpose is to spend another 50*l.* on him, and
have him printed by-and-by myself. I in some measure see
through the matter, not yet wholly. One thing I imagine to be
clear enough, that *bookselling,* slain by puffery, is dead, and will not
come alive again, though worms may for some time live in the car-
case. What method writers who have something to write shall
next take is now the question. In a generation or two the answer
(summed up from the procedure of wise, inventive men) will be
forthcoming. To us any way *martyrdom* is the thing appointed ;
in this and all other generations only the degree of it, the outward
figure of it, vary. Thank God we have still food and vesture, and

can still get a thing spoken out and printed ; more we need not covet, more is not necessary. I have a thing to send Napier on all this, but it is *in petto* yet. Meanwhile we get along tolerably enough ; all, as you fancied, is tight, tidy, and peaceable here—a flourishing garden, with blackbirds devouring the fruit, even apples a basket or two ; roses innumerable ; a park walled in (this was poor Alick's last act here) so that the ' rowantree gate' and all gates but the outer one are removed, and cow and horses graze at ease ; a monstrous peat-stack against grim winter ; money in one's purse, faith in one's heart. What is there wanting ? So we live here, a *wunderliches, abgesondertes Wesen.* Jane drives down to Dumfries to-morrow with the boy, and takes this letter. She is far enough from perfect health still, yet certainly improving. She greets you affectionately ; was much pleased with your letter, especially that part where you speak so sensibly about *a good wife* and the blessedness she brings. I have some thought that we shall be in Edinburgh this winter, printing of Dreck and what not. I have Mill, and Mrs. Austin Jane has, as occasional correspondents in London. Mill and Glen are acquainted, though it is mostly on Mill's side ; Glen is so *fencible,* a character, so near madness moreover. Mill's letters are too speculative ; but I reckon him an excellent person, and his love to *me* is great. He tells me Glen got your Naples letter, was much contented therewith, and well. His other news are the decease, or at least paralysis, of St. Simonianism ; and London politics, for which I care less every day. Buller is trying for Liskeard borough with hopes. The election will not be for several months ; no dissolution all winter. George Irving was at Annan at his father's funeral for two days. Edward, it seems, is summoned to answer for himself before the Annan Presbytery, and will come, and be deposed. The time is near ; whether I shall see him uncertain. He is preaching in the fields about London ; at Hampstead Heath, his precentor in a tree (last account I saw). There was also a paragraph about building him a new church. His old congregation have offered *somebody* 1,000*l.* a year. Whether he takes it, not said. The Dows are *both* out, the last of them resigned. It is wholly a beastly piece of ignorance and stupidity, too stupid even for the gross heads of England. That the high, the holy, can find no other lodging than that swinish one is even the misery. God mend it, and us. Of Badams no news since we left him in Bartlett's Buildings ; gone from Enfield, with no good outlook moral or domestic. Poor Badams, *wie gern möcht' ich Dich retten!* Graham is still in Glasgow, no tidings could I get of him farther. Burnswark unsold. So goes the world here, dear brother. The weather is hot, the year is fertile beyond all example. The simple hope from the Reform Bill. Electioneering .flourishes, in which I take no interest. Cholera is at Carlisle, and somewhat worse than ever in London. None of us are in the least *alarmed* at it. Be not you either. I paid Alick 45*l.* 8*s.* of your money. The 25*l.* 8*s.* was a tailor's account; and now you owe him nothing. I sent Jeffrey word that you had remitted the 43*l.* 10*s.* (specifying the items) to pay him, and that *I*, not you, was now (till I could get the Dumfries banker near) his debtor. He answers, gratified by your punctuality, and I will now clear him off the first time I am at Dumfries. He says you have justified what I thought unjustifiable. *Gott sey Dank!* I am in *no* need of money, otherwise I would freely take your help, and will continue as ready if you prove worthy. I can now pay the Advocate my own debt (had I once got my accounts in), and have a 50*l.* over. Another 100*l.*, to be earned as fast as may be, will clear Edinburgh and even print Dreck. As Dreck can be unprinted till the means be lent me, so one hand will wash the other, and we shall do very well. Jeffrey is perhaps on his way to Edinburgh to-day. He is a candidate for the Membership there, and has a Radical opponent and a Tory. All men are disappointed in him a little, but remember his *past* services.

Jane says she will write you a complete letter next time. This is the thing she *says*. Let us see whether she will perform. I will not fail to remind her, if that will do. And now, dear brother, adieu.

Valeas mei memor,

T. CARLYLE.

Extracts from Journal.

May 18.—About beginning an essay on Goethe's life. All still dark, or rather all void; yet thin films, of bulk enough had they become substances, hover here and there. Have been well nigh idle again for a fortnight. Nothing spurs me but an *evil conscience.*

I have often remarked that the present generation has lost the faculty of *giving names.* The modern streets of towns (London for a chief example) and innumerable other things are proofs of this. They are reduced to name streets by the owner of the land, by the builder, or in some other mechanical way, almost as if by formula. Thus in Dumfries they have made their old Lochmaben Gate into *English Street*, they have their *Irish Street*, and so forth. In Manchester they have taken the ready-made London names, have their Piccadilly and the like. In Liverpool they have named streets by herbs (Vine Street, &c., &c.), by poets (Pope Street), and by other desperate methods. What talent is specially requisite for giving a name? A certain geniality of insight, whereby some real property of the thing reveals itself. A very little will do, but some little is requisite; then, so useful are names, even an indifferent one sticks. We cannot now give so much as a *nickname*. Giving a NAME, indeed, is a poetic art; all poetry, if we go to that with it, is but a giving of *names*.

What a sad want I am in of libraries, of books to gather facts from! Why is there not a Majesty's library in every county town? There is a Majesty's jail and gallows in every one.

Wednesday, May 23.—Came news that Wellington has not been able to get on, so violent was the spirit of the country and Parliament, so had given up the concern, and 'our friends' were once more all in their places, with liberty to create peers or do what they liked. *A la bonne heure!* Democracy gets along with accelerated pace—whither? Old borough-mongers seemingly quite desperate; meetings, resolutions, black flags and white flags (some even mount a petticoat in reference to the Queen), threatenings, solemn covenants (to oust Toryism), run their course over all the Isles. I purely an on-looker, in any other capacity there being *no need* of me.

Thus, then, after eighteen months of discussion and concussion (enough to shake a far firmer than our worm-eaten constitution to pieces) is this grand question to be decided in the affirmative? Shall we give ourselves a chance to begin to try whether we can help the maladies of England, or shall we not give ourselves a chance?

Earl Grey and his squadron have moved along like honest, solid-lying—luggage. Tumbled back they had always fallen on a resolute unanimous people, and been borne forward again. Could they have passed a Catholic Bill, any 'Bill' requiring the smallest address or management? Wellington is at the stake (in effigy) in all market towns; undeservedly, as I imagine. The man seems a

Tory *soldier;* otherwise a person of great intrepidity, strategic-diplomatic faculty, soldierly (Dalgettyish) principle, and even directness and plainness of speech. Fond of employment doubtless, fond of power. Perhaps one of the most honest men in the House of Lords. Earl Grey can speak; act he apparently cannot. He should resign *directly* after passing his Bill, if he would avoid becoming the most unpopular man in England, which poor W. now is. *Basta!*

Wednesday, June 6.—Was at Templand yesterday; over the 'Bogra Craig' in the morning, and returned at night by the Lag road. Fine scent of hawthorns and green summer herbs; old-fashioned thatched cottages, clean, whitened, warm-looking in their *häusliche Eingezogenheit.* Woman with her children peeling potatoes by the water side, down in the chasm at Scarbridge. At night, hawthorn blossoms again, queen of the meadows, glowworms in Glenessland, a waning moon, and gusty north-easter. My own thoughts sad enough, yet not of that hateful *emptiness.* They are thoughts, not mere *sensations.* Mother and Jane waiting my (late) return.

Sir James Mackintosh is dead. A Whig of the highest order, the result of whose life is well-nigh exhausted with himself. Henceforth no man of such faculty is doomed to that unfortunate part of a 'supposer,' well paid for plainly *supposing,* and so *seeming* plausibly to act, but may become a *believer,* and actually set about doing. I saw Mackintosh only once, and never spoke to him, only heard him speaking.

Very kind letter from Mill, whose zealous and quite credible approbation and appropriation of *Johnson* gratifies me, I doubt, far more than it should. Unspeakable is the importance of man to man. A tailor at Thornhill, who had vehemently laid to heart the Characteristics, was also a glad phenomenon to me. Let a million voices cry out, 'How clever!' it is still nothing; let one voice cry out, 'How true!' it lends us quite a new force and encouragement.

I have no books, cannot by any convenient contrivance get any books; a little money in this, as in one or two other matters, might do something for me. Hast thou not the Book of Nature? A page of it; but here, in the Dunscore Moss, well-nigh a blank leaf. Not wholly so. Read it well.

The most stupendous of gigmen was Phaeton; drove the bravest gig, and with the sorrowfullest results. An instance, too, of
what the law of inheritance produces. He had built no sun chariot (could not build a wheelbarrow), but would and could insist
on *driving* one, and so broke his own neck and set fire to the
world.

July 21.—A strange feeling of *supernaturalism*, of 'the fearful-
ness and wonderfulness' of life, haunts me and grows upon me.
Saw Ben Nelson at Annan; long talk with him. Unluckily my
habit (and the people's habit with me) is rather to speak than to
listen; I mean it no wise so, but so I often find it has proved.

'Society for the Diffusion of Common Honesty' were the use-
fullest of all societies could it take *effect.*

July 22.—A foolish puppet figure, which I saw in a huckster's
shop-window at London in some lane, has awakened thoughts in
me which I have not yet found any words for! To imagine; *bil-
den!* That is an unfathomable thing.

As yet I have never risen into the region of creation. Am I approaching it? *Ach Gott! sich nähern dem unaussprechlichen.*

Was there ever a more merry-andrew-looking thing (if we consider it) than for a wretched creature named man, or gigman,
alighting for one instant on this 'everlasting earth,' to say, it is
mine! *It;* consider what *it* (the earth) properly is—*the reflex of
the living spirit of man,* the joint production of man and God—

> Natur ist Schall und Rauch
> Umnebelnd Himmelsgluth.

The greatest of all past or present anti-gigmen was Jesus Christ.
This age is quite especially wrecked and sunk in gigmanism.

Homer's 'Iliad' would have brought the author, had he offered
it to Mr. Murray on the half-profit system, say five-and-twenty
guineas. The Prophecies of Isaiah would have made a small article in a review, which, paying not under the rate of three guineas
a sheet (excluding extracts, whereof there are none in Isaiah), could
cheerfully enough have remunerated him with a five pound note.
To speak of paying the writer of a true book is, on the whole, delirium. The thing is unpayable; the whole world could not buy
it. Could the whole world induce him by fee or reward to write
it otherwise—opposite wise? Then is he no writer, only a deplo-

rable despicable scribbler, waiting till the besom of destitution sweep him away.

Authors are martyrs—witnesses for the truth—or else nothing. Money cannot make or unmake them. They are made or unmade, commanded and held back by God Almighty alone, whose inspiration it is that giveth them understanding ; yet for the world whom they address, for the fitness of their language towards it, their clearness of insight into its interests, and the ear *it* shall give them—for all in short that respects their revelation *of* themselves (not their existence *in* themselves)—money, as the epitome and magic talisman of all mechanical endeavour whatsoever, is of incalculable importance. Money cannot hire the writing of a book, but it can the printing of it. The existence of a public library, or non-existence thereof, in the circle where a thinker is born will forward his thinking or obstruct and prevent it. When the thinker has discovered truth, it depends on money whether the world shall participate in such discovery or not participate. In how many other ways (as when your nascent wise man is poor, solitary, uneducated, &c.) can the 'talisman of power' cut away impediments and open out the path ! Many a fallen spark too is quenched, or lives only as a spark, which could have been fanned into a cheerful light and fire. (No end to all this, which is to go into that paulo post future essay on *Authors*.)

Cholera at Carlisle ; a case talked of in Annandale. The cowardice or bravery of the world manifests itself best in such a season. Nothing lies in *cholera*, with all its collapses, spasms, blueness of skin, and what else you like, except *death*, which may lie equally in a common catarrh—in the wheel of the nearest hackney coach. Yet here death is original ; the dunce who, blinded by custom, has looked at it in the usual forms, heedless, unreasoning, now *sees* it for the first time, and shudders at it as a novelty.[1]

'The special, sole, and deepest theme of the world's and man's

---

[1] The cholera fell very heavily on Dumfries. For want of accommodation the sick were crowded together in a single large building, out of which few who had entered came out alive. The town was terror struck. Carlyle told me that the panic at last reached the clergy, who were afraid to go within the door of that horrible charnel house to help the dying in their passage into eternity, but preached to them from the outside through the open windows. He had no love for Catholic priests and what he called their poisoned gingerbread consolations ; but in this instance he bore an ungrudging testimony that the only minister of religion who ventured in among the sick beds was a poor priest ; and the poor priest, alas ! caught the infection and died.

history, whereto all other themes are subordinated, remains the conflict of unbelief and belief. All epochs wherein belief prevails, under what form it will, are splendid, heart-elevating, fruitful for contemporaries and posterity. All epochs, on the contrary, where unbelief, in what form soever, maintains its sorry victory, should they even for a moment glitter with a sham splendour, vanish from the eyes of posterity, because no one chooses to burden himself with a study of the unfruitful.'—'Goethe's Works,' vi. 159, on Moses and his Exodus.

These notes show how powerfully Carlyle's intellect was working, how he was cutting out an original road for himself, far away from the Radicalism of the day. But it is in the nature of such thoughts that they draw off a man's attention from what is round him, and prevent him from attending to the thousand little things and the many great things of which the commonplaces of life are composed. Vocal as he was—pouring out whatever was in him in a stream of talk for hours together—he was not the cheerfullest of companions. He spoke much of *hope*, but he was never hopeful. The world was not moving to his mind. His anticipations were habitually gloomy. The persons with whom he had come in contact fell short of the demands which the sternness of his temper was inclined to make on them, from the drudge who had ill-cleaned a vegetable dish, to the man of letters who had written a silly article, *or* the Phaeton who was driving the State chariot through the wrong constellations. Thus, although indigestion, which interfered with his working, recalled his impatience to himself, he could leave his wife to ill-health and toil, assuming that all was well as long as she did not complain; and it was plain to every one of her friends, before it was suspected by her husband, that the hard, solitary life on the moor was trying severely both her constitution and her nerves.

Carlyle saw, and yet was blind. If she suffered she concealed her trials from him, lest his work should suffer also. But she took refuge in a kind of stoicism, which was but a thin disguise for disappointment and at times for misery. It was a sad fate for a person so bright and gifted; and if she could endure it for herself, others, and especially Jeffrey, were not inclined to endure it for her. Jeffrey had been often in Ampton Street, claiming the privileged intimacy of a cousin. Eyes so keen as the Lord Advocate's could not fail to see how things were going with her. She herself perhaps did not hide from him that the thought of being again immured in Craigenputtock was horrible to her. Liking and even honouring Carlyle as he did, he did not like his faults, and the Lord Advocate was slightly irritated at the reception which Carlyle had met with in London, as tending to confirm him in the illusion that he was a prophet of a new religion. He continued to write to Mrs. Carlyle tenderly and even passionately, as he would have written to a daughter of his own. It was intolerable to him to think of her with her fine talents lost to all the enjoyments that belonged to her age and character, and provoking to feel that it was owing to moody fancies too long cherished, and fantastic opinions engendered and fed in solitude. She made the best of her position, as she always did. She had been greatly interested in the daughter of her landlady in Ampton Street, Miss Eliza Miles, who had so romantically returned Mrs. Carlyle's regard, that she had proposed to go back with her as a servant to Craigenputtock. Mrs. Carlyle knew too well what Craigenputtock was to allow her to accept Miss Miles's offer. She wrote to her occasionally, however, in the summer which followed their stay in London, and invited her to pay the place a visit.

To Miss Eliza Miles.

Craigenputtock: June 16, 1832.

My dear Eliza,—I could wager you now think the Scots a less amiable nation than you had supposed, least of all to be commended on the score of good faith. Is it not so? Has not my whole nation suffered in your opinion through my solitary fault. In February I made a voluntary engagement to write to you, which now in June remains to be fulfilled. Still I am fulfilling it, which proves that it is not altogether 'out of sight out of mind' with me; and could I give you an idea of the tumult I have been in since we parted, you would find me excusable if not blameless. I never forgot my gentle Ariel in Ampton Street; it were positive sin to forget her, so helpful she, so trustful, so kind and good. Besides, this is the place of all others for thinking of absent friends, where one has so seldom any present to think of. It is the stillest, solitariest place that it ever entered your imagination to conceive, where one has the strangest shadowy existence. Nothing is actual in it but the food we eat, the bed one sleeps on, and, praised be Heaven, the fine air one breathes. The rest is all a dream of the absent and distant, of things past and to come. I was fatigued enough by the journey home, still more by the bustling which awaited me there—a dismantled house, no effectual servants, weak health, and, worse than the seven plagues of Egypt, a necessity of painters. All these things were against me. But happily there is a continual tide in human affairs; and if a little while ago I was near being swept away in the hubbub, so now I find myself in a dead calm. All is again in order about us, and I fold my hands and ask what is to be done next?

'The duty nearest hand will show itself in course.' So my Goethe teaches. No one who lays the precept to heart can ever be at a stand. Impress it on your 'twenty' children (that I think was the number you had fixed upon). Impress it on the whole twenty from the cradle upwards, and you will spare your sons the vexation of many a wild-goose chase, and render your daughters for ever impracticable to *ennui*. Shame that such a malady should exist in a Christian land: should not only exist, but be almost general throughout the whole female population that is placed above the necessity of working for daily bread. If I have an antipathy for any class of people it is for *fine ladies*. I almost match my husband's detestation of partridge-shooting gentlemen. Woe to the fine lady who should find herself set down at Craigenputtock for the first time in her life left alone with her own thoughts—no '*fancy bazaar*' in the same kingdom with her; no place of amusement within a day's journey; the very church, her last imaginable resource, seven miles off. I can fancy with what horror she would look on the ridge of mountains that seemed to enclose her from all earthly bliss ; with what despair in her accents she would inquire if there was not even a ' charity sale ' within reach. Alas, no ! no outlet whatever for ' lady's work,' not even a book for a fine lady's understanding. It is plain she would have nothing for it but to die as speedily as possible, and so relieve the world of the expense of her maintenance. For my part I am very content. I have everything here my heart desires that I could have anywhere else, except society, and even that deprivation is not to be considered wholly an evil. If people we like and take pleasure in do not come about us here as in London, it is thankfully to be remembered that ' here the wicked cease from troubling, and the weary are at rest.' If the knocker make no sound for weeks together, it is so much the better for my nerves. My husband is as good company as reasonable mortal could desire. Every fair morning we ride on horseback for an hour before breakfast. My precious horse knew me again, and neighed loud and long when he found himself in his old place. And then we eat such a surprising breakfast of homebaked bread and eggs, &c. &c. as might incite anyone that had breakfasted so long in London to write a pastoral. Then Carlyle takes to his writing, while I, like Eve, ' studious of household good,' inspect my house, my garden, my live stock, gather flowers for my drawing-room, and lapfuls of eggs, and finally betake myself also to writing or reading or making or mending, or whatever work seems fittest. After dinner, and only then, I lie on the sofa (to my shame be it spoken), sometimes sleep, but oftenest dream waking. In the evening I walk on the moor—how different from Holborn and the Strand!—and read anything that does not exact much attention. Such is my life, agreeable as yet from its novelty if for nothing else. Now would you not like to share it? I am sure you would be happy beside us for a while, and healthy, for I would keep all drugs from your lips, and pour warm milk into you. Could you not find an escort and come and try? At all rates write and tell me how you are, what doing, what intending. I shall always be interested in all that concerns you. My health is slowly mending.

Yours affectionately,
Jane Carlyle.

This is pretty, and it shows Craigenputtock on its fairest side. But there was a reverse of the picture. I have not seen any of Mrs. Carlyle's letters to Jeffrey, but in one of them she sent some verses. It was summer, for there were rose leaves along with them, for which Jeffrey seems to have asked. That the verses below were written at Craigenputtock is certain, for they are dated from 'The Desert.' Time, circumstances, and Jeffrey's own acknowledgment that she had sent him verses of some kind, make it almost certain that they belong to this particular period. I find them among loose fragments in her own portfolio:—

To a Swallow building under our Eaves.

Thou too hast travelled, little fluttering thing—
Hast seen the world, and now thy weary wing
    Thou too must rest.
But much, my little bird, couldst thou but tell,
I'd give to know why here thou lik'st so well
    To build thy nest.

For thou hast passed fair places in thy flight ;
A world lay all beneath thee where to light ;
    And, strange thy taste,
Of all the varied scenes that met thine eye—
Of all the spots for building 'neath the sky—
    To choose this waste.

Did fortune try thee ? was thy little purse
Perchance run low, and thou, afraid of worse,
    Felt here secure ?
Ah, no ! thou need'st not gold, thou happy one !
Thou know'st it not.   Of all God's creatures, man
    Alone is poor !

What was it, then ? some mystic turn of thought,
Caught under German eaves, and hither brought,
    Marring thine eye
For the world's loveliness, till thou art grown
A sober thing that dost but mope and moan
    Not knowing why ?

Nay, if thy mind be sound, I need not ask,
Since here I see thee working at thy task
    With wing and beak.
A well-laid scheme doth that small head contain,
At which thou work'st, brave bird, with might and main,
    Nor more need'st seek.

In truth, I rather take it thou hast got
By instinct wise much sense about thy lot,
    And hast small care
Whether an Eden or a desert be
Thy home so thou remain'st alive, and free
    To skim the air.

God speed thee, pretty bird ; may thy small nest
With little ones all in good time be blest.
    I love thee much ;
For well thou managest that life of thine,
While I ! Oh, ask not what I do with mine !
    Would I were such !

The Desert.

CHAPTER XIII.

A.D. 1832. ÆT. 37.

JEFFREY carried Mrs. Carlyle's sad verses with him to the 'glades' of Richmond, to muse upon them, and fret over his helplessness. To him his cousin's situation had no relieving feature, for he believed that Carlyle was entered on a course which would end only less ruinously than Irving's—that he was sacrificing his own prospects, as well as his wife's happiness, to arrogant illusions. The fact was not as Jeffrey saw it. Carlyle was a knight errant, on the noblest quest which can animate a man. He was on the right road, though it was a hard one; but the lot of the poor lady who was dragged along at his bridle-rein to be the humble minister of his necessities was scarcely less tragic. One comfort she had—he had recovered her pony for her, and she could occasionally ride with him. His mother came now and then to Craigenputtock to stay for a few days; or when a bit of work was done they would themselves drive over to Scotsbrig. So far as Carlyle himself was concerned, his letters give an unusually pleasant impression of his existing condition.

To Mrs. Carlyle, Scotsbrig.

Craigenputtock: June 29, 1832.

My dear Mother,—You shall have a short note from me, though my task should stand half done all night. Peter Austin I expect will take you this on Monday, and tell you all about our last peat-leading, and what not; but I imagine you will not dislike a word under my own hand also.

Thank Jean for her letter: it gave us great relief to know that you were getting into your natural way again; that the rest were all in theirs. Let us hope this good state of matters still holds. As for yourself, I think you must go and have a plunge in the Solway this fine weather. When I come down next I will try to keep an eye on the moon, bring the clatch with me, and roll you along therein myself. I too want much to be bathed.

We are all going on as you saw us, or better. Jane is a little out-of-sorts these two or three days, but in general seems clearly improving. The boy has cleaned the garden, which looks well now, and is at this moment slashing like a Waterloo hero among the nettle and dock hosts over the paling. I hope they will not smother him up, but that his little arm and blunt hook will cut a way through them. Betty has got 'Noolly' (the cow) back again, little improved in temper, she says. Soft grass will soften her.

As for myself, I am doing my utmost, and seeing, as you counselled, not 'to make it too high.' In spite of 'the Taylors' applauses' I find myself but a handless workman too often, and can only get on by a dead struggle. This thing, I calculate, will be over in two weeks, and so the stone rolled from my heart again—for a little. I mean to run over and ask what you are doing shortly after; most probably I will write first, by Notman.[1] For the rest, I am well enough, and cannot complain while *busy*. I go riding every fair morning, sometimes as early as six, and enjoy this blessed June weather, oftenest on the Galloway side, the road being open and good now. My beast is wholly satisfactory: learns fast to *ride*, is already a good canterer, tame, quiet, and biddable as ever horse was. The boy has had it in the cart, too, and finds no difficulty in handling it. So, dear mother, on *that* head set your heart at rest.

No 'Examiner' came this week. I have charged Alick to send you over the 'Courier' by Peter. The following week you will find either *it* or something at the post office at the usual time. Any way there are no news of moment. The poor old King has been hit (by a solitary blackguard) with a stone. Wellington was peppered with 'mud and dead cats' along the whole length of London. I am sad for him, yet cannot but laugh to think of the business: the cast-metal man riding slowly five long miles, all the way like a pillar of *glass!* Every beast, you see, has its burden; every dog its day.

Now, dear mother, you see I must finish. My brotherly love to

[1] The carrier.

them all. Take care of yourself, and let me find you well. All good be with you all, now and ever!

Your affectionate son,
T. CARLYLE.

To John Carlyle, Naples.

Craigenputtock : July 2, 1832.

We are all well, and where we were. Our mother was here with us for a fortnight not quite three weeks ago, and I took her down in the gig, by Alick's, too, in whose house and farm [1] we found all prosperous. He was making a gate when we came up to the brae, but soon threw down his axes in a delight to see us. It is thought he has not changed for the worse, and may do well in the Water of Milk, which he looks like doing, for there is a great improvement in him, and increase not only of gravity, but of earnest sense and courage. His little girl is a queer, gleg, crowing creature, whom he takes much delight in. Jamie, too, and the sisters are doing well, and seem to go on judiciously enough together, a proper enough spirit seeming to pervade all of them. Our good mother is very serious, almost sad (as she well may be), yet not unhealthy, not altogether heavy of heart. She has her trust on what cannot die.

Such much for Annandale, where you see there are, as our mother piously says, many mercies still allotted to us.

As to Craigenputtock, it is, as formerly, the scene of scribble-scribbling. Jane is in a weakly state still, but I think clearly gathering strength. Her life beside me constantly writing here is but a dull one ; however, she seems to desire no other ; has, in many things, pronounced the word *Entsagen*, and looks with a brave if with no joyful heart into the present and the future. She manages all things—poultry, flowers, bread-loaves ; keeps a house still like a bandbox, then reads, or works (as at present) on some translation from Goethe. I tell her many times there is *much* for her to do if she were trained to it : her whole sex to deliver from the bondage of frivolity, dollhood, and imbecility, into the freedom of valour and womanhood. Our piano is quite out of tune, and little better than a stocking-frame ; this is an evil not remediable just yet, so we must want music. We have a boy servant named McWhir, a brisk, wise little fellow, who can scour knives, weed carrot beds, yoke gigs, trim saddle-horses, go errands, and

---

[1] New farm to which Alick Carlyle had removed, called Catlinns.

cart coals—a very factotum of a boy—at the rate of one sovereign per *semestre*. He brings the horses round every favourable morning (Alick and Jamie got *me* a noble gray mare at Longtown), and Jane and I go off riding, for which we have now *two* roads, the Glaister Hill one being remade and smoothed, and a bridge just about built over the Orr. Our weather in these mornings would hardly do discredit to Italy itself. Furthermore, a huge stack of the blackest peats was built up for us last week. McWhir has cleaned the garden, full of roses now, has hewn down innumerable nettle and dock weeds in the 'new wood,' where some of the trees are quite high, and is busy this day weeding the 'hedge' and the walk. We have had no visits but one of a day from John Welsh of Liverpool, who seemed happy and fished in the Orr. I have work enough; respect more than I deserve; am not without *thoughts* from time to time; and so *we* play our part. Of my writings this is the list: one often mentioned on *Samuel Johnson*, which you will one day read with a little pleasure; a *Trauerrede*, also often mentioned, on the Death of Goethe, printed in Bulwer's Magazine, never yet paid for, or seen by me in print; a speculative-radical discussion of some 'Corn-Law Rhymes' (bold enough, yet with an innocent smile on its countenance), of which I corrected the proof (twenty-four pages) the week before last for Napier; finally, this thing I am now at the thirtieth page of, on *Goethe's Works*, a *barocque* incongruous concern, which I am principally anxious to get *done* with. James Fraser is again willing to employ me (though at that double rate), the people having praised *Johnson*. With the editorial world, in these mad times, I stand at present on quite tolerable footing. I mean to be in Edinburgh some time before very long, and keep matters going. Here, too, let me mention that I am at no loss for money myself, and have safely received your remittance of 100*l.*, and written to Alick that I will bring it down with me next time, or send it sooner; to Jeffrey I will write a fit message on the same subject to-morrow.[1] All friends were touched with a kind of *wae* joy to see, as I said, 'the colour of Jack's money,' after so many misventures and foiled struggles. Poor Jack will be himself again, in spite of all that, and make the world stand about, stiff as it is, and make a little (straight) pathkin for him. Fear it not: you are already free of

---

[1] John Carlyle had received money from Jeffrey besides the advances which he had received from his brother. He was now diligently paying all his debts.

debt, and in that the miserablest of all millstones is rolled from off you. I too expect to pay the Advocate his money (perhaps along with yours) : then I too shall owe no man anything. Anti-gigmanism is the fixed unalterable Athanasian Creed of this house : Jane is almost stronger in it (and in Anti-fine-ladyism) than my-self. So while the fingers will wag, and the head and heart are uncracked, why should we care ? The world is a thing that a man must learn to despise, and even to neglect, before he can learn to reverence it, and work in it, and for it.

Of external persons or news we hear or see little. Mrs. Strachey sent an apologetic little letter to Jane the other week. She was just leaving Shooter's Hill, and about settling in Devonshire, I think at Torquay. She is earnest, sad, but not broken or dis-pirited. From John Mill I had a kind sheet of news and specula-tions. Mrs. Austin wrote lately that Goethe's last words were, *Macht die Fensterladen auf, damit ich mehr Licht bekomme!* Glori-ous man! Happy man! I never think of him but with reverence and pride. Jeremy Bentham is dead, and made his body be lec-tured over in some of their anatomical schools—by Southwood Smith, I think. You have likely seen this in the papers ; also that Sir Walter Scott lies struck with apoplexy, deprived of conscious-ness, and expected inevitably to die, at an hotel in Jermyn Street! He has a son and daughter there too ; and dies in an inn. I could almost cry for it. Oh all-devouring Time! Oh unfathomable Eternity! Edward Irving is out of his chapel, and seems to be preaching often in the fields. He has rented Owen's huge, ugly bazaar (they say) in Gray's Inn Road, at seven guineas a week, and lectures there every morning. Owen the Atheist, and Irving the Gift-of-Tongues-ist, time about : it is a mad world. Who our poor friend's audience are I hear not. It is said many even of his wo-men have given in. Some of his adherents seem to come before the police occasionally when they gather crowds on the street. His father, worthy old Gavin, was taken away, a few days ago, from sight of these perversities. Electioneering goes on here, in which I take no interest, more than in a better or worse terrier-fight. Reform-bill-ing is the universal business, not mine. . . .

I wholly understand your internal contentions at this period— the struggling, *Verwerfen*, and *Aufnehmen* that you have. It is a heavy burden on the shoulders of every true man, specially at this epoch of the world. It is by action, however, that we learn and attain certainty. The time for this with you is coming ; be ready for it. You have my deepest sympathy in these spiritual trials ; nevertheless I see them to be *necessary*. Not till now have you decidedly looked to me as if you were about becoming *a man*, and finding a manful basis for yourself. I have better hope than ever that it will turn for good. Keep up your heart, my dear brother ; show yourself a valiant man, worthy of the name you bear (for you too bear the name of a *brave man*), worthy of yourself. Trust in *me ;* love me. God forever bless you !

Your affectionate

T. CARLYLE.

So passed the summer. The Goethe paper (which did not please him : 'the time not having come to speak properly about Goethe') being finished and despatched, Carlyle took up Diderot. Diderot's works, five and twenty large volumes of them, were to be read through before he could put pen to paper. He could read with extraordinary perseverance from nine in the morning till ten at night without intermission save for his meals and his pipes. The twelfth of August brought the grouse shooting and young Welsh relations with guns, who drove him out of his house, and sent him on a few days' riding tour about the country. On returning he at once let the shooting of Craigenputtock, that he might be troubled with such visitors no more. A small domestic catastrophe followed, the maid-servant having misconducted herself and having to be sent away at an hour's notice. Her place could not be immediately filled, and all the work fell on Mrs. Carlyle. 'Oh mother, mother!' exclaimed Carlyle in telling her the story, 'what trouble the Devil does give us ; how busy he is wheresoever men are! I could not have fancied this unhappy, shameless, heartless creature would have proved herself so ; but she was long known for a person that did not *speak the truth*, and of such (as I have often remarked) there never comes good.'

Meanwhile 'he stuck,' as he said, 'like a burr to his reading, and managed a volume every lawful day (week day). On Sabbath he read to his assembled household (his wife, the maid, and the stable-boy) in the Book of Genesis.' And so the time wore on.

To John Carlyle, Naples.

Craigenputtock : August 31, 1832.

Your letters, I see, are all opened and re-sealed again before they arrive ; but it makes little difference, since such is the will of the Potentates, poor fellows. We have no Carbonari secrets to treat of, and are quite willing to let any biped or quadruped reign in Italy, or out of it, so long as he can.

All is well here in its old course. My article works are all published, and away from me. The Goethe, which was the last of them, went off in a printed shape to Catlinns on Wednesday. It is a poor, fragmentary thing ; some of it was put into Teufelsdröckh's mouth, and I had a letter from London since asking where Teufelsdröckh's great work ('Die Kleider') was to be fallen in with ! Did I say that the 'Corn-law Rhymes' was printed without the slightest mutilation ? So far well ! I have now written to Napier to pay me for it, and with the proceeds mean forthwith to clear scores with the 'Advocate,' and sign myself *Nemini Debens.* This is one fruit which springs from my labours ; and why should I calculate on any other ? There are two little translations of mine off to Fraser—the 'Mährchen,' with a Commentary ; a shorter piece named 'Novelle.' F. is very complaisant with me ; whether he accept or reject these trifles is left with himself. My next task is a very tedious one, an essay on *Diderot ;* as a preliminary for which I have twenty-five octavo volumes to read, and only some eight of them done yet. It will serve me till the end of September, and be worth next to nothing when done. I have engaged for it, and must accomplish it. For the rest, be under no fear lest I overwork myself. Alas ! quite the other danger is to be dreaded. I do not neglect walking or riding (as, for instance, this morning). Besides, the air here is quite specially bracing and good. I have had a kind of fixed persuasion of late that I was one day to get quite well again, or nearly so—some day, that is, between this and the Greek kalends. Indeed, on the whole, I am full of a sentiment which I name 'desperate hope,' and have long been getting fuller. We shall see what will come of it. Meanwhile, in my imprisonment here, whether for life or not, I have bethought me that I ought to get infinitely more *reading* than I have now means of, and *will* get it one way or other, though the Dumfries libraries I have been prying into the rules and state of as yet yield nothing. A very large mass of magazines, reviews, and such like, I have consumed like smoke within the last month, gaining, I think, no knowledge except of the *no*-knowledge of the writing world. Books produce a strange effect on me here : I swallow them with such unpausing impetuosity from early morning to late night, and get altogether filled and intoxicated with them. A little talk were wholesome dissipation for me, but it is not to be had, and one can do without it. My Janekin, if not a great speaker, is the best of listeners, and what she does say is in general real speech and not clatter.

On Monday, the 13th of this month, apprehending with reason an inroad of grouse-killers, I fled about six in the morning (as it had been previously arranged) into Galloway. I breakfasted with Skirving of Croys, rode through Castle Douglas with its withered ' Reform Jubilee' triumphal arch (most villages have had such), and about two o'clock was in the parlour of Kirk Christ. The Churches were in high spirits to see me ; I remembered with a kind of shudder that it was *nine* years since you and I went thither on my last previous visit. The old people are hardly changed, look healthy and prosperous ; all was trim about them, flourishing crops, and the hope of harvest just about to begin realising itself. Great change in the younger parties : two female infants become rather interesting young ladies ; John, whom I remembered in bib and tucker, shot up to six feet and more, a talking, prompt, rather promising young man, intended for the factor line. I could not but reflect, as I have done more than once of late, how small a proportion of mere *intellect* will serve a man's turn if all the rest be right. John Church, as I said, promises well ; James, of Calcutta, is doing admirably well ; and their heads are both of the smallest. Church was full of Herculaneum, and will question you strictly when he gets you. Poor Donaldson, the schoolmaster, my old comrade in Kirkcaldy, has had to put away his wife for the sin of drunkenness, and was a saddish kind of sight to me. I called on old Gordon ; terrified him much, but found him a very worthy and sensible man. Finally, on Thursday morning I departed for Girthon, and by rough ways and over deep rivers reached home that evening about six. Galloway was beautiful, all green and orange under the clear mellow sky. I had glanced into a peopled country, seen old friends, and not wholly wasted my time.

From Annandale I hear good news and nothing else three days ago. They are all well; our mother rather better than usual. Jamie had begun his harvest; the crops excellent, the weather rather damp.

Alick gets the ' Courier' newspaper from us weekly; our mother the 'Examiner,' of which she is exceedingly fond. In respect of this latter your punctuality is now and then desiderated; Tom Holcroft, who sends it to us, misses about one in the month, and I suppose cannot help it. I have just written to Mill, inquiring whether he can form no other arrangement for us. Holcroft has never written, and I hear not a word about him or Badams or any one *von diesem Geschlechte.* Neither has the 'noble lady' ever written, though she was written to months ago. Perhaps I should rather honour her for this omission or forbearance ; Jane and I had evidently become hateful to all that diabolic household, and on our side quite satisfied, not to say sated, of it. Nevertheless the noble lady, quick as a lynx to see this, stood by us faithfully and acted with friendliest regard and very reverence to the very last. Now perhaps she thinks such effort superfluous, and so do we. Her feeling, we know, is kindly, and *can* be translated into no action of importance. Poor old Montagu seemed wearied out and failing. Badams used to say he would not last long. Procter is an innocent kind of body, but not undeserving the name our little lady here used to give him, 'that dud.' A more entire *dud* it would perhaps be difficult to find in the poetical or periodical world. Mrs. P. is honest, keen, and shallow. God mend them and us! we can do them ' neither ill na' good.'

My British news are now nearly written. I need not trouble you with Reform Bill rejoicings—and then, alas! with the electioneerings. It is here that the Reform Bill comes to the test. Set the angel Gabriel to elect a Parliament : how shall he succeed when there is none to elect? However, a new generation will rise —and then. The 'Advocate' I find is at Edinburgh canvassing, and will succeed though the whole country (that had much hope in him) have been disappointed. They say he will be made a judge when any vacancy occurs and will be set free of politics. It were a happy change.

Of Edward Irving I hear nothing except through the newspapers. Last week it was said they had taken a large house (now used as an exhibition establishment) in Newman Street, Oxford Street, and were to put a gallery in it, and were to preach and shriek there. He has published three papers in 'Fraser' on his Tongues. I read the last yesternight, and really wondered over it. He says he cannot believe that God whom they had so prayed to, &c., would *cheat* them. Neither can I. Oh, my poor friend Irving, to what base uses may we come!

But you have enough of this. I must now turn for a moment to Naples.

We have every reason to be satisfied with the accounts you send us. All seems moving as it ought, or nearly so. If you be spared to come back to us, you will have means of settling yourself where you see fittest; above all, you will have *inward* means. We shall find you, I can well perceive, a new man in many things. All right; only do not *turn yourself inwards.* Man may doubt as he will, but the great fact remains: *He is here,* and 'not to ask questions, but to do work.' *Kein Grübeln! N'écoute toi! Cor ne edito!* Do not come back from Italy as if you had been living in a well; speak with all people; no mortal but has something to tell could you once get him to speak TRUTH. Continue to mind your duties; to write in your journal; to *see* and to *do* with utmost possible freedom. I write these things in the shape of *precept,* but I know they might as well be put down like commendations and encouragements, for you already practise and in great part accomplish them. Do it more and more. I am glad you like Naples, and find it strange and notable. Had I the Oriental wishing carpet I were soon beside you noting it too. Gell has proved a little worse than I expected—not much worse. Do you speak Italian perfectly? As for the English—once knowing them to be nonentities, you do right to heed them no more; their whole secret is already understood. Not so with Italians. Even nonentities and *simulacra* (who, as Fichte said, *gar nicht existiren*) of the human sort are worth studying till you see how they are painted and made up. But in any case you are not without society. Your own Countess can tell you innumerable things. You see there what multitudes are so anxious to see—an epitome of English fashionable life; and both for theory and practice can learn much from it. Tell me more about the inside of your household —what you talk of, what you read, what you do. Describe all your 'household epochs' till I can figure them. Did you ever see Thorvaldsen at Rome? Have you met any Italian of a literary cast? any of a *thinking* character, literary or not? Is there any 'Count Menso' now in Naples (Milton's friend and Tasso's)? Is

the blood of St. January now in existence ? Did you see it there ?
Where does Carlo Botta live, the historian ? What of Manzoni ?
Or are all these Lombards and unknown in your country ? I
could ask questions without end. Finally, dear Jack, be of good
heart, for better things are in store for thee. There is a task for
every mortal in this world of the Almighty's ; for thee there is one
greater than for most. Let us stand to our work full of ' desperate hope.' There is on the whole nothing to be afraid of. ' He
that has looked death in the face will start at no shadows.' Come
home to us when the time arrives—to us that love you. Many
hearts will give you welcome, and rejoice to see you in the way of
well-doing. Our dear mother you must consider, much against
her will, wishing and meaning to say many things but unable.
So for the rest you know the affection of them all. Jane will not
send compliments—scarcely even kind regards. ' She meant to
write the whole letter herself, but did not know there was such a
hurry, and now I have done it.' Patience ! there is a good time
coming. The good wifie is clearly very much improved in health
(though troubled with a little cold for the last week) ; and im-
putes her cure to no medicine so much as to an invaluable *three-
fold* (trefoil) which grows in the bogs here, and makes most excellent bitter infusion. Our old mother also is to have some of it.
I, too, have tried it, and find it a praiseworthy pharmacy.

Adieu.   T. C.

P.S.—Cholera is spreading ; is at Carlisle, at Ayr, at Glasgow ;
has hardly yet been in our county—at least, only as imported.
It is all over Cumberland. ' Four carriers, one of them from
Thornhill, breakfasted together at Glasgow, and *all* died on the
way home.' The Thornhill one did, we know. It has gone back
to Sunderland and Newcastle. Medical men can do *nothing*, except frighten those that are frightable. The mortality, after all,
is no wise so quick as in typhus form ; is seen every year ; but men
are natural blockheads, and *common* death is not death.

Extracts from Note Book.

August 8.—I cannot understand *Morals*. Our current Moral
Law (even that of philosophers) affronts me with all manner of
perplexities. *Punishment* neither is nor can be in proportion to
fault ; for the commonest of all examples take the case of an erring woman.

And then how strange is the influence of what we call *honour :* when our fellow men are once come to be asked for their vote, how strangely do they alter every thing ! Where are the limits of conscience and honour? what relation (even for the anti-gigman) do the two mutually bear? Moral *force* and moral *correctness*—how shall the litigation be settled between these? Ought there to *be* any unpardonable offence? Ought the judge in any case to say irrevocably, *Be thou outcast* (as proud fathers have done to erring daughters for instance)? The world has declared, Yes. Neither is there wanting some ground for it. Necessity rules our existence : Man should step in and be as stern as Necessity, and *take the word out of its mouth.* Perhaps ; yet not with clear certainty. This is 'the Place of Hope.' Should man's mind have sudden boundless transitions of that sort ; have *vaporific points*, and *freezing points*, or should it not? *Weiss nicht.* It is all confused to me : seems to be all refounding itself. Happily the practical is no wise dubious.

Toleration, too, is miserably mistaken; means for most part only indifference and contempt : *Verachtung, ja Nichtachtung.* What is bad *is* a thing to be the sooner the better *abolished.* Whether this imply *hatred* or not will depend on circumstances. Not toleration, therefore, but the quickest possible abolition : that were our rule. A wicked hatred, in abolishing, *substitutes* new badness (as bad or worse). The pure, *praiseworthy*, useful Hatred were that which abolished and did not substitute.[1]

I am getting very weary of the 'Nature of the Time,' 'Progress

---

[1] This sentence did not please Carlyle or adequately express his meaning. Suppose we put it in this way. A set of people are living in a village which threatens to fall about their ears. The thatch is rotting, the foundations sinking, the walls cracking. Is the village to be pulled down, and are the people to be left houseless? The shelter is bad; but still it is some shelter— better than none—and likely to serve till something sounder can be provided. If it be doing no harm otherwise, this would be clearly the rule. But suppose the village to be breeding the plague by generating poisonous vapours. Then clearly the people will be better off with no roof over them but the sky. Substitute for the village, Paganism, Romanism, or any other lingering creed which eager persons are impatient to be rid of. Is Romanism morally poisonous? Knox and Cromwell answered clearly, Yes ; and with good reason, and so did not tolerate it. We, with or without good reason, have found it no longer poisonous, and so do tolerate. Both may be right. In our toleration there is no indifference or contempt. In the intolerance of Cromwell there was a hatred of the intensest kind—hatred of evil in its concrete form.

of the Species,' and all that business. The Time is here; men should use it, not talk about it : while they talk and lay not hold, it is gone and returns not.

Great is self-denial! Practice it where thou needest it. Life goes all to ravels and tatters· where that enters not. The old monks meant very wisely : hit thou the just medium.

Thou complainest that enjoyments are withheld from thee, and thereby (thou caring nothing for *enjoyment* for its own sake) thy *culture* and experiences are in many ways obstructed. Be consistent: cultivate thyself in the want of enjoyment : gather quite peculiar experiences therein.

August 11.—A strange force of what I call 'desperate hope' is gathering in me : I feel a kind of defiant assurance that much shall yet be well with me, the rather as I care little *whether or not*.

It is true : evil must always continue: yet not this evil and that evil. *The* thing convicted of falsehood *must* be forthwith cast out : the Radical is a believer, of the gross, heathen sort ; yet our only believer in these times.

Politics confuse me—what my duties are therein? As yet I have *stood apart*, and till quite new aspects of the matter turn up, shall continue to do so. The battle is not between Tory and Radical (that is but like other battles) ; but between believer and unbeliever.

Am inclined to consider myself a most sorry knave ; but must cease *considering* and begin to work, whether at —— (?) or at Diderot? At the latter in any case *to-day;* and herewith enough.

> Oh! life turmoil—to-day—to-morrow
>   Unfathomed thing thou wert and art :
> In sight, in blindness, joy and sorrow
>   The wondrous Thomas plays his part.
>
> Awhile behold him flesh-clothed *spirit*,
>   He reaps and sows the allotted hours,
> Would much bequeath, did much inherit,
>   Oh ! help the helpless, heavenly powers.

Seneca was born to be of the Church of England. He is the father of all that work in sentimentality, and, by fine speaking and decent behaviour, study to serve God and Mammon, to stand well with philosophy and not ill with Nero. His *force* had mostly oozed out of him, or 'corrupted itself into *benevolence*, virtue, sensibility.' Oh! the everlasting clatter about virtue! virtue! In the Devil's name be virtuous, and no more about it! Seneca could have been a Bishop Heber; Dr. Channing, too, and that set, have some kindred with him. He was, and they are, better than nothing, *very greatly* better. *Sey gerade, sey verträglich.*

September 3.—Beautiful autumn days! I am reading Diderot, with intent to write on him; not at all in a very wholesome state of mind or body, but must put up with it, the thing needs to be *done.*

I thank Heaven I have still a boundless appetite for reading. I have thoughts of lying buried alive here for many years, forgetting all stuff about 'reputation,' success, and so forth, and resolutely setting myself to gain insight, by the only method not shut out from me—that of books. Two articles (of fifty pages) in the year will keep me living; employment in that kind is open enough. For the rest, I really find almost that I do *best* when *forgotten* of men, and nothing above or around me but the imperishable Heaven. It never wholly seems to me that I am to die in this wilderness : a feeling is always dimly with me that I am to be called out of it, and have work fit for me before I depart, the rather as I can do *either way.* Let not solitude, let not silence and unparticipating isolation make a savage of thee—these, too, have their advantages.

On Saturday (September 15), being summoned to Dumfries as a juryman, and my whole duty consisting in answering 'Here' when my name was called, I ran out to the Bank, got my draft from Cochrane (for 'Goethe') converted into cash, added to it what otherwise I had, and paid the Lord Advocate 103*l.* 10*s.*, my own whole debt, and John's (43*l.* 10*s.*, which had been already sent me for that end); a short, grateful letter accompanied the banker's cheque, and the whole would reach its destination at latest last Monday morning. I now once more owe no man any money, have 5*l.* in my possession still, and a matter of 50*l.* or 60*l.* due to me. Be thankful!

I must to Edinburgh in winter; the solitude here, generally very irksome, is threatening to get injurious, to get intolerable. Work, work! and gather a few pounds to take thee.

Opinions of the article, 'Goethe,' Cochrane writes, are all 'eminently unfavourable.' The 'eminently' he has inserted on second thoughts by means of a *caret*. He is a wondrous man to see editing, that Cochrane; what one might call an *Editing Pig*, as there are learned pigs, &c. He is very punctual in *paying*, and indeed generally; that is his only merit. Use him sharply, almost contemptuously, and he remains civil, and does better than most. Bibliopoly, bibliopoesy, in all their branches, are sick, sick, hastening to death and new *genesis*. Enough! *Ach gar zu viel.*

Great meaning that lies in *irrevocability*, as in ' eternal creeds,' ' eternal forms of government,' also in final irreversible engagements we make (marriage, for one). Worth considering this. The proper element of belief, and therefore of concentrated action. On a thing that were seen to be′ *temporary* (finite and not infinite), who is there that would spend and be spent?

Sir Walter Scott died nine days ago. Goethe at the spring equinox, Scott at the autumn one. A gifted spirit then is wanting from among men. Perhaps he died in good time, so far as his own reputation is concerned. He understood what *history* meant; this was his chief intellectual merit. As a thinker, not feeble—strong, rather, and healthy, yet limited, almost mean and *kleinstädtisch*. I never spoke with Scott (had once some small epistolary intercourse with him on the part of Goethe, in which he behaved not ′very courteously, I thought), have a hundred times seen him, from of old, writing in the Courts, or hobbling with stout speed along the streets of Edinburgh; a large man, pale, shaggy face, fine, deep-browed grey eyes, an expression of strong homely intelligence, of humour and good humour, and, perhaps (in later years among the wrinkles), of sadness or weariness. A solid, well-built, effectual mind; the merits of which, after all this delirious exaggeration is done, and the reaction thereof is also done, will not be forgotten. He has played his part, and left *none like* or second to him. *Plaudite!*

In the middle of October, the Diderot article being finished, the Carlyles made an expedition into Annandale. They stayed for a day or two at Templand. Carlyle, ' having nothing better to do,' rode over, with Dr. Russell, of Thornhill, to Morton Castle, ' a respectable old ruin, which looked sternly expressive, striking enough, in the pale October evening.' The castle had belonged to the Randolphs, and had been uninhabited for two centuries. The court was then a cattlefold. In the distance they saw the remains of the old Church of Kilbride, where Dr. Russell told Carlyle, 'there still lay open and loose on the wall a circular piece of iron framing, once used for supporting the baptismal ewer, and protected for 350 years by a superstitious feeling alone.' Leaving Templand, they drove round by Loch Ettrick, Kirkmichael, and Lockerby, stopping to visit Alex. Carlyle in his new farm, and thence to Scotsbrig. Here the inscription was to be fixed on old Mr. Carlyle's grave in Ecclefechan churchyard. It was the last light of dusk when they arrived at the spot where Carlyle himself is now lying. 'Gloomy empire of TIME!' he wrote, after looking at it. 'How all had changed, changed; nothing stood still, but some old tombs with their cross-stones, which I remembered from boyhood. Their strange *süss-schauerliche* effect on me! Our house where we had all *lived* was within stone cast; but this, too, knew us no more again at all for ever.'

After ten days they returned to Craigenputtock, bringing 'sister Jane' with them, who was followed afterwards by the mother. The winter they meditated spending in Edinburgh. The following pleasant letter to John Carlyle was written a day or two before they started on this tour.

To John Carlyle, Rome.

Craigenputtock : October 17, 1832.

I finished my 'composition' the day before yesterday. Am bound for Annandale in the end of the week ; and so here we are. I will not seal this till I have seen our mother, for I have *heard* nothing of them in a positive shape for many weeks.

There is little or nothing to be written of transactions, when the change of weather and of nervous sensibility are almost our only events. You can picture out Puttock, and how I sit here (in the library), with a blazing fire of peats and coals, careless of the damp, surly elements, having dulness only to struggle with. We keep a Famulus to go errands, yoke the gig, curry the cattle, and so forth; who proves very useful to us. Jane is sitting in the dining-room; reads, sews, rules her household, where cow, hens, human menials, garden crop, all things animate and inanimate, need looking to. She is not quite so brisk as she was, and the trefoil [1] has long been discontinued. However, she is certainly far better than while in London, and, on the whole, continuing to gather strength. The grey mare about six weeks ago kicked her harness to pieces with us, down at John McKnight's, without the slightest provocation, but did *us* no damage; I even brought the dame home on her back. However, such conduct was not to be dreamt of; so we despatched the animal to Alick, to màke ready for the 'rood fair,' who, as we since vaguely learn (for they have not even informed us of this), has sold her to Jamie, that he, in carts and plough-harness, may teach her 'another road to the well.' With unexampled dexterity, having procured an awl and thread from Dumfries, I mended the old harness again (indiscernibly to the naked eye); and now little Harry draws us, and makes no bones of the matter, being in good heart and well provided with fodder, both long and short : that is the way we manage. All is tight and sufficient round us, and need not be in disorder : we want for nothing in the way of earthly proviant, and have many reasons to be content and diligent. Recreation we have none; a walk, a ride, on some occasions a combined *drive* for health's sake alone. Miss Whigham (of Allanton) called here the other day, and this is simply our only call since we came from London ! Poor William Carson,[2] indeed, bounces up about once in the month to tea; but he is nigh distracted and one cannot count on him. I tried the schoolmaster, but he is a poor rawboned Grampus, whom I lent a book to, but could get no more good of. I have tried some of the peasants, but them also without fruit. In short, mortal communion is not to be had for us here. What, then, but do without it? Peter Austin (of Carstamon—Castra Montium—we, too, have had our Romans) is very useful to us; a decent, punctual man, the shrewdest of these parts. On the whole, I do not think I shall ever get anything better than a cheap and very peculiar *lodging* here; no home, I

---

[1] The supposed tonic made of the sorrel which grew freely in the Craigenputtock woods.

[2] A young neighbour.

imagine, has been appointed. For whom *is* such appointed ? The most have not even lodgings except by sufferance. The Advocate acknowledges his debt cleared ; it is the only thing we have heard of him for a great while. I imagine our relationship is a good deal cooled, and may now be visibly to him, as it has long been visibly to me, a rather fruitless one. His world is not our world : he dwells in the glitter of saloon chandeliers, walking in the 'vain show' of parliamenteering and gigmanity, which also he feels to be vain ; we, in the whirlwind and wild piping battle of fate, which, nevertheless, by God's grace, we feel to be not vain and a show, but true and a reality. Thus may each without disadvantage go his several ways. If Jeffrey's well-being ever lay in my reach how gladly would I increase it ! But I hope better things for him ; though he is evidently declining in the world's grace, and knows as well as the world that his political career has proved a nonentity. Often have I lamented to think that so genial a nature had been (by the *Zeitgeist* who works such misery) turned into that frosty, unfruitful course. But, as George Rae said, ' D—n you, be wae for yoursel',' so there we leave it. On that busy day I got the proof sheets of that Fraser concern, *The Tale by Goethe*, which is his leading item for this month, but has not got hither yet. It is not a bad thing ; the commentary cost me but a day, and does well enough. The produce belongs to my little dame to buy pins for her ; she got it as present long ago at the *Hill*, and reckoned it unavailable. Fraser applied for a paper on ' Walter Scott :' I declined, having a great aversion to that obituary kind of work—so undertaker-like ; but I said I might perhaps do it, afterwards. This thing I have been cobbling together last is a long paper on 'Diderot,' for Cochrane. I had an immense reading, to little purpose otherwise, and am very glad to have it all behind me. And now, after a few days' sight of friends, I must back hither into the wold, and dig a little more.

We are not for Edinburgh till six weeks hence, so there is time to do something previously. I shall have funds enough : there is this thing ; Napier, too, owes me above 60*l.*, some of it for nine or ten months, and seems to be shy of paying. I shall see better what he means in Edinburgh ; his ' Review,' except for Macaulay (who as yet has only sung old songs of Liberalism and the like, with a new windpipe) is the utterest ' dry rubbish shot here ;' yet by a kind of fatality it may linger on who knows how long, and perhaps Naso does not think my *moisture* would improve it. *A la bonne* *heure!* There are plenty of able editors zealous enough to employ me; this is all the fame (*Fama Diva!*) I fall in with, or need; so that when you come home, Doctor, there will be a considerable volume for you to read, and I, in the interim, have lived thereby. I do not mean to work much at Edinburgh for a while, but to *ask* and *look;* that makes me the busier at present. It is three years I have been absent, and several things will be changed.

Your offer, dear Jack, is kind, brotherly, suitable ; neither shall you be forbid to pay your ' debts,' and much more (if you come to have the means, and we both prove worthy) ; but in the meanwhile it were madness to reap corn not yet in the ear (or kill the goose for her golden eggs, if you like that figure better) ; your great outlook at present is to get yourself set up in medical practice, for which end all the money you can possibly save will be essential. I look to see you a faithful doctor, *real*, not an imaginary worker in that fold whereto God's endowment has qualified and appointed you. The rest I say honestly is within the merest trifle of indifferent to me. How *long* (were there nothing more in it) will it last ? Walter Scott is now poorer than I am ; has left all his *wages* behind. If he spoke the truth it was well for him ; if not, not well.

Adieu, dear brother ; adieu

T. CARLYLE.

Jeffrey's relations with Carlyle might be cooling. To his cousin his affection was as warm as ever, though they seemed to enjoy tormenting each other. He had been long silent, finding a correspondence which could not help Mrs. Carlyle exceedingly painful. He had been busy getting himself returned for Edinburgh ; but something more than this—impatience, provocation, and conscious inability to do any good—had stopped his pen. Now, however, he heard that the Carlyles were actually coming to Edinburgh, and the news brought a letter from him of warm anticipation.

The journey, which had been arranged for the beginning of December, was delayed by the illness of Mrs. Carlyle's grandfather, her mother's father, old Mr. Welsh of Templand, which ended in death. Mrs. Carlyle went

down to assist in nursing him, leaving her husband alone
with his mother at Craigenputtock, himself busy in charge
of the household economies, which his mother, either out
of respect for her daughter-in-law, or in fear of her, declined to meddle with. He had to congratulate himself
that the establishment was not on fire; nevertheless, he
wrote that his 'coadjutor's return would bring blessings
with it.' The illness, however, ended fatally, and she
could not come back to him till it was over.

To John Carlyle, Rome.

Craigenputtock: December 2, 1832.

Mrs. Welsh, I told you in my last letter, was not well; we had
driven over the moors out of Annandale, and seen her as we past,
apparently in a rather better state. But scarcely had sister Jane
after a week got conveyed home again, and our mother got up
hither, on pressing invitation, to see us, when a letter came from
Templand with intelligence that poor old grandfather was much
worse, and Mrs. Welsh, throwing by all her own ailments, had
started up to watch over him; whereupon my Jane thought it
right to set off without delay, and so left my mother and me by
ourselves here. It is needless to fill your sheet with long accounts of comings and goings, of agitations, sorrowings, and con-
fusions; enough to inform you that the old man now lies no more
on a sick bed, but in his last home beside his loved ones in the
churchyard of Crawford, where we laid him on Friday gone a
week. He had the gentlest death, and had numbered fourscore
years. Fond remembrances, and a mild long-anticipated sorrow
attended him. Man issues from eternity; walks in a 'Time Element' encompassed by eternity, and again in eternity disappears.
Fearful and wonderful! This only we know, that God is above it,
that God made it, and rules it for good. What change of life this
may produce for Mrs. Welsh we have not understood yet. Most
probably she will retain the home at Templand, and give up the
ground and farming establishment. Such at least were her wisest
plan. But Jane and I hastened off on the Saturday to relieve my
mother, who was watching here in total loneliness, agitated too
with change of servants and so forth.

For the rest receive thankfully the assurance that all continues

well. The cholera, of which I wrote to you,[1] is gone, taking about
500 souls with it, which from a population of 13,000, was, in the
space of some four weeks, rather an alarming proportion. The terror of the adjacent people, which was excessive and indeed dis-
graceful, has hardly yet subsided. Happily the pest does not
spread ; a few cases occurred in the Galloway villages, elsewhere
none, or hardly any, and so it went its way as mysteriously as it
had come. Nobody connected much with us has been taken, many
as were exposed. Death, however, in other shapes, is as of old
busy. James Thomson of Cleughside is gone lately. . . . Old
Wull Nay is dead ; his poor old wife (they say) bitterly lamented,
and 'hung by the hearse,' which, however, could not stay. . . . A
son of Davie Corrie, married about a year ago, is also dead. What
is this whole earth but a kind of Golgotha, a scene of Death-Life,
where inexorable *Time* is producing all and devouring all ? Happily there is a Heaven round it ; otherwise for me it were not in-
habitable. Courage ! courage !

Uns zu verewigen sind wir ja da.

On Wednesday I got your letter at Dumfries ; called also at the
bank, and found 135*l.* ready, for which I took a bank receipt that
shall be ready for you on your home-coming. I do not need the
money at present, and you will need it ; therefore, much as I rejoice in the spirit you display, let it *dabey bleiben* till we see how
times turn. You may by possibility become a moneyed man ; I
never. The relation between us in any case is already settled.

Alick is grown more collected, has lost none of his energy, nor
on occasion his biting satire, which however his wife is happily
too thick-skinned to feel. They will struggle on I think, and not
be defeated. Jamie too goes along satisfactorily, a shrewd sort of
fellow with much gaiety, who sometimes in his laughter-loving
moods reminds me slightly of you. No two of the house have such
a heart-relish for the ludicrous, though we all like it. Our good
mother is in tolerable health and heart. She improved much with
us here the first two weeks, but fell off again for want of exercise
and excitement. She read here about the persecutions of the
Scotch Church, and in some of Knox's writings I had ; not even
disdaining ' Fraser's Magazine,' or the *Reviews.* She is still very
zealous, and predicts black times (with us) for the world. It seemed

---

[1] As being at Dumfries.

to her that Lady Clare would be much amazed with your descriptions of Scotch life, and might learn much from it. From Almack's to Ecclefechan is a wide interval, yet strange things come together. Strictly speaking the wretched Ecclefechan existence is the more tolerable of the two, for in it there is a pre-ordination of Destiny, and something *done*, namely muslin woven, and savage bipeds boarded and bedded. Alas! the hand of the Devil lies heavy on all men. But days quite saturated with *Antigigmanism* are surely coming, and from these better will arise. The completest, profoundest of all past and present Antigigmen was Jesus Christ. Let us think of this, for much follows from it. Better times are coming, surely coming. Cast *thou* thy bread on the wild, agitated waters, thou wilt find it after many days. That is enough.

At Edinburgh I expect books, some conversation with reasonable, earnest, or even with unreasonable, baseless men; on the whole some guidance, economical if not spiritual. Sir William Hamilton is one I hope to get a little good of; of others, too, whom hitherto I have not personally known. Of my own acceptance with all manner of persons I have reason to speak with thankfulness, indeed with astonishment. It is little man can do for man, but of that little I am nowise destitute. In any case we will live in our own hired house, on our own earned money, and see what the world can show us. I get more earnest, graver, not unhappier, every day. The whole Creation seems more and more Divine to me, the Natural more and more Supernatural. Out of Goethe, who is my near neighbour, so to speak, there is no writing that *speaks* to me (*mir anspricht*) like the Hebrew Scriptures, though they lie far remote. Earnestness of soul was never shown as there. *Ernst is das Leben;* and even to the last, soul resembles soul. Here, however, speaking of Goethe, I must tell you that last week, as our mother and I were passing Sandywell, a little parcel was handed in which proved to be from Eckermann, at Weimar. It made me glad and sad. There was a medal in it, struck since the poet's death. Ottilie had sent it me. Then a gilt cream-coloured essay on Goethe's *Practische Wirksamkeit* by one F. von Müller, a Weimar *Kunstfreund* and intimate of deceased's, with an inscription on it by him. Finally the third *Heft* of the sixth volume of 'Kunst und Alterthum.,' which had partly been in preparation, and now posthumously produced itself; to me a touching kind of sight. Eckermann wrote a very kind letter, explaining how busy he was with reducing the fifteenth volume of *Nachgelassenen Schriften,* the titles of all which he gave me. There is a volume of 'Dichtung und Wahrheid,' and the completion of 'Faust.' These are the most remarkable. I have read Müller's essay, which is sensible enough—several good things also are in the *Heft,* towards the last page of which I came upon these words (by Müller, speaking of Goethe) : 'Among the younger British, Bulwer and Carlyle very especially attract him. The beautiful pure disposition of the last, with his calm, delicate perceptiveness, raises Goethe's recognition of him to the warmest regard : [1]' This of *liebevollste Zuneigung* was extremely precious to me. Alas ! *und das Alles ist hin.* Ottilie promises to write, but I think *not.*

And now, dear Jack, before closing let us cast a glance towards Rome. Your two last letters are very descriptive of your household ways, and give us all much satisfaction. We can figure you far better than before. Continue to send the like. I wish you were well settled for the winter. There seems nothing else to be wished at present. I can understand your relation to your patient to be a delicate one ; but you appear to have good insight into it, and to be of the most promising temper. ' *Geradheit, Urtheil und Verträglichkeit.*' I miss none of these three ; they make in all cases a noble mixture. Be of good cheer, *in omne paratus,* you will return home to us a much more productive kind of character than you were ; learned, equipped in *many* ways, with all that is worthy in your character developed into action, or much nearer development. Be diligent in business, fervent in spirit. What is all our life, and all its ill-success or good success, that we should fear it ? An eternity is already around us. Time (wherein is the disease we call Life), will soon be done, and then ! Let us have an eye on that city that *hath* foundations.

God ever bless you, dear brother,
T. CARLYLE.

A letter follows from Mrs. Austin :—

To Mrs. Carlyle, Craigenputtock.
26 Park Road, London : December 25, 1832.

Dearest Friend,—Writing to you, which ought from all natural causes to be one of my greatest and dearest pleasures, is become

---

[1] 'Unter den jüngern Britten ziehen Bulwer und Carlyle ihn ganz vorzüglich an, und das schöne reine Naturell des letztern, seine ruhige zartsinnige Auffassungsgabe steigern Goethe's Anerkennung bis zur liebevollsten Zuneigung.'

a sort of dread and pain and oppression. I feel as if I had no means of saying anything because I have so much to say ; because I would fain tell you how I love you and your husband ; how I look to you as objects that would console and refresh and elevate one to think of ; how I want your sympathy and approbation, and sometimes comfort ; because I have endless facts to tell and thoughts to communicate, requisitions to ask—and then—to write thus seems mocking myself and you. A quire of such sheets as these would not hold *all* I should like to write. But my business is not to do as I like ; and you and he will not think the worse of me for my self-denial. You may have seen somewhere or other that an early and long toil of mine is finished ; a selection from the Old Testament. If I knew how I should send you a copy, just that you might see that I *work !* Mr. Carlyle will think *that* worth praise, though there be many defects in the *how*. Also look, if by any chance the New Monthly Magazine comes in your way, for an article entitled 'On the recent attempts to revolutionise Germany.' I translated from a journal P. Pücklers sent me, with commendation. Other Germans admire it. I excite horror among my Radical friends for not believing that all salvation comes of certain organic forms of government ; and, as I tell Mrs. Jeffrey, am that monster made up ' of all we Whigs hate,' a Radical and an Absolutist.

Meantime Falk goes on. Falk *eigentlich* has long been done ; but matter keeps congregating around him. Frau von Goethe sent me by Henry Reeve, 'Goethe in seiner practischen Wirksamkeit,' by Von Müller, Kanzler of Weimar. She sent it 'with her best love,' and with the assurance that *He* was just about to write to me when he died—that one of the last things he read was my translation, with which he kindly said he was much pleased. You will be able to estimate the value I set upon this faint shadow of a communication with him.

How I wish Mr. Carlyle may like—in any degree—what I have done. And then you, like a loyal wife as you are, will like it too. And yet it is nothing but compilation and translation—mere drudgery. Well, dearest friend, there are men enough and women enough to dogmatise, and to invent, and to teach and preach all things, Political Economy included. I can write nothing, and teach nothing ; but if I can interpret and illustrate, it is something ; and I have the advantage of remaining, what a remnant of womanly superstition about me makes me think best for us—a woman. These are 'auld world notions.' You know that word in my vocabulary excludes no particle of strength, courage, or activity. But *a well-chosen field* is the thing. What say you?

My husband is tolerably; working or standing against the stream of washy violence which inundates us all. What is better, and what the practical many dream not of, he is ever daily and hourly converting, purifying, elevating—himself; for which small business your reformers of crowds have little time and less taste.

Lucy grows a tall, fair girl. At least, people call her handsome. She is, at any rate, intelligent and simple, and strong, and not like the children of the ' *upper classes.*' Mrs. Bulwer told me that her little girl of four said, in answer to some question about her little cousins, 'I suppose they have seen by the papers that I go to school.' Here is ' diffusion of knowledge' with a vengeance, and matter for the excellent Carlyle to moralise upon, ' auf seine Art und Weise.' Would I were there to hear. Henry Reeve is at Munich, and greatly attached to Schelling, who is quite fatherly to him.

And now God bless you. New years or old make no great difference in my wishes for you, which will outlast a year and I trust a world. Write to me, my dear friend, and believe that my affection and deep esteem are not the feebler for my want of time to tell of them.

Yours,

S. Austin.

CHAPTER XIV.

A.D. 1833. ÆT. 38.

Extracts from Journal.

Edinburgh, January 12, 1833.—Arrived here on Monday night last. Nasty fog; ghastly kind of light and silence in Dalveen Pass; the wearisome, dreaming-awake kind of day I always have in state coaches. Mill's letter awaiting me here. Village-like impression of Edinburgh after London. People are all kind; I languid, bilious, not very open to kindness. Dr. Irving advises immediate application for a certain Glasgow Astronomy Professorship. I shall hardly trouble myself with it. Deeply impressed with the transiency of time; more and more careless about all that time can give or take away. Could undertake to teach astronomy, as soon as most things, by way of honest day-labour : not otherwise, for I have no zeal now that way. To *teach* any of the things I am interested in were for the present impossible ; all is unfixed, nothing has yet grown ; at best, is but growing. Thus, too, the futility of founding universities at this time : the only university you can advantageously found were a public library. This is *never* out of season ; therefore not now, when all else in that kind is.

Have long been almost idle ; have long been out of free communion with myself. Must *suffer* more before I can begin thinking. Will try to write : but what? but when? On the whole, what a wretched thing is all fame ! A renown of the highest sort endures, say, for two thousand years. And then? Why, then, a fathomless *eternity* swallows it. *Work* for eternity : not the meagre rhetorical eternity of the periodical critics, but for the real eternity, wherein dwelleth the Divine ! Alas ! all here is so dark. Keep firm in thy eye what light thou hast.

Daily and hourly the world natural grows more of a world magical to me : this is as it should be. Daily, too, I see that there is no true poetry but in *reality*. Wilt thou ever be a poetkin? *Schwerlich :* no matter.

'I have long been almost idle.' The dark mood was back in Carlyle, and these words explain it. When idle he was miserable ; when miserable he made all about him miserable. At such times he was 'gey ill to live wi'' indeed.

Sick of Craigenputtock, sick of solitude, sick with thoughts of many kinds for which he could as yet find no proper utterance, Carlyle had gone to Edinburgh to find books and hear the sound of human voices. Books he found in the Advocates' Library, books in plenty upon every subject ; on the one subject, especially, which had now hold of his imagination. The French Revolution had long interested him, as illustrating signally his own conclusions on the Divine government of the world. Since he had written upon Diderot, that tremendous convulsion had risen before him more and more vividly as a portent which it was necessary for him to understand. He had read Thiers' history lately.[1] Mill, who had been a careful student of the Revolution, furnished him with memoirs, pamphlets, and newspapers. But these only increased his thirst.

In the Advocates' Library at Edinburgh he was able to look round his subject, and examine it before and after ; to look especially to scattered spiritual and personal phenomena ; to look into Mirabeau's life, and Danton's, and Madame Roland's ; among side pictures to observe Cagliostro's history, and as growing out of it the melodrama of 'The Diamond Necklace.' All this Carlyle devoured with voracity, and the winter so spent in Edinburgh was of immeasurable moment to him. Under other aspects the place was unfortunately less agreeable than he had expected to find it. In his choice of a future residence he had been hesitating between London and Edinburgh. In

---

[1] Carlyle once gave me a characteristic criticism of Thiers. It was brief. 'Dig where you will,' he said, 'you come to water.'

his choice of a subject on which to write he had been doubting between ' The French Revolution ' and ' John Knox and the Scotch Reformation.' On both these points a few weeks' experience of the modern Athens decided him. Edinburgh society was not to his mind. He discerned, probably, not for the first time in human history, that a prophet is not readily acknowledged in his own country. No circle of disciples gathered round him as they had done in Ampton Street. His lodgings proved inconvenient, and even worse. Neither he nor his wife could sleep for the watchman telling the hours in the street. When they moved into a back room they were disturbed by noises overhead. A woman, it appeared, of the worst character, was nightly entertaining her friends there. They could do with little money in Craigenputtock; life in Edinburgh, even on humble terms, was expensive. Napier was remiss in his payments for the articles in the ' Edinburgh Review.' He was generally six months in arrear. He paid only after repeated dunning, and then on a scale of growing illiberality. These, however, were minor evils, and might have been endured. They had gone up with light hearts, in evident hope that they would find Edinburgh an agreeable change from the moors. Carlyle himself thought that, with his increasing reputation, his own country would now, perhaps, do something for him. His first letter to his brother, after his arrival, was written in his usual spirits.

By Heaven's grace, he said, I nowise want merchants of a sort for my wares; and can still, even in these days, live. So long as that is granted, what more is there to ask? All gigmanity is of the Devil, devilish: let us rather be thankful if we are shut out even from the temptation thereto. It is not want of money or money's worth that I could ever complain of: nay, often too it seems to me as if I did *best* when no *praise* was given me, and I stood alone between the two eternities with my feet on the rock. But what I mourn over is the too frequent obscuration of faith within me; the kind of exile I must live in from all classes of articulate speaking men; the dimness that reigns over all my practical sphere; the etc., etc., for there is no end to man's complaining. One thing I have as good as ascertained: that Craigenputtock cannot for ever be my place of abode; that it is at present, and actually, one of the worst abodes for me in the whole wide world. One day I will quit it, either quietly or like a *muir-break;* for I feel well there are things in me to be told which may cause the ears that hear them to tingle! *Alles mit Mäss und Regel!* As yet I decide on nothing; will no wise desert the whinstone stronghold till I better see some road from it. I could live again in Edinburgh, perhaps still more willingly in London, had I means. My good wife is ready for all things, so we wait what the days bring forth. Perhaps the future may be kinder to us both; but is not the present kind? Full of work to do? Write me all things, my dear brother, and fear not that you shall ever want my sympathy. Keep diligent in business, fervent in spirit, serving God; that is the sum of all wisdom.

For the first week or two Edinburgh itself was not disagreeable. 'The transition was singular from the bare solitary moors to crowded streets and the concourse of men.' The streets themselves were 'orderly and airy.' 'The reek of Auld Reekie herself was the clearness of mountain tops compared to the horrible vapours of London.' Friends came about them, Jeffrey, Sir William Hamilton, Harry Inglis, and many more, all kind and courteous; but their way of thinking was not Carlyle's way of thinking, 'the things they were running the race for were no prizes for him,' and 'he felt a stranger among them.' 'When he gave voice' 'they stared at him.' 'When they had the word,' he said, 'he listened with a sigh or a smile.' [1] Then came another disappointment. A Professorship at Glasgow was vacant. Jeffrey, as Lord Advocate, had the appointment, or a power of recommending which would be as emphatic as a *congé d'élire.* Carlyle gave Jeffrey a hint about it, but Jeffrey left for Lon-

---

[1] Gibbon's expression.

don directly after, and Carlyle instinctively felt that he was not to have it. 'My own private impression,' he said, 'is that I shall never get any promotion in this world, and happy shall I be if Providence enable me only to stand my own friend. That is, or should be, all the prayer I offer to Heaven.'

Extracts from Journal.

February 1, 1833.—Have been exploring on all hands the foolish history of the Quack Cagliostro. Have read several books about him, searching far and wide after him ; learned, I ought to admit, almost nothing. Shall I study this enigma, then write my solution or no-solution.

Am quite bewildered, *déroute*, know not whither to address the little energy I have : sick, too, and on the whole solitary, though with men enough about me. Sir William Hamilton, the one that approaches nearest being earnest : he, too, does not attain earnestness, and his faculty is not of the instructive kind. 'Help thyself ; heaven will help thee ! '

The Advocate is gone : to join the new Reformed Parliament, where may he prosper ! Our relation is done, all but the outward shell of it, which may stick there as long as it can. *Respectability* and Fate-warfare march not long on one road. All is whiggery here, which means 'I will believe whatsoever I shall be forced to believe.' In this country, as in France, the main movement will come from the capital. Perhaps it may be sooner than one expects. The pressure of economical difficulty is rapidly augmenting ; misery of that and all kinds is prevalent enough here ; everything wears an uneasy, decaying aspect, yet far short of what strikes one in London. A sorrowful, poor, unproductive struggle, which nevertheless this Age was fated and bound to undertake. On with it then.

Wilson I have not seen. Is he afflicted with my Radicalism ? Is he simply too lazy to call on me, or indisposed to take the trouble of etiquette upon him, for object so little momentous ? Shall I stand on etiquette then ? It is of small consequence, though perhaps the issue will be that we stand not only apart but divided, which I have no wish to do. Moir has been here ; in all senses a *neat* man, in none a strong one. Great stupidity reigns here I think ; but what then ? Grow thou wiser ! Brewster has lost his canvass for Leslie's Professorship and is about entering the English Church, they say, being promised a living. 'Once a noble soap bell, now a drop of sour suds.' Such is the history of many men.

The bitter old Hebrew implacability of that couplet—

> On those that do me hate
> I my desire shall see.

One day they will be even *as I wish them!* Envy no man, for such, sooner or later, will be his hard fortune. Nay, in any case does he not at last die! One of my best moods (many are too *bad*) is that of sincere pity for all breathing men. Oftenest it is a sincere indifference. Yesterday it seemed to me death was actually a cheerful looking thing : such a boundless *Possibility;* no longer hampered by the so strait limits of this world's time and space. Oh for faith! Truly the greatest 'God announcing miracle' always is faith, and now more than ever. I often look on my mother (nearly the only genuine Believer I know of) with a kind of sacred admiration. Know the worth of Belief. Alas! canst thou acquire none?

That the Supernatural differs not from the Natural is a great Truth, which the last century (especially in France) has been engaged in demonstrating. The Philosophers went far wrong, however, in this, that instead of raising the natural to the supernatural, they strove to sink the supernatural to the natural. The gist of my whole way of thought is to do not the latter but the *former*. I feel it to be the epitome of much good for this and following generations in my hands and in those of innumerable stronger ones. *Belief*, said one the other night, has done immense evil : witness Knipperdolling and the Anabaptists, etc. 'True,' rejoined I, with vehemence, almost with fury (Proh pudor!), 'true belief has done some evil in the world; but it has done all the good that was ever done in it; from the time when Moses saw the Burning Bush and *believed* it to be God appointing him deliverer of His people, down to the last act of belief that you and I executed. Good never came from aught else.'

To John Carlyle.

Edinburgh : February 10.

I have not been idle during the last month though not employed in the way I most approve of. Since the article Diderot, written in October, I have never put pen to paper till last week, when I began a piece for Fraser to be entitled 'Cagliostro.' I had found some books about that quack here: it will take me about three weeks and do well enough as a *parergon*. A new fluctuation has come over my mode of publication lately: so that the things most at heart with me must lie in abeyance for some time. It begins to be presumable that the 'Edinburgh Review' can no longer be my vehicle, for this reason, were there no others, that Napier is among the worst of *payers*. What the poor man means I know not; most likely he is in utter *want of cash:* but at any rate he needs to be twice dunned before money will come from him; and at present owes me some 30*l.*, for which a third dunning will be requisite. This, then, simply will not do; I will look elsewhere, take new measures, as indeed solidity or permanence of any kind in authorship is at this time not to be looked for. Your foundation is like that of a man supporting himself in bog-lakes on floating sheaves or sods. The massiest will sink in a minute or two, and you must look out for new. Fraser, whose magazine I call the *mud* one (in contradistinction to Tait's, or the Sahara-sand one), is very fond of me, and at bottom an honest creature. Tait also would be glad to employ me, as poor Cochrane is. . . . On the whole we shall find means. . . . Meanwhile I have been reading violently, about the Scotch Kirk, in Knox, and others; about the French Revolution, in Thiers, which Mill sent me; about the Diamond Necklace, the Greek Revolt, and what not. I read with the appetite of one long starved; am oftenest of all in the Advocates' Library, and dig, not without result, there. My head is never empty; neither is my heart, though the contents of both are by times *rugged* enough. They must even be elaborated, made smooth and sweet. I could write whole volumes, were there any outlet: and will (if God spare me) both write them and find an outlet. These books, I fancy, will be one of our main conquests in Edinburgh. As to the men here, they are beautiful to look upon after mere black-faced sheep; yet not persons of whom instruction or special edification in any way is to be expected. From a Highlander you once for all *cannot* get breeches. Sir William Hamilton is almost the only *earnest* character I find in this city: we take somewhat to each other; meet sometimes with mutual satisfaction, always with good-will.

George Moir has got a house in Northumberland Street, a wife, too, and infants; is become a Conservative, settled everywhere into *dilettante;* not very happy, I think; dry, civil, and seems to

feel *unheimlich* in my company. *Aus dem wird Nichts.* Weir has
become a Radical spouter, and they say is gone or going to Glasgow to start as 'able Editor.' Did I tell you, by the way, that
London 'Spectator' Douglas had come to Dumfries in that capacity, and was weekly emitting a Radical 'Dumfries Times' there?
A company of malcontent writers and others had made a joint-stock
for that end; it is feared unsuccessfully. John Gordon is true
as steel to his old loves; otherwise a rather somnolent man; we
see him pretty often. He has got appointed College Clerk (or
some such thing), and has now 300*l.* a year and is happy enough.
Mitchell is quiet, in very poor health, yet cheerful, hopeful even,
a respectable schoolmaster now and henceforth. I saw a large
didactic company at dinner with him yesterday (for nothing else
would satisfy him), and astonished them I fear with my exposition of belief and Radicalism, as compared with opinion and Whiggism. There was an 'old stager,' a Doctor Brown, travelling
tutor college lecturer, statist, geologist, spiritual scratcher, and
scraper in all senses: a cold, sharp, hard, unmalleable 'logic
chopper' good to behold—at rare intervals. There was also an
advocate, Semple, an overfoaming Kantist, the best-natured and
liveliest of all small men; a very bottle of champagne (or soda
water) uncorked: we did well enough.

The Advocate came jigging up to us very often, but is now gone
to London. He asked kindly for you, and desired to be kindly
remembered to his 'old friend the Doctor.' I dined with him
once (Jane could not go). Napier (besides his being 'for ever in
the small debt court!') is a man of wooden structure limited in
all ways. I do not dislike him, but feel I can get no good of
him. Wilson, who is said to be grown far quieter in his habits,
has only come athwart me once. He, too, lion as he is, cannot
look at me as I look at him with *free* regard, but eyes me from
behind veils, doubtful of some mischance from me, political or
other. I suppose I shall see little of him, and at bottom need
not care.

As to our special *Befinden*, we are quite peaceable, content, for
the present; though both of us have a dirty under-foot kind of
catarrh for the last three weeks, whereby Jane in particular suffers
considerable—vexation, rather than pain. Otherwise she is at
least not worse. We go out not often, yet oftener than we wish;
have society enough; the best the ground yields: the time for
returning to Puttock will *too* soon be here. I have not abated in

my dislike for that residence, in my conviction that it is no longer good for me. Of solitude I have really had enough. You would be surprised, I am much surprised myself, at the wondrous figure I often make when I rejoin my fellow creatures. The talent of conversation, though I generally talk enough and to spare, has, as it were, quite forsaken me. In place of skilful, adroit fencing and parrying, as was fit and usual, I appear like a wild, monstrous Orson amongst the people, and (especially if bilious) smash everything to pieces. The very sound of my voice has got something savage-prophetic. I am as a John Baptist girt about with a leathern girdle, and whose food is locusts and wild honey. One must civilise; it is really quite essential. Here, too, as in all things, practice alone can teach. However, we will wait and watch, and do nothing rashly. Time and chance happen unto all men.

When you return to London you must see Mill; he is growing quite a believer, *mystisch gesinnt,* yet with all his old utilitarian logic quite alive in him; a remarkable sort of man, faithful, one of the faithfullest (yet with so much calmness) in these parts.

Carlyle, it will have been observed, had for some time spoken cheerfully of his wife, as not well, but as better than she had been. He observed nothing, as through his life he never did observe anything, about her which called away his attention from his work and from what was round him. A characteristic postscript in her own hand gives a sadly different picture of her condition.

My dear John,—If I kept my word no better in my daily walk and conversation than I do in this matter of writing, I should deserve to be forthwith drummed out of creation, but I beg you to believe my failure here an exception to the general rule.

In truth, I am always so sick now and so heartless that I cannot apply myself to any mental effort without a push from necessity; and as I get the benefit of your letters to Carlyle and see how faithfully he pays you back, I always persuade myself when the time comes that there is no call on me to strike into the correspondence. But I assure you my silence has nothing to do with indifference. I watch your *thun und lassen* with true and sisterly interest, and rejoice with my husband to see you in so hopeful a course. Everyone gets the start of poor me. Indeed, for the last year I have not made an inch of way, but have sate whimpering on a milestone lamenting over the roughness of the road. If you would come home and set my 'interior' to rights, it would wonderfully facilitate the problem of living. But perhaps it is best for me that it should not be made easier.

Edinburgh society pleased less the longer the Carlyles stayed. The fault partially, perhaps, was in Carlyle's own spiritual palate, which neither that nor anything was likely to please.

As for the people here (he tells his mother at the beginning of March), they are very kind, and would give us three dinners for one that we can eat; otherwise, I must admit them to be rather a barren set of men. The spirit of Mammon rules all their world— Whig, Tory, Radical. All are alike of the earth, earthy. They look upon me as a strong, well-intending, utterly misguided man, who must needs run his head against posts. They are very right. I shall never make any fortune in the world; unless it were that highest of all conceivable fortunes, the fortune to do, in some smallest degree, my All-wise Taskmaster's bidding here. May He, of His great grace, enable me! I offer up no other prayer. Are not my days numbered: a span's thrift in the sea of eternity? Fool is he who would speak lies or act lies, for the better or worse that can befall him for that least of little whiles. I say, therefore, lie away worthy brethren, lie to all lengths, be promoted to all lengths; but as for me and my house we will not lie at all. Again I say, God enable us! and so there it rests. Ought not my father's and my mother's son to speak even so?

A few days later he writes to his brother Alick.

Edinburgh continues one of the dullest and poorest, and, on the whole, paltriest of places for me. I cannot remember that I have heard one sentence with true meaning in it uttered since I came hither. The very power of thought seems to have forsaken this Athenian city; at least, a more entirely shallow, barren, unfruitful, and trivial set of persons than those I meet with, never, that I remember, came across my bodily vision. One has no right to be angry with them; poor fellows; far from it! Yet does it remain evident that 'Carlyle is wasting his considerable talents on impossibilities, and can never do any good'? Time will show. For the present, poor man, he is quite fixed to try. . . . At any rate, there are some good books here that one can borrow and read ; kindly disposed human creatures, too, who, though they cannot without a shudder see one spit in the Devil's face so, yet wish one well, almost love one.

To Mill also he had written a letter full of discontent, and looking, in the absence of comfort in Edinburgh society about him, for sympathy from his friend. But Mill rather needed comfort for himself than was in a situation to console others. He, like many others, had expected that the Reform Bill would bring the Millennium, and the Millennium was as far off as ever.

To his mother, whatever his humour, Carlyle wrote regularly. To her, more than even to his brother, he showed his real heart. She was never satisfied without knowing the smallest incidents of his life and occupation ; and he, on his part, was on the watch for opportunities to give her pleasure. He had sent her from Edinburgh a copy of ' Thomas à Kempis,' with an introduction by Chalmers. The introduction he considered ' wholly, or in great part, a *dud*.' Of the book itself he says : ' None, I believe, except the Bible, has been so universally read and loved by Christians of all tongues and sects. It gives me pleasure to think that the Christian heart of my good mother may also derive nourishment and strengthening from what has already nourished and strengthened so many.' In Edinburgh he described himself as at home, yet not at home ; unable to gather out of the place or its inhabitants the sustenance which he had looked for.

To Mrs. Carlyle, Scotsbrig.

Edinburgh : February 13, 1833.

From the first the appearance of the place, as contrasted with the boiling uproar of London, has seemed almost stagnant to us. There is no such thing as getting yourself properly *elbowed* in a ' flood of life.' The noise, too (except that of the watchman while we slept in a front room), is quite trifling and inadequate ! As for the people, they are now, as formerly, all of *one sort :* meet twenty of them in a day, they are all most probably talking of the same subject ; and that mostly an insignificant one, and handled in an insignificant way. And yet, poor fellows, how are they to be blamed? It is ' more their misfortune than their crime.' What sense is in them they no doubt honestly exhibit. Some cheering exceptions, too, one now and then falls in with ; indeed, for my own small share, I can no wise complain that honest sympathy, even love, and respect far beyond desert, is withheld from me here. This I receive with the greater clearness of appreciation, that (hardened by long custom) I had from of old *learned to do without it.* Nevertheless, that also is a mercy, and should be thankfully made use of. I think I have seen few people of note since I last wrote. I met Wilson in the street one day, and exchanged civilities with him. He is looking a little older ; was wrapped in a cloak for cold, and undertook to come and talk at home with me, ' if I would allow him,' the very first day he had leisure. I am glad we met, since now there need be no awkwardness or grudge between us : whether we meet a second time or not is of little or no moment. Henry Inglis has had my book reading,[1] and returns it with a most ecstatic exaggerated letter ; wherein this is comfortable, that he has seized the drift of the speculation, and can, if he pleases, lay it to heart. There are, perhaps, many such in this island whom it may profit ; so that I stand by the old resolution to print at my own risk so soon as I have 60*l.* to spare, but not till then. Meanwhile, my dear mother, I beg you again and again to take care of yourself ; especially in this wild, gusty February weather. Consider your welfare not as your own, but as that of others, to whom it is precious beyond price. I hope they are all kind, submissive, and helpful to you : it well beseems them and me. Forgive them if any of them offend ; for I know well no offence is intended : it is but the sinful infirmity of nature, wherein mortals should bear with one another. Oh ! ought we not to live in mutual love and unity, as a thing seemly for men, pleasing in the sight of God ! We shall so soon be parted, and *then,* Happy is he who has *forgiven much.*

From the Journal.

Friday, 15 *(March ?).*—Beautiful spring day ; the season of hope ! My scribble prospering very *ill.* Persevere, and thou wilt

---

[1] *Sartor* in MS.

improve. Sir Wm. Hamilton's supper (three nights ago) has done
me mischief; will hardly go to another. Wordsworth talked of
there (by Captain T. Hamilton, his neighbour). Represented
verisimilarly enough as a man full of English prejudices, idle,
alternately gossiping to enormous lengths, and talking, at rare intervals, high wisdom; on the whole, endeavouring to make out a
plausible life of *halfness* in the Tory way, as so many on all sides
do. Am to see him if I please to go thither; would go but a
shortish way for that end.

The brevity of life; the frightful voracity of *Time!* This is no
fancy; it is a wondrous unfathomable reality, and daily grows
more wondrous to me. 'Poor is what my lord doth say;' let him
to work then.

Beautiful that *I*, here and now, am alive! Beautiful to see so
many incorporated spirits, all six feet high (as in the oldest heroic
ages), all full of force, passion, impetuosity, mystery, as at the
first. 'The young new blood!' it flows and flows; the spirit host
marches unweariedly on—whither?

To Mrs. Carlyle, Scotsbrig.

March 16, 1833.

I have begun a kind of scribblement. It is for 'Fraser;' a foolish story about a certain Italian 'King of Quacks,' whom I have
long been curious about, and am now going to make known to all
the world—for some forty guineas, if I can get them. You will
see it in time. The long piece I did on the Frenchman in summer
came to be corrected very lately. It also will soon be out, and I
hope will give satisfaction at Scotsbrig. I have plenty of other
things to write; but should now rather lay myself out for getting
books and materials. Craigenputtock is the place for writing.
This same 'King of Quacks' ought to pay our expenses here and
back again. I am growing little richer, yet also no poorer. The
book can hardly be printed this season, but one ought to be content. I really am rather content; the rather as I do not imagine
there is any completer *anti-gigman* extant in the whole world at
present.

Among the new figures I have seen, none attracts me in any
measure except perhaps Knox's Dr. McCrie, whom I mean (as he
rather pressingly invited me) to go and call on were I a little at
leisure. A broad, large, stiff-backed, stalking kind of man, dull,
heavy, but intelligent and honest. We spoke a little about Scotch

worthies and martyrs, and I mean to ask him more. My notion of writing a book on that subject grows rather than decays.

If I tell you that our health is very much what it was (the old doctor still coming about Jane, but professing his inability to help her much), I think there is a very copious picture of our condition here. As for you, my dear mother, Alick would persuade me that you are in the usual way, 'resigned wonderfully, and even contented. . .' He says, 'it is only after having had something to do with this world that we can learn rightly to love and reverence such a life as hers.' Be resigned, my dear mother. '*Still* trust in God.' He will not leave us nor forsake us, not in death itself, nor in aught that lies between us and death. On *our* love, moreover, count always, as on a thing yours by good right. The longer I live, the more I feel how good is your right. Let us hope then to find you well in the early days of May, if not sooner; once again in this pilgrimage to meet in peace. Might we but meet in peace where there is parting no more! This also if it be for good will be provided us. God is great. God is good.

March 26.—I have finished my paper on the 'Quack of Quacks,' but got no new one fallen to, the house being in a kind of racket for the present. Mrs. Welsh is here, and Miss Helen Welsh from Liverpool; and though, if I determined on it, I can have my own fire and room, and bolt it against all people, it seems not worth while at present, for I am better resting. I had made myself *bilious* enough with my writing, and had need to recover as I am doing.

As for my own dame, she agrees but indifferently with these wild March winds: as I fear my mother does too. The advice I will always reiterate is, take care of yourself, dear mother. Such splashing and sleeting, with bright deceitful sun-blinks, and the firm, nipping north wind, need in all ways to be guarded against.

Napier has been obliged (by dunning) to pay me my money; he has paid rather stintedly, but it will do. We are to dine with him on Friday. My *writing* for him is probably over.

Did Alick show you Irving's speech at the Annan Presbytery? I read it with a mixture of admiration and deep pain; the man is of such heroic temper, and of head so distracted. The whole matter looked to me like a horrid kind of Merry Andrew tragedy. Poor Dow, I think, will end in a madhouse: Irving will end one cannot prophesy how; he must go from wild to wilder. This is

the issue of what once appeared the highest blessing for him—
Popularity!

Lady Clare was returning to England for the summer.
John Carlyle was coming with her, and the family were
looking eagerly forward to his arrival in Annandale.

To John Carlyle, Florence.

Edinburgh : March 29, 1833.

You will find much changed in Dumfriesshire, but not the affection of those that remain for you. There will be much to tell,
much to speculate upon and devise for the time that is to come.
. . I have thought much about your future of late ; see it like
all our futures, full of obstruction : nevertheless will not cease
to hope good. It is a most ruinous chaotic time, this of ours, a
time of confusion outward and inward, of falsehood, imbecility,
destitution, desperation, unbelief ; woe to him who has within
him no light of Faith, to guide his steps through it ! My main
comfort about you is to see the grand practical lesson of *Ertsagen*,[1]
impressing itself in ineffaceable devoutness on your heart ; herein,
it is well said, *eigentlich beginnt das Leben.* Whoso is a man may
in all seasons, scenes, and circumstances live like a man. Let us
take the world bravely then, and fight bravely to the end, since
nothing else has been appointed us. I have inquired with myself
often whether you should settle here, at London, or where. This
is but a pitiful place, but indeed all places are pitiful. In the
grand universal race towards ruin (economical) we are, as I judge,
almost a whole generation behind London. Nevertheless, here too
things are advancing with most rapid pace ; a few years will bring
us a long way. Universal Poverty is already here ; numerous persons, and these are the wisest, determine this season to fly over
seas, to America, Australia, anywhither where the famine is not.
Ruin economical is not far distant ; and then in regard to ruin
spiritual I should say that *it* was already triumphant among us ;
while in chaotic London there were blissful symptoms here and
there discernible of *palingenesia.* This makes the difference. In
London, amid its huge deafening hubbub of a Death-song, are to
be heard tones of a Birth-song ; while here all is putrid, scanda-

---

[1] This word, which so often occurs in Carlyle's letters, means briefly a resolution fixedly and clearly made to do without the various pleasant things—
wealth, promotion, fame, honour, and the other rewards with which the world
rewards the services which it appreciates.

lous, decadent, hypocritical, and sounds through your soul like lugubrious universal *Nœnia*, chaunted by foul midnight hags. There is misanthropy and philanthropy for you expressed with poetic emphasis enough.

In sober truth, however, it might almost surprise one to consider how infinitely small a quantity, not of enlightened speech, one catches here, but even of speech at all; for the jargon that is uttered without conviction from the teeth outwards, who would name that speech? Peace be with it! There are books to be got at; air to breathe; and, lastly, a coach to carry you back moorwards when that becomes more tolerable.

Most likely I mentioned last time that I was writing a paper on *Cagliostro*. I might, perhaps with advantage, have asked you some questions about his last scene of life, your Roman St. Angelo, but I did not recollect that possibility, and now the thing is all finished off, perhaps more carefully than it deserved to be. It is for Fraser, and may perhaps suit him well enough; otherwise I value the article below a pin's price; it will do no ill, and that is the most one can say of it. I am partly minded next to set forth some small narrative about the *Diamond Necklace*, once so celebrated a business, but must wait a day or two till I have *freies Feld*. It will serve me till about the time of our departure homewards, which we date a month hence. . . . . Wilson I have met only once; I had called on him before; as he never returned it, I could not go near him again, more especially after all the blathering stuff he had uttered on the matter for years past. I still read his Magazine palaver with an affectionate interest; believe that there is nothing to be got from him. We will not quarrel, but also we shall not agree. This night Gordon invites me to meet him at supper, but I cannot resolve to go; the man is not worth an indigestion. De Quincey, who has been once seen out this winter, sent me word he would come and see me; he will do no such thing, poor little fellow; he has hardly got out of his *cessio bonorum*, and for the present (little Moir, his friend, pathetically says) 'is living on game which has spoiled on the poulterer's hands,' having made a bargain to that effect with him, and even run up a score of fifteen pounds. Sir William Hamilton I like best of any, but see little of him. I even met the hash B . . . . ,' who has mounted a carriage now and rides prosperously. 'I saw the wicked great in power.' It was at Moir's, this rencounter, at dinner; the 'hash' somewhat reconciled to me by his presence;

I traced in him several features of my friend Cagliostro, and said honestly, Live then, enjoy thyself as subaltern quack. The devil is very busy with us all. Naso I visited in the dining way yester-night, for the first and probably last time. He affected to be ex-tremely kind, and our party (with an American anti-slave en-thusiast in it) went off quite happily; but Naso wants that first fundamental requisite of genius, I fear, common honesty. He has paid me, and shabbily, and on compulsion, that last debt of his; and now as I reckon our editorial relation may have terminated. That pecuniary defalcation of his again sorrowfully altered my scriptory method of procedure. But we cannot help it. Must even turn ourselves elsewhere.

The Reformed Parliament disappoints every one but me and the Tories. Endless jargon; no business done. I do not once a month look at the side of the world it sits on; let it go to the Devil its own way. . . . Of poor Edward Irving your Galignani will perhaps have told you enough; he came to Annan to be de-posed; made a heroico-distracted speech there, Dow finishing off with a Holy Ghost shriek or two; whereupon Irving, calling on them to 'hear that,' indignantly withdrew. He says, in a letter printed in the newspapers, that he ' did purpose to tarry in those parts certain days, and publish in the towns of the coast the great name of the Lord;' which purpose 'he did accomplish,' publish-ing everywhere a variety of things. He was at Ecclefechan, Jean writes us; gray, toilworn, haggard, with ' an immense cravat the size of a sowing-sheet covering all his breast;' the country people are full of zeal for him; but everywhere else his very name is an offence in decent society. 'Publish in the towns of the Coast!' Oh! it is a *Pickle-herring Tragedy:* the accursedest thing one's eye could light on. As for Dow, he must surely ere long end in a madhouse. For our poor friend one knows not what to predict.

Jane has walked very strictly by old Dr. Hamilton's law, with-out any apparent advantage. Her complaint seems like mine, a kind of seated dyspepsia; no medicine is of avail, only regimen (when once one can find it out), free air, and, if that was possible, cheerfulness of mind. She bears up with fixed resolution, ap-pears even to enjoy many things in Edinburgh, yet has grown no stronger of late. We must take the good and the ill together, and still hope for the better. She sends you her affection, and hopes we shall all meet at Craigenputtock once more. Be it so, if it pleases God. All things, as your faith tells you, *will* turn out for good if we ourselves prove good. Meanwhile, the only clear duty of man lies in this, and nothing else—work, work wisely, while it is called to-day. Nothing in this universe now frightens me, though yearly it grows more stupendous, more divine ; and the terrestrial life appointed us more poor and brief. Eternity looks grander and kinder if Time grow meaner and more hostile. I defy Time and the spirit of Time.

Farewell, dear John.

Ever your brother,
T. CARLYLE.

The account of the visit to Edinburgh began with an extract from Carlyle's Note-book. It may end with another.

March 31.

Wonderful, and alas ! most pitiful alternations of belief and unbelief in me. On the whole *no* encouragement to be met with here in Edinburgh; 'all men,' says John Gordon naively, 'are quite taken up with making a livelihood.' It is taken for granted, I find, that of me nothing can be made—that I am, economically speaking, but a lost man. No great error there, perhaps ; but if it is added by my friends themselves that therefore I am spiritually lost ? One's ears are bewildered by the inane chatter of the people; one's heart is for hours and days overcast by the sad feeling : 'There is none then, not one, that will believe in me !' Great in this life is the communion of man with man. Meanwhile, continue to believe in *thyself*. Let the chattering of innumerable gigmen pass by thee as what it is. Wait thou on the bounties of thy unseen Taskmaster, on the hests of thy inward *Dæmon*. Sow the seed field of Time. What if thou see no fruit of it ? another will. Be not weak.

Neither fear thou that this thy great message of the Natural *being* the Supernatural will wholly perish unuttered. One way or other it will and shall be uttered—write it down on paper any way ; speak it from thee—so shall thy painful, destitute existence not have been in vain. Oh, in vain ? Hadst thou, even thou, a message from the Eternal, and thou grudgest the travail of thy embassy ? O thou of little faith !

THE four months' experience of Edinburgh had convinced Carlyle that there at least could be no permanent home for him. If driven to leave his ' castle on the moor,' it must be for London—only London. In April he found that he had gathered sufficient materials for his article on the Diamond Necklace, which he could work up at Craig-enputtock. At the beginning of May he was again in Annandale on his way home, Mrs. Carlyle miserably ill, and craving like a wounded wild animal to creep away out of human sight. ' I left Edinburgh,' he wrote, ' with the grieved heart customary to me on visits thither ; a wretched infidel place; not one man that could forward you, co-operate with you in any useful thing. Scarcely one I could find (except Sir William Hamilton) that could speak a sin-cere word. I bought several books in Edinburgh, carried back with me materials enough for reflection ; the very contradictions, even unjust ones, you meet with, are ele-ments of new progress. My presence there was honoured with many a kind civility, too ; was publicly acknowledged by a kind of lampoon, laudative-vituperative (as it ought to be), by one Brown, editor of a newspaper, whom I have known at a distance as a blustering bubblyjock much given to fabrication ; on the other hand, I relieved Professor Wilson from the necessity of fabricating any more in my behalf by decidedly *cutting* him the day before we left town. I was quite wearied with the man, his deep desire to be familiar with me, his numerous evasions to meet me, his lies to excuse these; and so in mere Christian charity brought it to an end. My feelings to him remain, I hope, unchanged, as much as I can make them—admiration for a very superior talent, for many gleams of worth and generosity; contempt, pity for his cowardice, for his want of spiritual basis, which renders all his force a self-destructive one, properly no force at all. Thus did I finish off with Edinburgh, not in the most balsamic fashion.'

The work which Carlyle had done in the winter had more than paid his modest expenses. He was still undetermined how next to proceed, and felt a need of rest and reflection. It seemed, he said, as if 'the first act of his life was closing, the second not yet opened.' Means to go on upon were found in the hitherto unfortunate Teufelsdröckh. Unable to find an accoucheur who would introduce him to the world complete, he was to be cut in pieces and produced limb by limb in 'Fraser's Magazine.' Fraser, however, who had hitherto paid Carlyle twenty guineas a sheet for his articles (five guineas more than he paid any other contributor), had to stipulate for paying no more than twelve upon this unlucky venture. Ten sheets were to be allotted to Teufel in ten successive numbers. Thus 'Sartor Resartus' was to find its way into print at last in this and the following year, and sufficient money was provided for the Craigenputtock housekeeping for another twelve months.

The summer so begun was a useful and not unpleasant one. John Carlyle, returning from Italy, spent two months of it in his brother's house, intending at the end of them to rejoin Lady Clare and go again abroad with her. There were occasional visits to Scotsbrig. Many books were read, chiefly about the French Revolution, while from the Journal it appears that Carlyle was putting himself through a severe cross-examination, discovering, for one thing, that he was too intolerant, 'his own private discontent mingling considerably with his zeal against evildoers,' too contemptuously indifferent 'to those who were not forwarding him on his course;' wanting in courtesy, and 'given to far too much emphasis in the expression of his convictions.' It was necessary for him to ascertain what his special powers were, and what were the limits of them. 'I begin to suspect,' he wrote, 'that I have no *poetic* talent whatever, but of this, too, am no wise absolutely *sure*. It still seems as if a whole magazine of faculty lay in me all undeveloped; held in thraldom by the meanest physical and economical causes.'

One discovery came on him as a startling surprise.

'On the whole art thou not among the *vainest* of living men? At bottom among the very *vainest*? Oh, the sorry, mad ambitions that lurk in thee! God deliver me from vanity, from self-conceit, the first sin of this universe, and the last, for I think it will *never* leave us.'

Mrs. Carlyle continued ill and out of spirits, benefiting less than she had hoped from her brother-in-law's skill in medicine, yet contriving now and then to sketch in her humorous way the accidents of the moorland existence. She had an unlucky habit of dating her letters only by the day of the week, or sometimes not at all, and as those to Annandale were sent often by private hand, there is no post-mark to make good her shortcomings.

The following letter to her mother-in-law, however, is assigned by Carlyle to the summer of 1833. Written at what time it may, it will serve as a genuine picture of Craigenputtock life.

To Mrs. Carlyle, Scotsbrig.

Craigenputtock.

My dear Mother,—I am not satisfied it should be even so much as *whispered* that I have been scared from Scotsbrig by the *grate reform*, or by any other cause. Surely I have come through earthquakes enough in my time (and with an honourable, thorough bearing) to have acquired a character on that head more unimpeachable. But, to be sure, the calumny was no invention of yours, but of younger heads less eminent for charity. It was the long journey I boggled at on the last occasion, being in a despairing mood at the time with want of sleep, and dearly I rued, every hour of my husband's absence, that I had not accompanied him, when, if I must needs have been ill, I might at least have been so without molestation. Another time we will do better.

Carlyle is toiling away at the new article,[1] and though by no means content with the way he makes (when is he ever content?), still, as you used to say, 'what is down will not jump out again.' In three weeks or so it will be done and then we come. I am certainly mended since you were here; but 'deed Mrs. Carle's maist ashamed to say't,' a's still weakly and takes no unusual fatigue without suffering for it. The toil and trouble I had about Betty[2] did me great mischief, which I have scarcely yet got over; for the rest that explosion has had no unpleasant consequences. The woman I got in her stead, on an investigation of three minutes, proves to be quite as clever a servant as she was whom I investigated for the space of three half-years, and rode as I compute some hundred miles after. *Deaf* as a door nail, the present individual has nevertheless conducted herself quite satisfactorily, except that Carlyle's silk handkerchief is occasionally in requisition (oftener, I think, than there is any visible cause), wiping off particles of dust; and once, by awful oversight, a small *dead* mouse was permitted to insinuate itself into his bowl of porridge. We are not to keep her, however, because of her deafness, which in any other place, where her ears would be called into vigorous action, would make her the mere effigy of a servant. I got back the black button who was here when you came, whom I know to be ignorant as a sucking child of almost everything I require her to do, but whom I hope to find honest, diligent, good humoured, and quick in the up-take.

I had a very kind letter from Mrs. Montagu last week, reproaching me with forgetfulness of her.

We have not heard from or of Jeffrey for a very long time, but he will certainly write on Wednesday to acknowledge the repayment of his debt, which is a great load off our minds.[3]

---

[1] 'Diamond necklace.—T. C.'

[2] A misconducted maid.

[3] Carlyle's debt to Jeffrey had been paid the summer before. Either, therefore, Carlyle was mistaken in the date of this letter, and for 'Diamond Necklace' we should read Diderot; or there had been some further debt of John Carlyle's.

My mother writes in great alarm about cholera, which is at Penpont within three miles of her ; three persons have died. I have been expecting nothing else, and my dread of it is not greater for its being at hand. The answer to all such terrors is simply what Carlyle said a year ago to some one who told him in London, ' Cholera is here :' 'When is death not here?'

The next letter from Mrs. Carlyle bears a clear date of its own, and was written while John Carlyle was staying at Craigenputtock. It is to Eliza Miles.

Craigenputtock : July 15, 1833.

My dear Eliza,—I well remember the fine evening last year when I received your letter. I was riding alone across our solitary moor when I met my boy returning from the post-office, and took it from him and opened it and read it on horseback, too anxious for news about you to keep it for a more convenient place. Had anyone predicted to me *then* that the good, kind, trustful letter was to lie unanswered for a whole year, I should have treated such prediction as an injurious calumny which there was not the remotest chance of my justifying! Alas! and it is actually so! For a whole year I have left my dear little friend in Ampton Street to form what theory she pleased concerning the state of my mind towards her ; and finally, I suppose, to set me down for heartless and fickle, and dismiss my remembrance with a sigh ; for her gentle, affectionate nature is incapable, I believe, of more indignant reproach. And yet, Eliza (it was), neither the one thing nor the other. I am capable of as strong attachment as yourself (which is saying much), and if I do not abandon myself to my attachment as you do, it is only because I am older, have had my dreams oftener brought into collision with the realities of life, and learnt from the heart-rending jarring of such collision that ' all is not gold that glitters,' and that one's only safe dependence is in oneself—I mean in the good that is in one. As little am I fickle, which I must beg you to believe on trust; since my past life, which would bear me out in the boast, is all unknown to you. What is it, then, you will ask, that makes me fail in so simple a duty of friendship as the writing of a letter? It is sometimes sheer indolence, sometimes sickness, sometimes procrastination. My first impulse, after reading your letter, was to sit down and answer it by the very next post. Then I thought I will wait the Lord Advocate's return, that he may frank it. Then troubles thickened round me : my mother's illness, my grandfather's death, gave me much fatigue of body and mind. That, again, increased to cruel height my own persevering ailments. About the new year we removed to Edinburgh, where we stayed till the beginning of May. It was a fully more unhealthy winter for me than the previous one in London. I wrote to no one ; had enough to do in striving with the tempter ever present with me in the shape of headaches, heartache, and all kinds of aches, that I might not break out into fiery indignation over my own destiny and all the earth's. Since my home coming I have improved to a wonder, and the days have passed, I scarce know how, in the pleasant hopelessness that long-continued pain sometimes leaves behind.

Nay, I must not wrong myself. I have not been quite idle. I have made a gown which would delight Mrs. Page, it looks so neat and clean ; and a bonnet, and loaves of bread innumerable. At present I am reading Italian most of the day with my medical brother-in-law, who is home at present from Rome. It was my husband who, for all his frightening you with some books, raised me from Ariosto to-day, with the chiding words that it would be altogether shameful if I let his book parcel go without that letter for Miss Miles, which I had talked of writing these six months back. . . . . How is your health ? I hope you do not go often to Dr. Fisher's, or at all. The more I see of doctors the more I hold by my old heresy that they are all 'physicians of no value.' My brother-in-law is a paragon of the class, but he is so by—in as much as possible—undoctoring himself. He told me yesterday, ' Could I give you some agreeable occupation to fill your whole mind, it would do more for you than all the medicines in existence.'

I wish I had you here to drink new milk and ride my horse.

We are at home now for the summer and autumn, most likely for the winter also. We think of France next summer, and moving in the interim were scarce worth while. Surely your father might find some one travelling to Edinburgh by sea, who would take charge of you. It is the easiest and cheapest conveyance possible.

Write to me all that you are thinking and wishing, and never doubt my kind feelings towards you.

Your sincere friend,   Jane Carlyle.

John Carlyle remained at Craigenputtock for a month longer, and then left it to return with Lady Clare to Italy. Carlyle saw him off in the Liverpool steamer from Annan, and went back to solitude and work. He says that he was invariably sick and miserable before he could write to any real purpose. His first attempt at the Diamond Necklace had failed, and he had laid it aside. The entries in his journal show more than usual despondency.

Extracts from Journal.

August 24.—So now all this racketing and riding has ended, and I am left here the solitariest, stranded, most helpless creature that I have been for many years. Months of suffering and painful indolence I see before me ; for in much I am *wrong*, and till it is righted, or on the way to being so, I cannot help myself. Nobody asks me to work at articles, and as need does not drive me to do it for a while, I have no call in that direction. The thing I want to write is quite other than an article. Happily (this is probably my greatest happiness), the chief desire of my mind has again become to *write* a masterpiece, let it be acknowledged as such or not acknowledged. The idea of the universe struggles dark and painful in me, which I must deliver out of me or be wretched. But, then, How ? How ? We cannot think of changing our abode at present ; indeed, had we even the necessary funds for living in London itself, what better were it ? and I in such a want, in such a mood ! *Thyself* only art to blame. Take thyself vigorously to task. Cast out the unclean thing from thee, or *go deeper and deeper hellward with it.*

For the last year my faith has lain under a most sad eclipse ; I have been a considerably worse man than before.

At this moment I write only in *treble*, of a situation, of a set of feelings that longs to express itself in the voice of thunder. Be still ! Be still !

In *all* times there is a word which, spoken to men, to the actual generation of men, would thrill their inmost soul. But the way to find that word ? The way to speak it when found ? *Opus est consulto* with a vengeance.

On the whole it is good, it is absolutely needful for one to be humbled and prostrated, and thrown among the pots from time to time. Life is a school : we are *perverse* scholars to the last and require the rod.

Above me, as I thought last night in going to sleep, is the mute *Immensity ;* Eternity is behind and before. What are all the cares of this short little Platform of existence that they should give thee Pain? But on the whole man is such a *Dualism*, and runs himself into contradiction, the *second* step he makes from the beaten road of the practical. I may lament meanwhile that (for want of symbols?) those grand verities (the reallest of the real) Infinitude, Eternity, should have so faded from the view, from the grasp, of the most earnest, and left the task of *right living* a problem harder than ever.

Have to walk down to the smithy (my dame riding) and bring up a gig: thus are the high and the low mingled. I read books enough, but they are worthless and their effect worthless. Henry's *Britain, Poor Law Commission, Paris and Histor. Scenes*, &c., &c., all these are naught or nearly so; errand 'for the gig is better work for me. At any rate it is work; so to it.'

The next entry in the Journal is in another handwriting. It is merely a name—'Ralph Waldo Emerson.'

The Carlyles were sitting alone at dinner on a Sunday afternoon at the end of August when a Dumfries carriage drove to the door, and there stepped out of it a young American then unknown to fame, but whose influence in his own country equals that of Carlyle in ours, and whose name stands connected with his wherever the English language is spoken. Emerson, the younger of the two, had just broken his Unitarian fetters, and was looking out and round him like a young eagle longing for light. He had read Carlyle's articles and had discerned with the instinct of genius that here was a voice speaking real and fiery convictions, and no longer echoes and conventionalisms. He had come to Europe to study its social and spiritual phenomena; and to the young Emerson, as to the old Goethe, the most important of them appeared to be Carlyle. He had obtained an introduction to him from John Mill, in London, armed with which he had come off to Scotland. Mill had prepared Carlyle for his possible appearance not very favourably, and perhaps recognised in after years the fallibility of his judgment. Carlyle made no such mistake. The fact itself of a young American having been so affected by his writings as to have sought him out in the Dunscore moors, was a homage of the kind which he could especially value and appreciate. The acquaintance then begun to their mutual pleasure ripened into a deep friendship, which has remained unclouded in spite of wide divergences of opinion throughout their working lives, and continues warm as ever, at the moment when I am writing these words (June 27, 1880), when the labours of both of them are over, and they wait in age and infirmity to be called away from a world to which they have given freely all that they had to give.

Emerson's visit at this moment is particularly welcome, since it gives the only sketch we have of Carlyle's life at Craigenputtock as it was seen by others.[1]

From Edinburgh, writes Emerson, I went to the Highlands, and on my return I came from Glasgow to Dumfries, and being intent on delivering a letter which I had brought from Rome,[2] inquired for Craigenputtock. It was a farm in Nithsdale, in the parish of Dunscore, sixteen miles distant. No public coach passed near it, so I took a private carriage from the inn. I found the house amid desolate heathery hills, where the lonely scholar nourished his mighty heart. Carlyle was a man from his youth, an author who did not need to hide from his readers, and as absolute a man of the world, unknown and exiled on that hill farm, as if holding on his own terms what is best in London. He was tall and gaunt, with a cliff-like brow, and holding his extraordinary powers of conversation in easy command; clinging to his northern accent with evident relish; full of lively anecdote, and with a streaming humour which floated everything he looked upon. His talk, playfully exalting the most familiar objects, put the companion at once into an acquaintance with his Lars and Lemurs, and it was very pleasant to learn what was predestined to be a pretty mythology. Few were the objects and lonely the man, 'not a person to speak to within sixteen miles except the minister of Dunscore;' so that books inevitably made his topics.

[1] *English Traits*, Emerson's Prose Works, vol. ii. p. 165.
[2] From Gustave d'Eichthel. Emerson does not mention the note from Mill. Perhaps their mutual impressions were not dissimilar.

He had names of his own for all the matters familiar to his discourse. 'Blackwood's' was the 'Sand Magazine.' Fraser's nearer approach to possibility of life was the 'Mud Magazine;' a piece of road near by, that marked some failed enterprise was 'the Grave of the last Sixpence.' When too much praise of any genius annoyed him, he professed largely to admire the talent shown by his pig. He had spent much time and contrivance in confining the poor beast to one enclosure in his pen; but pig, by great strokes of judgment, had found out how to let a board down, and had foiled him. For all that, he still thought man the most plastic little fellow in the planet, and he liked Nero's death, *Qualis artifex pereo!* better than most history. He worships a man that will manifest any truth to him. At one time he had inquired and read a good deal about America. Landor's principle was mere rebellion, and *that* he feared was the American principle. The best thing he knew of that country was that in it a man can have meat for his labour. He had read in Stewart's book that when he inquired in a New York hotel for the Boots, he had been shown across the street, and had found Mungo in his own house dining on roast turkey.

We talked of books. Plato he does not read, and he disparaged Socrates; and, when pressed, persisted in making Mirabeau a hero. Gibbon he called the splendid bridge from the old world to the new. His own reading had been multifarious. 'Tristram Shandy' was one of his first books after 'Robinson Crusoe,' and 'Robertson's America,' an early favourite. 'Rousseau's Confessions' had discovered to him that he was not a dunce; and it was now ten years since he had learned German by the advice of a man who told him he would find in that language what he wanted.

He took despairing or satirical views of literature at this moment; recounted the incredible sums paid in one year by the great booksellers for puffing. Hence it comes that no newspaper is trusted now, no books are bought, and the booksellers are on the eve of bankruptcy.

He still returned to English pauperism, the crowded country, the selfish abdication by public men of all that public persons should perform. Government should direct poor men what to do. 'Poor Irish folk come wandering over these moors; my dame,' he said, 'makes it a rule to give to every son of Adam bread to eat, and supplies his wants to the next house. But here are thousands of acres which might give them all meat, and nobody to bid these poor Irish go to the moor and till it. They burned the stacks, and so found a way to force the rich people to attend to them.'

We went out to walk over long hills, and looked at Criffel, then without his cap, and down into Wordsworth's country. There we sat down and talked of the immortality of the soul. It was not Carlyle's fault that we talked on that topic, for he has the natural disinclination of every nimble spirit to bruise itself against walls, and did not like to place himself where no step can be taken. But he was honest and true, and cognisant of the subtle links that bind ages together, and saw how every event affects all the future. ' Christ died on the tree : that built Dunscore kirk yonder ; that brought you and me together. Time has only a relative existence.'

He was already turning his eyes towards London with a scholar's appreciation. London is the heart of the world, he said, wonderful only from the mass of human beings. He liked the huge machine. Each keeps its own round. The baker's boy brings muffins to the window at a fixed hour every day, and that is all the Londoner knows or wishes to know on the subject. But it turned out good men. He named certain individuals, especially one man of letters, his friend, the best mind he knew, whom London had well served.

Emerson stayed for a night and was gone in the morning, seeking other notabilities. Carlyle liked him well. Two days later he writes to his mother :—

Three little happinesses have befallen us : first, a piano tuner, procured for five shillings and sixpence, has been here, entirely reforming the piano, so that I can hear a little music now, which does me no little good. Secondly, Major Irving of Gribton, who used at this season of the year to live and shoot at Craigenvey, came in one day to us, and after some clatter offered us a rent of five pounds for the right to shoot here, and even tabled the cash that moment, and would not pocket it again. Money easilier won never sate in my pocket ; money for delivering us from a great nuisance, for now I will tell every gunner applicant, ' I cannot, sir ; it is let.' Our third happiness was the arrival of a certain young unknown friend, named Emerson, from Boston, in the United States, who turned aside so far from his British, French, and Italian travels to see me here ! He had an introduction from Mill and a Frenchman (Baron d'Eichthal's nephew), whom John knew at Rome. Of course we could do no other than welcome him ; the rather as he

seemed to be one of the most lovable creatures in himself we had
ever looked on. He stayed till next day with us, and talked and
heard talk to his heart's content, and left us all really sad to
part with him. Jane says it is the first journey since Noah's Deluge undertaken to Craigenputtock for such a purpose. In any
case we had a cheerful day from it, and ought to be thankful.

During these months, the autumn of 1833 and the beginning of the year which followed, a close correspondence was maintained between Carlyle and John Mill.
Carlyle's part of it I have not seen, but on both sides the
letters must have been of the deepest interest. Thinly
sprinkled with information about common friends, they
related almost entirely to the deepest questions which concern humanity ; and the letters of Mill are remarkable
for simplicity, humility, and the most disinterested desire
for truth. He had much to learn about Carlyle ; he was
not quick to understand character, and was distressed to
find, as their communications became more intimate, how
widely their views were divided. He had been bred a
utilitarian. He had been taught that virtue led necessarily
to happiness, and was perplexed at Carlyle's insistance on
Entsagen (renunciation of personal happiness) as essential
to noble action. He had been surprised that Carlyle liked
Emerson, who had appeared to him perhaps a visionary.
Carlyle, intending to write another book, was hesitating between a life of John Knox and the French Revolution.
Either subject would give him the opportunity, which he
wanted, of expressing his spiritual convictions. His in-
clination at this moment was towards the history of his
own country, and he had recommended Mill to write on
the Revolution. Mill felt that it would be difficult if not
impossible for him, without expressing completely his
views on Christianity, which the condition of public feeling in England would not allow him to do. He spoke
tenderly and reverently of the personal character of the

Founder of Christianity, and on this part of the subject he wrote as if he was confident that Carlyle agreed with him. But, below the truth of any particular religion, there lay the harder problem of the existence and providence of God, and here it seemed that Carlyle had a positive faith, while Mill had no more than a sense of probability. Carlyle admitted that so far as external evidence went, the Being of God was a supposition inadequately proved. The grounds of certainty which Carlyle found in himself, Mill, much as he desired to share Carlyle's belief, confessed that he was unable to recognise. So again with the soul. There was no proof that it perished with the body, but again there was no proof that it did not. Duty was the deepest of all realities, but the origin of duty, for all Mill could tell, might be the tendency of right action to promote the general happiness of mankind. Such general happiness doubtless could best be promoted by each person developing his own powers. Carlyle insisted that every man had a special task assigned to him, which it was his business to discover; but the question remained, by whom and how the task was assigned; and the truth might only be that men in fact were born with various qualities, and that the general good was most effectually promoted by the special cultivation of those qualities.

But I will not attempt to pursue further so interesting an exposition of Mill's views when I am forbidden to use his own language, and must express his meaning in a circuitous paraphrase. The letters themselves may perhaps be published hereafter by those to whom they belong. I have alluded to the correspondence only because it turned the balance in Carlyle's mind, sent him immediately back again to Marie Antoinette and the Diamond Necklace, and decided for him that he should himself undertake the work which was to make his name famous.

CHAPTER XVI.

A.D. 1833. ÆT. 38.

WHEN John Carlyle left Craigenputtock to rejoin Lady Clare, the parting between the brothers had been exceptionally sad. The popularity with Review editors which had followed Carlyle's appearance in London was as brief as it had been sudden. His haughty tone towards them, and his theory of 'the Dogs' Carrion Cart,' as a description of the periodicals of the day, could not have recommended him to their favour. The article on Goethe was received unfavourably, Cochrane said with unqualified disapproval. 'Sartor' when it began to appear in 'Fraser' piecemeal, met a still harder judgment. No one could tell what to make of it. The writer was considered a literary maniac, and the unlucky editor was dreading the ruin of his magazine. The brothers had doubtless talked earnestly enough of the threatening prospect. John, who owed all that he had and was to his brother's care of him, and was in prosperous circumstances, was leaving that brother to loneliness and depression, and to a future on which no light was breaking anywhere. Carlyle felt more for John than for himself, and his first effort after John was gone was to comfort him.

For me and my moorland loneliness (he wrote on the 27th of August) never let it settle in your heart. I feel assured from of old that the only true enemy I have to struggle with is the unreason within myself. If I have given such things harbour within me, I must with pain cast them out again. Still, then, still! Light will arise for my outward path, too ; were my inward light once clear again, and the world with all its tribulations will lie under my feet. ' Be of good cheer, I have *overcome* the world :' so said the wisest man, when what was his overcoming? Poverty, despite, forsakenness, and the near prospect of an accursed Cross. ' Be of good cheer ; I have overcome the world.' These words on the streets of Edinburgh last winter almost brought tears into my eyes. But, on the whole, quarrel not with my deliberate feeling that this wilderness is no wholesome abode for me ; that it is my *duty* to strive, with all industry, energy, and cheerful determination to change it for one less solitary. Consider also that I am far past the years for headlong changes, and will not rush out to the warfare without a plan and munitions of war. Nay, for a time my first duty must be composure ; the settling of innumerable things that are at sixes and sevens within myself.

I am writing nothing yet, but am not altogether idle. Depend upon it, I shall pass the winter here far more happily than you expect. So fear not for me, my dear brother ; continue to hope of me *that the work* given me ' to do may be done.'

Mrs. Carlyle, who was still ailing, was carried off by her mother a few days later, in the hope that change of air and relief from household work might be of use to her, and was taking a tour through the hills about Moffat. Carlyle himself was left in utter solitude at Craigenputtock. How he passed one day of it he tells in a letter, which he sent after his Goody Coadjutor, as he called her, soon after she had left him.

To Mrs. Carlyle, Moffat.

September 7.

Yesterday mornning, while the bright sun was welcoming you (I hope without headache) to the watering-place, I stirred little, yet was not wholly idle. I adjusted various small matters, wrote a long letter to poor Mrs. Swan[1]—a long one, yet the lamest utterance of my feeling on that sad matter, for I was stupid and could not even feel my feeling rightly, much less *think* it. After dinner I went to walk. Sitting with my back at the big stone in the ' Sixpence,' looking out over the void moor, I hear a little squeak of glad, unmelodious singing : and presently Midge, in red jacket

---

[1] Of Kirkcaldy. Her husband, 'Provost Swan,' who had been one of Carlyle's friends in the old days, was just dead.

with a bundle, heaves in sight, clashes back astonished into a kind of minuet, answers my questions with a ' *Sur !* ' and then to the repetition of it, ' How they were all at the hut ? ' chirps out with the strangest new old-woman's tone, ' Oh, bravely ! ' Poor little savage ! I met her again in the way back (she had been with Nancy's gown, I suppose), and did *not* kill her with my eyes, but let her shy past me. The red Midge in that vacant wilderness might have given Wordsworth a sonnet. All day, I must remark, Nancy had been busy as a town taken by storm, and, indeed, still is, though I know not with what : most probably washing, I think ; for yesterday there appeared once a barrow with something like clothes-baskets, and to-day white sheets hang triumphantly on the rope. She gets me all my necessaries quite punctually ; and as fit, no questions are asked. *Notybene,* after a long effort I remembered the shelling of your peas, and told her of it. After tea, I did—what think you ?—composed some beautiful doggerel on the Linn of Crichope and fair Ludovina (I hope she is fair) : quite a jewel of a piece, for which, however, there is no room on this page.[1]

Of the present Saturday the grandest event might be the following : Sickish, with little work, I took my walk *before* dinner. Reaching home at the corner of the house, I met a pig apparently

---

[1] Room was found for it on the margin of the lettter :—

CRICHOPE LINN.
(*Loquitur genius loci.*)

Cloistered vault of living rocks,
    Here have I my darksome dwelling ;
Working, sing to stones and stocks,
    Where beneath my waves go welling.

Beams flood-borne athwart me cast
    Arches see, and aisles moist gleaming ;
Sounds for aye my organ blast,
    Grim cathedral, shaped in dreaming.

Once a Lake, and next a Linn,
    Still my course sinks deeper ; boring
Cleft far up where rays steal in,
    That as ' Gullet ' once was roaring.

For three thousand years or more
    Savage I, none praised or blamed me ;
Maiden's hand unbolts my door—
    Look of loveliness hath tamed me.

in a state of distraction (grating harsh thunder, its lugs over its shoulders distractedly flow), pursued by Nancy in the same! The sow has not so much broken the gate as rent it, the side posts of it, into two, and left it hanging 'like a bundle of flails.' After dinner I, with a sublime patience, borrow 'Joseph's wimble,' and under ten thousand midge bites, with tools blunt as a wild Indian's, actually construct a brand-new, most improved gate, which you shall look upon not without admiration—if it swing so long. I sent a new message to the joiner, but do not in the least expect him. I had meant to excerpt from Bayle and such like, but the Fates, you see, had mostly ordered it *otherwise.* Night found me, like Basil Montagu, 'at my post,' namely, at my gate post, and nigh done with it. I had tea and Goody's letter, and so here we are.

But now, dear wifie, it is fit I turn a moment to thy side. Is my little Janekin getting any sleep in that unknown cabin? Is she enjoying aught, hoping aught, except the *end* of it, which *is*, and should be, one of her hopes? I shall learn 'all' on Wednesday (for she will write, as I do); and then 'all and everything.' When? I am patient as possible hitherto, and my patience will stretch if I know that you enjoy yourself, still more that your health seems to profit. Take a little amusement, dear Goody, if thou canst get it. God knows little comes to thee with me, and thou art right patient under it. But, courage, dearest! I swear better days are coming, *shall* come. The accursed, baleful cloud that has hung over my existence *must* (I feel it) dissipate, and let in the sun which shines on all. It *must*, I say. What is it but a

> Maiden mild, this level path
>   Emblem is of her bright being;
> Long through discord, darkness, scath,
>   Goes she helping, ruling, freeing.
>
> Thank her, wanderer, as thou now
>   Gazest safe through gloom so dreary:
> Rough things plain make likewise thou,
>   And of well-doing be not weary.
>
> 'Gullet' one day cleft shalt be,
>   Crichope cave have new sunk story;
> Thousand years away shall flee—
>   Flees not goodness or its glory.
>
> 'Ach Gott, wie lahm, wie krüppel-lahm!'

cloud, properly a shadow, a chimæra? Oh, Jeannie! But enough. If I am happy, art not thou, also, happy in my happiness? Hope *all* things, dearest, and be true to me still, as thou art. And so *felicissima Notte!* Sleep well, for it is now midnight, and dream of me if thou canst. With best love to mother and cousinkin,

Ever thy own husband,
T. CARLYLE.

To Mrs. Carlyle, Scotsbrig.

Craigenputtock : September 20, 1833.

My dear Mother,—Jack, as you will find, has got safe over the water, and begins his expedition as prosperously as could be desired. He goes into Germany, and then up the Rhine, towards the Swiss Alps, where that river springs, a beautiful road. Most likely he will pass through Constance, where our noble Huss testified to the death. He may tell us what he says to the 'scarlet woman,' and her abominations there! You and I shall not be with him to lecture from that text; but his own thoughts (for all that he talks so) will do it. The dumb ashes of Huss speak louder than a thousand sermons. . . . But I must tell you something of myself: for I know many a morning, my dear mother, you 'come in by me' in your rambles through the world after those precious to you. If you had eyes to see on these occasions you would find everything quite tolerable here. I have been rather *busy*, though the fruit of my work is rather inward, and has little to say for itself. I have yet hardly put pen to paper; but foresee that there is a time coming. *All* my griefs, I can better and better see, lie in good measure at my own door : were I right in *my own heart*, nothing else would be far wrong with me. This, as you well understand, is true of every mortal, and I advise all that hear me to *believe* it, and to lay it practically to their own case. On the whole, I am promising to occupy myself more wholesomely, and to be happier here all winter than I have been of late. Be 'diligent in well-doing;' that is the only secret for happiness anywhere : not a universal one or infallible (so long as we continue on earth), yet far the best we have.

For the last two weeks Jane has been away from me at Moffat. I led the loneliest life, I suppose, of any human creature in the king's dominions, yet managed wonderfully, by keeping myself continually at work. I clomb to the hill top on Sabbath day for my walk and saw Burnswark, and fancied you all at the sermon close by. On Monday morning I went over to Templand, and found my bit wifie altogether *défaite*, not a whit better, but worse, of Moffat and its baths, and declaring she would not leave me so soon again in a hurry.

To John Carlyle.

October 1, 1833.

If you ask what I have performed and accomplished for myself, the answer might look rather meagre. I have not yet put pen to paper. The *new chapter* of my history as yet lies all too confused. I look round on innumerable fluctuating masses: can begin to build no edifice from them. However, my mind is not empty, which is the most intolerable state. I think occasionally with energy; I read a good deal; I wait, not without hope. What other can I do? Looking back over the last seven years, I wonder at myself; looking forward, were there not a fund of tragical indifference in me, I could lose head. The economical outlook is so complex, the spiritual no less. Alas! the *thing* I want to do is precisely the thing I cannot do. My mind would so fain deliver itself adequately of that 'Divine idea of the world,' and only in quite inadequate approximation is such deliverance possible. I want to write what Teufelsdröckh calls a story of the *Time-Hat*, to show forth to the men of these days that they also live in the *age of miracles!* We shall see. Meanwhile, one of the subjects that engages me most is the French Revolution, which, indeed, for us is the subject of subjects. My chief errand to Paris were freer inquiry into this.[1] One day, if this mood continues, I may have something of my own to·say on it. But to stick nearer home. I have as good as engaged with myself not to go even to Scotsbrig till I have written something, with which view partly, on Saturday last, I determined on two things I could write about (there are twenty others if one had any vehicles): the first, 'A History of the Diamond Necklace;' the next, an 'Essay on the Saint Simonians.' I even wrote off to Cochrane as diplomatically as I could, to ask whether they would suit him. Be his answer what it may,[2] I think I shall fasten upon that Necklace business (to

[1] Carlyle had wished to spend the winter in Paris, but was prevented by want of means.

[2] The answer was unfavourable. All editors, from this time forward, gave Carlyle a cold shoulder till the appearance of the *French Revolution.* After the first astonishment with which his articles had been received, the world generally had settled into the view taken at Edinburgh, that fine talents,

prove myself in the narrative style), and commence it (sending for books from Edinburgh) in some few days. For the rest I have books enough; your great parcel came about a fortnight ago. I have already read what Mill sent for me. Finally, yesterday no farther gone, I drove over to Barjarg,[1] in the middle of thick small rain, to get the keys of the library, which I found most handsomely left for me, so that I could seize the catalogue and some half-dozen volumes to return at discretion. It is really a very great favour; there are various important works there, reading which I am far better than at any university. For the first time in my life I have free access to some kind of book-collection. I, a book-man! One way and another we look forward to a cheerfullish kind of winter here.

I will try for Winckelmann. . . . In my heterodox heart there is yearly growing up the strangest, crabbed, one-sided persuasion, that *art* is but a reminiscence now: that for us in these days prophecy (well understood), not poetry, is the thing wanted. How can we *sing* and *paint* when we do not yet *believe* and *see?* There is some considerable truth in this: how much I have not yet

which no one had denied him, were being hopelessly thrown away—that what he had to say was extravagant nonsense. Whigs, Tories, and Radicals were for once agreed. He was, in real truth, a Bohemian, whose hand was against every man, and every man's hand, but too naturally, was against him, and the battle was sadly unequal. If Carlyle had possessed the peculiar musical quality which makes the form of poetry, his thoughts would have swept into popularity as rapidly and as widely as Byron's. But his verse was wooden. Rhymes and metre were to him no wings on which to soar to the empyrean. Happy for him in the end that it was so. Poetry in these days is read for pleasure. It is not taken to heart as practical truth. Carlyle's mission was that of a prophet and teacher—and a prophet's lessons can only be driven home by prose.

[1] A large country house ten miles from Craigenputtock, the library of which had been placed at Carlyle's service. Scotland had grown curious about him, however cold or hostile; and the oddest questions were asked respecting his identity and history. Henry Inglis, an Edinburgh friend, writes to Mrs. Carlyle: 'Swift, I think it is, who says, "Truly you may know a great man by the crowd of blockheads who press round and endeavour to obstruct his path." A blockhead of my acquaintance (I have an extensive acquaintance amongst them) chose to ask me the other day whether the Carlyle who screams hebdomadally in the church in Carruthers Close was *our* Carlyle. I consider such a remark almost equal to receiving the hand of fellowship from Goethe. It is nearly the same thing to be the disclaimed or the misunderstood of an Ass, and the acknowledged of a Prophet.' The Barjarg acknowledgment of Carlyle's merits was a kind more honourable to its owner.

fixed. Now, what, under such point of view, is all existing art and study of art? What was the great Goethe himself? The greatest of contemporary men; who, however, is not to have any followers, and should not have any.

Extracts from Journal.

October 28.—No man in modern times, perhaps no man in any time, ever came through more confusion with less imputation against him than Lafayette. None can accuse him of variableness; he has seen the world change like a conjuror's pasteboard world; *he* stands there unchanged as a stone-pillar in the midst of it. Does this prove him a great man, a good man? Nowise—perhaps only a limited man.

The difference between Socrates and Jesus Christ! The great Conscious; the immeasurably great Unconscious. The one cunningly manufactured; the other created, living, and life-giving. The epitome this of a grand and fundamental diversity among men. Did *any* truly great man ever go through the world without *offence;* all rounded in, so that the current moral systems could find no fault in him? Most likely, never.

Washington is another of our perfect characters; to me a most limited, uninteresting sort. The thing is not only to avoid error, but to *attain* immense masses of truth. The ultra-sensual *surrounds* the sensual and gives it meaning, as eternity does time. Do I understand this? Yes, partly, I do.

If I consider it well, there is hardly any book in the world that has sunk so deep into me as 'Reinecke Fuchs.' It co-operates with other tendencies. Perhaps my whole speculation about 'clothes' arose out of that. It now absolutely haunts me, often very painfully, and in shapes that I will not write even here.

Yet, again, how beautiful, how true, is this other: 'Man is an incarnate word.' Both these I habitually feel.

'This little life-boat of a world, with its noisy crew of a mankind,' vanishing 'like a cloud-speck from the azure of the All.' How that thought besieges me, elevating and annihilating. What is 'fame'? What is life?

All barriers are thrown down before me; but then, also, all tracks and points of support. I look hesitatingly, almost bewilderedly, into a confused sea. The necessity of caution suggests itself. Hope *diminished* burns not the less brightly, like a *star* of hope. *Que faire? Que devenir?* Cannot answer. It is not I only that must answer, but Necessity and I.

Meanwhile, this reading is like a kind of manuring compost partly, of which my mind has need. Be thankful that thou hast it, that thou hast time for applying it. In *economics* I can yet hold out for a number of months.

Friday, November 1.—What a time one loses in these winter days lighting fires! lighting candles! I am in the dining-room, which would fain smoke, for it blows a perfect storm. Twelve o'clock is at hand, and not a word down yet!

'Edinburgh Review' came last night. A smart, vigorous paper by Macaulay on Horace Walpole. Ambitious; too antithetic; the heart of the matter not struck. What will that man become? He has more force and emphasis in him than any other of my British contemporaries (coevals). Wants the root of belief, however. May fail to accomplish much. Let us hope better things.

How confused, helpless; how dispirited, impotent; how miserable am I! The world is so vast and complex; my duty in it will not in the least disclose itself. One has to shape and to be shaped. It is all a perplexed imbroglio, and you have by toil and endeavour to *shape* it. 'Nothing would ever come to me in my sleep!'

Vain to seek a 'theory of virtue;' to plague oneself with speculations about such a thing. Virtue is like health—the harmony of the whole man. Some property of it traceable in every part of the man; its complete character only in the whole man. Mark this; it is not far from the truth, and as I *think* it, nearer than as I here express it.

My mode of writing for the last two days quite the old one, and very *far from the right.* How alter it? It must be altered. Could I not write more as I do *here?* My style is like no other man's. The first sentence bewrays me. How wrong is that? Mannerism at least!

Shall I go to London and deliver a course of lectures? Shall I

endeavour to write a *Time-Hat?* Shall I write a Life of Bona-
parte? A French Revolution? The decease of bookselling perplexes me. Will *ever* a good book henceforth be paid for by the
public? Perhaps; perhaps not. Never more in general. *Que
faire?* Live and struggle. And so now to work.

The dejected tone so visible in these entries was due to
no idle speculative distress, but to the menacing aspect
which circumstances were beginning to assume. The editors and booksellers were too evidently growing shy; and
unless articles could find insertion or books be paid for, no
literary life for Carlyle would long be possible. Employment of some other kind, however humble and distasteful,
would have to be sought for and accepted. Anything,
even the meanest, would be preferable to courting popularity, and writing less than the very best that he could;
writing ' *duds*,' as he called it, to please the popular taste.
An experienced publisher once said to me: 'Sir, if you
wish to write a book which will sell, consider the ladies'-
maids. Please the ladies'-maids, you please the great
reading world.' Carlyle would not, could not, write for
ladies'-maids.

The dreary monotony of the Craigenputtock life on
these terms was interrupted in November by interesting
changes in the family arrangements. The Carlyles, as
has been more than once said, were a family whose warmest affections were confined to their own circle. Jean, the
youngest sister, the 'little crow,' was about to be married
to her cousin, James Aitken who had once lived at Scotsbrig, and was now a rising tradesman in Dumfries; a
house-painter by occupation, of a superior sort, and possessed of talents in that department which with better opportunities might have raised him to eminence as an artist. 'James Aitken,' Carlyle wrote, ' is an ingenious,
clever kind of fellow, with fair prospects, no bad habit,
and perhaps *very* great skill in his craft. I saw a copied

Ruysdael of his doing which amazed me.' The 'crow' had not followed up the poetical promise of her childhood. She had educated herself into a clear, somewhat stern, well-informed and sensible woman. Hard Annandale farm-work had left her no time for more. But, like all the Carlyles, she was of a rugged, independent temper. Jean, her mother said, was outgrowing the contracted limits of the Scotsbrig household. Her marriage consequently gave satisfaction to all parties. Carlyle himself was present at the ceremony. 'A cold mutton pie of gigantic dimensions' was consumed for the breakfast; 'the stirrup-cup' was drunk, Carlyle joining, and this domestic matter was happily ended.

But Jean's marriage was not all. James Carlyle, the youngest brother, who carried on the Scotsbrig farm, had a similar scheme on foot, and had for himself fallen in love; 'nothing since Werter's time equalling the intensity of his devotion.' He, too, was eager to be married; but as this arrangement would affect his mother's position, Carlyle, as the eldest of the family, had to interfere to prevent precipitancy. All was well settled in the following spring, Carlyle making fresh sacrifices to bring it about. His brother Alick owed him more than 200*l.* This, if it could be paid, or when it could be paid, was to be added to his younger brother's fortune. His mother was either to continue at Scotsbrig, or some new home was to be found for her, which Carlyle himself thought preferable. His letter to the intending bridegroom will be read with an interest which extends beyond its immediate subject.

You have doubtless considered (he said) that such an engagement must presuppose one condition : our mother and sisters forming some other establishment also. I should not be surprised, indeed, if you had fancied that our mother and your wife might try to live together at Scotsbrig; but depend upon it, my dear brother, this will never and in no case do. The house must belong to your wife from the instant she sets foot in it; neither mother nor sister must any longer be there to contest it with her. The next question then for all of us, and for you too, is, What will my mother and the two lassies do ? I have thought of it often ; and though changes are always grievous, I think there are means to get a new way of life devised for our dear mother and those who yet need her guidance, and see them supported without burdening anyone. They must have, of course, a habitation of their own. With my mother's money, with the interest of the girls' money, with mine (or what was Alick's, now in your hands), which I think of adding to it, they will be able to live decently enough, I think, if we can be judicious in choosing some place for them.

In this latter ' if,' however, you yourself see that *Martinmas* is by no means the fit time ; that Whitsunday, the universal term-day of the country, is the soonest they can be asked to find new quarters. Now, as your wife cannot be brought home to Scotsbrig before that time, my decided advice were that you did not wed till then. I understand what wonderful felicities young men like you expect from marriage ; I know too (for it is a truth as old as the world) that such expectations hold out but for a little while. I shall rejoice much (such is my experience of the world) if in your new situation you feel *as* happy as in the old ; say nothing of happier. But, in any case, do I not know that you will never (whatever happens) venture on any such solemn engagement with a direct duty to fly in the face of ?—the duty, namely, of doing to your dear mother and your dear sisters *as you would wish that they should do to you.* Believe me, my dear brother, wait. Half a year for such an object is not long ! If you ever repent so doing, blame me for it.

And so now, my dear James, you have it all before you, and can consider what you will do. Do nothing that is *selfish*, nothing that you cannot front the world and the world's Maker upon ! May He direct you right.

Carlyle, perhaps, judged of possibilities by his own recollections. *He*, when it would have added much to his own wife's happiness, and might have shielded her entirely from the worst of her sufferings, had refused peremptorily to live with her mother, or let her live with them, except on impossible terms. He knew himself and his peremptory disposition, and in that instance was probably right. His own mother happily found such an arrangement *not* impossible. Her son married, and she did not leave her home, but lived out there her long and honoured life, and ended it under the old roof.

Carlyle himself, meanwhile, was soon back again with his 'Diamond Necklace' and his proof-sheets of 'Teufels-dröckh' at Craigenputtock, where his winter life stands pictured in his correspondence.

To John Carlyle.

Craigenputtock : November 18, 1833.

I will now record for you a little smallest section of universal history : the scene still Annandale. The Tuesday after the wedding I sate correcting the second portion of 'Teufelsdröckh' for 'Fraser's Magazine,' but towards night Alick, according to appointment, arrived with his ' little black mare' to drive me 'some-whither' next day. We after some consultation made it Annan, and saw ourselves there about one o'clock. A damp, still afternoon, quite Novemberish and pensive-making. The look of those old familiar houses, the *jow* of the old bell, went far into my heart. A struggling funeral proceeded up the street ; Senhouse Nelson (now Reform Bill Provost), with Banker Scott, in such priggish clothes as he wears, and two others of the like, stood on Benson's porch stairs gazing into inanity. Annan still stood there : and I—here. Ben was from home ; his little son gone to London, the maid thought, into some hospital, some navy appointment, into she knew not what. Finally, we determined on seeking out Waugh.[1] Old Marion, as clean and dour as ever, hobblingly admitted us. There sate the Doctor, grizzle-locked (since I saw him), yellow, wrinkled, forlorn, and outcast looking, with beeswax and other tailor or botcher apparatus on a little table, the *shell* of an old coat lying dismembered on the floor ; an-

[1] Son of a thriving citizen of Annan, who had been Carlyle's contemporary and fellow-student at Edinburgh, a friend of Irving, at whose rooms, indeed, Carlyle first became acquainted with Irving : who, with money, connections, and supposed talents, had studied medicine, taken his degree, and was considered to have the brightest prospects, had gone into literature, among other adventures, and now, between vanity and ill-fortune, had drifted into what is here described.

other not yet so condemnable, which with his own hand he was
struggling to rehabilitate ; a new cuff I saw (after he had huddled
the old vestment on) evidently of his own making ; the front button holes had all exploded, a huge rent lay under one armpit, ex-
tending over the back ; the coat *demanded* mending, since turning
was not to be thought of. *There* sate he ; into such last corner
(with the pale winter sun looking through on him) had *Schicksal
und eigne Schuld* hunted the ill-starred Waugh. For the first time
I was truly *wae* for him. He talked too with such meekness, yet is
still mad ; talking of 1,200*l.* to be made by a good comedy, and
such like. When we came out (since the state of his coat would
not allow him to come with us) Alick and I settled that at least
we would assure ourselves of his having food ; Alick, therefore,
got twenty shillings to take him four hundredweight of potatoes
and eight stone of meal ; three-fourths of which have been already
handed in (without explanation) ; the rest will follow at Candle-
mas. So goes it in native Annandale. A hundred times since has
that picture of Waugh, botching his old coat at the cottage window, stranded and cast out from the whole occupied earth, risen
in my head with manifold meaning.[1] His 'Prophecy Book' has
not paid its expenses. His 'Pathology' the Longmans, very naturally, would not have. I endeavoured to convince him that literature was hopeless, doubly and trebly hopeless for him. Further
advice I did not like to urge ; my sole consolation is to know that
for the present he has plenty of meal and potatoes, and salt cheap.
Perhaps it is likely he will fall into his mother's state, let an indolent insanity get the mastery over him, and spend his time
mostly in bed. I rather traced some symptoms of that : *Gott be-
hüte.*

Here at Craigenputtock everything is in its stillest condition.
I have read many books, put through me a vast multitude of
thoughts unutterable and utterable. In health we seem to improve, especially Janekin. We have realised a shower-bath at
Dumfries, and erected it in the room over this ; the little dame
fearlessly plunges it over her in coldest mornings. I have had it
only twice. Further, of external things, know that by science I
extracted the dining-room *lock*, had it repaired, and now it shuts
like a Christian lock ! This is small news, yet great. In my little
library are two bell-ropes (brass wire and curtain-ring), the daintiest you ever saw ; finally, the 'Segretario Ambulante' in fittest

[1] The fate of unsuccessful 'literature.'

framing hangs right behind my back (midway between the doors and the fire) and looks *beautiful;* really the piece of art I take most pleasure in of all my *Kunst-Vorrath.* He is a delightful fellow; shows you literature in its simplest quite steadfast condition, below which it *cannot* sink. My own portrait was to have been framed similarly and hung by him as counterpart, but Jane has put in rosewood and gilding, much to my dislike, and it hangs now on the other side of the wall (in the drawing-room), and keeps mostly out of my sight. If you think that our piano will still act, that one *reach* of the peat-stack is carried in, and all else in its old state, you may fancy us all tight and right, so far as the *case* of life goes. As to the kernel or spiritual part, there can hardly any description be given, so much of it has not yet translated itself into words. I am quiet; not idle, not unhappy; by God's blessing shall yet see how I can turn myself. Cochrane refuses both my projected articles. I have nevertheless written the 'Diamond Necklace;' at least, it is rough hewn in the drawer here, and only these marriages have kept me from finishing it. The other article I could not *now* have undertaken to write, the Saint Simonians, as you may perhaps know, having very unexpectedly come to light again, and set to giving missionary lectures of a most questionable sort in London. Mill is not there to tell me about them, but in Paris; so I can understand nothing of it, except that they are *not* to be written of, being once more in the fermenting state. Cochrane and I have probably enough done; but as Wull Brown says, 'perhaps it is just as well; for I firmly intended, &c.' I believe I must go back ere long and look at London again. In the meantime learn, study, read; consider thy ways and be wise! 'Teufelsdröckh,' as was hinted, is coming out in 'Fraser'—going 'to pot' probably, yet not without leaving me some money, not without making me quit of him. To it again! Try it once more! Alick was here since Saturday; came up with two sacks of old oats for Harry; went away this morning with a load of wood, &c. Not till Saturday last did we hear a word from the Advocate. He now writes to Jane in the frostiest, most frightened manner; makes honourable mention of you; to me he hardly alludes except from a far distance. Jane will have it that he took many things to himself in the article 'Diderot,' a possible thing, which corresponds, too, with the cessation of his letters. I love the Advocate, and partially pity him, and will write to him in such choicest mood as I can command at present.

To Mrs. Carlyle, Scotsbrig.

December 3, 1833.

My dear Mother,—I hope Notman delivered you the pills, so stupidly forgotten. The hasty scrawl that went with them would signify that we were here and little more; I was hardly this twelvemonth in such a hurry. Since then all goes on as it was doing; in spite of this most disastrous weather, the worst we have had for long, we indeed sit snug and defy the tempest; but Macadom's stable-slates jingling off from time to time suggest to us what many are suffering; some doubtless far out in the 'wide and wasteful main.' Both Jane and I go walking by *night*, if not by day, if there is a gleam of clearness. I take now and then a kind of *deck* walk to-and-fro at the foot of the avenue, in a spot where you know the wood shelters one from all winds that can blow.

We saw Jean and her man and household as we passed through Dumfries; it was all looking right enough; one could hope that they might do very well there. Aitken, I find, by a picture over his mantelpiece, has quite another talent for *painting* than I gave him the smallest credit for; it is really a *surprising* piece to have been executed there. As to Jean, we have always known her as a most reasonable, clear, and resolute little creature; of her, in all scenes and situations, good is to be anticipated. So we will wish them heartily a blessing with hope.

Ever since Alick left us I have been *writing* with all my old vehemence. This day too insisted on doing my *task*. It is about the 'Diamond Necklace,' that story you heard some hint of in Cagliostro; we shall see what it turns to. I am in the drawing-room to-night, with my big table (and side *half* to the fire, which is hot enough); Jane at my back also writing; *what* she will not tell me. We have been here together these three days; the rain had run down the vents actually in large streams and damped everything. This is what I call descriptive minuteness. Let me also say I have been reading in poor Waugh's book, and find your opinion of it verified; it is actually 'far better than one could have expected,' and contains some interesting things. Poor Waugh! Poor fellow—after all!

Alick's little letter (one of the smallest I ever read, but not the *emptiest*) informed us of what had been passing at Catlinns, and that you were there, he said, *well*. Have you returned from the expedition still well? I cannot too often impress on you the danger of winter weather; you have a tendency to apprehension for every one but yourself. Catlinns is not a good place in winter, and were Jenny not the healthiest of women, must have been very trying for *her*.

But there is another expedition, my dear mother, to which you are bound, which I hope you are getting ready for. Come up with Austin and Mary to Jean; stay with her till you rest; sending me up word *when;* on Wednesday or any other day I will come driving down and fetch you. In about a week hence, as I calculate, I shall be done with *this* scribblement, and then we can read together and talk together and walk together. Besides, this, in the horrid winter weather, is a better lodging for you than any other, and we will take better care of you—we promise. The blue room shall be dry as fire can make it; no *such* drying, except those *you* make at Scotsbrig, where on one occasion, as I remember, you spent the whole time of my visit in drying my clothes. Lastly, that when 'you come you may *come*.' Jane bids me communicate to Jamie that she wants three stone of meal, but will not take it unless he take pay for it.

And so, dear mother, this scribble must end, as others have done. To-morrow, I believe, is my eight-and-thirtieth birthday! You were then young in life: I had not yet entered it. Since then—how much! how much! They are in the land of silence (but, while we live, not of forgetfulness!) whom we once knew, and, often with thoughts too deep for words, wistfully ask of their and our Father above that we may again know. God is great: God is good! It is written ' He will wipe away all tears from every eye.' Be it as He wills: not as we wish. These things continually almost dwell with me, loved figures hovering in the background or foreground of my mind. A few years more and we too shall be with them in eternity. Meanwhile it is this *Time* that is ours: let us be busy with *it* and work, work, for the night cometh.

I send you all, young and old, my heart's blessing, and remain as ever, my dear mother, Your affectionate

T. Carlyle.

To John Carlyle, Rome.

Craigenputtock: December 24, 1833.

My dear Brother,—The description you give us of your Roman life is copious and clear: very gratifying to us; such matter as we like best to see in your letter. For myself, however, I can discern what perhaps our good mother does not so well, that with all favourable circumstances you have need of your philosophy there.

Alas! all modes of existence need such : we are, once for all, 'in a conditional world.' Your great grievance doubtless is that properly your office gives you nothing to do. Three hundred a year with sumptuous accommodation you have, but that is all. The days have to fly over you, and you seem to remain, as it were, windbound ; little more than an article of aristocratic state so far as your own household goes. This I can well see and sympathise in. It is hard, indeed, and grating to one's love of action ; a thing *intolerable*, did it threaten to continue for ever. But you are no longer a headstrong youth, but grown a deliberate man. Accordingly I see you adjust yourself to this also, from this also gather nourishment and strength. You are *equipping* yourself (in that strange way, so it was ordered) for your life voyage : patience, and the anchor is lifted. In the meanwhile, too, you know well *no* situation imposes on us the necessity of *idleness ;* if not in one way, if not in one of a hundred ways, you will work in the hundred and first. Continue, I beg you, to be mild, and either tolerant or *silently* intolerant. Let them go their way : go thou thine. What medical practice is to be come at, eagerly take. In defect of this read your Winckelmann, or any other solid book most appropriate to the place ; converse with all manner of mortals whose knowledge, as above ignorance, can directly or indirectly teach you aught. I should prefer Romans, I think, to any such a set of English as you have ; in any case if it is a man, and not a shadow of a man, one can get some good of him. My poor ' Segretario Ambulante,' actually converting disorder into order here in a small way, and realising victual for himself, is worth a hundred mere Clothes Horses and Patent Digesters, by what glorious name soever they may call themselves, that either do nothing, or the reverse of doing, which is even lower than nothing. Patience, therefore, my dear brother ! *Ohne Hast aber ohne Rast.* Let the cooks boil, and the tailors sew, and the shovel hat emit weekly his modicum of dishwater disguised as water of life ; it is all in the course of nature : ' like the crane's hoarse jingling flight that over our heads in long-drawn shriek sends down its creaking gabble, and tempts the silent wanderer that he look aloft at them a moment. These go their way and he goes his ; so likewise shall it be with us.'

And so now for a little Dumfriesshire news. Our good mother continues in her old state of health, or rather better, as they report to me. I expect her about Wednesday week. Austin and

Mary [1] will bring her to Jean's, and then on some appointed day I go down to fetch her with the gig. Austin can find no farm, he told us. What arrangement he will make for the coming year is not yet apparent. Many a time, I think, the foolish creatures, had they known better what stuff hope is made of, might as well have stayed where they were. But at any rate it was a change to be made—whether to-day or to-morrow is perhaps of little moment. A kind of sadness naturally came over our mother's mind at this new proof of terrestrial vicissitude, but withal she is quite peaceful and resolute, having indeed a *deeper* basis than earth and its vicissitudes to stand upon. I hardly know now another person in the world that so entirely believes and acts on her belief. Doubt not that all will shape itself, or be shapen, in some tolerable way. Jean, as you heard, is in her own house at Lochmaben Gate; to all appearances doing perfectly well. Alick has got a new son, whom he has named, or purposes naming, *Tom*, after me. He can get along amid the black mud acres of Catlinns, but with a continual struggle. One of his day-dreams for many a year has been America. I have ceased to oppose it so firmly of late; indeed, I often enough think what if I should go to America myself! Thousands and millions must yet go; it is properly but another section of our own country, though they rebelled very justly against George Guelph, and beat him, as they ought. We shall do or determine nothing rashly, the rather as for the present nothing presses.

As for Craigenputtock, it stands here in winter grimness, in winter seclusion. Nothing could exceed the violence of the December weather we have had; trees uprooted, Macadam slates jingling down, deluges of rain: Friday, in particular, did immense mischief to ships and edifices all over the island; such a day as has not been seen for a quarter of a century, they say. We nestled ourselves down here: '*better a wee bush than no bield.*' The shortest day is now behind us; we shall look forward to a spring which will be all the gladder. I continue to read great quantities of books. I have also, with an effort, accomplished the projected piece on the Diamond Necklace. It was finished this day week; really, a queer kind of thing, of some forty and odd pages. Jane, at first, thought we should print it at our own charges, set our name on it, and send it out in God's name. Neither she nor I are now so sure of this, but will consider it. My attempt was to make

[1] Carlyle's sister.

reality ideal; there is considerable significance in that notion of mine, and I have not yet seen the limits of it, nor shall till I have tried to go *as far* as it will carry me. The story of the *Diamond Necklace* is all told in that paper with the strictest fidelity, yet in a kind of *musical* way. It seems to me there is no epic possible that does not first of all ground itself on belief. What a man *does not believe* can never at bottom be of true interest to him. For the rest I remain in the completest isolation from all manner of editors. Teufelsdröckh is coming regularly out in 'Fraser's,' with what effect or non-effect I know not, consider not; and this is all I have to do with the world of letters and types. Before very long I shall most probably begin something else: at all events, go over again to the Barjarg library, and so use my time and not waste it. I have a considerable quantity and quality of things to impart to my brothers in this earth, if God see meet to keep me in it, and no editor, nor body of editors, nor, indeed, the whole world and the devil to back it out, can wholly prevent me from imparting them. Forward, then—*getrösten Muthes.*

My thirty-eighth birthday happened on the 4th last. I am fast verging towards forty, either as fool or physician. The flight of time is a world-old topic. I was much struck and consoled to see it handled quite in my own spirit in the Book of Job, as I read there lately. Oh! Jack, Jack, what unutterable things one would have to utter, had one organs. We have had some five or six letters from the Advocate: mostly unanswered yet. He asks me why I am not as cheerful a man as you? Babbles greatly about one thing and the other. They gave him a dinner at Edinburgh, listened patiently to his account of himself, pardoned him for the sake of *langsyne.* We hear now, not from himself, that some Lord Cringletie or other is about resigning, and that Jeffrey is to be made a JUDGE. It will be a happy change. Macaulay goes to India with 10,000*l.* a year. Jeffrey calls him the greatest (if I remember rightly) man in England, not excepting the Chancellor. How are we to get on without him at all? Depend upon it we shall get on better, or worse.

And now, my dear brother, leaving these extraneous things and persons, let me commend us all again to you, the absent, and therefore *best* loved. We shall not see you at our New Year's Day, but I here promise to think of you quite specially, and even drink your health (from my heart), though it were only in water, that day. Let us, as I said, be patient and peaceable. There

are other new years coming, when we shall not be so far apart.
Meanwhile, be strong. Remember always what you said of the
rush-bush here at Puttock on the wayside : 'It stands there because the whole world could not prevent its standing ;' one of the
best thoughts I ever heard you utter—a really true and pregnant
thought. So, too, with ourselves. Let us resist the devil, the
world, and the flesh. Alas! it is ill to do ; yet one should for
ever endeavour. Cheer up your low heart in the midst of those
Roman ruins. There is a time still young and fruitful, which
belongs to *us.* Get impatient with nobody. How easy it is to
bid you do this ; yet, really, it is right and true : the thing we
have to do were to abolish and abandon the worthless. If we
cannot do this all at once, let us, at least, not make it worse by
adding our own badness to it.

God be with you, my dear John.

BROTHER TOM.

Mrs. Carlyle writes a postscript between the lines—

My dear Brother,—I am told there is great space left for me to
add anything. Say, judge with your own eyes, where. If I had
known a letter was to go this week I should have been first in the
field. My good intentions, always unfortunate, were frustrated
last time ; but Carlyle always chooses a day for writing when I
am particularly engaged with household good and individual evil.
God bless you, however! Some day I shall certainly repay your
long, kind letter as it deserves. I continue to take your pills.
The prescription is in four pieces. I am better than last winter,
but 'association of ideas' is still hard on me.

CHAPTER XVII.

The economical situation of the Carlyles at Craigenputtock grew daily more pressing. The editors gave no sign
of desiring any further articles. 'Teufelsdröckh' was
still coming out in 'Fraser;' but the public verdict upon
it was almost universally unfavourable. The 'Diamond
Necklace,' which in my opinion is the very finest illustration of Carlyle's literary power, had been refused in its
first form by the editor of the 'Foreign Quarterly.' Fe-
vered as he was with the burning thoughts which were
consuming his very soul, which he felt instinctively, if
once expressed, would make their mark on the mind of
his country, Carlyle yet knew that his first duty was to
provide honest maintenance for himself and his wife—
somewhere and by some means; if not in England or
Scotland, then in America. His aims in this direction
were of the very humblest, not going beyond St. Paul's.
With 'food and raiment' both he and his wife could be
well content. But even for these, the supplies to be derived from literature threatened to fail, and what to do
next he knew not. In this situation he learnt from a
paragraph in a newspaper that a new Astronomy Professorship was about to be established in Edinburgh. Some
Rhetoric chair was also likely to be immediately vacant.
One or other of these, especially the first, he thought that
Jeffrey could, if he wished, procure for him. Hitherto
all attempts to enter on the established roads of life had

failed. He had little hopes that another would succeed;
but he thought it to be his duty to make the attempt.
He was justly conscious of his qualifications. The mathematical ability which he had shown in earlier times had
been so remarkable as to have drawn the attention of Le-
gendre. Though by the high standard by which he habitually tried himself Carlyle could speak, and did speak,
of his own capabilities with mere contempt, yet he was
above the affectation of pretending to believe that any
really fitter candidate was likely to offer himself. ' I will
this day write to Jeffrey about it,' he says in his Diary on
the 11th of January. 'Any hope? Little. My care for
it also not much. *Let us do what we can.* The issue not
with *us.*' He cared perhaps more than he had acknowledged to himself. He allowed his imagination to rest on
a possible future, where, delivered from the fiery unrest
which was distracting him, he might spend the remainder
of his life in the calm and calming study of the stars and
their movements. It was a last effort to lay down the
burden which had been laid upon him, yet not a cowardly
effort—rather a wise and laudable one—undertaken as it
was in submission to the Higher Will.

It failed—failed with an emphasis of which the effects
can be traced in Carlyle's Reminiscences of his connection
with Jeffrey. He condemns especially the tone of Jeffrey,
which he thought both ungenerous and insincere. Insincere it certainly was, if Jeffrey had any real influence, for
he said that he had none, and if he had already secured
the appointment for his own secretary, for he said that he
had not recommended his secretary. It may have been
ungenerous if, as Carlyle suspected, Jeffrey had resented
some remarks in the article on Diderot as directed against
himself, for he endeavoured to lay the blame of unfitness
for promotion upon Carlyle himself; but there is no proof
at all that Carlyle's surmise was correct.

Within the last few days (Carlyle wrote to his brother) I have made a proposal for a public office, and been rejected! There is to be an Astronomical Professor and Observer in Edinburgh, and no man of the smallest likelihood to fill it. I thought what an *honest* kind of work it was; how honestly I would work at it for my bread, and harmonise it with what tended infinitely higher than bread, and so wrote to the poor Advocate with great heartiness, telling him all this. He answered me by return of post in a kind of polite fishwoman shriek; adds that my doctrines (in literature) are 'arrogant, anti-national, absurd;' and to crown the whole 'in conclusion,' that the place withal is for an old secretary of his (who has not applied to *him*), unless I can convince the electors that I am fitter; which I have not the faintest disposition to do. I have written back to the poor body, suppressing all indignation, if there were any; diffusing over all the balm of pity, and so in a handsome manner terminate the business. One has ever and anon a kind of desire to 'wash away' this correspondent of ours; yet really it were not right. I can see him even in this letter to be very thoroughly miserable, and am bound to help him, not aggravate him. His censures, too, have something flattering even in their violence—otherwise impertinent enough; he cannot tolerate me, but also he cannot despise me; and that is the sole misery. On the whole, dear Jack, I feel it very wholesome to have my vanity humbled from time to time. Would it were rooted out forever and a day! My mother said when I showed her the purport of the letter, 'He canna hinder thee of God's providence,' which also was a glorious truth.

In this severe judgment there was possibly some justice. The doubt which Jeffrey pretended to feel, whether Carlyle was equal to the duties of handling delicate instruments without injuring them, cannot have been quite sincere. The supposition that a man of supreme intellectual qualification could fail in mastering a mere mechanical operation could only have originated in irritation. Carlyle already possessed a scientific knowledge of his subject. A few days' instruction might easily have taught him the mere manual exercise. It is possible, too, that if Jeffrey had gone out of his way to represent to Airy and Herschel, with whom the choice rested, what Carlyle's qualities really were, he might have saved to a Scotch university Scotland's greatest son, who would have made the School of Astronomy at Edinburgh famous throughout Europe, and have saved Scotland the scandal of neglect of him till his fame made neglect impossible.

In fairness to Jeffrey, however, whose own name will be remembered in connection with Carlyle as his first literary friend, we must put the Lord Advocate's case in his own way. If he was mistaken, he was mistaken about Carlyle's character with all the world. Everyone in Jeffrey's high Whig circle, the Broughams and Macaulays and such like, thought of Carlyle as he did. High original genius is always ridiculed on its first appearance; most of all by those who have won themselves the highest reputation in working on the established lines. Genius only commands recognition when it has created the taste which is to appreciate it. Carlyle acknowledged 'that no more unpromotable man than he was perhaps at present extant.'

Mrs. Carlyle had answered Jeffrey's *frosty* communication in the preceding November with a playfulness which, so far as she was concerned, had disarmed his anger with her, and he had fallen nearly back into his old tone.

Unpermitted though I am to publish Jeffrey's letters, I must, in allowing him to vindicate himself, adhere, as nearly as I can without trespassing, to his own language.

In the first week in December he had written affectionately to Mrs. Carlyle and kindly to Carlyle himself, pressing them to pay him a visit at Craigcrook. He professed and assuredly felt (for his active kindness in the past years places his sincerity above suspicion) a continued interest in Carlyle, some provocation, some admiration, and a genuine desire for his happiness. Carlyle thought that he did not please Jeffrey because he was so 'dreadfully in earnest.' The expression had in fact been used by Jeffrey; but what really offended and estranged him was Carlyle's extraordinary arrogance—a fault of which no one who knew Carlyle, or who has ever read his letters, can possibly acquit him.   He *was* superior to the people that he came in contact with.   He knew that he was, and being incapable of disguise or affectation, he let it be seen in every sentence that he spoke or wrote.   It was arrogance, but not the arrogance of a fool, swollen with conceit and vapour, but the arrogance of Aristotle's ' man of lofty soul,' ' who being of great merit,' knows that he is so, and chooses to be so regarded.   It was not that Carlyle ever said to himself that he was wiser than others.   When it came to introspection, never had anyone a lower opinion of himself ; but let him be crossed in argument, let some rash person, whoever he might be, dare to contradict him, and Johnson himself was not more rude, disdainful, and imperious ; and this quality in him had very naturally displeased Jeffrey, and had served to blind him, at least in some degree, to the actual greatness of Carlyle's powers.   In this letter Jeffrey frankly admitted that he disliked the wrangling to which Carlyle treated him.   Never having had much of a creed himself, he thought he had daily less ; and having no tendency to dogmatism and no impatience of indecision, he thought zeal for creeds and anxiety about positive opinions more and more ludicrous.   In fact, he regarded discussions which aimed at more than exercising the faculties and exposing intolerance very tiresome and foolish.

But for all that he invited Carlyle with genuine heartiness to come down from his mountains and join the Christmas party at Craigcrook.   Carlyle' professed to be a lover of his fellow-creatures.   Jeffrey said he had no patience with a philanthropy that drew people into the desert and made them fly from the face of man.

The good-humoured tone of his letter, and the pleasant banter of it, ending as it did with reiterated professions of a willingness to serve Carlyle if an opportunity offered, made it natural on Carlyle's part to apply to him when an opportunity did present itself immediately after. Jeffrey's letter had been written on December 8. Three weeks later the news of the intended Astronomy Professorship reached Craigenputtock, while Carlyle was told also that Jeffrey would probably have the decisive voice in the appointment. Carlyle wrote to him at once to ask for his good word, and there came by return of post the answer which he calls the 'fishwoman's shriek,' and which it is clear that he never forgave. For some reason—for the reason, possibly, which Carlyle surmised, that he expected the situation to be given to his own secretary—Jeffrey was certainly put out by being taken thus at his word when he had volunteered to be of use.

Impatiently, and even abruptly, he told Carlyle that he had no chance of getting the Astronomy Chair, and that it would be idle for him (Jeffrey) to ask for it. The appointment was entirely out of his own sphere, and he would be laughed at if he interfered. As a matter of fact, the most promising candidate was his secretary, a gentleman who had already been nominated for the Observatory at the Cape, and wished to go through some preliminary observing work at Edinburgh. But this gentleman, he said, had not applied to him for a recommendation, but trusted to his own merits. It was matter of notoriety that no testimonial would be looked at except from persons of weight and authority in that particular branch of science, and he was perfectly certain—indeed he *knew*—that the Government would be entirely guided by their opinions. The place would be given, and it was difficult to say that it ought not to be given, according to the recommendations of Herschel, Airy, Babbage, and six or seven other men of unquestionable eminence in the astronomical department, without the least regard to unprofessional advisers. If

Carlyle could satisfy *them* that he was the fittest person for the place, he might be sure of obtaining it; if he could not, he might be equally sure that it was needless to think of it. Whether Carlyle's scientific qualifications were such that he would be able to satisfy them, Jeffrey would not pretend to judge. But he added a further reason for thinking that Carlyle had no chance of success. He had had no practice in observing, and nobody would be appointed who was not both practised and of acknowledged skill. Sir David Brewster and Lord Napier looked on this as the most important qualification of all, and would abate much scientific attainment to secure tactical dexterity and acquired habits of observation. Herschel, it was said, was of the same opinion, and they were unlikely to trust the handling of their instruments to one who had not served an apprenticeship in the mechanical parts of the business. They were already crying out about the mischief which another professor had occasioned by his awkwardness, mischief which it would cost 500*l.* and many months of work to repair. The place to be given was, in fact, essentially an observer's place, there being little expectation that a class of practical astronomy would be formed out of the students at Edinburgh. It was not to be wondered at, therefore, that this qualification was regarded as indispensable.

Had Jeffrey stopped here, Carlyle would have had no right to complain. It is probable, but after all it is not certain, that Carlyle would have made a good observer, even if the technical knowledge could have been acquired without damage to the equatorials. Carlyle, no doubt, was a person whom the electors should have been grateful for the opportunity of choosing, if they had known what his intellectual powers were; but it is not clear that they could have known, or that Jeffrey could have persuaded them if he had tried. The 'secretary' was not only qualified as an

observer, but he had been already selected for a most responsible place at Capetown. Brewster could have spoken
for Carlyle's knowledge of mathematics; but mathematics
alone were insufficient; and in fact it is difficult to see by
what reasons any conceivable board or body of men would
have at that time been justified in preferring Carlyle.

But Jeffrey went beyond what was necessary in using
the occasion to give Carlyle a lecture. He was very sorry,
he said; but the disappointment revived and increased the
regret which he had always felt, that Carlyle was without
the occupation, and consequent independence, of some regular profession. The profession of *teacher* was, no doubt,
a useful and noble one; but it could not be exercised unless a man had something to teach which was thought
worth learning, and in a way that was thought agreeable;
and neither of those conditions was fulfilled by Carlyle.
Jeffrey frankly said that he could not set much value on
paradoxes and exaggerations, and no man ever did more
than Carlyle to obstruct the success of his doctrines by the
tone in which he set them forth. It was arrogant, obscure
vituperation, and carried no conviction. It might impress
weak, fanciful minds, but it would only revolt calm, candid,
and thoughtful persons. It might seem harsh to speak as he
was doing; but he was speaking the truth, and Carlyle
was being taught by experience to know that it was the
truth. Never, never would he find or make the world
friendly to him if he persisted in addressing it in so extravagant a tone. One thing he was glad to find, that
Carlyle was growing tired of solitude. He would be on
his way to amendment if he would live gently, humbly,
and, if possible, gaily, with other men; let him once fairly
come down from the barren and misty eminence where he
had his bodily abode, and he would soon be reconciled to a
no less salutary intellectual subsidence.

Disagreeable as language of this kind might be to Carlyle,

it was, after all, not unnatural from Jeffrey's point of view ; and there was still nothing in it which he was entitled to resent : certainly nothing of the ' fishwoman.' It was the language of a sensible man of the world who had long earnestly endeavoured to befriend Carlyle, and had been thwarted by peculiarities in Carlyle's conduct and character which had neutralised all his efforts. There was, in fact, very little in what Jeffrey said which Carlyle in his note-book was not often saying to and of himself. We must look further to explain the deep, ineffaceable resentment which Carlyle evidently nourished against Jeffrey for his behaviour on this occasion. The Astronomical chair was not the only situation vacant to which Carlyle believed that he might aspire. There was a Rhetoric chair—whether at Edinburgh or in London University, I am not certain. To this it appears that there had been some allusion, for Jeffrey went on to say that if he was himself the patron of that chair he would appoint Carlyle, though not without misgivings. But the University Commissioners had de-cided that the Rhetoric chair was not to be refilled unless some man of great and established reputation was willing to accept it, and such a man Jeffrey said he could not in his conscience declare Carlyle to be. Had it been Macaulay that was the candidate, then, indeed, the Commissioners would see their way. Macaulay was the greatest of living Englishmen, not excepting the great Brougham himself. But Carlyle was—Carlyle. It was melancholy and pro-voking to feel that perversions and absurdities (for as such alone he could regard Carlyle's peculiar methods and doc-trines) were heaping up obstacles against his obtaining either the public position or the general respect to which his talents and his diligence would have otherwise entitled him. As long as society remained as it was and thought as it did, there was not the least chance of his ever being admitted as a teacher into any regular seminary.

There was no occasion for Jeffrey to have written with such extreme harshness. If he felt obliged to expostulate, he might have dressed his censures in a kinder form. To Carlyle such language was doubly wounding, for he was under obligations to Jeffrey, which his pride already endured with difficulty, and the tone of condescending superiority was infinitely galling. He was conscious, too, that Jeffrey did not understand him. His extravagances, as Jeffrey considered them, were but efforts to express thoughts of immeasurable consequence. From his boyhood upwards he had struggled to use his faculties honestly for the best purposes; to consider only what was true and good, and never to be led astray by any worldly interest; and for reward every door of preferment was closed in his face, and poverty and absolute want seemed advancing to overwhelm him. If he was tried in the fire, if he bore the worst that the world could do to him and came out at last triumphant, let those who think that they would have behaved better blame Carlyle for his occasional bursts of impatience and resentment. High-toned moral lectures were the harder to bear because Goethe far off in Germany could recognise in the same qualities at which Jeffrey was railing the workings of true original genius.

Even so it is strange that Carlyle, after the victory had long been won when his trials were all over and he was standing on the highest point of literary fame, known, honoured, and admired over two continents, should have nourished still an evident grudge against the poor Lord Advocate, especially as, after the appearance of the 'French Revolution,' Jeffrey had freely and without reserve acknowledged that he had all along been wrong in his judgment of Carlyle. One expression casually let fall at the end of one of Jeffrey's letters, to which I need not do more than allude, contains a possible explanation. Jeffrey was always gentlemanlike, and it is not conceivable that he intended to affront Carlyle, but Carlyle may have taken the words to himself in a sense which they were not meant to bear ; and a misunderstanding, to which self-respect would have forbidden him to refer, may have infected his recollections of a friend whom he had once cordially esteemed, and to whom both he and his brothers were under obligations which could hardly be overrated. But this is mere conjecture. It may be simply that Jeffrey had once led Carlyle to hope for his assistance in obtaining promotion in the world, and that when an opportunity seemed to offer itself, the assistance was not given.

Never any more did Carlyle seek admission into the beaten tracks of established industry. He was impatient of *harness*, and had felt all along that no official situation was fit for him, or he fit for it. He would have endeavoured loyally to do his duty in any position in which he might be placed. Never would he have accepted employment merely for its salary, going through the perfunctory forms, and reserving his best powers for other occupations. Anything which he undertook to do he would have done with all his might; but he would have carried into it the stern integrity which refused to bend to conventional exigencies. His tenure of office, whether of professor's chair or of office under government, would probably have been brief and would have come to a violent end. He never offered himself again, and in later times when a professorship might have been found for him at Edinburgh, he refused to be nominated. He called himself a Bedouin, and a Bedouin he was ; a free lance owing no allegiance save to his Maker and his own conscience.

On receiving Jeffrey's letter, he adjusted himself resolutely and without complaining to the facts as they stood. He determined to make one more attempt, either at Craigenputtock or elsewhere, to conquer a place for himself, and earn an honest livelihood as an English man of letters. If that failed, he had privately made up his mind to try his fortune in America, where he had learnt from Emerson, and where he himself instinctively felt, that he might expect more favourable hearing. He was in no hurry. In all that he did he acted with a deliberate circumspection scarcely to have been looked for in so irritable a man. The words 'judicious desperation,' by which he describes the principle on which he guided his earlier life, are exactly appropriate.

Including Fraser's payments for 'Teufelsdröckh' he was possessed of about two hundred pounds, and until his brother John could repay him the sums which had been advanced for his education, he had no definite prospect of earning any more—a very serious outlook, but he did not allow it to discompose him. At any rate he had no debts; never had a debt in his life except the fifty pounds which he had borrowed from Jeffrey, and this with the Advocate's loan to his brother was now cleared off. The 'Diamond Necklace' had proved unsaleable, but he worked quietly on upon it, making additions and alterations as new books came in. He was not solitary this winter. In some respects he was worse off than if he had been solitary. With characteristic kindness he had taken charge of the young Scotchman whom he had met in London, William Glen, gifted, accomplished, with the fragments in him of a true man of genius, but with symptoms showing themselves of approaching insanity, in which after a year or two he sank into total eclipse. With Glen, half for his friend's sake, he read Homer and mathematics. Glen, who was a good scholar, taught Carlyle Greek. Carlyle taught Glen Newtonian geometry; in the intervals studying hard at French Revolution history. His inward experience lies written in his Diary.

Saturday, Jan. 11, 1834.—So long since my pen was put to paper here. The bustle, the confusion has been excessive. Above three weeks ago by writing violently I finished the 'Diamond Necklace,' a singular sort of thing which is very far from pleasing me. Scarcely was the 'Necklace' laid by when the Glens arrived, and with them the entirest earthquake. Nothing could be done, nothing so much as thought of. Archy [1] often only went off on Sunday; William not near so ill as we anticipated. I have him at geometry, which he actually learns; mean to begin reading Homer with him. Will he ever recover? We have hope and ought to endeavour.

Wednesday gone a week I went down to Dumfries and brought up my mother, who is still here reading and sewing. She is wonderfully peaceful, not unhappy; intrinsically an admirable woman whom I ought to be right thankful that I have for mother.

Letter from Mill about a new Radical Review in which my co-operation is requested. Shall be ready to give it if they have any payment to offer. Dog's-meat Bazaar which you enter muffled up, holding your nose, with 'Here, you master, able editor, or whatever your name is, take this mess of mine and sell it for me—at the old rate, you know.' This is the relation I am forced to stand in with publishers as the time now runs. May God mend it.

Magazine Fraser writes that 'Teufelsdröckh' excites the most unqualified disapprobation—*à la bonne heure.*

Feb. 9.—Nothing done yet—nothing feasible devised. Innumerable confused half-thoughts; a kind of *moulting* season with me; very disconsolate, yet tending, as I believe or would fain believe, to profit. Almost all things go by systole and diastole, even one's spiritual progress. Neglect, humiliation, all these things *are* good, if I will use them wisely. From the uttermost deeps of darkness a kind of unsubduable hope rises in me; grows stronger and stronger.

Began *Homer* two weeks ago : nearly through the first book now—like it very considerably. Simplicity, sincerity, the singleness (not quite the word) and massive repose as of an ancient picture. Indeed, all the engravings of Pompeii antiques, and such like, that I have seen grow singularly present with me as I read. A most quieting wholesome task too ; will persist in it. Poor Glen is my

[1] Brother of William Glen.

very sufficient help here. Have sent for Heyne, Blackwell, and other books, as further helps. Dacier here, but nearly unproductive for me.

Read 'Beattie's Life,' by Sir Wm. Forbes (from Barjarg, where I was some days ago), *Schneidermässig*, religious 'Gigmanity,' yet lovable, pitiable, in many respects worthy. Of all literary men, Beattie, according to his deserts, was perhaps (in those times) the best rewarded; yet alas! also, at length, among the unhappiest. How much he enjoyed that is far from *thee!*—converse with minds congenial; an element not of *black cattleism*, but of refinement, plenty, and encouragement. Repine not; or, what is more to be dreaded, *rebel not*.

Feb. 13.—Reading in those larger quartos about the *Collier*. Nearly done with it now. View of the rascaldom of Paris, tragical at this distance of time (for where is now that reiving and stealing, that squeaking and jabbering—of lies?) : otherwise unprofitable. What to do with that 'Diamond Necklace' affair I wrote? must correct it in some parts which these new books have illuminated a little.

Letter from Jeffrey indicating that *he* can or will do nothing in the 'Rhetoric Professor' business had I resolved on trying him. Better to be done with all that business, and know that I have *nothing* to hope for in that quarter, or any such, and adjust myself thereto. Rebel not; be still; still and strong!

Finished the first book of *Homer* last night. Pleasantest most purely poetical reading I have had for long. Simplicity (not multiplicity), almost vacuity, yet sincerity, and the richest toned artless music. The question at present with me, *What* does he mean by his gods? In the question of *belief* some light to be sought from Homer still; he is still far from clear to me.

Bulwer's 'England and the English' :

> Weightiest of harrows, what horse will ply it?
> Cheeriest of sparrows meanwhile will try it.

Intrinsically a poor creature this Bulwer; has a bustling whisking agility and restlessness which may support him in a certain degree of significance with some, but which partakes much of the nature of *levity*. Nothing truly notable can come of him or of it.

Sunday, Feb. 16.—Beautiful days; this is the third of them. Unspeakably grateful after the long loud howling deluge of a winter. Blackbirds singing this morning—had I not been so sick!

Friday, Feb. 21.—Still reading, but with indifferent effect. *Homer* still grateful—grows easier; one hundred lines have been done more than once in an evening. Was Thersites intended to have any wit, humour, or even fun in his raillery? Nothing (with my actual knowledge of Greek) comes to light but mere beggarly abuse, and miry blackguardism. When Ulysses weals his back with that bang of his sceptre, how he sinks annihilated like a cracked bug! Mark too the sugar-loaf head, bald but for down; the squint, the shoulders drawn together over his back: a perfect beauty in his kind. How free otherwise is Ulysses with his sceptre! 'Whatever man of the Δῆμος he met' he clanked him over the crown. It does not seem to me so incredible as it did, that opinion of Voss's. The 'characters' in Homer, might they not be like the pantaloon, harlequin, &c. of the Italian comedy, and sustained (what is there meant by sustaining?) by various hands? One thing is clear, and little more to *me* at present. The whole is very *old*. 'Achilles sitting weeping by the hoary beach looking out into the dark-coloured sea;' still, *einfach*, with a kind of greatness.

Mein Leben geht sehr übel: all dim, misty, squally, disheartening, at times almost heart-breaking. Nevertheless it seems to me clear that I am in a growing state: call this a *moulting season* for the mind; say I shall come out of it new coated, made young again!

Yesterday we for the first time spoke seriously of setting off for London to take up our abode there next Whitsunday. Nothing but the wretchedest, forsaken, discontented existence here, where almost your whole energy is spent in keeping yourself from flying out into exasperation. I had never much hope of foreign help: perhaps the only man I put even a shadow of dependence upon was Jeffrey; and he has, two or three weeks ago, convinced me that he will never do anything for me; that he dares not; that he cannot; that he does not wish to do it. Why not try for ourselves, while as yet we have strength left, and old age has not finally lamed us? *Andar con Dios!* Unutterable thoughts are in me, and *these* words are but faint chirpings. May God direct us and go with us! My poor mother! But once for all one must cut himself loose though his heart bleed; it is better than perennial torpor which ends in death.

March 25.—Strange days these are; again quite original days in my life. Cannot express any portion of their meaning in words; cannot even try it.

I dig the garden flower-beds, though not hoping to see them spring. It is a bodeful, *huge* feeling I have, like one to be delivered from a Bastille; and who says, delivered? or cast out?

Thousand voices speak to me from the distance out of the dim depths of the old years. I sit speechless. If I live, I *shall* speak.

Many things are sad to me : the saddest is to forsake my poor mother; for it is kind of *forsaking*, though she, too, sees well the necessity of it. May He to whom she ever looks not forsake her !

Be still, be wise, be brave ! The world is all before thee; its *pains* will soon (how very soon) be over; the *work* to be done in it will continue—through eternity. Oh, how fearful, yet how great !

So far the Diary. The letters, or portions of them, fill the interval between the notes, and wind up the story of the Carlyles' life in the Dumfriesshire highlands.

To John Carlyle, Rome.

Craigenputtock : January 21, 1834.

On Wednesday gone a fortnight I drove down to Dumfries to fetch up our mother, who had been waiting at Jean's there for several days. We got home betimes; found Archy Glen and William, the former of whom went off on the following day and left us a little more composure. My mother was wonderfully cheerful and composed. She read various things—Campan's 'Memoirs,' and such like, with great interest; sewed a little, smoked and talked, and, on the whole, was very tolerably off. Her calmness in the midst of so many vicissitudes, and now while her immediate future is still so problematical, was very gratifying to me; showed the admirable spirit she is of. It is one of the saddest possibilities now that lies before me, the losing of such a parent. One thing with another, and altogether apart from natural affection, I have seen no woman in the whole world whom I would have preferred as a mother. On the following Sunday Alick and Jamie both arrived, so that again we had a full house. They stayed till Wednesday morning, when I accompanied them as far as Stroquhan ; it had been arranged that Alick was to come next Saturday to Dumfries and meet our mother there if the day was tolerable. She and I accordingly set off; met Alick there, who had his cart, and I reyoked poor Harry and turned back again to the solitude of our moors. Our mother was wrapped to all lengths, and, having the wind favourable, I hope would not suffer much from cold.

As for our household it is much as you can fancy it. Jane continues in a tolerable, in an improving state of health, though the last five weeks of bustle have done her no good. I, when I take walking enough, get along as I was wont in that particular. Continued sickness is a miserable thing, yet one learns to brave it. . . .

What you say of periodicals is mournfully true ; yet it is true also that a man must provide food and clothes for himself as long as he honestly can. While you write down a truth you do an honest duty, were the devil himself your editor, and all fellow contributors mere incubi and foul creatures. One loses repute by it, but nothing more ; and must front that loss for a gain which is indispensable. Indeed, had I (written) the best book possible for me, I see not, such is the condition of things, where I could so much as get it printed. *Your* money, my dear boy, I will not take at this time till you are settled with it, and making more. Come home, and let us settle in London together, and front the world together, and see whether it will beat us ! Let us try it. And in the meanwhile never fear but I hold on ; now as ever it lies with myself. Mill tells me that he and Buller and a number of Radicals with money capital, and what they reckon talents, have determined on a new Radical Review, which they want me to write in. Unitarian Fox is to be editor. I calculate that it may last three years at any rate, for money is found to that length. If they pay me rightly they shall have a paper or two ; if not, not. The Radicals I say always are barren as Sahara, but *not* poisonous. In my prophecy of the world they are my *enfants perdus*, whom I honestly wish well to. James Fraser writes me that ' Teufelsdröckh ' meets with the most unqualified disapproval, which is all extremely proper. His payment arrives, which is still more proper. On the whole, dear Jack, it is a contending world ; and he that is born into it must fight for his place or lose it. If we are under the *right flag*, let the world do its worst and heartily welcome.

God bless thee, dear brother! *Auf ewig.*   T. CARLYLE.

To Mrs. Carlyle, Scotsbrig.

January 28, 1834.

I wrote to poor Jeffrey, but not till any anger I felt had gone off, and given place to a kind of pity. ' Poor fellow ! ' I thought : ' what a miserable *fuff* thou gettest into, poor old exasperated politician ! I will positively have pity on thee, and do thee a little good if I can ! ' In this spirit was my letter written; a short careless letter winding up the business handsomely, not ravelling it further. He is off to London to-day I fancy, to worry and be worried in that den of discord and dishonesty; actually, I doubt, to lose his last allotment of health, almost his life, if he be not soon delivered. 'He cannot hinder thee of God's providence,' is also a most precious truth : not he nor the whole world with the Devil to back it out! *This* is a fact one ought to lay seriously to heart and see into the meaning of. Did we see it rightly, what were there beneath the moon that should throw us into commotion? Except writing letters, I have not put pen to paper yet. I sent word to Mill that I *would* write two essays for his new periodical, the second of which is perhaps to be on John Knox; but I suppose there is no great hurry.

To Alexander Carlyle.

February 18, 1834.

. . . Poor Mrs. Clow it seems has been called away. She was not long left a *superfluity* in the world, but has found a home beside her old partner where there will be none to grudge her. Oh Time! Time! how it brings forth and devours! And the roaring flood of existence rushes on for ever similar, for ever changing! Already of those that we looked up to as grown men, as towers of defence and authority in our boyhood, the most are clean gone. We ourselves have stept into their position, where also we cannot linger. Unhappy they that have no footing in eternity; for here in time all is but cloud and the baseless fabric of a vision!

But to turn back to the earth; for in the earth too lies the pledge of a higher world—namely, a *duty* allotted us. Tell me, my dear brother, how you fare on that wild Knowhead, what kind of cheer you are of. The little children I imagine must be your chief blessing; and surely you are thankful for them, and will struggle with your whole strength to instruct them and protect them, and fit them for the long journey (long, for it is as long as eternity) that lies before them. Little Jane will be beginning to have many notions of things now. Train her to this as the corner-stone of all morality : to stand by the *truth; to abhor a lie as she does hell-fire.* Actually the longer I live I see the greater cause to look on falsehood with detestation, with terror, as the beginning of all else that is of the Devil. *My* poor little namesake has no knowledge of good or evil yet; but I hope he will grow to be a strong man and do his name credit. For yourself, I am glad to see you make so manful a struggle on that uncomfortable clay footing, which however you must not quite quarrel with. In the darkest weather I always predict better days. The world is God's world, and wide and fair. If they hamper us too far we will try another side of it. Meanwhile I will tell you a fault you have to guard against, and is not that the truest friendship that I can show you? Every position of man has its temptation, its evil tendency. Now yours and mine I suspect to be this : a tendency to imperiousness, to indignant self-help, and if nowise theoreti-cal, yet practical, forgetfulness and tyrannical contempt of other men. This is wrong; this is *tyranny,* I say ; and we ought to guard against it. Be merciful; repress much indignation ; too much of it will get vent after all. Evil destiny is nothing ; let it labour us and impoverish us as it will, if it only do not lame and distort us. Alas! I feel well one cannot wholly help even this ; but we ought unweariedly to endeavour.

To John Carlyle, Rome.

Craigenputtock : February 25, 1834.

We learned incidentally last week that Grace, our servant, though ' without fault to us,' and whom we with all her inertness were nothing but purposing to keep, had resolved on ' going home next summer.' The cup that had long been filling ran over with that smallest of drops. After meditating on it for a few minutes, we said to one another : ' Why not *bolt* out of all these sooty des-picabilities, of *Kerrags* and lying draggle-tails of byre-women, and peat-moss and isolation and exasperation and confusion, and go at once to London ? *Gedacht, gethan!* Two days after we had a letter on the road to Mrs. Austin, to look out among the ' houses to let ' for us, and an advertisement to Mac Diarmid to try for the letting of our own. Since then, you may fancy, our heads and hearts have been full of this great enterprise, the greatest (small as it is) that I ever *knowingly* engaged in. We bring anxiously together all the experience we have gathered or got reported, look back and look forward, make the bravest resolutions, and in fine seem to see a trembling hope that we may master the enterprise (of an honest life in London); at all events, a certainty that we ought to try it. Yes, we must try it! Life here is but a kind of life-in-death, or rather, one might say, a not-being-born : one sits as in the belly of some Trojan horse, weather screened, but pining, inactive, neck and heels crushed together. Let us burst it in the name of God! Let us take such an existence as He will give us, working where work is to be found while it is called to-day. A strange shiver runs through every nerve of me when I think of taking that plunge ; yet also a kind of sacred faith, sweet after the dreary vacuity of soul I have through long seasons lived in as under an eclipsing shadow. I purpose to be *prudent,* watchful of my words, to look well about me, and with all the faculty I have pick my steps in that new arena. Thousands of sillier fellows than I flourish in it : the whole promotion I strive for is simplest food and shelter in exchange for the honestest work I can do.

We purpose for many reasons to make this a whole measure, not a half one : thus the first thing will be to give up our establishment here, to sell off all the furniture but what will equip a very modest house in the suburbs of London ; to let *this* house if we can ; if we cannot, to let it stand there and not waste more money. This Jane calls a 'burning of our ships,' which suits better with our present aims than anything else would. For indeed I feel this is as if the *last* chance I shall ever have to redeem my existence from pain and imprisonment, and make something of the faculty I have, before it be for ever hid from my eyes. No looking back then! Forward! Advance or perish! We imagine some suburban house may be got for 40*l.* Leigh Hunt talked much about a quite delightful one he had (for 'ten children' too) at Chelsea, all wainscoted, &c., for thirty guineas. With 200*l.* we fancy the *rigour of economy* may enable us to meet the year. I must work and seek work ; before sinking utterly I will make an 'a-fu' struggle.

Our dear mother has not heard of this ; for though I wrote to Alick a week ago, it was not then thought of. It will be a heavy stroke, yet not quite unanticipated, and she will brave it. My brother and she are the only ties I have to Scotland. I will tell her that though at a greater distance we are not to be disunited. Regular letters—frequent visits. I will say who knows but what you and I may yet bring her up to London to pass her old days waited on by both of us? Go whither she may, she will have her Bible with her and her faith in God. She is the truest Christian believer I have ever met with; nay I might almost say the only true one.

P.S. from Mrs. Carlyle:—

My dear Brother,—Here is a new prospect opened up to us with a vengeance! Am I frightened? Not a bit. I almost wish that I felt more anxiety about our future; for this composure is not *courage*, but *diseased indifference*. There is a sort of incrustation about the inward me which renders it alike insensible to fear and to hope. I suppose I am in what Glen calls the *chrysalis state* or the *state of incubation*. Let us trust that like all other states which have a beginning it will also have an end, and that the poor Psyche shall at last get freed. In the meantime I do what I see to be my duty as well as I can and wish that I could do it better. It seems as if the problem of living would be immensely simplified to me if I had health. It does require such an effort to keep oneself from growing quite wicked, while that weary weaver's shuttle is plying between my temples. Unhappy Melina, &c.! I have reason to be thankful that I have had less sickness this winter than in the two preceding ones, which I attribute partly to the change in my pills. Your recipe is worn to tatters, but Glen copied it for me. The note book you gave me is half filled with such multifarious matter! No mortal gets a glimpse of it. I wish Carlyle would let me begin a letter instead of ending it. He leaves me nothing but dregs to impart. Would you recommend me to sup on porridge and beer? Carlyle takes it. We have got a dear little canary bird which we call Chico, which sings all day long 'like—like anything.'

So ends the last letter from Craigenputtock. 'The ships were burnt,' two busy months being spent in burning them —disposing of old books, old bedsteads, kitchen things, all the rubbish of the establishment. The cows and poultry were sold. Mrs. Carlyle's pony was sent to Scotsbrig. Friends in London were busy looking out for houses. Carlyle, unable to work in the confusion, grew unbearable, naturally enough, to himself and everyone, and finally, at the beginning of May, rushed off alone, believing that house letting in London was conducted on the same rule as in Edinburgh, and that unless he could secure a home for himself at Whitsuntide he would have to wait till the year had gone round. In this hurried fashion he took his own departure, leaving his wife to pack what they did not intend to part with, and to follow at her leisure when the new habitation had been decided on. Mill had sent his warmest congratulations when he learnt that the final resolution had been taken. Carlyle, who had settled himself while house hunting at his old lodgings in Ampton Street, sent his brother John a brief account of his final leave-taking of Scotland.

To John Carlyle.

4 Ampton Street : May 18.

With regard to our dear mother, I bid you comfort yourself with the assurance that she is moderately well. She adjusts herself with the old heroism to the new circumstances; agrees that I *must* come hither; parts from me with the stillest face, more touching than if it had been all beteared. I said to Alick as we drove up the Purdamstown brae that morning, that I thought if I had all the mothers I ever saw to choose from I would have chosen my own. She is to have Harry,[1] and can ride very well on him, will go down awhile to sea-bathing at Mary's, and will spend the summer tolerably enough. For winter I left her the task of spinning me a plaid dressing gown, with which if she get too soon done she may spin another for you. She has books, above all her *Book.* She trusts in God, and shall not be put to shame. While she was at Craigenputtock I made her train me to two song tunes ; and we often sang them together, and tried them often again in coming down into Annandale. One of them I actually found myself humming with a strange cheerfully pathetic feeling when I first came in sight of huge smoky Babylon—

> For there's seven foresters in yon forest.
> And them I want to see, see,
> And them I want to see.

I wrote her a little note yesterday and told her this.

[1] The pony.

Thus the six years' imprisonment on the Dumfriesshire moors came to an end. To Carlyle himself they had been years of inestimable value. If we compare the essay on Jean Paul, which he wrote at Comely Bank, with the 'Diamond Necklace,' his last work at Craigenputtock, we see the leap from promise to fulfilment, from the immature energy of youth to the full intellectual strength of completed manhood. The solitude had compelled him to digest his thoughts. In 'Sartor' he had relieved his soul of its perilous secretions by throwing out of himself his personal sufferings and physical and spiritual experience. He had read omnivorously far and wide. His memory was a magazine of facts gathered over the whole surface of European literature and history. The multiplied allusions in every page of his later essays, so easy, so unlaboured, reveal the wealth which he had accumulated, and the fulness of his command over his possessions. His religious faith had gained solidity. His confidence in the soundness of his own convictions was no longer clouded with the shadow of a doubt. The 'History of the French Revolution,' the most powerful of all his works, and the only one which has the character of a work of art, was the production of the mind which he brought with him from Craigenputtock, undisturbed by the contradictions and excitements of London society and London triumphs. He had been tried in the furnace. Poverty, mortification, and disappointment had done their work upon him, and he had risen above them elevated, purified, and strengthened. Even the arrogance and self-assertion which Lord Jeffrey supposed to have been developed in him by living away from conflict with other minds, had been rather tamed than encouraged by his lonely meditations. It was rather collision with those who differed with him which fostered his imperiousness; for Carlyle rarely met with an antagonist whom he could not overbear with the torrent of his metaphors, whilst to himself his note-books show that he read many a lecture on humility.

He had laid in, too, on the moors a stock of robust health. Lamentations over indigestion and want of sleep are almost totally absent from the letters written from Craigenputtock. The simple, natural life, the wholesome air, the daily rides or drives, the poor food—milk, cream, eggs, oatmeal, the best of their kind—had restored completely the functions of a stomach never, perhaps, so far wrong as he had imagined. Carlyle had ceased to complain on this head, and in a person so extremely vocal when anything was amiss with him, silence is the best evidence that there was nothing to complain of. On the moors, as at Mainhill, at Edinburgh, or in London afterwards, he was always impatient, moody, irritable, violent. These humours were in his nature, and could no more be separated from them than his body could leap off its shadow. But, intolerable as he had found Craigenputtock in the later years of his residence there, he looked back to it afterwards as the happiest and wholesomest home that he had ever known. He could do fully twice as much work there, he said, as he could ever do afterwards in London; and many a time, when sick of fame and clatter and interruption, he longed to return to it.

To Mrs. Carlyle Cragenputtock had been a less salutary home. She might have borne the climate, and even benefited by it, if the other conditions had been less ungenial. But her life there, to begin with, had been a life of menial drudgery, unsolaced (for she could have endured and even enjoyed mere hardship) by more than an occasional word of encouragement or sympathy or compassion from her husband. To him it seemed perfectly natural that what his mother did at Scotsbrig his wife should do for him. Every household duty fell upon her, either directly, or in supplying the shortcomings of a Scotch maid-of-all-work.

She had to cook, to sew, to scour, to clean ; to gallop down alone to Dumfries if anything was wanted; to keep the house, and even on occasions to milk the cows. Miss Jewsbury has preserved many anecdotes of the Craigenputtock life, showing how hard a time her friend had of it there. Carlyle, though disposed at first to dismiss these memories as legends, yet admitted on reflection that for all there was a certain foundation. The errors, if any, can be no more than the slight alterations of form which stories naturally receive in repetition. A lady brought up in luxury has been educated into physical unfitness for so sharp a discipline. Mrs. Carlyle's bodily health never recovered from the strain of those six years. The trial to her mind and to her nervous system was still more severe. Nature had given her, along with a powerful understanding, a disposition singularly bright and buoyant. The Irving disappointment had been a blow to her ; but wounds which do not kill are cured. They leave a scar, but the pain ceases. It was long over, and if Carlyle had been a real companion to her, she would have been as happy with him as wives usually are. But he was not a companion at all. When he was busy she rarely so much as saw him, save, as he himself pathetically tells, when she would steal into his dressing-room in the morning when he was shaving, to secure that little of his society. The loneliness of Craigenputtock was dreadful to her. Her hard work, perhaps, had so far something of a blessing in it, that it was a relief from the intolerable pressure. For months together, especially after Alick Carlyle had gone, they never saw the face of guest or passing stranger. So still the moors were, that she could hear the sheep nibbling the grass a quarter of a mile off. For the many weeks when the snow was on the ground she could not stir beyond the garden, or even beyond her door. She had no great thoughts, as Carlyle had, to occupy her with the administration of the universe. He had deranged the faith in which she had been brought up, but he had not inoculated her with his own; and a dull gloom, sinking at last almost to apathy, fell upon her spirits. She fought against it, like a brave woman as she was. Carlyle's own views of the prospects of men in this world were not brilliant. In his 'Miscellanies' is a small poem, written at Craigenputtock, called 'Cui Bono?' giving a most unpromising sketch of human destiny :—

Cui Bono?

What is Hope? a smiling rainbow
   Children follow through the wet;
'Tis not here, still yonder, yonder!
   Never urchin found it yet.

What is Life? a thawing iceboard
   On a sea with sunny shore.
Gay we sail—it melts beneath us!
   We are sunk, and seen no more.

What is Man? a foolish baby;
   Vainly strives, and fights, and frets;
Demanding all—deserving nothing!
   One small grave is what he gets.

In one of Mrs. Carlyle's note-books, I find an 'Answer' to this, dated 1830 :—

Nay, this is Hope: a gentle dove,
   That nestles in the gentle breast,
Bringing glad tidings from above
   Of joys to come and heavenly rest.

And this is Life: ethereal fire
   Striving aloft through smothering clay;
Mounting, flaming, higher, higher!
   Till lost in immortality.

And Man—oh! hate not nor despise
   The fairest, lordliest work of God!
Think not He made the good and wise
   Only to sleep beneath the sod!

Carlyle himself recognised occasionally that she was not happy. Intentionally unkind it was not in his nature to be. After his mother, he loved his wife better than anyone in the world. He was only occupied, unperceiving, negligent; and when he *did* see that anything was wrong with her, he was at once the tenderest of husbands.

In some such transient state of consciousness he wrote, on January 29, 1830 :—

The Sigh.

Oh! sigh not so, my fond and faithful wife,
　In sad remembrance or in boding fear :
This is not life—this phantasm type of life !
　What is there to rejoice or mourn for here ?

Be it no wealth, nor fame, nor post is ours—
　Small blessedness for infinite desire ;
But has the King his wish in Windsor's towers ?
　Or but the common lot—meat, clothes, and fire ?

Lone stands our home amid the sullen moor,
　Its threshold by few friendly feet betrod ;
Yet *we* are here, we two, still true though poor :
　And this, too, is *the world*—the ' city of God ' !

O'erhangs us not the infinitude of sky,
　Where all the starry lights revolve and shine ?
Does not that universe within us lie
　And move—its Maker or itself divine ?

And we, my love, life's waking dream once done,
　Shall sleep to wondrous lands on other's breast,
And all we loved and toiled for, one by one,
　Shall join us there and, wearied, be at rest.

Then sigh not so, my fond and faithful wife,
　But striving well, have hope, be of good cheer ;
Not rest, but worthy labour, is the soul of life ;
　Not that but this is to be looked and wished for here.

If the occasional tenderness of these lines could have been formed into a habit Mrs. Carlyle might have borne Craigenputtock less impatiently, and as her bodily ailments were chiefly caused by exposure and overwork, she would probably have escaped the worst of them, because she would have thought it worth while to take care of herself.

Of the solitude and of the strange figures moving about the moor, to make the desolation more sensible, Carlyle has left a singular picture.

Old Esther, whose death came one of our early winters, was a bit of memorability in that altogether vacant scene. I forget the old woman's surname, perhaps McGeorge, but well recall her heavy lumpish figure, lame of a foot, and her honest, quiet, not stupid countenance of mixed ugliness and stoicism. She lived above a mile from us in a poor cottage of the next farm.[1] Esther had been a laird's daughter riding her palfrey at one time, but had gone to wreck father and self; a special 'misfortune' (so they delicately name it) being of Esther's producing. Misfortune in the shape ultimately of a solid tall ditcher, very good to his old mother Esther, had just before our coming perished miserably one night on the shoulder of Dunscore Hill (found dead there next morning), which had driven his poor old mother up to this thriftier hut and silent mode of living in our moorland part of the parish. She did not beg, nor had my Jeannie much to have given her of help (perhaps on occasions milk, old warm clothes, &c.), though always very sorry for her last sad bereavement of the stalwart affectionate son. I remember one frosty kind of forenoon, while walking meditative to the top of our hill, the silence was complete, all but one 'click clack' heard regularly like a far-off spondee or iambus, a great way to my right, no other sound in nature. On looking sharply, I discovered it to be old Esther on the highway, crippling along, towards our house most probably. Poor old soul! thought I. What a desolation! But you will meet a kind face too perhaps. Heaven is over all.

Not long after poor old Esther sank to bed—deathbed, as my Jane, who had a quick and sure eye in these things, well judged it would be. Sickness did not last above ten days: my poor wife

---

[1] 'Carson's, of Nether Craigenputtock, very stupid young brother used to come and bore me at rare intervals.—T. C.'

zealously assiduous and with a minimum of fuss and noise. I remember those few poor days full of human interest to her, and
through her to me ; and of a human pity not painful, but sweet
and genuine. She went walking every morning, especially every
night to arrange the poor bed, &c.—nothing but rudish hands,
rude though kind enough, being about ; the poor old woman evidently gratified by it, and heart thankful, and almost to the very
end giving clear sign of that. Something pathetic in old Esther
and her exit ; nay, if I rightly bethink me, that ' click clack ' pilgrimage had in fact been a last visit to Craigenputtock with some
poor bit of crockery, some grey-lettered butter-plate, which I
used to see ' as a wee *memorandum* o' me, mem, when I am gone.'
' Memorandum ' was her word, and I remember the poor little
platter for years after. Poor old Esther had awoke that frosty
morning with the feeling that she would soon die, that the ' bonny
leddy ' had been ' unco guid ' to her, and that there was still that
' wee bit memorandum.' Nay, I think she had, or had once had,
the remains or complete ghost of a ' fine old riding habit,' once
her own, which the curious had seen, but this she had judged it
more polite to leave to the parish.

Enough of Craigenputtock. The scene shifts to London.

CHAPTER XVIII.

A.D. 1834. ÆT. 39.

Extracts from Journal.

London: May 24, 1834.—What a word is there! I left home on Thursday last (five days ago), and see myself still with astonishment here seeking houses. The parting with my sister Jean, who had driven down with me to Dumfries, was the first of the partings; that with my dear mother next day, with poor Mary at Annan, with my two brothers Alick and Jamie—all these things *were* to be done. Shall we meet again? Shall our meeting again be for good? God grant it. We are in his hands. This is all the comfort I have. As to my beloved and now aged mother, it is sore upon me,—so sore as I have felt nothing of the sort since boyhood. She paid her last visit at Craigenputtock the week before, and had attached me much, if I could have been more attached, by her quiet way of taking that sore trial. She studied not to sink my heart; she shed no tear at parting; and so I drove off with poor Alick in quest of new fortunes. May the Father of all, to whom she daily prays for me, be ever near her! May He, if it be his will, grant us a glad re-meeting and re union in a higher country. But no more of this. Words are worse than vain. I am here in my old lodging at Ampton Street, wearied, and without books, company, or other resource. The Umpire coach from Liverpool. Through the arch at Holloway came first in sight of huge smoky London, humming, in a kind of defiance, my mother's tune of 'Johnny O'Cox.' Find this lodging. Mrs. Austin very kind. See several houses. Disappointed in all. Kensington very dirty and confused. Sleep—sweet sleep. This day busy, with little work done; my feet all lamed, and not above one house seen that in any measure looks like fitting.

Went to Mrs. Austin, through the Park and Gardens. Find a Mrs. Jamieson—a shrewd-looking, hard-tempered, red-haired woman, whom I care little about meeting again. Look at many houses with them. Edward Irving starts up from a seat in Kensington Gardens, as I was crossing it with these two, and runs towards me. The good Edward! He looked pale, worn, unsound, very unhealthy. At the house we were going to no key could be got: no this, no that. Miss my dinner. Innkeepers can give me none. Dine with a dairyman on bread and milk beside his cows —a most interesting meal. Charge three halfpence, I having furnished bread. Gave the man sixpence, because I liked him. Will see the poor fellow again, perhaps. Hunt's [1] household in Cheyne Row, Chelsea. Nondescript! unutterable! Mrs. Hunt asleep on cushions ; four or five beautiful, strange, gipsy-looking children running about in undress, whom the lady ordered to get us tea. The eldest boy, Percy, a sallow, black-haired youth of sixteen, with a kind of dark cotton nightgown on, went whirling about like a familiar, providing everything : an indescribable dreamlike household. Am to go again to-morrow to see if there *be* any houses, and what they are. Bedtime now, and so good night, ye loved ones. My heart's blessing be with all!

Those who have studied Carlyle's writings as they ought to be studied, know that shrewd practical sense underlies always his metaphorical extravagances. In matters of business he was the most prudent of men. He had left his wife at Craigenputtock to pack up, and had plunged, himself, into the whirlpool of house-hunting. He very soon discovered that there was no hurry, and that he was not the best judge in such matters. He understood—the second best form of wisdom—that he did not understand, and forebore to come to any resolution till Mrs. Carlyle could join him. He wrote to her, giving a full account of his experiences.

The female head (he said) is not without a shrewdness of its own in these affairs. Moreover, ought not my little *coagitor* to have a vote herself in the choice of an abode which is to be *ours?* The sweet word *ours!* The blessed ordinance—let Hunt say what he will [2]—by which all things are for ever one between us and

[1] Leigh Hunt.
[2] Leigh Hunt advocated ' women's rights ' in marriage arrangements.

separation an impossibility. Unless you specially order it, no final arrangement shall be made till we both make it.

Carlyle had not been idle—had walked, as he said, till his feet were lamed under him. He had searched in Brompton, in Kensington, about the Regent's Park. He had seen many houses more or less desirable, more or less objectionable. For himself he inclined on the whole to one which Leigh Hunt had found for him near the river in Chelsea. Leigh Hunt lived with his singular family at No. 4 Upper Cheyne Row. About sixty yards off, about the middle of Great Cheyne Row, which runs at right angles to the other, there was a house which fixed his attention. Twice he went over it. 'It is notable,' he said, 'how at each new visit your opinion gets a little hitch the contrary way from its former tendency. Imagination has outgone the reality. I nevertheless still feel a great liking for this excellent old house. Chelsea is unfashionable: it was once the resort of the Court and great, however; hence numerous old houses in it at once cheap and excellent.'

A third inspection produced a fuller description—description of the place as it was fifty years ago, and not wholly incorrect of its present condition; for Cheyne Row has changed less than most other streets in London. The Embankment had yet forty years to wait.

The street (Carlyle wrote) runs down upon the river, which I suppose you might see by stretching out your head from the front window, at a distance of fifty yards on the left. We are called 'Cheyne Row' proper (pronounced *Chainie* Row), and are a 'genteel neighbourhood;' two old ladies on one side, unknown character on the other, but with 'pianos.' The street is flag pathed, sunk storied, iron railed, all old fashioned and tightly done up; looks out on a rank of sturdy old *pollarded* (that is, beheaded) lime trees standing there like giants in *tawtie* wigs (for the new boughs are still young); beyond this a high brick wall; backwards a garden, the size of our back one at Comely Bank, with trees, &c., in bad culture; beyond this green hayfields and tree avenues, once a bishop's pleasure grounds, an unpicturesque yet rather cheerful outlook. The house itself is eminent, antique, wainscoted to the very ceiling, and has been all new painted and repaired ; broadish stair with massive balustrade (in the old style), corniced and as thick as one's thigh ; floors thick as a rock, wood of them here and there worm-eaten, yet capable of cleanness, and still with thrice the strength of a modern floor. And then as to rooms, Goody ! Three stories beside the sunk story, in every one of them three apartments, in depth something like forty feet in all—a front din-ing-room (marble chimney piece, &c.), then a back dining-room or breakfast-room, a little narrower by reason of the kitchen stairs ; then out of this, and narrower still (to allow a back window, you consider) a china-room or pantry, or I know not what, all shelved and fit to hold crockery for the whole street. Such is the ground area, which of course continues to the top, and furnishes every bedroom with a dressing-room or second bedroom ; on the whole a most massive roomy sufficient old house with places, for ex-ample, to hang, say, three dozen hats or cloaks on, and as many crevices and queer old presses and shelved closets (all tight and new painted in their way) as would gratify the most covetous Goody—rent, thirty-five pounds ! I confess I am strongly tempted. Chelsea is a singular heterogeneous kind of spot, very dirty and confused in some places, quite beautiful in others, abounding with antiquities and the traces of great men—Sir Thomas More, Steele, Smollett, &c. Our row, which for the last three doors or so is a street, and none of the noblest, runs out upon a 'Parade' (perhaps they call it) running along the shore of the river, a broad highway with huge shady trees, boats lying moored, and a smell of ship-ping and tan. Battersea Bridge (of wood) a few yards off ; the broad river with white-trowsered, white-shirted Cockneys dashing by like arrows in thin long canoes of boats ; beyond, the green beautiful knolls of Surrey with their villages—on the whole, a most artificial, green-painted, yet lively, fresh, almost opera-look-ing business, such as you can fancy. Finally, Chelsea abounds more than any place in omnibi, and they take you to Coventry Street for sixpence. Revolve all this in thy fancy and judgment, my child, and see what thou canst *make* of it.

The discovery of this Chelsea house had been so gratify-ing that more amiable views could be taken, and more in-terest felt, with the other conditions of London life.

Let me now treat thee to a budget of small news (he goes on). Mill I have not yet seen again; we could make no appointment, being so unfixed as yet. Mrs. Austin had a tragical story of his having fallen *desperately in love* with some young philosophic beauty (yet with the innocence of two sucking doves), and being lost to all his friends and to himself, and what not ; but I traced nothing of this in poor Mill; and even incline to think that what truth there is or was in his adventure may have done him good. Buller also spoke of it, but in the comic vein. Irving I have not again seen, though I have tried four times ; yesterday twice (at Bayswater), and the second time with great disappointment. He seems to be under the care of a Scotch *sick nurse* there ; was said to be 'asleep' when I called first, then gone (contrary to my appointment) when I called the second time. He rides twice a day down to that Domdaniel in Newman Street, rises at five in the morning, goes to bed at nine, is '*very weak.*' I had refused dinner at the Austins for his sake ; it seemed to me as if I might have clutched him from perdition and death, and now we were not to meet again. My poor Edward! *Heu, quantum mutatus!* But I will make a new trial. Heraud said to me, quite in the cursory style, 'Aaving (Irving) is dying and a—a—!' Heraud himself ('mad as a March hare,' Fraser said) lives close by Ampton Street, and is exceedingly *kedge* about me, anxious beyond measure for golden opinions of his God-dedicated Epic—of which I would not tell him any lie, greatly as he tempted me.

Fraser did not open freely to me, yet was opening. Literature still all a mystery ; nothing 'paying;' 'Teufelsdröckh' beyond measure unpopular; an oldest subscriber came in to him and said, 'If there is any more of that d—d stuff I will, &c. &c.;' on the other hand, an order from America (Boston or Philadelphia) to send a copy of the magazine *so long* as there was anything of Carlyle's in it.' 'One spake up and the other spake down :' on the whole, Goody, I have a great defiance of all that. As to 'fame' and the like, in *very truth*, in this state of the public, it is a thing one is always better without; so I really saw and felt the other night, clearly for the first time. Miss Martineau, for example, is done again ; going to America to try a new tack when she returns—so are they all, or *will* inevitably all be *done;* extinguished and abolished ; for they are *nothing*, and were only *called* (and made to fancy themselves) something. Mrs. Austin herself seems to me in a kind of trial-state ; risen or rising to where she cannot hope to stand ; where it will be well if she feels no giddiness, as indeed I really hope she will. A most excellent creature, of surveyable limits ; her goodness will in all cases save her. Buller is better and went yesterday (I fancy) to ' the House.' We have had two long talks (on occasion of the franks) with great mutual delight. An intelligent, clear, honest, most kindly vivacious creature ; the genialest Radical I have ever met. He throws light for me on many things, being very *ready* to speak. Mrs. Austin spoke ominously of his health, but to my seeing without much ground. Charlie, I think, will be among my little comforts here.

The Duke, now plain Mr. Jeffrey, but soon to be Lord Jeffrey, is still here for a week ; he has left his address for me with Mrs. Austin. I determined to call some morning in passing, and did it on Monday. Reception anxiously cordial from all three ; hurried insignificant talk from him still at the breakfast table ; kindness playing over ' iron gravity ' from me. I felt it to be a farewell visit, and that it should be ' hallowed in our choicest mood.' The poor Duke is so tremulous, he bade me ' good evening ' at the door ; immense jerking from Mrs. Jeffrey, yet many kind words and invitations back. . . . And so ends our dealing with bright Jeffreydom, once so sparkling, cheerful, now gone out into darkness—which shall not become foul candlestuff vapour, but darkness only. Empson is still alive ; but I surely will not seek him. Napier, too, is here, or was ; him, too, I will nowise seek or meddle with—the hungry *simulacrum.*

To Mrs. Carlyle, Scotsbrig.

4 Ampton Street, London : May 30, 1834.

My dear Mother,—How often have I thought of you since we parted, in all varieties of solemn moods, only seldom or never in a purely sad or painful one. My most constant feeling is one not without a certain sacredness : I determine to live worthily of such a mother ; to know always, like her, that we are ever in our great Taskmaster's eye, with whom are the issues not of time only, which is but a short *vision,* but of eternity, which ends not and is a reality. Oh that I could keep these things for ever clear before me ! my whole prayer with regard to life were gratified. But these things also should not make us gloomy or sorrowful : far from that. Have we not, as you often say, ' many mercies ' ? Is not the light to see that they are mercies the first and greatest of these ?

Assure yourself, my dear mother, that all goes well. In regard to health, this incessant toil and even irregular living seems to agree with me. I take no drugs. I really feel fresher and stronger than I used to do among the moorlands. Moreover, I never was farther in my life from '*tining heart*,' which I know well were to 'tine all.' Not a bit of me! I walk along these tumultuous streets with nothing but a feeling of kindness, of brotherly pity, towards all. No loudest boasting of man's strikes any, the smallest, terror into me for the present; indeed how should it when no loudest boasting and threatening of the Devil himself would? He nor they '*cannot* hinder thee of God's providence.' No, they cannot. I have the clearest certainty that if work is appointed me here to do, it must and will be done, and means found for doing it. So fear nothing, my dear mother. Tom will endeavour not to disgrace you in this new position more than in others.

I have seen some book-publishing persons, some 'literary men' also. The great proportion are indubitablest *duds:* these two we must let pass, and even welcome when they meet us with kindliness. By far the sensiblest man I see is Mill, who seems almost fonder of me than ever. The class he belongs to has the farther merit of being genuine and honest so far as they go. I think it is rather with that class that I shall connect myself than with any other;[1] but still in many important respects I have to expect to find myself alone. Charles Buller is grown a very promising man, likely to do good in the world, if his health were only better, which as yet hampers him much. He evidently likes me well, as do all his household, and will be a considerable pleasure to me. I was dining there this day week. I saw various notable persons—Radical members, and such like; among whom a young, very rich man, named Sir William Molesworth, pleased me considerably. We have met since, and shall probably see much more of one another. He seems very honest: needs, or will need, guidance much, and with it may do not a little good.

I liked the frank manners of the young man; so beautiful in contrast with Scottish gigmanity. I pitied his darkness of mind, and heartily wished him well. He is, among other things, a vehement smoker of tobacco. This Molesworth is one of the main men that are to support that Radical Review of theirs with which

---

[1] 'No poison in the Radicals. If little apprehension of positive truth, no hypocrisy; no wilful taking up with falsehood.'

it seems likely that I may rather heartily connect myself, if it take a form I can do with. The rest of the reviews are sick and lean, ready for nothing, so far as I can see, but a gentle death. I also mean to write a *new book ;* and in a serious enough style, you may depend upon it. By the time we have got the flitting rightly over I shall have settled what and how it is to be. Either on the French Revolution, or on John Knox and our Scottish Kirk.

By dint of incessant industry I again got to see Edward Irving, and on Saturday last spent two hours with him. He seemed to have wonderfully recovered his health, and I trust will not perish in these delusions of his. He is still a good man, yet wofully given over to his idols, and enveloped for the present, and nigh choked, in the despicablest coil of cobwebs ever man sate in the midst of.

Mrs. Strachey I have seen some three times, but not in very advantageous circumstances. She is the same true woman she ever was, indignant at the oppressing of the poor, at the wrong and falsehood with which the earth is filled ; yet rather gently withdrawn from it, and hoping in what is beyond it than actively at war with it.

Carlyle was not long left alone. Mrs. Carlyle arrived—she came by Annan steamer and the coach from Liverpool at the beginning of June; old Mrs. Carlyle, standing with a crowd on the Annan pier, waving her handkerchief as the vessel moved away. Carlyle, as he returned from his walk to his lodgings in Ampton Street, was received by the chirping of little Chico, the canary bird ; his wife resting after her journey in bed. They had been fortunate in securing a remarkable woman, who was more a friend and a companion than a servant, to help them through their first difficulties—Bessy Barnet, the daughter of Mr. Badams's housekeeper at Birmingham, whom Carlyle had known there as a child. Badams was now dead, and this Bessy, who had remained with him to the last, now attached herself to Carlyle for the sake of her late master. The Chelsea house was seen by Mrs. Carlyle, and after some hesitation was approved ; and three days after they had taken possession of their future home, and Pickford's

vans were at the door unloading the furniture from Craigenputtock.

Thirty-four years later Carlyle wrote :—

Tuesday, 10th of June, 1834, was the day of our alighting, amidst
heaped furniture, in this house, where we were to continue for life.
I well remember bits of the drive from Ampton Street : what
damp-clouded kind of sky it was ; how in crossing Belgrave
Square Chico, whom *she* had brought from Craigenputtock in her
lap, burst out into singing, which we all (Bessy Barnet, our romantic maid, sate with us in the old hackney coach) strove to accept
as a promising omen. The business of sorting and settling with
two or three good carpenters, already on the ground, was at once
gone into with boundless alacrity,[1] and under such management
as hers went on at a mighty rate ; even the three or four days of
quasi camp life, or gipsy life, had a kind of gay charm to us ; and
hour by hour we saw the confusion abating—growing into victorious order. Leigh Hunt was continually sending us notes ; most
probably would in person step across before bedtime, and give us
an hour of the prettiest melodious discourse. In about a week, it
seems to me, all was swept and garnished, fairly habitable, and
continued incessantly to get itself polished, civilised, and beautiful to a degree that surprised me. I have elsewhere alluded to
all that, and to my little Jeannie's conduct of it. Heroic, lovely,
mournfully beautiful as in the light of eternity that little scene of
time now looks to me. From birth upwards she had lived in opu-
lence, and now for my sake had become poor—so nobly poor. No
such house for beautiful thrift, quiet, spontaneous—nay, as it were,
unconscious minimum of money reconciled to human comfort and
dignity, have I anywhere looked upon where I have been.

[1] Carlyle's memory was perfectly accurate in what it retained. His account
to his brother at the time gives fuller detail to the picture : 'A hackney coach,
loaded to the roof and beyond it with luggage and the passengers, tumbled us
all down here at eleven in the morning. By all I mean my dame and myself,
Bessy Barnet, who had come the night before, and little Chico, the canary
bird, who *multum jactatus* did nevertheless arrive living and well from Puttock, and even sang violently all the way, by sea and land, nay, struck up his
lilt in the very London streets whenever he could see green leaves and feel the
free air. There we sate on three trunks. I, however, with a match-box soon
lit a cigar, as Bessy did a fire ; and thus with a kind of cheerful solemnity we
took possession by "raising reek," and even dined in an extempore fashion on
a box lid covered with some accidental towel.' (To John Carlyle, June 17,
1834.)

The auspices under which the new life began, not from Chico's song only, were altogether favourable. The weather was fine; the cherries were ripening on a tree in the garden. Carlyle got his garden tools to work and repaired the borders, and set in slips of jessamine and gooseberry bushes brought from Scotland. To his mother, who was curious about the minutest details, he reported—

We lie safe at a bend of the river, away from all the great roads, have air and quiet hardly inferior to Craigenputtock, an outlook from the back windows into mere leafy regions with here and there a red high-peaked old roof looking through; and see nothing of London, except by day the summits of St. Paul's Cathedral and Westminster Abbey, and by night the gleam of the great Babylon affronting the peaceful skies. The house itself is probably the best we have ever lived in—a right old, strong, roomy brick house, built near 150 years ago, and likely to see three races of these modern fashionables fall before it comes down.

The French Revolution had been finally decided on as the subject for the next book, and was to be set about immediately; Fraser having offered, not indeed to give money for it, but to do what neither he nor any other publisher would venture for 'Sartor'—take the risk of printing it. Mill furnished volumes on the subject in 'barrowfuls.' Leigh Hunt was a pleasant immediate neighbour, and an increasing circle of Radical notabilities began to court Carlyle's society. There was money enough to last for a year at least. In a year he hoped that his book might be finished; that he might then give lectures; that either then or before some editorship might fall to him—the editorship, perhaps (for it is evident that he hoped for it), of Mill's and Molesworth's new Radical Review. Thus at the outset he was—for him—tolerably cheerful. On the 27th of June he sent a full account of things to Scotsbrig.

To Alexander Carlyle.

5 Cheyne Row, Chelsea : June 27, 1834.

The process of installation is all but terminated, and we in rather good health and spirits, and all doing well, are beginning to feel ourselves at home in our new *hadding*. We have nothing to complain of, much to be piously grateful for ; and thus, with a kind of serious cheerfulness, may gird ourselves up for a new career. As it was entered on without dishonest purposes, the issue, unless *we* change for the worse, is not to be *dreaded*, prove as it may.

One of the greatest moments of my life, I think, was when I waved my hat to you and Jamie from on board the steamboat. My two brothers, the last of my kindred I had to leave, stood *there*, and I stood *here*, already flying fast from them. I would not desecrate so solemn an hour by childish weakness. I turned my thoughts heavenward, for it is in heaven only that I find *any* basis for our poor pilgrimage on this earth. Courage, my brave brothers all ! Let us be found faithful and we shall not fail. Surely as the blue dome of heaven encircles us all, so does the providence of the Lord of Heaven. He will withhold *no* good thing from those that love Him ! This, as it was the ancient Psalmist's faith, let it likewise be ours. It is the Alpha and Omega, I reckon, of all possessions that can belong to man.

Neither my mother nor you will interpret these reflections of mine as if they betokened gloom of temper—but indeed rather the reverse. I hope we have left great quantities of gloom safe behind us at Puttock, and indeed hitherto have given little harbour to such a guest here. It is strange often to myself, with what a kind of not only fearlessness, but meek contempt and indifference, I can walk through the grinding press of these restless millions, 'listening,' as Teufelsdröckh says, ' to its loudest threatenings with a still smile.' I mean to work according to my strength. As to riches, fame, success, and so forth, I ask no questions. Were the work laid out for us but the kneading of a clay brick, let us, in God's name, *do it faithfully*, and look for our reward elsewhere. So, on the whole, to end moralising, let us sing—

> Come, fingers five, come now be live,
> And stout heart fail me not, not—

or, what is far before singing, let us do it, and go on doing it.

In respect of society we have what perfectly suffices—having indeed here the best chance. Mill comes sometimes; the Bullers were all here, paying us their first visit, Mrs. Austin, &c. There is really enough, and might easily be to spare. Things go in the strangest course in that respect here. A man becomes for some reason, or for no reason, in some way or other notable. Straightway his door from dawn to dusk is beset with idlers and loungers, and empty persons on foot and in carriages, who come to gather of his supposed fulness one five minutes of tolerable sensation; and so the poor man (most frequently it is a poor woman) sits in studied attitude all day, 'doing what he can do,' which is, alas! all too little; for gradually or suddenly the carriage and foot empty persons start some other scent and crowd elsewhither; and so the poor notable man, now fallen into midnight obscurity, sits in his studied attitude within forsaken walls, either to rise and set about some work (which were the best), or mournfully chant *Ichabod!* according to his convenience.

On the whole, as I often say, what is society? What is the help of *others* in any shape? None but *thyself* can effectually help thee, can effectually hinder thee! A man must have lived to little purpose six years in the wilderness of Puttock if he have not made this clear to himself.

Hunt and the Hunts, as you have heard, live only in the next street from us. Hunt is always ready to go and walk with me, or sit and talk with me to all lengths if I want him. He comes in once a week (when invited, for he is very modest), takes a cup of tea, and sits discoursing in his brisk, fanciful way till supper time, and then cheerfully eats a cup of porridge (to sugar only), which he praises to the skies, and vows he will make his supper of at home. He is a man of thoroughly London make, such as you could not find elsewhere, and I think about the *best* possible to be made of his sort: an airy, crotchety, most copious clever talker, with an honest undercurrent of reason too, but unfortunately not the deepest, not the most practical—or rather it is the most *un*practical ever man dealt in. His hair is grizzled, eyes black-hazel, complexion of the clearest dusky brown; a thin glimmer of a smile plays over a face of cast-iron gravity. He never laughs—can only titter, which I think indicates his worst deficiency. His house excels all you have ever read of—a *poetical Tinkerdom*, without parallel even in literature. In his family room, where are a sickly large wife and a whole shoal of well-conditioned wild children, you will find half a dozen old rickety chairs gathered from half a dozen different hucksters, and all seemingly engaged, and just pausing, in a violent *hornpipe.* On these and around them and over the dusty table and ragged carpet lie all kinds of litter—books, papers, egg-shells, scissors, and last night when I was there the torn heart of a half-quartern loaf. His own room above stairs, into which alone I strive to enter, he keeps cleaner. It has only two chairs, a bookcase, and a writing-table ; yet the noble Hunt receives you in his Tinkerdom in the spirit of a king, apologises for nothing, places you in the best seat, takes a window-sill himself if there is no other, and there folding closer his loose-flowing 'muslin cloud' of a printed nightgown in which he always writes, commences the liveliest dialogue on philosophy and the prospects of man (who is to be beyond measure 'happy' yet) ; which again he will courteously terminate the moment you are bound to go : a most interesting, pitiable, lovable man, to be used kindly but with discretion. After all, it is perhaps rather a comfort to be near honest, friendly people—at least, an honest, friendly man of that sort. We stand sharp but mannerly for his sake and for ours, and endeavour to get and do what good we can, and avoid the evil.

To John Carlyle, Naples.

5 Cheyne Row : July 22, 1834.

We are getting along here as we can without cause of complaint. Our house and whole household, inanimate and rational, continue to yield all contentment. Bessy is a clever, clear-minded girl ; lives quietly not only as a servant, but can cheer her mistress as a companion and friend. Most favourable change. Jane keeps in decidedly better health and spirits. Within doors I have all manner of scope. Out of doors, unhappily, the prospect is vague enough, yet I myself am not without fixed aim. The bookselling world, I seem to see, is all but a hopeless one for me. Periodical editors will employ me, as they have employed me, on this principle : for the sake of my name, and to help them to season a new enterprise. That once accomplished, they want little more to do with me. Amateurs enough exist that will dirty paper gratis, and puffery, and so forth, is expected to do the rest. Thus they kept a *gusting bone* in the four towns, and lent it out to give a flavour to weak soup ; otherwise hung it in the nook. I am much dissatisfied with the arrangement and little minded to continue it. Meanwhile, by Heaven's blessing, I find I can get a book printed with my name on it. I have fixed on my book, and am labouring (*ohne Hast, ohne Rast*) as yet afar off to get it ready. Did I not tell you the subject? The French Revolution. I mean to make an artistic picture of it. Alas! the subject is high and huge. *Ich zittre nur, ich stottre nur, und kann es doch nicht lassen.* Mill has lent me above a hundred books; I read continually, and the matter is dimly shaping itself in me. Much is in the Museum for me, too, in the shape of books and pamphlets. I was there a week ago seeking pictures; found none; but got a sight of Albert Dürer, and (I find) some shadow of his old—*teutschen*, deep, still soul, which was well worth the getting. This being my task till the end of the year, why should I curiously inquire what is to become of me next? 'There is aye life for a living body,' as my mother's proverb has it; also, as she reminded me 'if thou tine heart, thou tines a'.' I will do my best and calmest; then wait and ask. As yet, I find myself much cut off from practical companions and instructors; my visitors and collocutors are all of the theoretic sort, and worth comparatively little to me, but I shall gradually approach the other sort, and try to profit by them. With able editors I figure my course as terminated. Fraser cannot afford to pay me, besides seems more and more bent on Toryism and Irish reporterism, to me infinitely detestable.

With regard to neighbourhood I might say we were very quiet, even solitary, yet not oppressively so. Of visitors that merely *call* here we have absolutely none; our day is our own, and those that do come are worth something to us. Our most interesting new friend is a Mrs. Taylor, who came here for the first time yesterday, and stayed long. She is a living romance heroine, of the clearest insight, of the royalest volition, very interesting, of questionable destiny, not above twenty-five. Jane is to go and pass a day with her soon, being greatly taken with her. Allan Cunningham with his wife and daughter made us out last night. We are to dine there some day. Hunt is always at hand; but, as the modestest of men, never comes unless sent for. His theory of life and mine have already declared themselves to be from top to bottom at *variance*, which shocks him considerably; to me his talk is occasionally pleasant, is always clear and lively, but all too *foisonless*, baseless, and shallow. He has a theory that the world is, or should, and shall be, a gingerbread Lubberland, where evil (that is, pain) shall never come: a theory in very considerable favour here, which to me is pleasant as streams of unambrosial dishwater, a thing I

simply *shut my mouth* against, as the shortest way. Irving I have
not succeeded in seeing again, though I went up to Bayswater once
and left my name. I rather think his wife will incline to secrete
him from me, and may even have been capable of suppressing my
card. I will try again, for his sake and my own. Mill is on the
whole our best figure, yet all too narrow in shape, though of wide
susceptibilities and very fond of us. He hunts me out old books,
does *all* he can for me ; he is busy about the new Radical Review,
and doubtless will need me there, at least as 'gusting bone.'
Ought he to get me ? Not altogether for the asking perhaps, for
I am wearied of that. *Voyons.* Thus, dear brother, have you a
most full and artless picture of our existence here. You do not despair of us ; your sympathies are blended with hopes for us. You
will make out of all this food enough for musing. Muse plenti-
fully about us : to me, also, you continue precious. With you I
am *double* strong. God be with you, dear Jack ! Jane stipulated
for a paragraph, so I stop here.

P.S. by Mrs. Carlyle :—

Again only a postscript, my dear John, but I will write one time
or other. I *will :* as yet I am too unsettled. In trying to write or
read, above all things, I feel I am in a new position. When I look
round on my floors once more laid with carpets, my chairs all in a
row, &c., I flatter myself the tumult is subsided. But when I
look within ! alas, I find my wits by no means in a row, but still
engaged at an uproarious game of 'Change seats, the king's coming.' I read dozens of pages, and find at the end that I have not
the slightest knowledge what they were about. I take out a note-
book day after day and write the day of the week and month, and
so return it. Pity the poor white woman. She will find herself
by-and-by and communicate the news to you among the first : for
I am sure you care for her, and would rejoice in her attainment of
a calm, well-ordered being for her own sake. At all rates we are
well out of Puttock everywhere.

These first letters from London would seem to indicate
that Carlyle was tolerably 'hefted' to his new home and
condition ; but the desponding mood was never long absent. Happy those to whom nature has given good animal spirits. There is no fairy gift equal to this for helping a man to fight his way, and animal spirits Carlyle

never had. He had the keenest sense of the ridiculous; but humour and sadness are inseparable properties of the same nature; his constitutional unhopefulness soon returned upon him, and was taking deeper hold than he cared to let others see. The good effects of this change wore off in a few weeks: the old enemy was in possession again, and the entries in his diary were more desponding than even at Craigenputtock.

Saturday night (sunset), July 26, 1834.—Have written nothing here for above a month; my state has been one of those it was almost frightful to *speak* of: an undetermined, unspeakable state. Little better yet; but the book being open I will put down a word.

Nothing can exceed the *gravity* of my situation here. 'Do or die' seems the word; and alas! what to do? I have no practical friend, no confidant, properly no companion. For five days together I sit without so much as speaking to anyone except my wife. Mood tragical, gloomy, as of one forsaken, who had nothing left him *but to get through his task and die.* No periodical editor wants me: no man will give me money for my work. Bad health, too (at least, singularly changed health), brings all manner of dispiritment. Despicablest fears of coming to absolute beggary, &c. &c. besiege me. On brighter days I cast these off into the dim distance, and see a world fearful, indeed, but grand: a task to do in it which no poverty or beggary shall hinder.

Can friends do much for one? Conversing here I find that I get almost nothing; the utmost, and that rarely, is honest, clear reception of what I give. Surely I go wrong to work. I question everybody too, but none, or almost none, can answer me on *any* subject. Hunt is limited, even bigoted, and seeing that I utterly dissent from him fears that I despise him; a kindly clever man, fantastic, brilliant, shallow, of one topic, loquacious, unproductive. Mrs. A. (alas!) a 'Niagara of gossip;' in certain of my humours fearful! Mill is the best; unhappily he is *speculative* merely; can open out for me no practical road, nor even direct me where I may search after such. The Unitarian-philosophic fraternity (likely to open through Mrs. Taylor) also bodes little. Alone! alone! 'May we say' (my good father used to pray), 'may we say we are not alone, for the Lord is with us.' True! true!

Keep thy heart resolute and still ; look prudently out, take diligent advantage of what time and chance *will* offer (to thee as to all) ; toil along and fear nothing. Oh thou of little faith ! Weak of faith indeed ! God help me !

For about a month past, finding that no editor had need of me, that it would be imprudent to *ask* him to have need of me, and moreover that booksellers now would *print* books for nothing, I have again been *resolute* about the writing of a book, and even working in the direction of one. Subject, ' The French Revolution.' Whole boxes of books about me. Gloomy, huge, of almost boundless meaning ; but obscure, dubious—all too deep for me ; will and must *do my best.* Alas ! gleams, too, of a work of art hover past me ; as if this should be a *work of art.* Poor me !

In the midst of innumerable discouragements, all men indifferent or finding fault, let me mention two small circumstances that are comfortable. The first is a letter from some nameless Irishman in Cork to another here (Fraser read it to me without names), actually containing a *true* and one of the friendliest possible recognitions of me. One mortal then says I am *not* utterly wrong. Blessings on him for it. The second is a letter I got to-day from Emerson, of Boston in America ; sincere, not baseless, of most exaggerated estimation. Precious is man to man.

It was long ago written, ' Woe to them that are at *ease* in Zion.' Such woe at least is not thine !

Tout va bien ici, le pain manque.

August 12.—Good news out of Annandale that they are all well; the like from Jack. I still lonely, how lonely ! Health and with it spirits fluctuating, feeble, usually bad. At times nothing can exceed my gloom. Foolish weakling ! However, so it is ; light alternates with darkness ; sorrow itself must be followed by cessation of sorrow : which is joy. As yet no prospect whatever. Mill, I discern, has given Fox the editorship of that new Molesworth periodical; seems rather ashamed of it—*à la bonne heure ;* is it not probably better so? Trust in God and in thyself ! Oh, could I but ! all else were so light, so trivial ! Enough now.

August 13.—Weary, dispirited, sick, forsaken, every way heavy laden ! cannot tell what is to become of that ' French Revolution ;' vague, boundless, without form and void—*Gott hilf mir !*

The idea of not very distant death often presents itself to me, without satisfaction, yet without much terror, much aversion—*ein verfehltes Leben?* Poor coward! At lowest I say nothing; what I suffer is, as much as may be, locked up within myself. A long lane that has *no* turning? Despair *not.*

How to keep living was the problem. The 'French Revolution,' Carlyle thought at this time, must be a mere sketch; finished and sold by the following spring if he was to escape entire bankruptcy. He had hoped more than he knew for the editorship of the new Review. It had been given to Fox, 'as the safer man.'

I can already picture to myself the Radical periodical (he wrote to his brother John), and can even prophesy its destiny. With myself it had not been so; (but) the only thing certain would have been difficulty, pain, and contradiction, which I should probably have undertaken; which I am far from breaking my heart that I have missed. Mill likes me well, and on his embarrassed face, when Fox happened to be talked of, I read both that editorship business, and also that Mill had *known* my want of it, which latter was all I desired to read. As you well say, disappointment on disappointment only simplifies one's course; your possibilities become diminished; your choice is rendered easier. In general I abate no jot of confidence in myself and in my cause. Nay, it often seems to me as if the extremity of suffering, if such were appointed me, might bring out an extremity of energy as yet unknown to myself. God grant me faith, clearness, and peaceableness of heart. I make no other prayer.

No doubt it was hard to bear. By Mill, if by no one else, Carlyle thought that he was recognised and appreciated; and Mill had preferred Fox to him. The Review fared as Carlyle expected: lived its short day as long as Molesworth's money held out, and then withered. Perhaps, as he said, 'With him it had not been so.' Yet no one who knows how such things are managed could blame Mill. To the bookselling world Carlyle's name, since the appearance of 'Sartor Resartus' in 'Fraser,' had become an abomination, and so far was Mill from really altering his own estimate of Carlyle that he offered to publish the

'Diamond Necklace' as a book at his own expense, 'that he might have the pleasure of reviewing it!' Carlyle at bottom understood that it could not have been otherwise, and that essentially it was better for him as it was. Through his own thrift and his wife's skill, the extremity of poverty never really came, and his time and faculties were left unencumbered for his own work. Even of Fox himself, whom he met at a dinner-party, he could speak kindly; not unappreciatively. The cloud lifted now and then, oftener probably than his diary would lead one to suppose. Carlyle's sense of the ridiculous—stronger than that of any contemporary man—was the complement to his dejection. In his better moments he could see and enjoy the brighter side of his position. On the 15th of August, two days after he had been meditating on his *verfehltes Leben,* he could write to his brother in a happier tone.

To John Carlyle, Naples.

5 Cheyne Row : August 15.

All of us have tolerable health, Jane generally better than before; I certainly not worse, and now more in the ancient accustomed fashion. I am diligent with the shower-bath ; my pilgrimages to the Museum and on other town errands keep me in walking enough ; once or twice weekly on an evening Jane and I stroll out along the bank of the river or about the College, and see white-shirted Cockneys in their green canoes, or old pensioners pensively smoking tobacco. The London street tumult has become a kind of marching music to me ; I walk along following my own meditations without thinking of it. Company comes in desirable quantity, not deficient, not excessive, and there is talk enough from time to time. I myself, however, when I consider it, find the whole all too *thin,* unnutritive, unavailing. All London-born men, without exception, seem to me narrow built, considerably perverted men, rather fractions of a man. Hunt, by nature a *very* clever man, is one instance ; Mill, in quite another manner, is another. These and others continue to come about me as with the cheering sound of temporary *music,* and are right welcome so. A

higher co-operation will perhaps somewhere else or some time
hence disclose itself.

> There was a piper had a cow,
>   And he had nought to give her;
> He took his pipes and played a spring,
>   And bade the cow consider.

Allan Cunningham was here two nights ago: very friendly, full
of Nithsdale, a pleasant *Naturmensch.* Mill gives me logical de-
velopments of *how* men act (chiefly in politics); Hunt, tricksy de-
vices and crotchety whimsicalities on the same theme. *What* they
act is a thing neither of them much sympathises in, much seems
to know. I sometimes long greatly for Irving—for the old Irving
of fifteen years ago; nay, the poor actual gift-of-tongues Irving
has seemed desirable to me. We dined with Mrs. (Platonica)
Taylor and the Unitarian Fox one day. Mill was also of the
party, and the husband—an obtuse, most joyous-natured man, the
pink of social hospitality. Fox is a little thickset, bushy-locked
man of five and forty, with bright, sympathetic, thoughtful eyes,
with a tendency to pot-belly and *snuffiness.* From these hints you
can construe him; the best *Socinian philosophist* going, but not a
whit more. I shall like well enough to meet the man again, but
I doubt he will not me. Mrs. Taylor herself did not yield un-
mixed satisfaction, I think, or receive it. She affects, with a kind
of sultana noble-mindedness, a certain girlish petulance, and felt
that it did not wholly prosper. We walked home, however, even
Jane did, all the way from the Regent's Park, and felt that we
had done a duty. For me, from the Socinians as I take it, *wird
nichts.*

The 'French Revolution' perplexes me much. More books on
it, I find, are but a repetition of those before read; I learn nothing, or almost nothing, further by books, yet am I as far as possible from understanding it. *Bedenklichkeiten* of all kinds environ
me. To be *true* or not to be true: there is the risk. And then
to be *popular*, or not to be popular? That, too, is a question that
plays most completely with the other. We shall see; we shall
try. *Par ma tête seule!*

My good Jack has now a clear view of me. We may say, in the
words of the Sansculotte Deputy writing to the Convention of the
Progress of Right Principles, *Tout va bien ici, le pain manque!*
Jane and I often repeat this with laughter. But in truth we live
very cheap here (perhaps not much above 50*l.* a-year dearer than

at Puttock), and so can hold out a long while independent of chance. Utter poverty itself (if I hold fast by the faith) has no terrors for me, should it ever come.

I told you I had seen Irving. It was but yesterday in Newman Street, after four prior ineffectual attempts. William Hamilton, who was here on Saturday, told me Irving was grown worse again, and Mrs. Irving had been extremely ill; he, too, seemed to think my cards had been withheld. Much grieved at this news, I called once more on Monday: a new failure. Yesterday I went again, with an insuppressible indignation mixed with my pity; after some shying I was admitted. Poor Irving! he lay there on a sofa, begged my pardon for not rising; his wife, who also did not, and, probably, could not well rise, sate at his feet all the time I was there, miserable and haggard. Irving once lovingly ordered her away; but she lovingly excused herself, and sate still. He complains of biliousness, of pain at his right short rib; has a short, thick cough, which comes on at the smallest irritation. Poor fellow, I brought a short gleam of old Scottish laughter into his face, into his voice; and that, too, set him coughing. He said it was the Lord's will; looked weak, dispirited, partly embarrassed. He continues toiling daily, though the doctor says rest only can cure him. Is it not mournful, hyper-tragical? There are moments when I determine on sweeping in upon all tongue work and accursed choking cobwebberies, and snatching away my old best friend, to save him from death and the grave.

So passed on the first summer of Carlyle's life in London. 'The weather,' he says, ' defying it in hard, almost brimless *hat*, which was *obligato* in that time of slavery, did sometimes throw me into colic.' In the British Museum lay concealed somewhere ' a collection of French pamphlets' on the Revolution, the completest in the world, which, after six weeks' wrestle with officiality, he was obliged to find ' inaccessible' to him. Idle obstruction will put the most enduring of men now and then out of patience, and Carlyle was not enduring in such matters; but his wife was able on the first of September to send to Scotsbrig a very tolerable picture of his condition.

To Mrs. Carlyle, Scotsbrig.

Chelsea : September 1, 1834.

My dear Mother,—Could I have supposed it possible that any mortal was so stupid as not to feel disappointed in receiving a letter from *me* instead of my husband, I should have written to you very long ago. But while this humility becomes me, it is also my duty (too long neglected) to send a little adjunct to my husband's letters, just to assure you 'with my own hand' that I continue to love you amidst the hubbub of this 'noble city'[1] just the same as in the quiet of Craigenputtock, and to cherish a grateful recollection of your many kindnesses to me ; especially of that magnanimous purpose to 'sit at my bedside' through the night preceding my departure, 'that I might be sure to sleep.' I certainly shall never forget that night, and the several preceding and following : but for the kindness and helpfulness shown me on all hands I must have traiked,[2] one would suppose. I had every reason to be thankful then to Providence and my friends, and I have had the same reason since.

All things since we came here have gone more smoothly with us than I at all anticipated. Our little household has been set up again at a quite moderate expense of money and trouble ; wherein, I cannot help thinking, with a *chastened vanity*, that the superior shiftiness and thriftiness of the Scotch character has strikingly manifested itself. The English women turn up the whites of their eyes and call on the 'good heavens' at the bare idea of enterprises which seem to me in the most ordinary course of human affairs. I told Mrs. Hunt one day I had been very busy *painting.* 'What ?' she asked ; 'is it a portrait ?' Oh no, I told her, something of more importance : a large wardrobe. She could not imagine ; she said, 'how I could have patience for such things.' And so, having no patience for them herself, what is the result ? She is every other day reduced to borrow my tumblers, my teacups ; even a cupful of porridge, a few spoonfuls of tea are begged of me, because 'Missus has got company, and happens to be out of the article ;' in plain, unadorned English, because 'missus' is the most wretched of managers, and is often at the point of not having a copper in her purse. To see how they live and waste

---

[1] Phrase of Basil Montagu's.—T. C.'

[2] '"Traiked" means perished. Contemptuous term, applied to cattle, &c. Traik = German *dreck.*—T. C.'

here, it is a wonder the whole city does not 'bankrape [1] and go out of sicht;' flinging platefuls of what they are pleased to denominate 'crusts' (that is, what I consider the best of the bread) into the ashpits. I often say with honest self-congratulation, 'In Scotland we have no such thing as crusts.' On the whole, though the English ladies seem to have their wits more at their finger-ends, and have a great advantage over me in that respect, I never cease to be glad that I was born on the other side of the Tweed, and that those who are nearest and dearest to me are Scotch.

I must tell you what Carlyle will not tell of himself, that he is rapidly mending of his Craigenputtock gloom and acerbity. He is really at times a tolerably social character, and seems to be regarded with a feeling of mingled terror and love in all companies, which I should think the diffusion of Teufelsdröckh will tend to increase.

I have just been called away to John Macqueen, who was followed by a Jock Thomson, of Annan, whom I received in my choicest mood to make amends for Carlyle's unreadiness,[2] who was positively going to let him leave the door without asking him in, a neglect which he would have reproached himself for after.

My love to all. Tell my kind Mary to write to me; she is the only one that ever does.

Your affectionate,
JANE W. CARLYLE.

Carlyle's letter under the same cover (franked by Sir John Romilly) communicates that the writing of the ' French Revolution' was actually begun.

Of Chelsea news we have as good as none to send you, which, indeed, means intrinsically good enough news. We go on in the old fashion, adhering pretty steadily to our *work*, and looking for

---

[1] ' To "bankrape" is to "bankrupt" (used as a *verb* passive). "And then he bankrapit and gaed out of sicht." A phrase of my father's in the little sketches of Annandale biography he would sometimes give me.—T. C.'

[2] ' Macqueen and Thomson were two big graziers of respectability—Macqueen a *native* of Craigenputtock. Thomson, from near Annan, had been a schoolfellow of mine. They had called here without very specific errand; and I confess what the letter intimates (of my silent wish to have evaded such interruption, &c.) is the exact truth.—T. C.'

our main happiness in that. This is the dull season in London, and several of our friends are fled to the country. However, we have still a fair allowance of company left us; and what is best, the company we have is none of it *bad*, or merely 'a consuming of time,' but rational and leads to something. The best news I have is that this day (September 1) I mean to begin *writing* my book; nay, had it not been for the present sheet, would already have been at it! Wish me good speed; I have meditated the business as I could, and must surely strive to do my best. With a kind of trembling hope I calculate that the enterprise may prosper with me; that the book may be at least a true one, and tend to do God's service, not the Devil's. It will keep me greatly on the stretch these winter months, but I hope to have it printed and out early in spring; what is to be done next, we shall then see. The world must be a tougher article than I have ever found it, if it altogether beats me. I have defied it, and set my trust *elsewhere*, and so it can do whatsoever is permitted and appointed it. As to our other doings and outlooks, I have written of them all at great length to Alick the other day, so that as you are likely to see his letter I need not dwell on them. I have seen Mill and various other agreeable persons since (for our company comes often in rushes), but met with no further adventure.

The close of the letter refers to economics, and to the generous contributions furnished by Scotsbrig to the Cheyne Row establishment.

The sheet is fading very fast; Jane's little note too is ready, and I have still some *business* to do. We spoke long ago about a freight of eatable goods we wanted out of Annandale at the fall of the year. As you are the punctuallest of all, I will now specify the whole to you, that you may bestir yourself, and stir up others in the proper quarter to be getting them ready. Here is the list of our wants, as I have extracted it by questions out of Jane. First, sixty pounds of butter in two equal *pigs* (the butter here is 16*d*. a pound!); secondly, a moderately-sized sweet-milk cheese; next, two smallish bacon-hams (your beef-ham was just broken into last week, and is in the best condition); next, about fifteen stone of right oatmeal (or even more, for we are to give Hunt some stones of it, and need almost a pound daily: there is not now above a stone left); and after that, as many hundredweights of potatoes as you think will keep (for the rule of it is this: we take two pounds daily, and they sell here at three halfpence, or at lowest a penny, a pound, and are seldom good) : all this got ready and packed into a hogshead or two will reach us by Whitehaven, and we will see how it answers.

John Carlyle meanwhile was prospering with Lady Clare, and was in a position to return to his brother the generosity of earlier days. It was perfectly true, as Carlyle had said, that what any one of the family possessed the others were free to share with him. In September John sent home 130*l.* for his mother.[1]

To John Carlyle, Rome.

Chelsea : September 21, 1834.

Your kind letter, my dear Jack, was read over with a feeling such as it merited : it went nearer my heart than anything addressed to me for long. I am not sure that there were not *tears* in the business, but they were not sad ones. Your offers and purposes are worthy of a brother, and I were but unworthy if I met them in any mean spirit. I believe there is no other man living from whom such offers as yours were other to me than a pleasant sound which I *must disregard;* but it is not so with these; for I actually can (without damage to any good feeling in me), and will, if need be, make good use of them. We will, as you say, stand by one another; and so each of us, were all other men arranged against us, have one friend. Well that it is so. *Wohl ihm dem die Geburt den Bruder gab.* I will not speak any more about this, but keep it laid up in my mind as a thing to act by. I feel, as I once said, *double*-strong in the possession of my poor *Doil,*[2] and so I suppose we shall quarrel many times yet, and instantly agree

[1] Carlyle carried it to the City to be forwarded to the bank at Dumfries, and he enlarged his experiences of London on the way. 'In my perambulations,' he said, 'I came upon a strange anarchy of a place—the Stock Exchange. About a hundred men were jumping and jigging about in a dingy, contracted apartment, and yelping out all manner of sounds, which seemed to be auctioneer's offers, not without much laughter and other miscellaneous tumult. I thought of the words " trades' contentious hell"; but had no room for reflections. A rednecked official coming up with the assurance that this place was " private, sir," I departed with a "thousand pardons " and satisfaction that I *had* seen the Domdaniel. These were my discoveries in the city.'

[2] Family nickname for John Carlyle.

again, and argue and sympathise, and on the whole stand by one
another through good and evil, and turn *two* fronts to the world
while we are both spared in it. *Amen!* There are many wallow-
ing in riches, splendent in dignities, who have no such possession
as this. Let us be thankful for it, and approve ourselves worthy
of it.

I have not yet earned sixpence since I came hither, and see not
that I am advancing towards such a thing: however, I do not
'tine heart.' Indeed, that money consideration gives me wonderfully little sorrow; we can hold out a *long time* yet. It is very
true also what you say, that soliciting among the bibliopoles were
the *worst* policy. Indeed I have no deeper wish than that bread
for me of the brownest sort were providable elsewhere than with
them. We shall not cease to try. One comfortable thing is the
constant conviction I have that here or nowhere is the place for
me. I must swim or sink *here*. Withal, too, I feel the influences
of the place on me *rebuking* much in my late ways of writing and
speech: within my own heart I am led to overhaul many things,
and alter or mourn for them. I might say generally that I am
leading a rather painful but not unprofitable life. *At spes in-
fracta!* I look up to the everlasting sky, and with the azure infinitude all around me cannot think that I was made in vain.
These things, however, I do not well to speak of yet, or perhaps
at all. The best news is that I have actually *begun* that 'French
Revolution,' and after two weeks of blotching and bloring have
produced—two clean pages! *Ach Gott!* But my hand is out;
and I am altering my style too, and troubled about many things.
Bilious, too, in these smothering, windless days. It shall be *such*
a book: quite an epic poem of the Revolution: an apotheosis of
Sansculottism! Seriously, when in good spirits I feel as if there
were the matter of a very considerable work within me; but the
task of shaping and uttering will be frightful. Here, as in so
many other respects, I am alone, without models, without *limits*
(this is a great want), and must—just do the best I can.

The expected provision barrels from Scotsbrig were long
in arriving, and Carlyle had to quicken the family movements in the end of October by a representation of the
state of things to which he and his wife were reduced.
'It will seem absurd enough to tell you,' he wrote to his

mother, ' that we are in haste now after waiting so long;
but the truth is, our meal has been done for a fortnight,
and we have the strangest shifts for a supper. Amongst
others, flour porridge, exactly shoemaker's paste, only
clean; and at last have been obliged to take to some of
the Scotch oatmeal sold in the shops here—very dear—
fivepence a quart by measure—which though rough, is
quite sound, which therefore we can thankfully use; so
you need not suppose us starving. The butter too is almost always excellent (churned I believe out of milk),
at the easy rate of sixteenpence a pound! In regard to
provision I shall only add that the beef-ham daily plays its
part at breakfast, and proves thoroughly *genuine.* The
butcher came here one day to saw the bone of it, and
asked with amazement whether it was pork or not. He
had never heard of any ham but a bacon one, and departed
from us with a new idea. N.B.—We get coffee to breakfast (at eight or nearly so), have very often mutton-chops to
dinner at three, then tea at six; we have four pennyworth
of cream, two pennyworth of milk daily. This is our diet,
which I know you *would* rather know than not know.'

For the rest, life went on without much variety. ' Bessy
Barnet ' left Cheyne Row after two months, being obliged
to return to her mother, and they had to find another servant among the London maids of all work. Carlyle
crushed down his dispiritment; found at any rate that
' nothing like the *deep sulkiness* of Craigenputtock ' troubled him in London. He felt that ' he was in the right
workshop if he could but get acquainted with the tools.'
' Teufelsdröckh,' circulating in a stitched-up form, made
out of the sheets of ' Fraser,' was being read, a few persons really admiring it; the generality turning up their
eyes in speechless amazement. Irving had departed, having gone to Scotland, where he was reported as lying ill at
Glasgow, and, to Carlyle's very deep distress, likely to die.

Among minor adventures, Carlyle was present at the burning of the Houses of Parliament. 'The crowd,' he says, 'was quiet, rather pleased than otherwise; whewed and whistled when the breeze came, as if to encourage it. "There's a flare-up for the House of Lords!" "A judgment for the Poor Law Bill!" "There go their *Hacts!*" Such exclamations seemed to be the prevailing ones: a man *sorry* I did not see anywhere.'

Horny-handed Radicalism gave Carlyle a grim satisfaction. He considered modern society so corrupt that he expected, or rather desired, an immediate end to it. But Radicalism, too, had its unfavourable aspects, especially when it showed itself in the direction of female emancipation.

Mill and one or two of his set (he said) are on the whole the reasonablest people we have. However, we see them seldom, being so far off, and Mill himself, who would be far the best of them all, is greatly occupied of late times with a set of quite opposite character, which the Austins and other friends mourn much and fear much over; Fox the Socinian, and a flight of really wretched-looking 'friends of the species,' who (in writing and deed) struggle not in favour of duty being *done*, but against duty of any sort being *required*. A singular creed this; but I can assure you a very observable one here in these days: by me deeply hated as the GLARE which is its colour (*die seine Farbe ist*) and substance likewise mainly. Jane and I often say, 'Before all mortals beware of friends of the species'! Most of these people are very indignant at marriage and the like, and frequently, indeed, are obliged to divorce their own wives, or be divorced; for though this world is already blooming (or is one day to do it) in everlasting 'happiness of the greatest number,' these people's own *houses* (I always find) are little hells of improvidence, discord, and unreason. Mill is far above all that, and I think will not sink into it; however, I do wish him fairly far from it, and though I cannot speak of it directly, would fain help him out. He is one of the best people I ever saw.

The next letter is from Mrs. Carlyle, which Carlyle interprets.

'Mournfully beautiful,' he says, 'is this letter to me; a clear little household light shining pure and brilliant in the dark obstructive places of the past. The two East Lothian friends are George Rennie the sculptor, and his pretty sister, wife of an ex-Indian ship captain.'

'Eliza Miles and the Mileses are the good people in Ampton Street with whom we lodged. Eliza, their daughter, felt quite captivated with my Jane, and seems to have vowed eternal loyalty to her almost at first sight; was for coming to be our servant at Craigenputtock; actually wrote proposing it then—a most tempting offer to us, had not the rough element and the delicate aspirant been evidently irreconcilable! She continued to visit us here at moderate intervals, wrote me, after my calamity befell, the one letter of condolence I could completely read. She was a very pretty and to us interesting specimen of the London maiden of the middle classes; refined, polite, pious, clever both of hand and mind. No gentlewoman could have a more upright, modest, affectionate, and unconsciously high demeanour. Her father had long been in a prosperous upholsterer's business, but the firm had latterly gone away. He was a very good-natured, respectable man, quietly much sympathised with in his own house. Eliza, with her devout temper, had been drawn to Edward Irving, went daily alone of her family to his chapel in those years 1831-2, and was to the last one of his most reverent disciples. She did in her soft, loyal way right well in the world; married poorly enough, but wisely, and is still living a rich man's wife and the mother of prosperous sons and daughters.

' " Buller's Radical-meeting " was a meeting privately got up by Charles Buller, but ostensibly managed by others, which assembled itself largely and with emphasis at the London Tavern, to say what it thought of the first re-appearance of Peel and Co. after the Reform Bill—" first Peel Ministry," which lasted only a short time. I duly attended the meeting (never another in my life), and remembered it well. Had some interest—not much. The two thousand human figures, wedged in the huge room into one dark mass, were singular to look down upon, singular to hear their united voice coming clearly as from one heart, their fiery " Yes," their sternly bellowing " No." I could notice too what new laws there were of speaking to such a mass : no matter how intensely consentaneous your two thousand were, and how much you *agreed* with every one of them, you must likewise begin where they began, follow pretty exactly their *sequence* of thoughts, or they lost sight of your intention, and for noise of contradiction to you and to one another you could not be heard at all. That was new to me, that second thing, and little or nothing else was. In the speeches I had no interest except a phenomenal ; indeed, had to disagree throughout more or less with every part of them. Roebuck knew the art best, kept the two thousand in constant reverberation, more and more rapturous, by his adroitly correct series of commonplaces. John Crawford, much more original, lost the series, and had to sit down again ignominiously unheard. I walked briskly home much musing. Found her waiting, eager enough for any news I had.—T. C.'

To Mrs. Carlyle, Scotsbrig.

Chelsea : November 21, 1834.

My dear Mother,—Now that franks are come back into the world, one need not wait for an inspired moment to write ; if one's letter is worth nothing it costs nothing ; nor will any letter that tells you of our welfare and assures you of our continual affection be worth nothing in your eyes, however destitute of news or anything else that might make it entertaining.

The weather is grown horridly cold, and I am chiefly intent, at present, on getting my winter wardrobe into order. I have made up the old black gown, which was dyed puce for me at Dumfries, *with my own hands.* It looks twenty per cent. better than when it was new ; and I shall get no other this winter. I am now turning my pelisse. I went yesterday to a milliner to buy a bonnet. An old, very ugly lady, upwards of seventy I am sure, was bargaining about a cloak at the same place; it was a fine affair of satin and violet; but she declared repeatedly that 'it had *no air*,' and for her part she could not put on such a thing. My bonnet, I flatter myself. *has* an *air.* A little brown feather nods over the front of it, and the crown points like a sugar-loaf! The diameter of the fashionable ladies at present is about three yards; their *bustles* are the size of an ordinary sheep's fleece. The very servant girls wear bustles. Eliza Miles told me a maid of theirs went out one Sunday with *three* kitchen dusters pinned on as a substitute.

The poor Mileses are in great affliction. Mr. Miles about the time we came to London got into an excellent situation, and they were just beginning to feel independent, and look forward to a comfortable future, when one morning, about a week ago, Mr. Miles, in walking through his warerooms, was noticed to stagger, and one of the men ran and caught him as he was falling. He was carried to a public-house close by, his own house being miles off, and his wife and daughter sent for. He never spoke to them, could never be removed, but there, in the midst of confusion and riot, they sate watching him for two days, when he expired. I went up to see them so soon as I heard of their misfortune. The wife was confined to bed with inflammation in her head. Poor Eliza was up and resigned-looking, but the picture of misery. A gentleman from Mr. Irving's church was with her, saying what he could.

Mrs. Montagu has quite given us up; but we still find it possible to carry on existence. I offended her by taking in Bessy Barnet, in the teeth of her vehement admonition, and now I suppose she is again offended that I should receive a discharged servant of her daughter-in-law's. I am sorry that she should be so whimsical, for as she was my first friend in London I continue to feel a sort of tenderness for her in spite of many faults which cleave to her. But her society can quite readily be dispensed with nevertheless; we have new acquaintances always turning up, and a pretty handsome stock of old ones.

A brother and sister, the most intimate friends I ever had in East Lothian, live quite near (for London), and I have other East Lothian acquaintances. Mrs. Hunt I shall soon be quite terminated with, I foresee. She torments my life out with borrowing. She actually borrowed one of the brass fenders the other day, and

I had difficulty in getting it out of her hands; irons, glasses, tea-cups, silver spoons are in constant requisition, and when one sends for them the whole number can never be found. Is it not a shame to manage so with eight guineas a week to keep house on? It makes me very indignant to see all the waste that goes on around me, when I am needing so much care and calculation to make ends meet; when we dine out, to see as much expended on a dessert of fruit (for no use but to give people a colic) as would keep us in necessaries for two or three weeks. My present maid has a grand-uncle in town with upwards of a hundred thousand pounds, who drives his carriage and all that; at a great dinner he had he gave five pounds for a couple of pine-apples when scarce; and here is his niece working all the year through for eight, and he has never given her a farthing since she came to London.

My mother gave a good account of your looks. I hope you will go and see her again for a longer time; she was so gratified by your visit. I have just had a letter from her, most satisfactory, telling me all she knows about any of you. She gives a wonderful account of some transcendentally beautiful shawl which Jean had made her a present of. I am sure never present gave more contentment.

Carlyle is going to a Radical meeting to-night; but there is no fear of his getting into mischief. Curiosity is his only motive; and I must away to the butcher to get his dinner. I wish you may be able to read what I have written. I write with a steel pen, which is a very unpliable concern, and has almost cut into my finger. God bless you all. A kiss to Mary's new baby when you see it.

Yours affectionately,

JANE CARLYLE.

'Above a month before this date,' Carlyle adds, 'Edward Irving rode to the door one evening, came in and stayed with us some twenty minutes—the one call we ever had of him here; his farewell before setting out to ride towards Glasgow, as the doctors, helpless otherwise, had ordered. He was very friendly, calm, and affectionate; chivalrously courteous to *her*, as I remember. "Ah, yes," looking round the room, "you are like an Eve—make every place you live in beautiful." He was not sad' in manner, but was at heart, as you could notice, serious, even solemn. Darkness at hand and the weather damp, he could not loiter. I saw him mount at the door; watched till he turned the first corner, close by the rector's garden door, and had vanished from us altogether. He died at Glasgow before the end of December.'

Irving was dead, and with it closed the last chapter of Jane Welsh's early romance. Much might be said of the effect of it both on Irving and on her. The characters of neither of them escaped unscathed by the passionate love which had once existed between them. But all that is gone, and concerns the world no longer. I will add only an affectionately sorrowful letter which Carlyle wrote at the time to his mother when the news from Glasgow came.

To Mrs. Carlyle, Scotsbrig.

Chelsea: December 24, 1834.

Poor Edward Irving, as you have heard, has ended his pilgrimage. I had been expecting that issue, but not so soon; the news of his death, which Fraser the bookseller (once a hearer of his) communicated quite on a sudden, struck me deeply; and the *wae* feeling of what it has all been, and what it has all ended in, kept increasing with me for the next ten days. Oh, what a wild, weltering mass of confusion is this world! how its softest flatterings are but bewitchments, and lead men down to the gates of darkness! Nothing is clearer to me than that Irving was driven half mad, and finally killed, simply by what once seemed his enviable fortune, and by the hold it took of him; killed as certainly (only a little more slowly) as if it had been a draught of sweetened arsenic! I am very sad about him: ten years ago, when I was first here, what a rushing and running; his house never empty of idle or half-earnest, wondering people, with their carriages and equipments; and *now*, alas, it is all *gone*, marched like a deceitful vision; and all is emptiness, desertion, and his place knows him no more! He was *a good man* too; that I do heartily believe; his faults, we may hope, were abundantly expiated in *this* life, and now his memory—as that of the just ought—shall be hallowed with us. One thing with another, I have not found another such man. I shall never forget these last times I saw him; I longed much to help him, to deliver him, but could not do it. My poor first friend—my first, and best! Fraser applied to me to write a word about him; which I did, and, after much hithering and thithering, I ascertain to-day that it is at last to be printed [1] (in some tolerable neighbourhood, for we discorded about that) in his magazine. I will send you a copy of it, and another for his mother, which you may deliver her yourself. Go and see the poor old forsaken widow: it will do her good, and yourself. Tell her that her son did not live for Time only, but for Eternity too; that he has fought the good fight, as we humbly trust, and is not *dead* but sleepeth. There are few women whom I pity more than poor old Mrs. Irving at this moment: few years ago all was prosperous with her: she had sons, a cheerful household; could say, *Oh, Edward, I am proud of ye:* now 'ruin's ploughshare' has passed over her, and it is all fled.

Tenderly, beautifully, Carlyle could feel for his friend. No more touching 'funeral oration' was ever uttered over a lost companion than in the brief paper of which here he spoke; and his heart at the time was heavy for himself also. He had almost lost hope. At no past period of his life does the Journal show more despondency than in this autumn and winter. He might repeat his mother's words to himself, ' tine heart, tine a'. ' But the heart was near ' tined' for all that.

Extracts from Journal.

Monday, September 8, 1834.—Pain was not given thee merely to be miserable under; learn from it, turn it to account.

Yesterday set out to go and see Mrs. Taylor—Jane with me. Broke down in the park; *könnte nichts mehr*, being sick and weak beyond measure; sate me down in a seat looking over the green with its groups, Jane gone to make a call in the neighbourhood; Mrs. Taylor with her husband make their appearance, walking; pale she, and passionate and sad-looking: really felt a kind of interest in her.

'French Revolution' begun, but, alas! not in the right style, not in the style that can stand. The mind has not yet grappled

[1] Republished in the fourth volume of Carlyle's *Miscellanies*.

with it heartily enough : must seize it, crush the secret out of it, and make or mar.

Acknowledgments of 'Teufelsdröckh' worthless to me one and all. 'Madam,' said I the other night to poor hollow Mrs. ——, ' it is a work born in darkness, destined for oblivion, and not worth wasting a word on.'

September 10.—'French Revolution' shapeless, dark, unmanageable. Know not this day, for example, on what side to attack it ; yet *must* forward. One of the things I need most is to subdue my polemics, my ill-nature.

September 27.—Walk in the evening by Millbank and the dusty, desolate shore with Jane : gloom ; rest. One day in the little garden see a huge spider kill a fly ; see it kill a second, lift something and angrily kill *it*. Consider what a world of benevolence this is ; how many forces are at work in Nature ; how multiplex, unfathomable is she.

October 1.—This morning think of the old primitive Edinburgh scheme of *engineership ;* [1] almost meditate for a moment resuming it *yet !* It were a method of gaining bread, of getting into con tact with men, my two grand wants and prayers. In general, it may be said no man ever so wanted any practical adviser, or shadow of one ; it is utterly, from of old (and even the very appearance of it), withheld from me. Sad ; not irremediable now. My isolation, my feeling of loneliness, unlimitedness (much meant by this), what tongue shall tell ? Alone, alone ! Woes too deep —woes which cannot be written even here. Patience, unwearied endeavour !

Surprised occasionally and grieved to find myself not only so disliked—suspected—but so known. Though at Puttock I saw no audience, I had one, and often (in all Whig circles) a most writhing one. *Dommage ?* Yes and no.

Didst thou ever hitherto want bread and clothes ? No. Courage, then ! But above all things, *diligence.* And so to work.

Sunday, October 5.—Calm, smoky weather.' A pale sun gets the better of the vapours towards noon, the sad sinking year. See M'Culloch and speak with him. Promise to see him again. A

---

[1] After throwing up the law, Carlyle had for a few days thought of becom‐ ing an engineer.

hempen man, but.*genuine* hemp. Hunt *invites* us over pressingly for the evening. Go, and sit talking; not miserable, yet with the deepest sea of misery lying in the background. 'Remote, unfriended, solitary, low.' Courage! Do not tine *heart*. On the whole, how *much* have I to learn! Let me not think myself too old to learn it.

Meanwhile here is another blessed, still day given me. Let me work wisely therein while it lasts. Oh that I could weep and pray! Does a God hear these dumb troublous aspirations of my soul? *Credamus ! ut vivamus !*

November 1.—What a long-drawn wail are these foregoing pages, which I have just read! Why add another note to it at present? In general, except when writing, I never feel myself that I am *alive*. So the last week too has been a doleful one. Complain not. Struggle, thou weakling.

November 27.—It is many days since I have written aught here ; days of suffering, of darkness, despondency ; great, not yet too great for me. Ill-health has much to do with it, ill-success with the book has somewhat. No prospect, no definite hope nor the slightest ray of such. Stand to thy tackle! Endure! Endeavour·! It must alter, and shall ; but on with this present task, at any rate. That thou hast clear before thee.

Radical meeting (Buller's) at the City of London Tavern on Friday night last. Meaning of a multitude of men : their fierce *bark* (what in Annandale we call a *gollie*) primary indispensability of *lungs*. Radical Murphy, with cylindrical high head (like a water-can), pot-belly, and voice like the Great Bell of Moscow. All in earnest. Can Wellington stay in? for long, may be doubted. Peel not yet heard of.

1835.—Twelve o'clock has just struck : the last hour of 1834, the first of a new year. Bells ringing (to me dolefully). A wet wind blustering. My wife in bed, very unhappily ill of a foot which the puddle of a maid scalded three weeks ago. I, after a day of fruitless toil, reading and re-reading about that Versailles 6th of October still. It is long time since I have written anything here. The future looks too black round me, the present too doleful, unfriendly. I am too sick at heart, wearied, wasted in body, to complain, even to myself. My first friend Edward Irving is dead above three weeks ago. I am friendless here, or as good as that. My book cannot get on, though I stick to it like a *bur*. Why should I say Peace, peace, when there is no peace ? May God grant me strength to do or to endure aright what is appointed me in this coming, now commencing, division of time. Let me not despair—nay, I do not in general. Enough to-night, for I am *done !* Peace be to my mother and all my loved ones that yet live. What a noisy inanity in this world.

With these words I close the story of Carlyle's apprenticeship. His training was over. He was now a master in his craft, on the eve, though he did not know it, of universal recognition as an original and extraordinary man. Henceforward his life was in his works. The outward incidents of it will be related in his wife's letters and in his own explanatory notes. My part has been to follow him from the peasant's home in which he was born and nurtured to the steps of the great position which he was afterwards to occupy ; to describe his trials and his struggles, and the effect of them upon his mind and disposition. He has been substantially his own biographer. But no one, especially no one of so rugged and angular a character, sees the lights and shadows precisely as others see them. When a man of letters has exercised an influence so vast over successive generations of thinkers, the world has a right to know the minutest particulars of his life ; and the sovereigns of literature can no more escape from the fierce light which beats upon a throne, than the kings and ministers who have ruled the destinies of states and empires. Carlyle had no such high estimate of his own consequence. His poor fortunes he considered to be of moment to no one but himself ; but he knew that the world would demand an account of him, and with characteristic unreserve he placed his journals and his correspondence in my hands with no instructions save that I should tell the truth about him, and if shadows there were, that least of all should I conceal them.

If in this part of my duty I have erred at all, I have erred in excess, not in defect. It is the nature of men to dwell on the faults of those who stand above them. They are comforted by perceiving that the person whom they have heard so much admired was but of common clay after all. The life of no man, authentically told, will ever be found free from fault. Carlyle has been seen in these volumes fighting for thirty-nine years—fighting with poverty, with dyspepsia, with intellectual temptations, with neglect or obstruction from his fellow-mortals. Their ways were not his ways. His attitude was not different only from their attitude, but was a condemnation of it, and it was not to be expected that they would look kindly on him. His existence hitherto had been a prolonged battle ; a man does not carry himself in such conflicts so wisely and warily that he can come out of them unscathed ; and Carlyle carried scars from his wounds both on his mind and on his temper. He had stood aloof from parties ; he had fought his way *alone*. He was fierce and uncompromising. To those who saw but the outside of him he appeared scornful, imperious, and arrogant. He was stern in his judgment of others. The sins of passion he could pardon, but the sins of insincerity, or half-sincerity, he could never pardon. He would not condescend to the conventional politenesses which remove the friction between man and man. He called things by their right names, and in a dialect edged with sarcasm. Thus he was often harsh when he ought to have been merciful ; he was contemptuous where he had no right to despise ; and in his estimate of motives and actions was often unjust and mistaken. He, too, who was so severe with others had weaknesses of his own of which he was unconscious in the excess of his self-confidence. He was proud—one may say savagely proud. It was a noble determination in him that he would depend upon himself alone; but he would not only accept no obligation, but he resented the offer of help to himself or to anyone belonging to him as if it had been an insult. He never wholly pardoned Jeffrey for having made his brother's fortune. His temper had been ungovernable from his childhood; he had the irritability of a dyspeptic man of genius; and when the Devil, as he called it, had possession of him, those whose comfort he ought most to have studied were the most exposed to the storm: he who preached so wisely ' on doing the duty which lay nearest to us,' forgot his own instructions, and made no adequate effort to cast the Devil out. Nay, more: there broke upon him in his late years, like a flash of lightning from heaven, the terrible revelation that he had sacrificed his wife's health and happiness in his absorption in his work; that he had been oblivious of his most obvious obligations, and had been negligent, inconsiderate, and selfish. The fault was grave and the remorse agonising. For many years after she had left him, when we passed the spot in our walks where she was last seen alive, he would bare his grey head in the wind and rain—his features wrung with unavailing sorrow. Let all this be acknowledged; and let those who know themselves to be without either these sins, or others as bad as these, freely cast stones at Carlyle.

But there is the other side of the account. In the weightier matters of the law Carlyle's life had been without speck or flaw. From his earliest years, in the home at Ecclefechan, at school, at college, in every incident or recorded aspect of him, we see invariably the same purity, the same innocence of heart, and uprightness and integrity of action. As a child, as a boy, as a man, he had been true in word and honest and just in deed. There is no trace, not the slightest, of levity or folly. He sought his friends among the worthiest of his fellow-students, and to those friends he was from the first a special object of respect and admiration. His letters, even in early youth, were so remarkable that they were preserved as treasures by his correspondents. In the thousands which I have read, either written to Carlyle or written by him, I have found no sentence of his own which he could have wished unwritten, or, through all those trying years of incipient manhood, a single action alluded to by others which those most jealous of his memory need regret to read, or his biographer need desire to conceal. Which of us would not shiver at the thought if his own life were to be exposed to the same dreadful ordeal, and his own letters, or the letters of others written about him, were searched through for the sins of his youth? These, it may be said, are but negative virtues. But his positive qualities were scarcely less beautiful. Nowhere is a man known better than in his own family. No disguise is possible there; and he whom father and mother, brother and sister love, we may be sure has deserved to be loved.

Among the many remarkable characteristics of the Carlyle household, whether at Mainhill or Scotsbrig, was the passionate affection which existed among them and the special love which they all felt for 'Tom.' Well might Jeffrey say that Carlyle would not have known poverty if he had not been himself a giver. His own habits were Spartan in their simplicity, and from the moment when he began to earn his small salary as an usher at Annan, the savings of his thrift were spent in presents to his father and mother and in helping to educate his brother. I too can bear witness that the same generous disposition remained with him to the end. In his later years he had an abundant income, but he never added to his own comforts or luxuries. His name was not seen on charity lists, but he gave away every year perhaps half what he received. I was myself in some instances employed by him to examine into the circumstances of persons who had applied to him for help. The stern censor was in these instances the kindest of Samaritans. It was enough if a man or woman was miserable. He did not look too curiously into the causes of it. I was astonished at the profuseness with which he often gave to persons little worthy of his liberality.

Nor was there even in those more trying cases where men were prospering beyond their merits any malice or permanent ill-will. He was constitutionally atrabilious and scornful; but the bitterness with which he would speak of such persons was on the surface merely. 'Poor devil,' he would say of some successful political Philistine, 'after all, if we looked into the history of him, we should find how it all came about.' He was always sad: often gloomy in the extreme. Men of genius rarely take cheerful views of life. They see too clearly. Dante and Isaiah were not probably exhilarating companions; but Carlyle, when unpossessed and in his natural humour, was gentle, forbearing, and generous.

If his character as a man was thus nobly upright, so he employed his time and his talents with the same high sense of responsibility—not to make himself great, or honoured, or admired, but as a trust committed to him for his Maker's purposes. 'What can you say of Carlyle,' said Mr. Ruskin to me, 'but that he was born in the clouds and struck by the lightning?'—'struck by the lightning'—not meant for happiness, but for other ends; a stern fate which nevertheless in the modern world, as in the ancient, is the portion dealt out to some individuals on whom the heavens have been pleased to set their mark. Gifted as he knew himself to be with unusual abilities, he might have risen to distinction on any one of the beaten roads of life, and have won rank and wealth for himself. He glanced at

the Church, he glanced at the Bar, but there was something working in him like the *Δαίμων* of Socrates, which
warned him off with an imperious admonition, and insisted
on being obeyed.   Men who fancy that they have a 'mission' in this world are usually intoxicated by vanity, and
their ambition is in the inverse ratio of their strength to
give effect to it.   But in Carlyle the sense of having a
mission was the growth of the actual presence in him of
the necessary powers.   Certain associations, certain aspects
of human life and duty, had forced themselves upon him
as truths of immeasurable consequence which the world
was forgetting.   He was a *vates*, a seer.   He perceived
things which others did not see, and which it was his business to force them to see.   He regarded himself as being
charged actually and really with a message which he was
to deliver to mankind, and, like other prophets, he was
'straitened' till his work was accomplished.   A Goethe
could speak in verse, and charm the world into listening to
him by the melody of his voice.   The deep undertones of
Carlyle's music could not modulate themselves under
rhyme and metre.   For the new matter which he had to
utter he had to create a new form corresponding to it.   He
had no pulpit from which to preach, and through literature alone had he any access to the world which he was to
address.   Even 'a man of letters' must live while he
writes, and Carlyle had imposed conditions upon himself
which might make the very keeping himself alive impossible; for his function was sacred to him, and he had laid
down as a fixed rule that he would never write merely to
please, never for money, that he would never write anything save when especially moved to write by an impulse
from within; above all, never to set down a sentence which
he did not in his heart believe to be true, and to spare no
labour till his work to the last fibre was as good as he
could possibly make it.

These were rare qualities in a modern writer whose bread depended on his pen, and such as might well compensate for worse faults than spleen and hasty temper. He had not starved, but he had come within measurable distance of starvation. Nature is a sharp schoolmistress, and when she is training a man of genius for a great moral purpose, she takes care by ' the constitution of things ' that he shall not escape discipline. More than once better hopes had appeared to be dawning. But the sky had again clouded, and at the time of the removal to London the prospect was all but hopeless. No man is bound to fight for ever against proved impossibilities. The ' French Revolution ' was to be the last effort. If this failed Carlyle had resolved to give up the game, abandon literature, buy spade and rifle and make for the backwoods of America. ' You are not fit for that either, my fine fellow,' he had sorrowfully to say to himself. Still he meant to try. America might prove a kinder friend to him than England had been, in some form or other. Worse it could not prove.

For two years the writing of that book occupied him. The materials grew on his hands, and the first volume, for the cause mentioned in the 'Reminiscences,' had to be written a second time. All the mornings he was at his desk ; in the afternoons he took his solitary walks in Hyde Park, seeing the brilliant equipages and the knights and dames of fashion prancing gaily along the Row. He did not envy them. He would not have changed existences with the brightest of these fortune's favourites if the wealth of England had been poured into the scale. But he did think that his own lot was hard, so willing was he to do anything for an honest living, yet with every door closed against him. ' Not one of you,' he said to himself as he looked at them, ' could do what I am doing, and it concerns you too, if you did but know it.'

They did not know it and they have not known it. Fifty years have passed since Carlyle was writing the ' French Revolution.' The children of fashion still canter under the elms of the Park, as their fathers and mothers were cantering then, and no sounds of danger have yet been audible to flutter the Mayfair dove-cotes. ' They call me a great man now,' Carlyle said to me a few days before he died, ' but not one believes what I have told them.' But if they did not believe the prophet, they could worship the new star which was about to rise. The Annandale peasant boy was to be the wonder of the London world. He had wrought himself into a personality which all were to be compelled to admire, and in whom a few recognised, like Goethe, the advent of a new moral force the effects of which it was impossible to predict.

INDEX.

ERRATUM.

Vol. ii. page 167. line 3 from top, *for* Mary Wollstonecraft's 'Life of Godwin,' *read* 'Mary Wollstonecraft's Life,' by Godwin.